Wole Soyinka

Illustration by Kazeem Oyetunde Ekeolu.

BLACK LITERARY AND CULTURAL EXPRESSIONS

Bloomsbury's **Black Literary and Cultural Expressions** series provides a much-needed space for exploring dimensions of Black creativity as its local expressions in literature, music, film, art, etc., interface with the global circulation of culture. From contemporary and historical perspectives, and through a multidisciplinary lens, works in this series critically analyze the provenance, genres, aesthetics, intersections, and modes of circulation of works of Black cultural expression and production.

SERIES EDITORS
Toyin Falola and Abimbola A. Adelakun,
University of Texas at Austin, USA

ADVISORY BOARD
Nadia Anwar, University of Management and Technology, Lahore, Pakistan
Adriaan van Klinken, University of Leeds, UK
Alain Lawo-Sukam, Texas A&M University, USA
Nathaniel S. Murrell, University of North Carolina, Wilmington, USA
Mukoma wa Ngugi, Cornell University, USA
Bode Omojola, Mount Holyoke and the Five College Consortium, USA
Nduka Otiono, Carleton University, Canada
Bola Sotunsa, Babcock University, Nigeria
Nathan Suhr-Sytsma, Emory University, USA

VOLUMES IN THE SERIES:
Wole Soyinka: Literature, Activism, and African Transformation
by Bola Dauda and Toyin Falola

Wole Soyinka

Literature, Activism, and African Transformation

Bola Dauda and Toyin Falola

BLOOMSBURY ACADEMIC
NEW YORK • LONDON • OXFORD • NEW DELHI • SYDNEY

BLOOMSBURY ACADEMIC
Bloomsbury Publishing Inc
1385 Broadway, New York, NY 10018, USA
50 Bedford Square, London, WC1B 3DP, UK
29 Earlsfort Terrace, Dublin 2, Ireland

BLOOMSBURY, BLOOMSBURY ACADEMIC and the Diana logo are trademarks
of Bloomsbury Publishing Plc

First published in the United States of America 2022

Copyright © Bola Dauda and Toyin Falola, 2022

For legal purposes the Acknowledgments on p. x constitute
an extension of this copyright page.

Cover design: Eleanor Rose
Cover image © Kazeem Ekeolu

All rights reserved. No part of this publication may be reproduced or
transmitted in any form or by any means, electronic or mechanical, including
photocopying, recording, or any information storage or retrieval system,
without prior permission in writing from the publishers.

Bloomsbury Publishing Inc does not have any control over, or responsibility for,
any third-party websites referred to or in this book. All internet addresses given
in this book were correct at the time of going to press. The author and publisher
regret any inconvenience caused if addresses have changed or sites have
ceased to exist, but can accept no responsibility for any such changes.

Library of Congress Cataloging-in-Publication Data
Names: Dauda, Bola, author. | Falola, Toyin, author.
Title: Wole Soyinka : literature, activism, and African transformation /
Bola Dauda and Toyin Falola.
Description: New York : Bloomsbury Academic, 2021. |
Series: Black literary and cultural expressions | Includes
bibliographical references and index.
Identifiers: LCCN 2021011690 (print) | LCCN 2021011691 (ebook) | ISBN
9781501375767 (hardback) | ISBN 9781501375750 (paperback) |
ISBN 9781501375774 (epub) | ISBN 9781501375781
(pdf) | ISBN 9781501375798
Subjects: LCSH: Soyinka, Wole. | Soyinka, Wole–Criticism and
interpretation. | Authors, Nigerian–20th century–Biography. |
LCGFT: Biographies. | Literary criticism.
Classification: LCC PR9387.9.S6 Z613 2021 (print) |
LCC PR9387.9.S6 (ebook) | DDC 822/.914–dc23
LC record available at https://lccn.loc.gov/2021011690
LC ebook record available at https://lccn.loc.gov/2021011691

ISBN:	HB:	978-1-5013-7576-7
	PB:	978-1-5013-7575-0
	ePDF:	978-1-5013-7578-1
	ePUB:	978-1-5013-7577-4

Series: Black Literary and Cultural Expressions

Typeset by Integra Software Services Pvt. Ltd.
Printed and bound in the United States of America

To find out more about our authors and books visit www.bloomsbury.com
and sign up for our newsletters.

Our heroic Grandpa:
Pasitor Eleepo
who was gunned down and died in my presence for
refusing to be silent in the face of tyranny
during the Agbekoya revolt in Western State in 1969.

CONTENTS

List of Figures ix
Acknowledgments x
Preface xi

Part 1 Introduction and Context

1 Studies on Wole Soyinka 3

2 Wole Soyinka in Historical Perspective 33

Part 2 Historical and Cultural Background

3 Abẹokuta: The City of Innovations and Creativity 51

4 Collective Traditions, Childhood, and Rites of Passage 79

5 Nobel Laureate: Literary Scholarship and Nation-building 95

6 Relationships, Beliefs, and Values 113

Part 3 Literary Works

7 Soyinka's Novels 135

8 Dramatic Oeuvre 159

9 Soyinka's Poetry 177

10 The Politics of Soyinka's Literature 195

Part 4 Legacies and Conclusion

11 Soyinka's Contribution to Literature 217

12 Soyinka's Literary Achievements and the Use of Language 239

13 Conclusion: Will Soyinka's Works Outlive Him? 259

Bibliography 276
Index 290

FIGURES

Title Page	Wole Soyinka in the late 1990s	i
7.1	Soyinka in the 1980s	134
8.1	Soyinka working on *The Lion and the Jewel*	158
10.1	Fighting for justice	194
12.1	Writing in the 1990s	238
14.1	Wole Soyinka	296

Illustrations by Dr. Kazeem Ekeolu, Michael Efionayi, and Olasunmade Akano.

ACKNOWLEDGMENTS

We are indebted to many people in our humble effort to encapsulate over sixty of Wole Soyinka's published works, and his more than sixty years of political activism into a 120,000-word format for this book. We would like to thank Sarah Skinner, Amy Martin, Ben Doyle, Rebecca Willford, and their team at Bloomsbury Academic. We are grateful to Professor Adeshina Afolayan for his preliminary research work in fishing out scores of academic articles, books, and resource materials on Wole Soyinka.

While we would like to acknowledge the many authors that have instructed and influenced our understanding and analysis of Soyinka's corpus, we regret that we cannot list all. We want to thank Michael Afolayan, Mike Vickers, Augustine Agwuele, Akin Alamu, Kenneth Harrow, Ben Lindfors, James Gibbs, Olajumoke Yacob-Haliso, Aderonke Adesanya, Omobola Dauda, and Ademola Dasylva for reading some draft chapters and for their useful comments. We are grateful to Michael Efionayi, Olasunmade Akano, and Oyetunde Ekeolu for the illustrations. We are grateful to the anonymous reviewers for their time and their unanimous compliments and praise for the book. We appreciate our families for bearing with the solitary demands of being writers' spouses! To many others, who we could not list here, we are most grateful.

Toyin Falola, Texas, USA, November, 2020
Bola Dauda, Crystal Palace, UK, November, 2020

PREFACE

On July 13, 1934, Wole Soyinka was born in Abẹokuta, Nigeria, to a Yoruba mother who actively served in Nigeria's women's liberation movement and to a Yoruba father who was a principal of a school and an Anglican priest. Before his university years, Soyinka attended college preparatory school at Government College in Ibadan. He then attended the University of Leeds in England, from where he completed his degree and later received an honorary degree. During his studies at the University of Leeds, he was very active in drama and theater. Between 1958 and 1959, Soyinka was a dramaturgist at London's Royal Court Theatre and, in 1960, Soyinka received a Rockefeller bursary. At this point, he chose to go back to Nigeria in order to study African drama. During this pursuit, he also taught literature and drama at universities in Lagos, Ibadan, and Ife. He, in the meantime, founded two theater groups: "The 1960 Masks" in 1960 and the "Orisun Theatre Company" in 1964. Soyinka not only acted in these groups but also engaged in his own productions.[1]

We would like to use this opportunity to say that this work is an unauthorized biography of Wole Soyinka, and we are indebted to Kitty Kelley for her advocacy of the authenticity of unauthorized biography. In a foreword to her biography of Oprah Winfrey, Kitty Kelley, a biographer of international repute, mused that the challenge of each biography has been to answer the question, "What is the person like?"

> [T]he unauthorized biography avoids the pureed truths of revisionist history—the pitfall of authorized biography. Without having to follow the dictates of the subject, the unauthorized biographer has a much better chance to penetrate the manufactured public image, which is crucial. For, to quote President Kennedy again, "The great enemy of the truth is very often not the lie—deliberate, contrived and dishonest—but the myth—persistent, persuasive and unrealistic."[2]

---

[1] The Nobel Prize, "Wole Soyinka," *The Nobel Prize*, 1986, https://www.nobelprize.org/prizes/literature/1986/soyinka/biographical/.
[2] Kitty Kelley, *Oprah: A Biography* (New York: Three Rivers Press, 2010), xi.

Wole Soyinka is not an exception in biographical revisionism and political equivocation. In other words, what he says depends on the debate in which he is engaged. In his five-volume autobiography, one senses that Soyinka has taken liberties to tell his own story in his own way: sometimes like a fiction, emphasizing his heroics along the way and at others revealing that he is hardly a saint. For example, Soyinka wrote *Aké* in part to prove that he is "earthed." After all, even in fiction, and much more so in real life, "there are no heroes with flawless character!" He too has some "flaws" that have been pointed out by numerous others. Ironically, however, Soyinka also has a global followership and hagiographic admirers.

Thus, as the low and high pressures and the cold and warm winds from the high seas result in British weather that feels like four seasons in a day, it is so with Soyinka's life and works. His person and personality are skewed and shrouded in his swinging moods and the nature of the task and issue he had at hand at any point in time. In addition, as he confronted different subject matter, he deployed different and differing methods and instruments. Hence, both his hard-to-read books (e.g., *The Man Died: Wole Soyinka's Prison Notes*; and *A Dance of the Forests*), and the easy-to-read ones (e.g., *Aké: The Years of Childhood*; *Ibadan: The Penkelemes Years*; *Işara: The Voyage Around Essay*; and *You Must Set Forth at Dawn*) not only present the two sides—indeed, the multifaceted sides—of Wole Soyinka but also seem to have been written by different authors.

Consequently, the perception of Soyinka as a man with split personalities and contradictory feelings who still manages somewhat revolutionary positive action and political activism are situated in his never-ending internal struggles. As he confronts the proverbial hydra-headed snake of postcolonial and post-independence Nigerian geopolitics, he projects the struggle of a drowning man in a hostile sea. As the problems he confronts continually metamorphose so, too, does he seem to project and act out the melodrama, the restlessness, and the dilemma of a drowning man trying to hold his breath and remain afloat while struggling to make sense of the human condition, people's inhumanity to one another, and the "irrational world of adults."[3] He is perpetually disillusioned and frustrated as he desperately wants to do something that makes a difference, despite the difficult odds, including occasions of solitary imprisonment, exiles, and a death sentence!

In four parts, this book examines Wole Soyinka's works and life with a view not only to transcend the pure truths of revisionist history but also to demystify some presumed conventional myths that often shroud his iconic persona. The breadth and depth of the life and works of Wole Soyinka are, therefore, examined as issues rather than events. Thus, in Parts 1 and 2 "Introduction and Context," and "A Historical and Cultural

---

[3] Wole Soyinka, *Aké: The Years of Childhood* (Ibadan: Bookcraft, 2014), 319.

Background," we offer a key to help decode or decipher the studying, reading, interpretation, and the understanding of Soyinka's life and works. Indeed, a clue to demystifying the driving force that propels his writings, plays, and political activism lies in mining the interconnectedness of the "collective reality" of African history and traditions, and the "oppressive weight" of his lifelong experiences,[4] especially as they are encoded in Wole Soyinka's birthplace, "Abẹokuta: The City of Innovations and Creativity."

Arguably, Wole Soyinka is the greatest literary mind from Africa. In Part 3 "Literary Works," we examine the recurring themes in his novels, drama, poetry, and the recurring themes in the politics of Soyinka's literature. We review Soyinka's use of mythopoesis, syncretic culture, and diglossia to recreate, reconstruct, and reproduce a modernist hybridization and yet universal genre of African (alas! Yoruba) literature in English. The aim, for example in Soyinka's novels, is to show that there are themes that are worthy of vexed concentration and analysis. These themes are historically, politically, philosophically, and culturally relevant to the Nigerian reality. This part of the book also explores the thematic concerns in Wole Soyinka's novels, drama, poetry, and political treatises on themes of culture, politics, history, struggle, religion, and philosophy. This is an exploration of the perspectives of Soyinka and a linear yet interwoven plot of his life, imagination, worship, and overall, his reflections on social issues. Without doubt, Soyinka's efforts in his literary works aim to analyze issues through characters and sometimes through narration of events, and in most cases, he has placed himself (sometimes with pseudonyms) at the center of it all.

Soyinka's works can simply be defined as writing about everyday life, of the rituals of Nigeria and Nigerians, and of the collective traditions of Africa and Africans. The explorations of the thematic concerns in Soyinka's corpus aim to examine the relevance of his literary works to Africa, that is, the Pan-Africanist concerns. Soyinka's literary oeuvre is also culturally, politically, historically, and philosophically relevant to African geopolitics and reality.

African literature is essentially a committed literature. It is born out of the society in which the writer lives. In other words, African literature and African society are inextricably linked. The creation of African literary works is usually influenced by the realities of African society at any point in time. In this part, therefore, we also examine the artful and crafty ways that Wole Soyinka manifests the different layers of commitment in his plays.

Literature and stagecraft constitute a stimulus, platform, and means for the realization of Soyinka's chosen mission as a vanguard for human rights, nationalism, political activism, cultural humanism, and responsible governance. Throughout his life, Soyinka has engaged in political activism. His writings span different genres of literature, including stagecraft, to offer

---

[4] Wole Soyinka, *The Man Died: Prison Notes of Wole Soyinka* (Ibadan: Bookcraft, 2014), 319.

alternative public policy options and to inform, mobilize, and sometimes incite civil action. In the politics of Soyinka's literature, this study also investigates tropes that are commonplace in the development of his literary journey from post-independence to twenty-first century plays that classify him as a modern African playwright.

Drama texts from different periods are employed in this part in order to account for the dominant thematic preoccupations of the literary giant and how the plays from these periods manifest their social, political, cultural, economic, and existential commitment. These themes include: corruption, neocolonialism, postcolonial disillusionment, the irresponsibility of African leaders, cultural dilemma, and cultural universalism, among others. This study also identifies Yoruba cosmology, Ogun pantheon, multiplicity of meaning, and satire as the major devices Soyinka uses to foreground and discuss salient issues that are prevalent in African society.

In Part 4 "Legacies and Conclusion," we note that the legacies of Wole Soyinka's works and life are beyond the borders of Nigeria, and indeed beyond the borders of Africa, and beyond any presumed encomium of his Nobel laureate. Yes, and indisputably in part because of his personal fame, Wole Soyinka's life and social activism are of interest to audiences beyond Nigeria and the African continent. Even more important, he is unstoppable and unrelenting in acting out his moral philosophy: "That the man dies in all who keep silent in the face of tyranny."[5] Thus, his legacies will, for posterity, remain flagged and alive as the voice of the voiceless and the conscience of humanity. Indeed, it is his lifelong devotion and his Spartan commitment, if need be, to pay the supreme sacrifice for being the voice of the oppressed or "the wretched of the earth"[6] and also for the global impact of the issues that he engages and the targets of his civil actions—from sleazy insider trading, to false corporate accounting, to kleptomaniac politicians— and their fundamental significance for human conditions that reflect upon not only the North-South divide and the postcolonial conditions of Africa's independent nations but also Soyinka's status as a global icon.

---

[5] Soyinka, *The Man Died*, 3.
[6] Frantz Fanon, *The Wretched of the Earth* (New York: Grove Press, 1963).

PART 1

Introduction and Context

1

Studies on Wole Soyinka

As a student of African history in the 1970s, my supervisor, John Iliffe, advised us all that there was one African writer we had to read, "the closest Africa has come to its own Shakespeare." His name was Wole Soyinka.
NICHOLAS WESTCOTT, "SOYINKA'S CULTURAL ANTIPHONIES," 2014[1]

Introduction

Wole Soyinka is one of the greatest writers Africa has ever produced, remaining an imposing figure whose ideological convictions have been espoused in his many writings. Culturally and politically informed, Soyinka continues to command enormous social and intellectual attention within and outside the continent because of what he represents. Culturally, Wole Soyinka is a "conservative," with an obvious bias for African cultural expressions and their applications. His adeptness in Western scholarship does not dogmatically influence his views on the African ontological and epistemological viewpoint, as he effortlessly compartmentalizes the two perspectives and considers them different in their inalienable rights, in terms of who is covered by them, their makeup, or the arenas in which they are applicable. Soyinka represents the African cultural compass directed toward

---

[1] Nicholas Westcott, "Soyinka's Cultural Antiphonies," in *Crucible of the Ages: Essays in Honour of Wole Soyinka at 80*, edited by Ivor Agyeman-Duah and Ogochukwu Promise (Ibadan: Bookcraft, 2014), 27.

cultural heritages and their acceleration as the path toward self-fulfillment. He also became a cultural activist and the theme of cultural revolution reverberates in most of his intellectual product. From the perspective of Wole Soyinka, the African ontological reality has been the victim of a malicious narrative from the West and efforts to suppress it yielded predetermined results. For a very long time, Africans viewed their culture through the lens of Europeans and passed a negative judgment, hence their gravitation away from it.

Politically, Soyinka presents himself as an irrepressible voice that challenges both colonial and postcolonial political actors. On many occasions, he has solitarily engaged the Nigerian political class through his writing and physical activism. It is irrefutable that Wole Soyinka is one of those foresighted Africans who envisioned an African continent that is devoid of dependency on external aid and is capable of producing for itself the essential materials required for economic independence. It is entrenched within Soyinka's philosophy that the slow pace of development in Africa cannot be separated from its continued dependence on the Western world, or any other external power for that matter. Any expectation for the redemption of the continent's image cannot be based on the efforts of the same party that was responsible for its denigration in the first place. The people need to channel their collective revolutionary actions toward a more effective direction, where their political activities can present solutions to their existential challenges. Soyinka understands that the estrangement of African ontological values that encapsulate all of their cultural expressions is an effort to keep them in a constantly inferior position.

Soyinka became a compelling character of the twentieth century, establishing himself as a culturally and politically radical African writer whose anti-imperialism pierced through the heart of totalitarian colonial and postcolonial leaders. As if eternally blessed by his muse, Ogun, Wole Soyinka survived countless acts of deliberate brutality unscathed and he has continued his activism into the twenty-first century with a more refined approach. This explains why scholars from various academic fields dedicate so much attention to looking at the life and works of Soyinka in order to advance understanding about the African environment and the sociopolitical currency that necessitated the emergence of such an enigma.

We are attracted by the growing body of study on the intellectual giant and intend to concentrate on the analysis given of Soyinka by different writers to see how their various evaluations of him represent his ideological convictions and revolutionary action and combine to produce a portrait of him and his work. In what follows, we identify many of the most important works.

Scars of Conquest/Masks of Resistance: The Invention of Cultural Identities in African, African-American, and Caribbean Drama by Tẹjumọla Ọlaniyan

Ọlaniyan's material,[2] although laden with exposition about African drama and its evolution, also offers an overlapping experience with Eurocentric, Afrocentric, and post-Afrocentric perspectives and reveals the intellectual depth of Wole Soyinka as demonstrated through his distinctive literary style and methods that are usually drawn from African epistemic perception. Ọlaniyan observes that the literary productions of his selected African writers, including Soyinka, are an enunciation of their racial and political experiences interlaced with power politics from the hegemonic structure. Ọlaniyan contends that Soyinka is a cultural purist who specifically roots for Afrocentric cultures or values, as it enables African cultural emancipation from the complex politics of nuanced identities. Although Soyinka tends toward repudiating the erroneous mindset that African drama is a branch of its Western counterpart, as the system and form are an offshoot, Ọlaniyan notes that at the heart of Soyinka's drama is a conscious effort in support of an African inscription of its unique identity and the independent formation of its style.

In his examination of the work of selected dramatists including Soyinka, Derek Walcott, Amiri Baraka, and Ntozake Shange, Ọlaniyan reveals the various individual cultural struggles that collectively serve as the pretext for these writers' revolution protesting the inferiorization of African identity through their plays. It is against this background that Soyinka uses his literary ingenuity to challenge the hegemonic agenda of the Universalist, who views African drama exclusively through the Eurocentric lens. It indicates something interesting about Eurocentric interpretations of African drama or other indices of culture through which the identification of people is possible. This book argues that the affixation of the historical rise of African drama within the ambit of European exploitation in Africa underrepresents the African indigenous ontological expertise in this discourse and unduly promotes the Western bias against African epistemology, especially in the dramaturgical domain. Whereas the intellectual product of Wole Soyinka and others continues to reveal that this one-sided interpretation reeks of pompous arrogance because African drama is different in its own right and constitutes an independent canon, not a dependent variable or an

---

[2] Tẹjumọla Ọlaniyan, *Scars of Conquest/Masks of Resistance: The Invention of Cultural Identities in African, African-American, and Caribbean Drama* (New York: Oxford University Press, 1995).

appendage to its Western counterpart. Making that kind of claim is an indirect validation of a master-subordinate relationship.

Here, the author demonstrates that Soyinka, among others, is irrevocably convinced that the styles, techniques, and aesthetic values of African drama are distinct from other traditions and therefore invalidates the assumption that they are only worthy of being treated as a dangling appendage behind European drama.[3] Wole Soyinka believes that the application of an inferior status placed on African drama is another subtle front in the war for superiority, which seeks to impose Western dominance on the African people, as was done in religion, politics, and then in science and technology. Those who would seek such an imposition are working from unfounded claims and their generalizations often made about African drama are demonstrations of hegemonic dominance in the sense that they attempt to force the African identity out of currency. Knowing this allows African dramatists, chiefly Soyinka, to shape their dramatic techniques, aesthetic, and other aspects of their work in ways that reveal Africanness and establish their essential capacity for difference rather than deference to Western traditions. When Frantz Fanon remarks that "there is a fact: White men consider themselves superior to black men,"[4] he was alluding to the underlying imperialism of Europeans in Africa and its resulting convoluted politics of dominance imposed on Africans and their epistemological existence. Accordingly, writers like Wole Soyinka use their art to protest this insidious condescension, which seeks to establish that Africans are grossly incapable of equaling the cultural establishment.

To the extent that the contention of the validity of independent African "drama" was a widespread discursive engagement, Ruth Finnegan, one of the foremost researchers on African oral legacies, lends her voice to the existing controversy surrounding it. She questions the originality of the form, owing to her understanding that Africans historically tended toward oral heritages like poetry, panegyrics, and others.[5] This understanding is premised on the unsupported conclusion that the elements of African drama are derivations of their European counterparts, since they share certain similarities and so are not independent concepts on their own. The maintenance of this mindset instigates divisive thinking about the originality of African drama and tries to smash its prospects by concluding that its points of difference with the Western domain are indications of weakness and inferiority. This inferiorization of African drama discredits its identity and inaptly places it below its European counterparts as an appendage of minimum or zero

---

[3] Olaniyan, *Scars of Conquest*.
[4] Frantz Fanon, *A Dying Colonialism*, trans. Haakon Chevalier (New York: Grove Press, 1967).
[5] Ruth Finnegan, *Oral Literature in Africa* (Nairobi: Oxford University Press, 1970).

value. Consequently, the ascription of tragedy to African drama is derisively discredited.

This, coupled with the systematic racism embodied in the struggle for hegemonic dominance in scholarship, becomes the existential hurdle that African dramatists must jump over. Wole Soyinka produced a chronological sequence of dramas that not only disarmed these misconceptions but also unmasked the underlying imperialism that motivated them. African drama evolved from the cultural pressure to establish a dramaturgical difference that reflects not only the African identity but also validates its racial essentialism against the impression that it is an extension of the European formulation—and its consequent erroneous misrepresentation as residue in the hegemonic structure and dominance of the West. The centuries-old relationship has reconfigured many African practices so much that the separation of facts and fictions appears difficult, which necessitates the hybridization of their ideas and cultures, and this informs the West's misrepresentation that Africans do not have a specific cultural history from which the genre of drama can be drawn. This misconception is disrobed though by the production of dramas that do not share Eurocentric characteristics, such as Soyinka's plays.

The valorization of Wole Soyinka comes from the understanding that his works make a distinct departure from such uninformed conclusions as they betray the collective identity understood in the Western world. Because their prolonged imperialism created an unbalanced relationship, the Europeans believe that the only cultural space from which Africans can negotiate their existence is the one handed to them by their colonizers. Therefore, when Africans did come up with a dramatic identity in which the identifiable common characteristics of Europeans' identity is cleverly rejected, the counter-reaction became necessary to avoid the appearance that they were giving up their quest to be considered as the foundation of progress and civilization from which every other expression of humans, especially Africans, is drawn. It is for this reason that Soyinka's dramatic productions are exclusively nationalistic, espousing cultural traditions that are neither produced in Europe or its imagined or real territories. Based on the reality that African drama is actually an intersection of Eurocentric, Afrocentric, and then the post-Afrocentric discourses, Olaniyan contends that "many manifestations of the post-Afrocentric, on the other hand, evince suggestions of a performative cultural identity."[6] Africa, regardless of the fact of even a racial category that seemingly brings the people together tied to the experience of slavery in which the Europeans played essential roles to sustain, is an environment where heterogeneous cultural traditions are rife and the idea of diverse sociopolitical realities is inevitable.

---

[6] Olaniyan, *Scars of Conquest*, 34.

It is exciting that Wole Soyinka is a cultural purist who chooses to expound on an aspect of African culture that should be retained and celebrated by his generation. He prepares the mind of his audience for the dangers to African culture inherent in the visitation of Europeans in Africa. He laments its dislocation, which is a byproduct of their racist prejudices and the corresponding hegemonic relationships, and rebuffs the idea that European cultural praxis is the very foundation for African practices because of his conviction that African culture is self-sufficient. Therefore, it became imperative for Africans to fight against traces of the Eurocentric hegemony that roots for constant dislocation of the African identity. The fact that the Western world denied for ages the existence of anything under the tag of "African Literature" became the very point of resistance because the promulgation of such unsubstantiated ideas could only destroy African knowledge systems further. Soyinka's negation of this superstructure seeks to achieve a very subtle goal: the essentialization of African knowledge systems, especially in the literary industry. Soyinka continues to make known in his works and ideology that the glorification of African history does not necessarily mean the devaluation of its European counterparts, but that this celebration is necessary because it enables the shattered African identity to be reclaimed and for the world to accept their self-dependency.

Principally, Soyinka contends with the racial prejudice inherent in European exceptionalism, which seeks bragging rights for some unwarranted sense of superiority. In his own words, as quoted by Ọlaniyan, and given in reaction to the idea that drama originated from Europe:

> I remember my shock as a student of literature and drama when I read that drama originated in Greece. What is this? I couldn't quite deal with it. What are they talking about? I never heard my grandfather talk about Greeks invading Yorubaland. I couldn't understand. I've lived from childhood with drama. I read at the time that tragedy evolved as a result of the rites of Dionysus. Now we all went through this damn thing, so I think the presence [sic] of eradication had better begin.[7]

In essence, he found it irreconcilable that the dramatic productions that he and many other Africans, had access to in his childhood are attributed to Europeans—even to groups that have not gained any access to Africa. He became very uncomfortable with such an uninformed conclusion and decided to challenge its authenticity in his intellectual productions. As such, Soyinka's drama shows Afrocentric cultures and patterns, without being indebted to Western styles and systems. He considered them complementary.

---

[7] Wole Soyinka, as quoted in Ọlaniyan, *Scars of Conquest*, 45.

Wole Soyinka: Politics, Poetics, and Postcolonialism by Biọdun Jeyifo

Predominantly, Biọdun Jeyifo[8] explores the interconnectedness of Soyinka's writings and their political essence, bolstered by the understanding that his works evince radicalism against every structure of domination and subjugation. The Nigerian environment in which Soyinka was raised has had different phases of colonization and, by extension, imperialism that saw the subjugation of the people's resolve and their quest for democratic leadership. Although he was too young to use his literary ingenuity to challenge colonial power in the heyday of the colonial occupation of Nigeria and the turn against colonialism in the wake of the Second World War that necessitated or compelled the British disengagement from its colonies, and accepting the imminent reality of the need to prepare for Nigeria's self-government, Soyinka dedicated his revolutionary works to the excoriation of hegemonic dominance of both the West and neocolonial Africans, which continued beyond the era of colonization. Jeyifo's book examines how the different experiences of political brutality culminated in the commitment to challenge power regardless of the inherent consequences.[9] The acrimonious relationship between Wole Soyinka and the Nigerian government was caused by his uncompromising dedication to struggles for political emancipation from all predatory actors, whether the colonial power, their neocolonial accessories, or others of the same mindset.

Jeyifo provides the political background that encouraged the literary radicalism of Soyinka, just as it did for the majority of African writers of this period. African countries had been experiencing an overwhelming rise of political recognition, secured for them by their successful dislocation from European imperialists in their political arena, through either persuasion or some show of resistance. The reality that they remained immersed in the Western strategy of governance, however, brought them into another phase of their evolutionary process, as they mostly functioned using the philosophies of their erstwhile imperialists. This means that they operated through values and virtues representative of the European expansionists to the detriment of their African identity, which inevitably led to the resuscitation of dissent and resistance from the radical activists who used their different media to protest the marginalization of the African masses and their unwarranted estrangement and disenfranchisement. Soyinka can comfortably be classed as one of these vociferous antagonists against the systematic subversion of the Nigerian people and the denial of their fundamental rights. He was acutely

---

[8] Biọdun Jeyifo, *Wole Soyinka: Politics, Poetics, and Postcolonialism* (New York: Cambridge University Press, 2004).
[9] Jeyifo, *Wole Soyinka: Politics*.

dedicated to the emancipation struggles of the people if the government continued to show indifference to the travails of the defenseless masses.

Soyinka's progression in the activist movement is well-documented. He fully participated in the struggles against totalitarian regimes from Britain that oversaw the subjugation of Africa and the continued exploitation of its resources. Joined by a group of passionate Africans who prioritized the welfare of their fellows, Soyinka set a very sturdy foundation for his future activism, which would later be given unfettered attention upon his return to Africa where he had the opportunity to rub minds with Afrocentric scholars with similar interests. These experiences constituted the background to the development of his participation in anti-progressive struggles on Nigerian sociopolitical terrain.

The author celebrates Soyinka's ability to respond to the growing challenges on both political and intellectual fronts. Politically, the new Nigeria was confronted with massive incompetence in leadership, which was negatively reflected in the day-to-day lifestyles of Nigerians. Simultaneously, the European bias was growing inadvertently because, for a very long time, many Africans had to conform to European misconceptions, spread across the board, aimed at the delegitimization of African ontological reality. With these problems at hand, it was evident that Soyinka's generation was confronted by challenges to which they had to rise, both reflexively and appropriately.

Jeyifo explores Soyinka's artistic lifestyle and commends the commitment he has toward the repudiation of the political class, who seek to continue the process of intimidation and misrule without restraint. Soyinka has faced challenges and risks on many occasions in his quest to ensure political reform and the enthronement of a political culture that would focus on a governance prioritizing good policies designed to help the helpless masses. He serves as an amalgam of radical philosophy and activism, considering his revolutionary efforts and wise instincts in arresting situations that appear complexly problematic. Given the country's level of moral shortcomings, radical activism for Soyinka goes beyond what can be comfortably limited to his books. So, in his commitment to fight for the rights of ordinary individuals and healthy democratic processes, Soyinka undertook some courageous steps. For example, just like the fourteenth-century Robin Hood's civic action, Soyinka boldly intercepted the pickpockets who attempted to rob an old woman in Ibadan, and also invaded a radio station to block the premier's recorded broadcast claiming victory in a rigged election. In the early 1960s, concluding that the Western Nigerian government was impeding true democracy, Soyinka served as a maverick to destroy the government's plans to wrongfully deploy executive power for personal benefit. Immediately after the breakdown of law and order in Western Region and the subsequent crises that emerged after the two military coup d'états in 1966, Soyinka interfered in the impending secessionist quest of the Biafran struggle, both intervening and playing a mediatory role.

These bold steps provide evidence of his aversion to tyrannical leadership and incompetence in the domain of politics. For this reason, he was recognized in the country as one of the most dedicated activists in the cause of economic and political freedom. When examined closely, virtually all of Soyinka's works are demonstrations of protest and resistance, employing his usual radical use of satire to provoke political self-evaluation. In whatever medium or style he chose, Soyinka was uncompromising in his dedication to emancipation struggles and there is sufficient evidence demonstrating this commitment beyond many of his contemporaries. Whatever the struggle for freedom required monetarily, ideologically, morally, or physically he always made himself available to the revolution of African democracy. Although Soyinka belongs to an elite social cartel, who believe themselves qualified for special sociopolitical benefits and treatment in society, philosophically, he has always shown his revolutionary orientation against his own class by identifying with the masses. The sustained protest by admirers of his writing about the relative obscurity of his literary works has always been mollified by their acclaim for his sacrificial actions consistently directed against oppressive and tyrannical regimes.

Stylistically, Jeyifo, like many critics, sees Soyinka as an unyieldingly activist writer with an exceptional willingness to accept the obscurity of his writing. Whenever it appeared that the Nigerian political class was unconcerned by his campaigns against them in his intellectual productions, Soyinka accompanied his revolutionary messages with physical protests to ensure that he achieved his mass-oriented intentions. In the service of what he believes in, he has spearheaded many protests and actions of sometimes quixotic resistance against the government, most of which came with unimaginable consequences for his freedom. Soyinka's artistic competence and his political and intellectual ruggedness are indicative of his rough-hewn views and approach to issues that bear the mark of social injustice. Soyinka will not bow to pressure, regardless of the many ways that his liberty is threatened. Instead of reneging on his calls for social emancipation, in difficult situations, he can bend his style and methods to ensure that he continues his fearless engagement with oppressors. It is genuinely inspiring that Soyinka's works combine artistic mastery with political radicalism to produce a force for change in Nigeria, and indeed the whole of Africa by extension, to promote the recognition of people's rights. Attracting this level of controversy and social contradiction to himself eventually paved the way for his ascension into stardom. The articulation of people's rights has never failed to invite personal sacrifice and the experience of Soyinka could not be any different.

Jeyifo explores Soyinka's theoretical evolution, identifying him as a man who gravitated from anti-Negritudism to becoming a neo-Negritudist in his later works that depict a celebration of a precolonial African past, with his many characters trying to locate their philosophical essence within the nucleus of their being. Soyinka has continued to grow in acceptance of the inherent reality that true African development lies in the appreciation of the past and the exploration of its ideas. One instructive way to understand this purposeful shift is to interrogate the characters in his earlier works, during the 1950s to the 1960s. The majority of them demonstrate aversion to customs and the conventional institutions of African society, remaining indifferent to their cultural identity. According to Jeyifo, these early works of Soyinka, including *A Dance of the Forests* (1960), *The Strong Breed* (1963), *The Swamp Dwellers* (1963), and *The Interpreters* (1965), as well as essays such as "The Future of West African Writing" (1958), and "Towards a True Theatre" (1962), contain characters that are aloof to their Africa identity and represent an entirely different philosophical construct. Inevitably, this stance has an undertone of resistance to the establishment of the popular movement available during the period.[10]

Soyinka, whose early works are a revelation in their utter criticism of the romanticizing of the African past, suddenly transformed his artistic productions to project the image of the precolonial African world filled with celebration and adoration of its historical beginnings. This is not done for the mere aggrandizement of the past, as can be erroneously perceived or imagined. Instead, it is a smart, suggestive way toward the enthronement of resistance to the hegemonic or imperialistic dispositions of the West. Consciously or otherwise, imperialism can be actively confronted with the apparent reification of African cultural traditions through their affirmation. This book, therefore, educates us about the transposition of the African identity into Soyinka's later characters, who now embrace their indigenous identity and are unapologetic about it. Jeyifo notes that works such as *Poems of Black Africa* (1974), *Death and the King's Horseman* (1975), and *Ogun Abibiman* (1976) give hints about Soyinka's ideological evolution, as they are more of an indictment of the Western characters and explore the lives of the African people.[11] For example, the core idea shared in *Death and the King's Horseman* is the affirmation of the African communal humanitarian tradition in which individuals make sacrifices for the good of their community or humanity. Without a doubt, Wole Soyinka is not only seen by Jeyifo as a political activist, rather he is accordingly considered as a postcolonial critic.

Wole Soyinka by James Gibbs

James Gibbs[12] offers a biographical approach to Soyinka and presents helpful information about the man and his revolutionary works. The chronological sequence of his artistic productions is combined with exploration of his

---

[10] Jeyifo, *Wole Soyinka: Politics*, 280–4.
[11] Jeyifo, *Wole Soyinka: Politics*, 280–4.
[12] James Gibbs, *Wole Soyinka* (London: Macmillan Publishers, 1986).

philosophical conventions and it gives a commendable summary of the man in question. Soyinka's formative years were spent in Abẹokuta and his elementary education was provided in a Yoruba society where he had access to the culture and traditions that would eventually become the foundation and pillars of his artistic competence. He moved to Ibadan when approaching adulthood, where he was introduced to tertiary education, which was again garnished with the societal culture and systems available in the city. Between 1954 and 1959, Soyinka went to England to continue his academic pursuits and set his career in the right direction,[13] but after his education in Leeds and his professional work in London, he decided to return to his cultural home of Nigeria to conduct research and expand his intellectual horizons. Gibbs looks into some of the autobiographical accounts provided by Soyinka himself to reveal the sociocultural or religious-cultural background of the foremost African writer and concludes that resistance to every establishment of superiority has been present from the beginning of his journey.

Gibbs clinically establishes that the town of Aké was symbolic in the making of the man, as it was the spatial setting that enhanced his access to the expansive Yoruba culture, which he considered the source of his inspiration. As we have highlighted in Chapter 4, Aké constitutes an ideological environment and society that can introduce the curious to the Yoruba cultural traditions and systems, leaving them to locate their identity within the temporal space. At the same time, Aké's immersion in Yoruba culture is relatively limited because it was a refugee settlement that allowed a mix of different individuals with varying cultural and religious philosophies, modestly and purposefully contaminated by the influx of diverse people into the space. Soyinka got further cultural marination in his father's hometown of Iṣara, which was descriptively distant from the influence of European Christianity and culture, deciding to gain access to that environment so that his quest for the acquisition of his cultural traditions could be gladly achieved.

Soyinka's childhood exploits charted his way to the greatness he eventually was synonymous with. His enrollment in schools in childhood and interest in obtaining a university education, with his exploits made in the process, are indicative of his unusual dedication to a productive future. Wole Soyinka's ascension to fame was sprinkled with various experiences capable of consuming some individuals. For example, according to Gibbs, while he was at the University of Leeds, Soyinka decided to pursue an interest in politics and offer his contributions to the administration of the school. However, his lofty ambition was smashed because of the underlying racism woven into the fabric of the European world. He began to develop the understanding that Africans and Europeans possessed two different cultures that are each meant

---

[13] Gibbs, *Wole Soyinka*.

to be protected with political power. His artistic proclivity would therefore earn him some respect and attention from his academic environment in England, as his artistic skill became a point of attraction. No sooner had he completed his academic pursuits, than he was offered the opportunity to participate in the activities of their theater in London.[14]

One of Wole Soyinka's outstanding characteristics has been his ability to maneuver the media into airing his opinions. He has been an essential voice, making significant contributions to the effacement of political and moral decadence that has engulfed his country, and he did not concede to pressure from the authorities whenever they intended to manipulate the people. For his principles, predominantly centered on the improvement of conditions of the people, he became the enemy of the state in his adamance about pursuing his worthy goals. Having begun his career as a promising lecturer at Ife's University College in 1962, he lent his voice to addressing the controversies relating to the issues of academic freedom and university autonomy on one hand, and the politicization of the university community and governmental interference in the affairs of the university on the other, that have overtaken the Nigerian sociopolitical space and, in some cases, made efforts to create some himself. This placed unpleasant pressure on the federal government, who did everything to employ very combative tactics against him, attempting to crush his engagement and frustrate his efforts. However, Soyinka has never shown any sign of weakness, even before his appointment as a university lecturer, and his refusal to bow to the pressure of the Nigerian government in this period invited the state punishment of him that was manifested in the continual and intimidating pressure exerted on him. Instead of compromising his standards, he peacefully resigned his position as a lecturer.[15]

His system of managing oppressors and the victimization engendered in the process of their oppression is remarkably different. Leaving the school premises where he contributed to the correction of the residual rot in Nigerian leadership did not mean Soyinka bowed to pressure; instead, it allowed him to become more creative in handling his situation. Immediately after his resignation, Soyinka next embraced drama as the appropriate medium through which his critical assessment of the government would garner further interest. This time around, the nature of the work and using the media allowed him to reach out to a broader audience, who would consume his many satiric productions and feel innately disappointed in the ways that the political class handled their collective welfare in the postcolonial environment. Since the early postcolonial period was filled with contradictions and intense controversies, Soyinka's plays represented

---

[14] Gibbs, *Wole Soyinka*, 4.
[15] Gibbs, *Wole Soyinka*, 6.

events that countered the government on many fronts, given that they were too prone to violence, provoking political expediencies. Soyinka primarily committed to the exposition of this underlying debacle with consistent intensity.

Gibbs also records one of Soyinka's significant experiences of activism, when he courageously challenged the abrasive political decisions that were subverting the will of the masses for the interests of elites. This was the insidiously and cavalierly planned installation of Chief S. L. Akintọla, the then premier of the Western Region, in an electoral process that was marred by violence and the disproportionate arrogance of the power brokers. This commodification of justice using state power was considered a breach of the trust that the public had reposed in their constituted authority, and citizens like Wole Soyinka would not sit helplessly by without introducing his dramatic contributions to address the situation. As in the case of the invasion of the radio station, Soyinka decided to stage a counteraction that was intended to check the premier in his excessive use of power. The remarkable Soyinka's reversal of Akintọla's announcement of victory, along with a solemn warning of civil revolt, on Western Nigerian Radio made Soyinka famous as he eventually won despite his methods.[16]

The book *Wole Soyinka* reveals that the man is a social liberator in his own right. Indeed, there are sufficient reasons to consider him as one of the chief moral police officers in Nigerian society. He confidently challenged the government and has consistently encouraged them to adopt better political views and philosophies to advance the country and the African people as a whole. From *Opera Wonyosi*, which was produced in 1976, to *Requiem For a Futurologist*, the challenge for good leadership devoid of corruption was thematically highlighted. Soyinka continues to express the ideological convictions that shaped his plays and writings. His dedication to the development of a Nigerian society where corruption and the abuse of power are reduced to a minimum makes him remain socially relevant even long after the climax of his intellectual productions. Inevitably, Soyinka's growing body of work came with multiple benefits, as his unfettered commitment to the writing of plays aimed at containing the excesses of the Nigerian government, along with his introduction of new styles and systems to Nigerian drama, won him attention and accolades around the world.

When creative writers decide to correct a growing anomaly in their society, they are inclined to use their work to address the situation. In the case of Wole Soyinka, many of his plays are an indictment of the political elite and the detached middle-class, who follow their responsibility to society with spurious attention. The Nigerian elites never accepted the

---

[16] Justice Eso dismissed the case against Wole Soyinka on technical grounds. For details, see Wole Soyinka, *You Must Set Forth at Dawn* (Ibadan: Bookcraft, 2006, 2014), 102–3.

responsibility to develop their social values or upgrade them using the benefit of the exposure to international governance good practices that their privileged education accorded them. Instead, they denounce their culture and distance themselves from their African identity. For example, the character of Lakunle in Soyinka's *The Lion and the Jewel* comes across as someone who demonstrates excessive Eurocentrism. Lakunle, an educated man, instantly departed from the cultural traditions governing the roles of a would-be suitor toward his intended bride. His awareness of the established culture and norms notwithstanding, Lakunle decides to adopt European values in a situation where African tradition is expected to be followed. As the possibility of being the chosen groom becomes very uncertain, he decides to ridicule and denigrate the bride-price tradition as akin to buying a heifer.

For the arrogant political elite, Soyinka has equally corrective plays that speak to their apparently maladjusted positions on the well-being of the people. The connivance of spiritual fathers within the political elite gives room for expanded corruption that places people on the wrong trajectory in the long run. *The Trials of Brother Jero*, produced in 1960, is a clear statement of condemnation of the spiritual leaders who deliberately serve as the political accessories to the influential elite. Their decision to provide this needed support, both moral and spiritual, has some unbearable consequences for the development of society. The play reflects the extensive corruption in Nigerian politics and its spiritual aspect, interacting to deny the citizens their fundamental human rights. There can be no mistaking Soyinka's intention to engage the leaders of the country to show them the consequences of irresponsible leadership and the overwhelmingly destructive ways by which the people are generally affected as a result. Gibbs's work projects the intellectual as an asset of inestimable value to Nigeria and Africa at large. The fact that Soyinka continues to attract further studies is an allusion to his unique greatness.

"'The Story We Had To Tell': How Chinua Achebe and Wole Soyinka Reclaimed Nigerian Identity Through Their Writing" by Clara Brodie

Clara Brodie,[17] who carried out a comparative study on two of the foremost Nigerian writers, remarks on the contributions of Wole Soyinka, which

---

[17] Clara Brodie, "'The Story We Had To Tell': How Chinua Achebe and Wole Soyinka Reclaimed Nigerian Identity Through Their Writing," *Honors Thesis Collection*, Wellesley College, Paper 89, 2013, https://repository.wellesley.edu/thesiscollection/89.

therefore warrants its entry here. Chinua Achebe and Wole Soyinka are arguably two of the most talented literary minds from Nigeria, who used their intellectual productions to challenge the European imperialists and promote African identity as a means of protest. Soyinka's experience as a Nigerian growing up under the influence of Christianity was developed alongside mixed religious experiences, leading to his hybrid identity. His access to an English education provided him with the material to challenge the supremacy of European identity by considering it through his native systems and establishing the originality and essentialness of the African epistemology. Brodie comments that the underlying philosophy and activism of Soyinka are geared toward the reconstruction of African identity through the excavation of its history, situating the continent on an appropriate pedestal in preparation for future advancement. As a cultural revolutionary, Soyinka confronts the hegemonic interpretation of African history and the devaluation of its identity, which has become the primary focus of the supremacist ideologies.

The acknowledgment of Soyinka's profound status is reinforced by the commendations which several literary critics direct toward him. Apart from being highly successful in the production of plays and dramas, Soyinka has authored several works of prose and poetry which makes him unique among writers of Nigerian ancestry. As if the fame he has acquired for himself in the literary world was not enough, he also commands impressive recognition in Nigeria's political realm because of his many engagements with the political elite of the country, especially during their shows of moral shortcomings. Soyinka intervened in various political conflicts, which would have had severe consequences for the fragile unity of the country, by playing the role of a maverick and producing works that mounted pressure on the ruling class at various times. It is not an exaggeration to conclude that his prolific nature was instrumental in the conferment of the much-coveted literary title of Nobel laureate in 1986. In this piece, Brodie has staked the position of Soyinka in the reclamation of the lost African identity and demonstrates how relentlessly committed he was to the cause of Africa. Without a doubt, the communicative personality for which he is known is spotlighted by his political activism.

Interestingly, Soyinka's writings continue to comment on the dislocation of colonial philosophy and he has committed the majority of his ongoing efforts to the project of the African Cultural Revolution. There can be no mistaking the works of Soyinka, which subtly reject the overindulgence of the West by diplomatically producing the African alternative and thereby advocating for African heritage as the necessary philosophical base from which Africans must develop their environment and view of the world. The works of Soyinka and their Afrocentric sentiments are geared toward identity politics and political freedom, invalidating the erroneous conclusions of Europeans about the non-standardization of African values and the purported subordination of them. Soyinka's writing has shown that Africans are people with an impressive history, but his exploration of various genres demonstrates that nothing is alien to them, including that which the West has brought. Therefore, any attempt to discredit the people on account of their history is at best malicious or hateful and, at worst, suppressive. Repudiating the Western hegemonic narrative, Africans are duty-bound to resist the cultural deracination attempts that were disguised through the misrepresentation of their history and Soyinka is one of the African writers that was at the forefront of this struggle.

Brodie considers Soyinka's classic, *Death and the King's Horseman*, as an instrument for confronting the sweeping European generalization about African religion and its spiritual disposition. She sees Soyinka as someone with a force of ideas that are usually dressed within democratic conventions, where the adherent of the culture is left to determine their choice without coercion. The Yoruba world philosophizes sacrifice as something necessary and essential to the advancement of the people, required for the circulation of events to occur and the distribution of equality in society. In this paradigm, the success of a community is to an extent determined by the readiness of the people to make the necessary sacrifices. From the individual level to the broader context of society, there can be no avoidance of sacrifice, as that is the essential requirement for humans and ideas to be recycled. While Christianity, introduced by Europeans, celebrates the sacrifice of their religious figure, Jesus Christ, they are appalled by the sociocultural necessity of Ẹlẹṣin Ọba, the protagonist in the play, to sacrifice himself for the lives of the people in order to experience tranquility. The reservations of these Europeans led to the eruption of controversy,[18] as they were interested in attacking such cultures out of parochial or political sentiment.

Creatively, Soyinka considers the sacrifice of an individual who is culturally interpreted as serving as a judge keeping societal peace and how failure to conform to the established norms would perhaps lead to the loss of many more lives. The author creatively questions the social ethics of the West, who pry into African affairs and pass judgment on them based on their cultural perspective of life. While it is tenable that one can interpret other people's culture from their own standpoint, it is bewildering that an individual would decide to impose their cultural view on others. Brodie concludes that

> Soyinka comments that he has backdated the play so that the action takes place during World War II; as a result, the violence abroad highlights the dramatic contrast between a local dispute and the backdrop of an entire

---

[18] Wole Soyinka, *Death and the King's Horseman* (London: Secker and Warburg, 1975).

world turned upside down. It proves the question of why the sacrifice of one man according to Yoruba tradition should be considered so barbaric when western patriots simultaneously glorify the slaughtering of millions of troops in the name of nationalism.[19]

In essence, Wole Soyinka has posed a moral question to the interventionist West, which turns a blind eye to the massacres of the Second World War but decides to interfere with the cultural traditions of the African people.

The play draws a convergence between Yoruba culture and traditions with their religious philosophy. Against the incorrect assessment that Ẹlẹṣin's impending death should be associated with murder or suicide, Soyinka clarifies that it is neither. When Joseph remarks in the play, "He will not kill anybody, and no one will kill him. He will simply die,"[20] he was referring to the apparent differences that exist with the European understanding of deaths of that nature. Ẹlẹṣin is neither murdered, nor did he commit suicide by following the cultural mandate to embark on a spiritual journey with the dead king. Looking at this situation from a very different philosophical standpoint, Soyinka cleverly establishes that two cultures are different and one does not deserve being wrongly described because it does not conform to the styles and systems of the other. The play embodies the beliefs of Africans about the afterlife; they culturally understand that the journey of man continues beyond the physical realm, and therefore the continuation of traditions beyond death must be considered. Against this background, they ready special preparations for dying kings, who they believe are carrying the image of their culture and traditions into the afterlife. European Christians believe very differently; the stoppage of man's physical existence is seen as an end, at least until the events of the world are brought to a final halt. This was the motivation behind their intervention in the fulfillment of the conflicting cultural traditions in the Yoruba world.

Interestingly, Soyinka also addresses the many philosophical challenges tied to the employment of the Western education system for the development of an African mind. Rather than bringing about the desired changes and improvements, he reports that they are always a pastiche of contradictions, as their ideas and the ideologies they acquire are mostly irreconcilable. *The Interpreters* becomes symbolic when it talks about the various views of the characters about a similar topic, caused by their variegated experiences within the respective places from where they obtained their knowledge. Even when interpreters are expected to serve as competent mediators between people and their supposed messages, the delivery of their messages is challenged by their irreconcilable experience. This captures the postcolonial situation of

---

[19] Brodie, "The Story We Had To Tell," 32.
[20] Soyinka, *Death and the King's Horseman*, 22.

the majority of African countries where people, upon their acquisition of Western knowledge, became determined to contribute to the improvement of their society. Generally, these people may have the intention to make their society a cynosure to all eyes, but the fact remains that they are prone to conflicts of interest because of their different perceptions and understanding of life.

Soyinka's language is usually esoteric and this explains why many critics refer to him as an obscurantist literary scholar. Soyinka agrees that the adoption of European languages has contextual shortcomings in transmitting the cultural messages of Africans. The adoption of colonial languages has automatically influenced the cultural direction of the people and it is only logical that they should domesticate the language in order to express their traditions and systems and avoid becoming vulnerable to losing their language and cultural identity in the general scheme of things. Despite the obvious downsides of using European languages to express African culture, Soyinka considered it desirable to construct the African experience using them in order that their messages get across to the appropriate quarters. The available reality does not allow for the adoption of African languages to confront the hegemonic West, as it would restrict its coverage. Without using the language of the colonizers, radical activism against the extension of colonization would be immediately defeated. Several controversies arise from the employment of the English language in Africa, as it is another effort toward the deterioration of African language and then culture, but there is no mistaking Soyinka's conclusion about the inevitability of such a situation.

"The Theatre of Wole Soyinka: Inside the Liminal World of Myth, Ritual and Postcoloniality" by Oluwakẹmi Atanda Ilọri

Here, Wole Soyinka's works are examined through the lens of their mythic, liminal, and postcolonial focuses as Ilọri argues that their contents are replications of expressions of the African worldview and colonial experience.[21] Africans' established belief systems are woven around the structure of myth and Ilọri draws the connection between African philosophy and the mythification of some of their cultural indexes, which

---

[21] Oluwakẹmi Atanda Ilọri, "The Theatre of Wole Soyinka: Inside the Liminal World of Myth, Ritual and Postcoloniality" (PhD diss., University of Leeds, 2016), http://etheses.whiterose.ac.uk/15733/1/ILORI%2C%20O.A.%20School%20of%20Performance%20%26%20Cultural%20Industries%20PhD%202016.pdf.

in turn provides sociological significance in building a morally vibrant society, a politically advanced environment, and also a spiritually informed group of people. Immersed in the culture of the African people, the author understands the undeniable place of mythical creation in social engineering toward a particular direction. It is inarguable that the establishment of myths and their sustenance serves all the purposes highlighted because the life of an average African, regardless of their professed Christian or Islamic faith, is evidence in this mythical belief system. Therefore, it is not surprising that the imposition of Western systems does not automatically put an end to new structures with precolonial roots, seen in how the mythical representation of Soyinka's world is tethered to his dedication to ideas and purposes, which ultimately usually provoke a certain rebirth of the primordial African myths and beliefs.

Identified as the physical manifestation of his mythical muse, Ogun, Soyinka's works never depart from the ideological convictions of the Yoruba ancestral figure, who is saddled with bringing about creation and the destruction of every existence considered unproductive and vain. As such, it is not odd that Soyinka is regarded as a dominant force for the introduction of the desired environment in Nigerian society. Just as Ogun uses metallic objects to conduct its metaphysical exercise in the process of rebirth, Soyinka is a literary icon who uses his artistic productions to force society toward rejuvenation and recreation. His works, especially his plays, are critical of the government and always address the excesses of power and the need to reconsider collective indulgence in morally condemnable activities, which are presented as indicators of imminent destruction. His mythical influence is appropriately represented by the level of commitment Soyinka has to his struggles and convictions. In the process of fighting for a rebirth and renewal of social ideas, there are examples of his personal sacrifices when he faced odd and extreme experiences in order to send his revolutionary messages to society.

The convergence of the mythical figure Ogun with Wole Soyinka is seen in how Ogun usually undertakes assignments that promise the emancipation of the masses against intemperate oppressors. Similarly, Soyinka has shown through different embarkations that he is committed to the struggles of the common people despite whatever personal sacrifices are called for. Whatever it required, Soyinka provided his revolutionary works with matching energy off the page, when he confronted the government on numerous occasions. One significant example is when he was clamped down on by the government for taking some courageous steps to approach the Biafran leaders to reconsider their decision to secede from Nigeria, which were deliberately misinterpreted because of their ill intentions. It is difficult to understand how he escaped the rough experiences that threatened his life. On many occasions, Soyinka succeeded in the face of unimaginable catastrophe because he was unbending in his determination to ensure that the environment be changed for the betterment of the masses. It is hard to believe he always made himself available to serve the people because of an inherent interest in fame. Rather, because of his mythic disposition, he considered every act of sacrifice as necessary for him to achieve his goals for freedom in all senses. In Nigeria alone, there are a multitude of cases he was entangled in, but he was always triumphant, just like his mythical muse, the Ogun.

Soyinka is portrayed as a man with broad general knowledge and a wide-ranging approach to literary and political expeditions embedded into his work. His childhood experience as a Christian informed his fabrication of characters who are Christian-influenced and, by implication, West-centric. When one sees the inflexible nature of Lakunle in *The Lion and The Jewel*, for instance, one can understand his detachment from his cultural background because of his exposure to British education. The deracination of his cultural roots was complete and absolute, such that he prioritizes Western traditions above all other things and tends toward the imposition of the hegemonic structure over his African identity. This reveals the playwright as someone with a level of preference for the predominant Western culture. Nevertheless, Soyinka's experience with Yoruba culture, which initially informed his identification with the Ogun as the god of creation and destruction, also considerably influenced his thematic structuration. One is continuously bound to see the oscillation of his characters—from embodying Christian theology to representing core African (Yoruba) cultural values. This background experience, therefore, renders him a literary artist with an eclectic approach.

In addition, Soyinka grew up within the colonial experience, and its destructive effects on African identity. From politics to the education system, the foundation of Africa's knowledge was uprooted, to be substituted with strange foreign philosophies and structures. The African people have thenceforth been confronted with an acute reality of social contradictions that immediately threatened their continued existence and survival. There is a severe point of intersection of these varying experiences, where post-coloniality meets with cultural discontinuity, and there is the road where they bifurcate. Similarly, there are corresponding meeting points of Western theoretical models and knowledge and those energies for activism. Soyinka was radically orientated against the establishment, especially having realized that there was a close relationship between it and the subordination of African epistemic and ontological reality, reflected in his works as he gave his thoughts and experiences the critical medium for information transmission. Rather than being seen as an instance of conflict, one can recognize a level of mutuality in the work he produced, as a common theme of cultural redemption and revolution usually reverberates throughout it.

Soyinka's writing reflects the difficulties of radicalism and activism and the urgency of the form of protest that emerged in his works and those of his contemporaries. African mythical creations, which have been the only source for molding the social and political philosophy of the people, became helplessly entrapped in the project of colonization, where they suffered maximum deracination. Through continuous criticism and denigration, African mythical creations lost their relevance and became a small, disposable inheritance with their potency and usefulness stripped away by the alternative epistemic perception offered by European systems and Christian evangelism. Yoruba culture and values traditionally had no problems with transmission because they are easily accessible in society, where everyone is a potential custodian of it. Things experienced a radical change with the consummate Europeanization of African epistemology through education and then politics. One can conclude that the eruptive nature of Soyinka's brain is a reaction to the chaotic mixed religious experiences he had as a child and through his maturation into adulthood, which forced him to accept the responsibility of correcting the anomalous colonial presence in Yorubaland and its considerable influence on Yoruba cultural directions and identity. The milieu of his childhood emitted the philosophy of Christianity, but the larger society of the outside world introduced him to his ancestral heritage and activated controversial and contradictory thoughts.

For a life that started from this pedestal, it is unsurprising that Soyinka's eventual artistic productions were revelations of protest and radicalism. This was laid out from his childhood and its conflicting dynamic of two opposing philosophies in both the religious and the intellectual world. When he penned one of his early memoirs (*Aké, The Years of Childhood*, 1981; *Işara: A Voyage Around Essay*, 1989; *Ibadan: The Penkelemes Years*, 1994), there was a glaring indication of his future philosophy of resistance. Protests in Aké formed against the imposition of taxes on the people and the young Soyinka was seen running errands for the protesters. Before we dismiss such juvenile engagement as irrelevant to his eventual dedication to struggles and resistance, note that it was staged against colonial politics, which were primarily concerned with the exploitation of the people economically. Growing up in such an environment contributed to his understanding of the societal realities of colonial Africa, where the colonizers determined essential parts of people's lives. Instructively, he began to reflect on the situation and continued to imagine what its causes were. Assuredly, the early reflection on this reality inevitably encouraged the kind of life which he committed to achieving.

In the postcolonial environment, Soyinka has matured in his literary ingenuity. His writings now have strong and persistent themes of emancipation and revolution. The chronological sequence of his works and their development attests that protest and resistance are essential to his intellectual productions. The ways in which Soyinka engages every hegemonic structure in his later works shows that the foundation of protest, which gathered formidable standing during his formative years, now produces a beautiful result. In Nigerian society, Soyinka is known both as a literary engine and a political conscience that takes African development as the core reason for his anti-establishment principles. Culturally, Soyinka believes that African values have already mixed with European traditions and that denial of this reality will adversely affect the exponential rise of African identity. Rather than taking an entirely purist opinion about the retrieval of precolonial African culture, he appreciates its flexibility and fecundity. Unavoidably, this creates conflict, which is why Ilọri says that "Soyinka's characters are jammed in certain horns of dilemma": whether they are "revolutionary" ideologues such as Kongi (*Kongi's Harvest*), Professor (*The Road*), Demoke (*A Dance of the Forests*), Igwezu (*The Swamp Dwellers*, 1958), Eman (*The Strong Breed*, 1964), Dr. Bero (*Madmen and Specialists*, 1971), or Olunde (*Death and the King's Horseman*).[22]

"Modernism in James Joyce's *Ulysses* and Wole Soyinka's *The Interpreters*: A Comparative Study" by Bourahla Djelloul

Bourahla Djelloul offers a fresh perspective to the interrogation of Soyinka's works and style and eventually establishes the linking chain that connects him and James Joyce.[23] In what we understand is a modernist technique, Soyinka's employment of literary theory to address the problems of the country and the continent is tied to the manner in which the types of situations and circumstances that ordinarily call forth the use of such systems surfaced in the country, as did the appropriate way to contain them through introducing a corresponding literary movement to address these raging problems. By seeing Soyinka as a modernist, literary scholars that align their thoughts along this direction generally consider Soyinka as far removed from the reality of the country through his appropriation of a style that is most obviously far from the grasp of the common folk. This argument is embedded within the comments of some Nigerian critics, such as Chinweizu, Onwuchekwa Jemie, and Ihechukwu Madubuike, who conclude that Wole Soyinka slavishly and condescendingly adopts the modernist style of the Europeans against the moral expectations of bowing

---

[22] Ilọri, "The Theatre of Wole Soyinka," 35.
[23] Bourahla Djelloul, "Modernism in James Joyce's *Ulysses* and Wole Soyinka's *The Interpreters*: A Comparative Study" (MA diss., University M'hamed Bougara at Boumerdes, 2008), http://dlibrary.univ-boumerdes.dz:8080/jspui/bitstream/123456789/4835/1/bourahla.pdf.

to African demand for contextual clarity of issues.[24] Due to his adoption of this literary technique to address contemporary Nigerian issues, Soyinka is declared a detached intellectual elite.

What is missing from the comments of these critics is an understanding that in the global economy of literature, movements are bound to rise on special occasions as a reaction to prevailing circumstances, although conditioned by their historical context. This means that the change of ideas and structures that arise as a critical response to a popular tradition will die out when the prompting challenges are collectively addressed, but the new styles and systems that accompany them do not also have existential finitude. The development of a style presupposes the possibility that it may be reincarnated when circumstances surface in a similar archetypal mode elsewhere. Therefore, the accusation that modernism as a literary and social movement pulled from English history should find no reference or reinforcement in another culture does not consider the broader, global appeal of various attributes of literature. For this reason, the scholars within the ideological frame of modernism identify Soyinka not only as a modernist archetype but also a literary engine that understands the appropriate styles and modes required to tackle occasions as they appear. The reality in Nigeria reveals a disorderly society, anarchy, and chaos, all of which are perfect call outs for a modernist approach.

For a vibrant modernist, the appropriation of creation myths to describe the issues and matters ravaging Nigerian and, by extension, African society corresponds to the styles and techniques common to modernist literature when seeking to represent those issues in metaphor by employing substitution as the mode to express this information. Considering this, one can place the writings of Wole Soyinka within the context of modernist literature and understand that they were meant to parody the situation of the country for satirical purposes. From *The Lion and the Jewel* to *The Trial of Brother Jero*, Soyinka employs metaphor to depict the depth of decadence that has permeated Nigerian society. To discountenance the style or literary system employed by the writer on account of failing to carry the people or audience along is to deny their modernist franchise. While it is within the intellectual right of a realist to depict a condition through attempting to paint it in a literal or direct manner, those who are on the modernist matrix also have the freedom to represent events via parody and metaphor with the aim of creating so vibrant a picture that people who read it can relate to the truth of what is being presented. If they are successful, it will make the work archetypal modernism or the writer gain more popularity with time.

---

[24] Djelloul, "Modernism in James Joyce's *Ulysses*."

Some literary critics consider modernism as the melting pot of other literary theories,[25] all-encompassing because it does not reject characteristics drawn from other critical theories. Apart from the genuineness of modernist writers, the fact that they are uniquely original and creatively distinct makes them very appealing to those who are conversant with the style. Robert Scholes, in an article titled "In the Brothel of Modernism," expounds on this: "From Romanticism, modernism gets its emphasis on originality, on the need to make things 'new'—to be perpetually innovative at the level of both form and content."[26] Under Scholes's rubric, one finds difficulty in denying Wole Soyinka the accolades he deserves as a well-established modernist literary scholar in Africa. Further assessment of modernist literature reveals a commonality of employing mythical creations within the literary movement and the works of Soyinka similarly bring to the fore the use of myths and supernatural archetypes.

Perhaps the modernist disposition of Wole Soyinka can be better appreciated with the understanding that modernist writers challenged the existing writing traditions of their time, as did the ingenious African writer Soyinka. His works and ideology deviate from the writing traditions of Nigerian and African society, a philosophy that is arguably still enduring in him. One could counter this assertion by raising the argument that there was no extensive evidence of much of a writing tradition in Nigeria at the ascent of Soyinka into literary stardom, but it is impossible to deny that there were brilliant African writers, including from Nigeria, whose popularity preceded his: D. O. Fagunwa, Isaac Delano, and Chinua Achebe, among others, are Africans who already made notable contributions in the continent's literary tradition. There can be no argument about the ideological departure of Soyinka from the established system laid down by the likes of these authors. While they all wrote to achieve the same result, his position was radical and energetic relative to those he met on the literary protest scene, so one cannot deny the reality that Soyinka is indeed a modernist scholar.

Another definitive attribute of the modernist writers is their employment of a style where their characters engage in stream of consciousness. This enables them to reveal who and what they are to the audience without the author imposing their characteristics directly and without prying into their privacy at the same time. Wole Soyinka's characters in *The Interpreters* unquestionably come to mind; most reveal themselves through their

---

[25] See for example, James Smethurst, *The African American Roots of Modernism: From Reconstruction to the Harlem Renaissance* (Durham, NC: University of North Carolina Press, 2011).

[26] Roberts Scholes, "In the Brothel of Modernism: Picasso and Joyce," *American Journal of Semiotics* 8, no. 1 & 2 (1991): 5–25.

thoughts and their nature, and the audience gets to understand them through these conversations. The style enables the author to project the situation of society without forcing an interpretation onto the audience. The modernist author distances themself from literal, proscribed narratives and instead allows the work to flow in their intended direction. In its convergence with Freud's psychoanalytical theory, the idea that the unbound thoughts of the characters is a beautiful way to understand them is very important to understanding the modernist technique. Since the majority of the wishes and desires of people are filtered through social constraints, individuals always express themselves more in unconscious thoughts than can be imagined.

Apart from the obvious determination to reveal the intentions of the characters through the exposition of their thoughts and experiences that informs the use of modernist style, there is an understanding that getting into the collective consciousness of the people in the audience is another motivating factor. For example, the people of a society are aware of the sociopolitical currency of their environment, but they are usually hampered in projecting their grievances and their ideas and protests are ultimately repressed in the process. The production of literary material provides them with a possibility of staging their protest without raising their voice, because modernist literature expresses their opinions and carries the message to the appropriate quarters in their stead. Hence, the target of works of modernism is reached without struggles. Considering these available benefits, it becomes clear why modernist literature is popular, especially by practitioners like Wole Soyinka. Modernism deviates from the old structures, where attention is focused on artistic orderliness, by creating something radically different and thematically delineated.

Generally, the mythification of Soyinka's characters comes from the intention to give the metaphysical account of some strange phenomenon. Without departing from this principle focus, his works are explicit expressions of sociopolitical issues and the need to arrest them. Even when parts of modernist literature are directed toward the appropriation of archetypes, they do not deny the reality that this must conform to established norms. Examination of Soyinka's writings attests that he has comfortably shown that the post-independence decay that pervades Nigerian society requires modernist evaluation, provided by Soyinka himself. By being aggressively metaphorical, he paints the picture of the rot in the Nigerian political landscape using caricature and parody as needed. That the Nigerian bourgeoisie has decided to continue the marginalization agenda of the West necessitates calling them out in the works of the author, using the literary technique that best answers this need. The mimicry of the popular Nigerian elite through the characters in *The Interpreters* shows how they are anti-progressive and this qualifies them for their representation as agents of social destruction.

"Linguistic Imperialism: A Study of Language and Yoruba Rituals in Wole Soyinka's *Death and the King's Horseman*" by Golnar Karimi

To understand the messages and cultural significance of Soyinka's play, *Death and the King's Horseman*, Karimi provides a semantic extension of the concept of language.[27] Predominantly, language is used as a vehicle to communicate one's thoughts and emotions to an audience. The most basic understanding of language covers all human sounds and, by extension, these extralinguistic cues signal the meaning of an expression as used in a certain context. From the beginning, Karimi's examination of this play argues that music, songs, and other cultural activities are employed as instruments of communication within it, serving the purpose of a language themselves. The establishment of this fact has an essential influence on the interpretation of Yoruba's mythic existence. The place of music and dance is well established in the Yoruba's cosmo-cultural environment as there are hardly any social activities or engagements where the people do not show their close relationship with musical language, using it for communication.

There is no misunderstanding Karimi's conceptual clarity about linguistic imperialism, which he considered as inherent in Soyinka's play. For one, the imperialistic tendency is demonstrated in the way that the musical and dance elements of the language used in the context of Ẹlẹṣin and the market-women signal far more than the social appurtenances of their outside appearance could reveal. Beyond the merriment, the music seeks to communicate to Ẹlẹṣin and society at large about the imminent sacrificial actions that are involved in the spiritual journey with the dead king. Again, the immanence of his willful acceptance of this duty is underscored by the common knowledge of the people about its spiritual significance. Therefore, when the man is dancing and cavorting joyfully in the market, he was seen as choosing to mourn himself in preparation for such encounters indirectly. For an outsider, the ability to make this connection to a communication strategy is predictably tricky. Only the immersion into the people's customs could lead them to connect the dots. Ritual, or more accurately, sacrifice, is primary to the people's social practices as it is believed that the renewal of life and others is dependent on sacrificing some things.

Soyinka's adoption of the English language to express the sociocultural realities of the Yoruba people in the play is borne out of the idea that it enables his audience to understand the epistemological independence of

---

[27] Golnar Karimi, "Linguistic Imperialism: A Study of Language and Yoruba Rituals in Wole Soyinka's *Death and the King's Horseman*" (PhD diss., Université de Montréal, 2015), https://core.ac.uk/download/pdf/55655298.pdf.

the two cultures: African and European. Although the play is set in the postcolonial world, it illustrates how the colonizing West has different cultural convictions from that of the colonized Africans. While there may be instances of intertextuality, they are ultimately separate and unique in their own right. It is not surprising that the sudden invasion of the people's space by the West came with the immediate emergence of cultural discontinuity, demonstrated in the cultural scenery of the people. Whereas this would have had a devastating impact on the cultural traditions of the people, Africans are depicted in *Death and the King's Horseman* as self-evaluative and corrective. This is embodied in the deliberate decision of the playwright to introduce Olumide, the son of Ẹlẹṣin, who understands the culture and knows the implications of avoidance. Here, the essence of the Yoruba ritual world is depicted; Olumide is portrayed as someone who has sufficient exposure to Western systems yet chooses to toe the line of African culture by taking such courageous measures in supporting the tradition that his father, Ẹlẹṣin, should comply with the tradition to die with the king. Rather than the colonial actors present solutions, they instead import complications by their unsolicited interventions.

Karimi's exploration of language, in this sense, looks at the very different ways through which the culture of the Yoruba is represented and, at the same time, affected. For one, the West ably represented by Simon Pilkings sees the death of Ẹlẹṣin as a murder, stemming from the practice of a barbaric culture, while the Yoruba considers it as "fate," according to Karimi. This reinforces the argument of the cultural incompatibility of the two worlds of the African and the European. The essence of using language in this manner is to correct the common misconception that African cultures and traditions are inherently evil and anachronistic. That the West does not have the cultural material or knowledge to understand the sociocultural importance of Ẹlẹṣin's roles leads them to make wild statements and generalizations about the people and their culture that reek of hegemonic arrogance and grandstanding condescension. Every culture has its aspects and practices that appear odd and primitive to outsiders without the cultural context to understand and interpret them appropriately, but the insistence of these colonizers to impose their views on the people leads to a sudden social breakdown.

Very artfully, Soyinka has employed language to distance his Western readership and the audience from that cultural background as well. While the language is English, the process of their finding meaning in the narrative is difficult, evident in the manner that some of the Western characters are quite flummoxed about Yoruba culture. This is achieved using different techniques, such as the translation of local proverbs into English stripped of contextual significance which suspends the outsider's ability to relate to them easily. The proverbs help to validate the Yoruba cultural identity and, in the process, reveal why different aspects of human cultures require adequate knowledge before applying judgment. The apparent ignorance of Simon Pilkings and other Western characters is one of the causes of conflicts in the work, mirrored by the ignorance of the European audiences and their engagement with Nigerian society. In essence, while there is a division between groups who contemplate appropriating African languages as an instrument of communication in their writing and those rooting for the employment of the English language as their instrument of information dissemination, Soyinka abridges these two groups and compresses their approaches.

The resistance of Soyinka to the philosophical focus of the Negritude movement is inspired by his understanding of the limitations inherent in following such ideological convictions. Soyinka has continuously warned against it because of what he sees as crafty colonization of African history under imperialism. Karimi notes that "Soyinka cautions readers not to consign the African experience to the moment when the European colonizer arrives to inscribe it into the written word. Therefore, among his critiques of negritude, Soyinka states that African works of literature are too often designed as 'an appendage of English Literature.'"[28] The perspective that the narratives promoted by Africa writers should reflect African interior history reverberates through the writings of the intellectual giant. Similarly, Femi Osofisan lends his critical assessment to the topic; quoting him, Karimi states that "post-Négritude" serves the productive purpose of further developing the postcolonial African subject because it "seeks to identify, emphasize, and promote certain cultural aspects of the black African world which it believes have been under threat of erasure by first, colonialism, and secondly, by the present global (translate: 'American') cultural incursions".[29]

Conclusion

Soyinka remains one of the most versatile and admirable intellectuals and literary artists ever produced in Africa. Seen as a radical purist against hegemonic dominance by some of his colleagues, Soyinka is better understood by many as a political activist and intimidating detractor to various administrations in Nigeria. He has a commendable history of engaging military and democratic governments who have made strenuous efforts to disenfranchise the people or consume their commonwealth greedily. Soyinka took his resistance struggles beyond the pages of his writing and sacrificed his peace and freedom several times to bring anomalous situations

---

[28] Karimi, "Linguistic Imperialism," 18.
[29] Karimi, "Linguistic Imperialism," 19.

to redress. At one point, he tested his courage by sabotaging the plan of a sitting premier of then Western Nigeria, who intended to impose himself on the people against the collective will demonstrated in electoral results. In a conflagration that was full of suspense, Soyinka's successful expedition brought him more political limelight as he not only became a popular topic of domestic discussion, he also won international recognition.

As noted by Biọdun Jeyifo, the sociopolitical challenges of the Nigerian environment provide the setting for the creation of the wild Soyinka and his postcolonial radicalism. The post-independence of many African countries did not bring about the anticipated liberation as envisioned by many of the people. Instead, their neocolonialist leaders were distracted by the intoxicating influence of power and inevitably became contemporary imperialists. Their failure to set African society on the right path has meant that the protests of various revolutionaries have not ended. Instead, they have had to be strategically redefined. Accordingly, Soyinka has been one of the critical voices that continue to challenge the powerful political elites of Nigeria, charging them to assume their duty as leaders with vision and foresight. In the process, he was arrested, his intentions were misinterpreted, and his methods were condemned. Rather than bow out, Soyinka became more determined and committed to the struggles of emancipation. Culturally and politically, he was active and continued to influence the sociopolitical landscape of the country with his intellectual works geared toward this aim. Before long, he established himself as a force of nature that cannot be ridiculed or disrespected in light of his enormous impact.

2

Wole Soyinka in Historical Perspective

We in the middle of the twentieth century are like pilots in the transatlantic flight who have passed the point of no return, who do not have fuel enough to go back but must push on regardless of storms or dangers. What, then, is the task before us? The implications are clear ... we must rediscover the sources of strength and integrity within ourselves. This, of course, goes hand in hand with the discovery and affirmation of values in ourselves and in our society which will serve as the core of unity. ... This the individual must do, and in this way he will help lay the groundwork for the new constructive society which will eventually come out of this disturbed time, as the Renaissance came out of the disintegration of the Middle Ages.

ROLLO MAY[1]

History is full of individuals out-performing their contemporaries, making monumental contributions to society and all facets of human endeavor. History does not glorify those who make average contributions, and the majority of people in every society are steered and influenced by the overwhelming impact of a select few. Writing one's name on the slate of history requires extraordinary accomplishments.

Even when would-be historical giants set out to inscribe their names in the record books, their social standing—developed as they make great

---

[1] Rollo May, *Man's Search for Himself* (New York: W.W. Norton, 1953), 53–54.

strides within the social spaces of their communities—requires them to meet a certain standard of conduct. They are expected to respond or contribute to ongoing social issues, even during times of chaos or disarray. Their free expression can comfort masses who feel stifled by oppressive leadership. When these voices gather enough political and social weight, they can occupy an influential position.

In most cases, these people sacrifice their freedom, and sometimes even their lives, in exchange for the admiration of the vulnerable masses. Society calls them activists as a way of acknowledging their altruism. The explicit encomium that they receive for their priceless contributions can encourage further effort, sealing their irrevocable commitment to the majority's cause. They devote their time to social issues, stopping at nothing to confront dysfunctional systems, and the enforcers that enable those systems, steering society in a direction that will lead to positive growth. These people have immeasurable importance in their societies because of their criticism, evaluation, and appraisals, as well as their refusal to back down in the face of glaring injustice. One such person is the Nigerian literary giant and icon, Akinwande Oluwole Babatunde Soyinka, popularly called Wole Soyinka.[2] Born into the Soyinka family in 1934,[3] this future icon comes across as an enigmatic intellectual with unique qualities that set him apart from his contemporaries.

Wole Soyinka's global influence can be linked to the timeline of his birth and the environment that nurtured him. He was born during a time when colonial intruders maintained a firm grip on African countries, applying methods of governance that discredited indigenous knowledge and discouraged native creativity. Soyinka received a blend of Western and indigenous education that gave him a bird's-eye view of the sociopolitical emergencies and cultural terrorism perpetrated on African heritage.

Soyinka is a walking African library, even in the contemporary world. His power to distinctively navigate between the twentieth and the twenty-first centuries speaks of an unmatched dynamism that characterizes his life. Soyinka has carried the torch for a substantial part of protest literature's history, refusing to allow its fire to dwindle either through his resignation or by distancing himself from relevant issues that steer social development. In the face of political upheaval, he has never stopped challenging the African government, as a collective, doing something great and important for the people—even when his age has meant that he does not stand to benefit from those efforts in the future.

---

[2] Tyler Wasson and Gert H. Brieger, *Nobel Prize Winners: An H. W. Wilson Biographical Dictionary* (vol. 1) (New York: H. W. Wilson, 1987), 993.
[3] Wasson and Brieger, *Nobel Prize Winners*.

The flame of sociopolitical and cultural relevance, carried by a proverbial Amalinze who refuses to let his back touch the earth, proves Soyinka's fecundity not only in academic endeavors, but also in political, cultural, and social arenas. He has risked his life on many occasions to speak the truth to power, even when others of his age and caliber trembled in submission under the draconian leadership of those in power. His scars are a testament to his doggedness, and his aims and focus are unwavering.

These qualities make it inevitable for Soyinka's name to be written in gold in his country's history and the history of the world at large. The dearth of activist critics in the social fabric of contemporary society proves that individuals like Wole Soyinka are rare and precious. It explains why Africans past and present, who have been privileged enough to access his works, have been proud to associate themselves with his genius and the artistry that delivers his material through its own unique style. Soyinka has done more than enough to earn the social status that he enjoys today.

Soyinka is considered highly productive in his chosen career; his literary disciples describe him as prolific. They reserve this identity exclusively for him, because he has produced works in all genres with a brilliance and impact that would leave anyone dumbfounded. Soyinka has organized numerous plays in Nigeria and Britain, the two most formative sites for his educational experience. The satiric assaults of his work have delighted discerning audiences and antagonized his intended targets. Soyinka has been harassed by those in power, from many political dispensations, because the critical attacks of his literary and theatrical works have sent shivers of fear through their spines. He is one of the hardest nuts to crack for anyone seeking to take advantage of Africans for parochial or provincial interests. Soyinka will stop at nothing to register his displeasure, and in voicing his concerns, he wreaks havoc on the culprits. Soyinka has gained his popularity not by creating a nuisance in the social space, but by making genuine contributions not only to literary scholarship, but to the development of the African people and the world. It is difficult to understate his relevance.

Soyinka's eclectic philosophy has had a profound impact on his own life and the lives of people in his world. He specializes in comparative literature, consistently developing the lives of younger generations through the Nigerian school system and the world at large.[4] Despite the rigidity of his philosophical standpoint, he retains high moral standards and strong ethical convictions.

Soyinka has won various local and international awards that testify to his robust academic work and his many social contributions. By repeatedly locking horns with people in authority, he has won the hearts of many

---

[4] Theresia de Vroom, *The Many Dimensions of Wole Soyinka*. Archived June 5, 2013, at the Wayback Machine, Vistas, Loyola Marymount University.

devotees, either enthused by the organic nature of his work or affected by his uncompromising philosophy. Virtually every stage of his life is marked by his characteristic energy. Soyinka went to school by himself at a very young age, which amazed his parents. They felt that a child of his age would flourish in an environment of informal, domestic learning instead of the formal atmosphere found inside a school's four walls. However, Soyinka was a youth brimming with ideas and energy; he used them to affect his surroundings.

Soyinka has a strong foundation in spiritual matters. His childhood offered opportunities for his combinatorial energy, allowing him to explore the religion of his native identity and that which had been brought by Western influences. A popular misconception holds that Soyinka became an atheist at one point during his youth, which highlights how a forced Eurocentric interpretation can misrepresent things that do not align with a universalist ideology. An atheist according to the Eurocentric ideological concept of God is someone who does not believe in the existence of God. But, Soyinka has overtly adopted one of the gods from the Yoruba pantheon, identifying this connection as the source of his literary prowess. He has aligned his religious philosophy with one that is recognized by the epistemology of his native identity, renouncing the predatory identity orchestrated by Western education and interests. It is misleading to summarize him as an atheist— one who rejects the concept of a cosmic intelligence.

Wole Soyinka as a Literary Soldier

Wole Soyinka is a fighter who has dedicated his freedom and personal welfare to the cause of protecting the powerless, identifying with them and their suffering whenever they are oppressed by the government of the day. Throughout Africa in general, and Nigeria in specific, the masses have suffered from misrule and indiscriminately high-handed methods applied by the people who are statutorily compelled to protect and serve their interests. Security operations, conducted by governments, ostensibly protect the interests of their citizens, but the men in uniform usually take instructions from the custodians of power, and their interests can be the most selfish and parochial. The twentieth century was marred by governmental violence enacted against the helpless man on the street, first by European colonial officers, and later by African military forces—it was also the century when the world encountered the climactic rise of Soyinka's literary genius. This fearless warrior stood up to challenge the government, especially military rule, refusing to allow his voice to be swept under the carpet of irrelevance.

The use of force to achieve sinister aims is detrimental to public peace and social order, wreaking untold psychological havoc. Forceful methods are targeted to serve a singular purpose: to imprint a psychology of war on the mind of the people. It is a calculated effort to enable future shows of blatant immorality, establishing a resolve to apply violence whenever their criminally dubious acts require protection. In response to these disturbances, in which government officials exercise power without consequence, Wole Soyinka has audibly called for justice and due process. And he reliably pitches his tent in the common people's camp when rallying to their defense. It generates an overbearing reaction from corrupt government actors who feel threatened by the intervention of voices such as his. Soyinka has been unyielding in the face of attempts to crush him or cow him into silence, which has made him popular worldwide and established him as a burning flame of global importance.

Wole Soyinka's role as a soldier has been simultaneously metaphoric and symbolic. He uses his creative ingenuity to drag the government onto a battleground where the munitions are wits and tact. It is difficult to beat him on this field without using force to silence him, and political leaders have attempted to silence him with violence countless times. Soyinka has bravely employed his skills to demand justice for the vulnerable in every society where his voice counts, both inside and outside of Africa. Soldiers are expected to mount this kind of brave offensive, armed with the munitions to engage recalcitrant members of society. Soyinka's endless commitment to the cause of the people has also earned this title; he has never faltered in undertaking these responsibilities. He is a man who consistently opposes people who profit from the misdeeds of the ruling class, which has paved the way for his popularity among the masses.

Protest literature is the reaction of people whose sociopolitical environment has conditioned their mind and affected their views about life and politics. It is birthed and groomed in an environment with little choice other than to direct creative works toward emancipation from the grip of political mercenaries. In 1965, Wole Soyinka took a daring step in opposing the government's obvious falsification of election results. By exchanging the planned government announcement with a message of his own, he ruffled feathers and invited reprisal. In an interview with the media, he said, "And so with some assistance, some of my usual collaborators, I managed to stop the broadcast, substitute my—I pre-recorded my own statement. So, I went to the studio and I took the premier's tape off and substituted my own and went away. And so, I was tried—very, very nasty charge."[5] Soyinka understood that he was bound to face consequences, but he was obligated to oppose the government's attempt to issue falsehoods.

---

[5] Academy of Achievement, *Wole Soyinka: The Literary Lion*, https://www.achievement.org/achiever/wole-soyinka/#interview.

Later, Soyinka was arrested, charged with armed robbery, and targeted by character assassination attempts. His release came shortly after incarceration, but his concerns about the falsified election results were validated: the nation was plunged into war, and its citizens endured anarchy and government corruption. The civil war exposed the resentment that had been building under the flawed policies of the political class, and it revealed the accuracy of Soyinka's predictions and the importance of the warnings that he had issued to avert misfortune. His ability remains undimmed by age, allowing him to undertake actions that would be dismissed as incredible or impossible. To understand his unwavering commitment, one must understand the biting criticism he levels against the government for its lax approach to good governance and its unceasing efforts to milk the public dry and exploit every last economic resource.

Wole Soyinka is a progressive whose solitary efforts take greater significance against the backdrop of larger issues that threatened the unity of his country. In 1966, despite his relatively recent experience with arrest and intimidation, he refused to remain silent. Soyinka intervened in the civil war, putting his life on the line to seek a compromise between the aggrieved parties and to negotiate a resolution to the issues of violence and secession. In his view, violence would escalate an already tense situation, and it would provide an excuse for the enraged government to justify excessive force.

Soyinka risked his own safety in an attempt to avoid conflict. As a youth brimming with ideas and energy, he always spoke out in favor of the oppressed masses. Regardless of his intention of traveling to the east, a region that was burning with a desire for freedom, Soyinka was arrested and detained once again.[6] His literary career was built on this incident and many others.

Traces of Soyinka's ideology can be found in his works, offering a greater understanding of his role as a fighter in the country's cultural and sociopolitical landscape. In one of his canonical poems, *Civilian and Soldier*, Soyinka challenges men who jump to answer an order without understanding the reason behind it. It is a metaphor that refers to innocent soldiers who have been coerced into carrying out orders without question, believing that they are defending the integrity and sovereignty of their state. The poem reminds the stone-hearted soldier that he should not forget the blood running through his veins, and he should not kill the components of his biology that respond to stimuli. When the people in power order him to exterminate other human beings, he should remember that following such an order may be his own undoing. His ignorance of the motives behind the orders make him vulnerable to political leaders who deploy state security in pursuit of a personal agenda.

---

[6] Academy of Achievement, *Wole Soyinka: The Literary Lion*.

In one of his recent creative works, Soyinka instigates mobilization against oppressive governments. *King Baabu*, written in 2001, invokes public reaction against the anti-democratic tendencies of people in power. The culture of "sit-tight syndrome," which pervades Africa's political system, is one of the reasons for the continent's regression. More often than not, leaders want to retain power indefinitely, achieving this goal through manipulation and subversion of the normal democratic process. Soyinka's pattern of protest demonstrates that the masses are aware of their democratic rights and responsibilities. It challenges the authority of government actors who have attempted to replace the public interest with their own overwhelming greed. The king in Soyinka's work, who obviously symbolizes those occupying positions of power in Nigeria's political system, is not only undemocratic, but also antithetical to the society's plans for development.

Nigeria's current body politic is the product of ceaseless trials and constant confrontation with those who would marginalize citizens, continuously displaying disdain for purposeless leadership. Soyinka and many other progressives in society have made unmatched efforts in their quest for justice and equality in a society whose leaders oppose those values.

Soyinka's records have already been archived in the hearts of Nigerians and other admirers of his creative works. He has been recognized as a strong political activist who fears no one in his crusade for transparency and political decency. His fight against unaccountable government figures has forced him to find safety in foreign lands, but he continues to strike his targets with the smarting influence of his creative archery. General Sani Abacha, an erstwhile military dictator, felt the heat of Soyinka's criticism and would have hunted him down if it was possible. However, Soyinka escaped to a foreign enclave where he could breathe easily.

Wole Soyinka: The Compass of Yoruba's Ontology

Wole Soyinka's work is inspired by the cultural epistemology available through his Yoruba cultural praxis; the rich Yoruba system has influenced his perception of the world and shaped his creative accomplishments. Soyinka's creativity has made him a world-renowned cultural icon, showcasing historical legacies through written plays and staged dramas. It is difficult to separate an indigenous system of knowledge from the person who has been exposed to its rich legacy, but the works of Soyinka are a blend of native knowledge and global experiences, which he received through education and travel. By incorporating these influences, he reaches distant audiences that are far removed from his cultural and geographical position. The two dominating philosophies of the foreign religions in Soyinka's upbringing allowed him to adopt a form of religious eclecticism that influenced his decisions. As he matured, exploring and experimenting with new ideas, Soyinka was able to place these philosophies side by side to examine their points of convergence and their areas of dissimilarity.

Soyinka's interpretation sees these two similar-but-not-identical religions as familiar systems in the world of his ancestors, his Yoruba ontology. Although he aligned his own religious principles with those of his indigenous background, he was not criticized by his Christian parents. This is partly because Yoruba religious attitudes are notably tolerant of philosophies that do not match with their own—this level of understanding has ensured mutual respect and encouraged religious syncretism in their socio-geographical space for a very long time. Soyinka's anger at European imperialism was fueled by the idea that they considered all the aspects of the Yoruba world as inherently incapable of living up to their own standards. This bias was applied by European views of all African people, dismissing their politics, morality, culture, religions, and social structures. Soyinka himself is an example of the values that are overlooked and dismissed by an imperialist mindset.

In the twentieth century, writers in an African context were saddled with a preconceived responsibility to set the record straight, dispelling the illusions that had been cultivated to conceal the imperial oppression of innocent African cultures. When Soyinka was asked whether there were democratic practices in Africa prior to the intrusion of the European world, he unequivocally responded,

> Many people don't understand this outside, but actually the Yoruba system of Ọbaship, that's kingship, is really a pretty democratic one. There are severe limitations to what a king can do and not do. There is a council of chiefs who wield a lot of power, they're like a cabinet and if the king misbehaves or uses excessive power, this Ogboni council can actually meet, the enclave can meet and dethrone him.[7]

Soyinka was countering the idea that Africans did not have democracy before the arrival of the colonizers, challenging the assumption that African cultures received a benefit from the "timely" intrusion of the West. He had gathered enough native knowledge to expose the deliberate efforts to submerge African ontologies.

Soyinka tailors his works to show that he has not just identified with his native identity, he has come to accept it unapologetically. There are

---

[7] Simon Stanford, *Transcript from an Interview with Wole Soyinka*, https://www.nobelprize.org/prizes/literature/1986/soyinka/25230-interview-transcript-1986/.

frequent representations of indigenous knowledge and social institutions in his works, particularly when he handles African-related worldviews. His literary production, *Death and the King's Horseman*, relates the story of a traditional chief who is culturally obligated to escort the king on his transitory journey into the great beyond; it remains one of the greatest works explaining the full nuance of this cultural perspective. It has also gathered a cloud of critical dust while people all across the world are enthused by such cultural uniqueness. In the play, Soyinka implicitly reveals the ominous consequences of inspecting a cultural frame with the lens of an outsider. It is far from being the justification for the willing sacrifice made by Ẹlẹṣin Ọba, the play's major character, but it expatiates the Yoruba perspective on life's futility.

In *Death and the King's Horseman*, the chief is trapped within his own life of affluence, but the story explores how people undertake daunting tasks—even when recognizing the futility of their actions—to ensure the orderly function of society. This selfless ideal captivates the audience, because they understand that people are naturally averse to giving up their own freedom and peace. Ẹlẹṣin Ọba is intent on fulfilling his duty, presenting himself for sacrifice during the cultural rite that would end his existence. However, as a living human who has tasted the life of opulence that accompanies his position, Ẹlẹṣin Ọba falters. This is a commentary on the unstable nature of human beings; people can make decisions at a specific point in time and reverse them later, which speaks to the erratic nature of humanity. People are especially prone to change when their decision brings an unfavorable outcome.

Death and the King's Horseman is not a call for Eurocentric readers to pass judgment on the culture. Instead, it underscores the arbitrary nature of many cultural practices across the globe. Every culture has its fair share of benign customs, and they are all prone to evolution, especially after receiving more detailed knowledge about the world around them. Ultimately, the jaundiced understanding of the West leads to an intervention that forestalls the sacrifice of Ẹlẹṣin Ọba and obliterates the associated traditional practices. It leads to a double tragedy—the aftermath is even more debilitating. The unsolicited intervention, driven by a deformed understanding, not only enables the death of an innocent, it speeds the demise of Ẹlẹṣin Ọba himself. This sublime work shows the Yoruba perspective on existence and their ontological understanding of sacrifice.

By personally adopting *Ogun*, one of the Yoruba God-characters, Soyinka leads a cultural group. As their defender, he stands against external pundits with no knowledge of tradition. By incorporating these traditionally revered deities into his works, he has adopted a semantic coloration showing that he both believes in and receives motivation from them. Soyinka is a cultural ambassador who flexes his artistic muscle through his creative productions. Many of his works include local content that is beautifully designed.

Soyinka's play *The Lion and the Jewel* discusses the culture shock that can happen to individuals who acquire a new cultural perspective, exploring their efforts to bridge the gap or merge the two in an attempt to appear eclectic. Three characters—Lakunle, Sidi, and Baroka—hold different perspectives on traditional culture, and they exhibit inherently conflicted views about the evolutionary tendencies of different human cultures.

Lakunle is a young man looking for a bride, and he sets his sights on Sidi, the village belle. Sidi's mind holds a naive understanding of marriage, but before she accepts his proposal, she asks him to perform the cultural rite of paying the dowry. It is a core custom of the Yoruba society in which the narrative is set. Lakunle objects, considering the custom to be backward and refusing to maintain it in the contemporary period. Sidi is fearful of her community's scorn and afraid of inviting mockery from an act that would be considered cultural genocide. She becomes willing to accept anyone who could meet her traditional requirements, regardless of whether or not they had received a Western education—Lakunle had assumed that his education would be an attractive asset to the locals. His derogatory comments, referring to the people as uncivilized, turn out to be his undoing.

King Baroka understands and applies cultural practices in his daily routine, and he readily shows interest in paying the price required to secure the heart of the beautiful Sidi. Baroka's age is irrelevant to Sidi, and the benefits of his social position offset the risk that he might later find another object for his affections. What matters to Sidi is the approval of her society, and she is not willing to become a cultural outcast that brings shame to her family due to personal desires. Lakunle's unsuccessful attempt to secure Sidi's love has adverse effects—he is caught in a web of mental explosion because of the contradictory philosophies that cannot be reconciled in his own mind. He has been abandoned by a lady who he believes should rightfully be his, and the shock from that experience leaves him incapable of moving forward. His inability to achieve his goals stems from his inability to compromise when it is necessary.

The Lion and the Jewel addresses the clash of cultures in a postcolonial society; people are ensnared in the adoption of European cultural affectations and fail to adapt them to native issues. Their unconscious goal of superimposing Western customs over local ones is a nucleus of concern for writers, explaining why Soyinka addresses the idea in his captivating literary work. In addressing local and international audiences, Soyinka explains the need to understand the pluralities of perspective that are inherent in addressing experiences that are shared across societies. We cannot obliterate alternate views of life that do not conform with our own. Attempting to place every single culture under the scrutiny of a single, inflexible logic is a futile attempt at rationality. People adopt the cultural practices that have relevance for their own lives, and they take action that is likely to advance their own interests. The Eurocentric efforts of Lakunle, made in his indigenous culture, have little or no impact. His unsuccessful attempts to court Sidi show his community's adherence to existing cultural practices.

Writers must awaken the collective consciousness of the people. Soyinka excavates history, hunts cultural practices, and seeks epistemic heritages in the pursuit of this goal. For every social experience, Soyinka examines his cultural background and draws inspiration; it fuels his creative ingenuity and develops the fascinating literary materials that he shares with the world. He always takes care to craft them in ways that show the uniqueness of his world.

Soyinka the Social Engineer

Society is the physical result of abstract planning and philosophical efforts. In every society, human relationships and political administration are guided by the physical manifestation of efforts to establish practical philosophical constructs. Every social space and setting has organized structures to allow peaceful coexistence without resort to violence. Without these structures, order quickly disintegrates into chaos that wipes the society out of existence. The people creating ideologies to help these societies survive are regarded as social engineers; they provide alternate perspectives for social issues and call public attention to different lines of thought or highlight the dangers of ignoring them. These people often put up their own lives as collateral, because they are not elected to undertake the role. The commitment that they show, and the brilliance of their thoughts in addressing society's contemporary issues, allow them to secure the love and trust of the people.

Not many people have the creative talent required to produce works that force society to redirect its focus on collective development. Some of those who have the talent are intimidated by the unbearable pressure that powerful incumbents can wield in response to critical rebuke. But the writers who have accepted this responsibility to guide society, even when leaders relentlessly try to abandon their responsibilities, remain steadfast in their pursuit of justice and equity. They ensure that the system is not oppressive and that it does not exploit the powerless members of society. Wole Soyinka is one of these select few who stands up for the masses at great personal cost. Drastic measures can be required to force the government to recognize justice and due process; it takes people with guts to stand their ground when they are protesting against a state that can retaliate indiscriminately against those who are perceived as threats.

Literature has boundless capacity to reshape perspectives. Some works fall short of inciting social change, especially when they have difficulty attracting an audience. Other works fail to compel the physical activities that could prevent political classes from marginalizing the voices of the oppressed. True activism is born from direct engagement with people on the street, championing their interests when the need arises. A purposeful writer who identifies with the people can help elevate their standards of living and remain unwavering even as conflicts become more heated. Wole Soyinka is one such writer. He has dedicated his life to the masses, and he cannot be called anything other than a social engineer. Most of his works confront governments directly, whether they be democratic or military, demanding that they consider the interests of the people as their primary concern.

Soyinka has faced threats, public embarrassment, harassment, and even confinement without trial. He has accepted the daunting challenge of leading people to political safety, through protest and continuous media engagement, and educating the public about their constitutional rights. Soyinka exposes how their rights are trampled by harsh government policies or the outright subversion of justice to serve the goals of selfish leaders. For a man who faced down General Sani Abacha,[8] the oppressive military dictator, he can only be described as society's moral compass. And yet this label still fails to explain the enigmatic personality of Wole Soyinka. In an interview, he said that

> The problem with literature, with writing, is that it works sometimes in terms of correction of social ills. Other times, it just does not suffice. The proof of that is the ability of a dictator to snuff out the life of a writer as happened to my colleague, Ken Saro-Wiwa, the Ogoni environmental activist who was hanged after a kangaroo trial by this brutal dictator, Sani Abacha, he and eight of his companions.[9]

Wole Soyinka is genuinely committed to improving society. His daring act of exposing political mercenaries, sabotaging their attempt to rig elections, made him the target of power politics. Social engineering requires not only strategic planning, but also careful execution to achieve the intended effects. Nigeria's social activists, and activists in other African countries during the early period of post-independence, were conscious of the people. They employed a variety of means to achieve desirable outcomes. Although Soyinka is unique among his contemporaries, the era was characterized by activists who were unable to write and sleep in the comfort of their own homes. They accompanied their works with follow-up social commentary, mounting physical protests and carrying the people with them on their journey of activism. Christopher Okigbo, Ken Saro-Wiwa, and many other

---

[8] Stanford, *Interview with Wole Soyinka*.
[9] Stanford, *Interview with Wole Soyinka*.

popular writers and activists made their presence felt through works and actions in defiance of oppressive governments and inhumane policies.[10]

Soyinka is a diplomatic planner, demonstrating his skill in rallying the masses whenever he embarks on an activist campaign. His work always ruffles the feathers of the country's political heavyweights. He has been smuggled out of the country to avoid death sentences and other threats to his safety. The confidence that he shows in defying the powerful is uncommon in an environment where people have developed mechanisms to cope with oppression; those who wield power only speak the language of oppression in the socioeconomic space of African communities. Serial arrests and mass incarceration did not muffle Soyinka's criticism. On many occasions, he wrote from prison and shared his works with audiences outside the walls. During one period of confinement, he received the Jock Campbell New Statesman Literary Award.[11] Soyinka has been heard clearly throughout the world.

Wole Soyinka's Prolific Creativity

One way to recognize Soyinka's incredible nature is by considering the sheer volume of his literary and creative works; it is difficult to find other writers with his pace of production. He has consistently produced volumes of work that remain rich in content while insightfully addressing contemporary issues. And his works were created even as he endured a series of harsh consequences orchestrated by unscrupulous state actors, often with the tacit approval of foreign interests that were victims of his criticism. Soyinka lives up to a standard embodied in a cliché that is popularly ascribed to him: "A tiger does not proclaim his tigritude, he pounces." His zeal has been unrelenting, even at the peak of his career. His aggressive pace of production makes him stand out among other writers of his age. He makes critical work seem effortless, bringing local perspective to a position of comparison with European counterparts and putting African literary material on the map of global reverence.

In his works and his life philosophy, Soyinka has attracted legions of followers that zealously model his engagements and nurture hopes of similarly impressive achievements. Soyinka has received national and global accolades and recognition for his scintillating contributions to the literary world, his critical engagement, and his role as an activist. He has written his name in gold, and his ingenious ability has already been recorded for

---

[10] Stanford, *Interview with Wole Soyinka*.
[11] Uzor Maxim Uzoatu, "The Essential Soyinka," African Writing Online, http://www.african-writing.com/seven/uzoruzoatu.htm.

posterity. In 1986, Martin Banham had the following to say in praise of Soyinka:

> Since he published his first short story, 'Madame Etienne's Establishment' in the Leeds University journal *The Gryphon* in March 1957, Wole Soyinka has gone on to produce over fifteen plays, three novels, an autobiography of his childhood, a record of his prison experiences (when detained without trial in Nigeria), volumes of poetry, major critical essays and a host of other various works. He has established himself not only as one of the foremost writers of post-independence Africa, but also as one of the most creative and exciting playwrights in the English language. His plays, in their theme and tone, reflect the world in which Soyinka has lived, which, for him, has become increasingly harsh. In the early plays (sometimes known as 'the Leeds plays' because initial drafts were made during his time here) he offers a gentle satire (*The Lion and the Jewel*) and a sensitive concern with the tensions of a rapidly changing Nigerian world (*The Swamp Dwellers*). By the 1970s the satire has become fierce and the tone full of anger, and sometimes contempt. In plays like *Madmen and Specialists* he uses the image of cannibalism to attack the military politicians of his country, and in *A Play of Giants* he projects a grotesque picture of corruption and violence as he depicts some of modern Africa's more awful dictators holding the United Nations to ransom.[12]

Banham's remarks were delivered when Soyinka received his honorary degree from Leeds University. These reports, from local and international communities, attest to his unique creative nature. Wole Soyinka is a writer and social icon who addresses integral issues of well-being for society and the African continent, without censoring negative images to promote an African identity. The unbiased nature of his works is part of the reason why he has received global recognition.

Conclusion

Wole Soyinka's work as a Nigerian writer and political activist is relevant for the entire world. His life is punctuated with a series of events that simultaneously tarnished his image and increased his popularity. He stands out among his contemporaries for a clairvoyant ability to predict future events, taking proactive measures to curb or abate their intensity. Instead of earning respect from the political class, Soyinka's ability has invited harsh

---

[12] Martin Banham, "Wole Soyinka: An Appreciation," Leeds African Studies Bulletin, https://lucas.leeds.ac.uk/article/wole-soyinka-an-appreciation-martin-banham/

reprisals for his willingness to make them uncomfortable. He is a genius with uncompromising standards of fairness and justice. Soyinka is one of the few Africans who dared the raging political atmosphere of his time to speak truth in the face of power. He has continuously advocated for just, transparent leadership that allows citizens to enjoy the dividends of democracy and the protection of the law.

Wole Soyinka's early years were marred by the impairment of his personal freedom and individual rights; he was framed by governments that saw him as a threat to their personal ambitions. Soyinka's writing has transformed the creative hub of literary engagement in the continent, gaining disciples from near and far. His role as a moral compass has earned him the respect of the public. Soyinka is a man who considers his African heritage as a resource, from which he draws inspiration and ideology. African societies, whose survival was threatened during the colonial and postcolonial era, have benefited from his critical overview, and he has offered solutions to their problems—their warped political understanding and lack of foresight made it difficult to design workable solutions on their own to deal with the anomalies that arose within their environments. Soyinka has been a social engineer, organizing society's systems for effective action. By constantly reminding the people of what a model society should be, he has guided them through a tunnel of despair.

Wole Soyinka's literary protests and public activism have earned envy and recognition across the globe. Few people have dared to defy national and international power structures to the same extent. His fearlessness paves the way for his efforts in ways that are difficult to anticipate. At the height of civil war, Soyinka put his life on the line in an appeal to the group that had been sidelined in national issues. He traveled into a war zone in pursuit of peace. His willingness to put his life at risk has come to define him; it displays his enormous courage and enthusiasm for fairness. As noted in the above epigraph, Wole Soyinka has figuratively over the years taken on Rollo May's challenging task before the twentieth century transatlantic pilots. Soyinka's works and life have been devoted not only to "rediscover the sources of strength and integrity within [himself, but also] to the discovery and affirmation of values in ourselves and in our society which will serve as the core of [Nigerian] unity."[13] The historical undertakings of Soyinka are marked by active participation in the social issues that define Nigeria today, along with global issues that affect the African world in general. He has made magnificent contributions to improve the well-being of the African family. We now move on to review Soyinka's road to Nobel laureate, looking at Soyinka's scholarship and his patriotic involvements in nation-building and citizenship in Nigeria.

---

[13] May, *Man's Search for Himself*, 53–4.

PART 2

Historical and Cultural Background

3

Abẹokuta: The City of Innovations and Creativity

*Think not that I am come to send peace on earth: I come
not to send peace, but a sword.
For I am come to set a man at variance against his father,
and the daughter against her mother, and the daughter
in law against her mother in law.
And a man's foes shall be they of his own household.
He that loveth father or mother more than me is not worthy
of me: and he that loveth son or daughter more than me
is not worthy of me.
And he that taketh his cross, and followeth after me,
is not worthy of me.
He that findeth his life shall lose it: and he that loseth
his life for my sake shall find it.*
(MATTHEW 10:34-39, KING JAMES VERSION)

Introduction

Wole Soyinka was born to Ẹgba and Ijẹbu (what he has coined as Ijẹgba) parents, from the city of Abẹokuta. Today, he lives in the city of Abẹokuta. In talking about his early history, we want to start from his place of birth. Born on July 13, 1934 to Yoruba parents in Abẹokuta, Soyinka is a prolific and profound Nigerian writer known globally for his adept literary scholarship. He had his formative education in the same city, which he later complemented with further academic pursuits at the University College, Ibadan, and the University of Leeds, United Kingdom. The city of Abẹokuta, which today serves as the capital city of Ogun State, Nigeria, continues to attract scholarly engagement for the right reasons. Owing to the relevance of the city-state in the development of Yoruba history and civilization, contemporary scholarship on the city keeps growing in exciting proportions. There are very many instances of history that point to the greatness of Abẹokuta as the city has always been valuable to the historical continuity of the Yoruba people and cardinal to their collective growth. In the early period of the nineteenth century, it was both a military and economic success. However, Abẹokuta has also seen the rise of resourceful individuals who became pioneers in different areas of life. The exponential rise in the number of successful Abẹokutan indigenes who are making invaluable contributions in their different walks of life raises important questions about whether there is any relationship between the city and the making of legends, or the place of the sociopolitical space in the molding of ideas-filled individuals. In no part of the world is success or progress considered a product of luck. For this reason, it is objectionable to think the progress accomplished by the indigenes of Abẹokuta is a product of coincidence.

When Henri Brunschwig asserts that the Ẹgba people (one of the subcultures making up Abẹokuta) are truly modernized sets of individuals, considering their pragmatic organization and the sequential arrangement of their political, social, and economic activity before the incursion of the Europeans,[1] he was alluding to the evolutionary brilliance of the Abẹokuta people. There can never be any contention that the introduction of British expansionists in Yoruba spaces remains the very reason for the slow pace of their development, given the historical discoveries that point to the systematic development of the people prior to the invasion of their space. This was what Brunschwig further meant when he categorically said that "modernization was many cases frustrated rather than accelerated by the European conquest."[2] It remains incontestable to scholars who conduct anthropological and sociological research about Abẹokuta that people in the city-state are a proper definition of civilization and modernization, given their impressive level of political administration, economic organization, and social philosophies. They are united in the face of struggles, adroit in making scientific discoveries, and were great individuals in the formulation of good political philosophy. Abẹokuta continues to serve as motivation for its indigenes who usually strive very hard to achieve gargantuan goals in very many endeavors.

---

[1] Henri Brunschwig, "L'Avenement de l'Afrique Noire," in *West Africa Under Colonial Rule*, ed. M. Crowder (London: Hutchinson, 1968).
[2] Brunschwig, "L'Avenement de l'Afrique."

As will be revealed shortly, the city of Abẹokuta has produced and continues to produce a modernist archetype of African expertise in various fields. In isolation, the city remains distinct in Yoruba political history for its immense contributions to shaping it. In the country today, generally, the city has produced numerous pioneers in various fields with admirable quality and records worthy of intense study. Geographically speaking, Abẹokuta has been a fortunate environment located on the east bank of the Ogun River with useful proximity to a wooded savanna.[3] On productivity, it has been seen to be the making of great warriors of history whose exploits are deserving of intellectual study. Considerable numbers of men and women of notable influence in the country come from the city of Abẹokuta, and the fact that their political virtues and philosophy contributed to the enhancement of internal democracy among the Yoruba people prior to the Europeans' arrival makes their place a golden one. Given the level at which Abẹokuta makes important people who, in turn, make indispensable contributions to nation-building, this segment, therefore, looks into the relationship between the space as a geographical entity and the making of these individuals. To do this, we inevitably reflect on some of the history of the space.

Abẹokuta: A Brief History

The eighteenth-century war-torn Old Ọyọ Empire witnessed the breakdown of peace and the inevitable scramble for survival, which among many other things, instigated the migration of Ẹgba people into the geographical space that today is called Abẹokuta.[4] Internal intermittent struggles led to the dissolution of the political force holding the people together and as a result, seeking refuge in a more peaceful environment was inevitably necessary. Sodeke became the founder of the geographical entity in c.1830 and after that, other migrants spread across the same territory to form a confederacy, which allows the different migrants to maintain a formidable loyalty to their culture and the traditions of their parents' hometowns. This historical reference establishes the Ẹgba people as the original settlers in Abẹokuta, whose source of initial migration was the Old Ọyọ. Before getting settled finally in Abẹokuta, the descendants of these people had experienced a series of relocations from one place to another until they discovered the rocky environment holding the prospect of protection, especially against external

---

[3] Britannica, "Abẹokuta," https://www.britannica.com/place/Abeokuta.
[4] Earl Phillips, *The Ẹgba at Abẹokuta: Acculturation and Political Change, 1830–1870* (Cambridge: Cambridge University Press: 2009), 117.

aggression. Being a time when the people faced continuous turbulence and hostility from the Fulani expansionists, seeking to conquer them for economic and political domination, they were bound to seek survival.

Upon settlement, the nineteenth century became the most gracious one for the Abẹokutans, whose progressive shift from being raided continuously and intimidated by groups seeking domination to being one of the economic epicenters of the Yoruba world was historic. Having the geographical advantage and topographical edge, the town attracted colonial merchants seeking economic and political expansion; however, with a different and friendly business relationship. Its openness underscores the locational value of Abẹokuta to economic development through its potential for agricultural production such as palm trees and many others. This convinced the Europeans of the likely impact that their relationship with the Ẹgba, the subcultural occupants of Abẹokuta, would yield. The existing tension among different settlements during this period, therefore, escalated for purely economic reasons. For example, the Dahomey people, who are the inhabitants of what is politically known today as the Benin Republic, coveted the economic transformation that came with the establishment of a good relationship between the Ẹgba and the European merchants, and, therefore, triggered them to launch an attack to overthrow the Ẹgba politically and put them under Dahomey control—a plan that would see them being in control of the economic activity of the people.[5]

This graduated to an incurable hostility, which unavoidably led to the escalation of the mutual tension that caused the 1851 war between the Dahomey and the Ẹgba people.[6] Interestingly, Abẹokuta began to demonstrate its invincible character and self-confidence by decidedly dealing with the detractors led by King Gezo, forcing them back into their own geographical habitat, defeated and humbled. The habit of repudiating external aggression and matching every hostile invader with equal energy was once again displayed when the missionaries, who had already established strong roots in Lagos, decided to harness the resources of Ẹgba town. This annexation agenda was firmly rejected and dispelled by the people, who immediately got the missionaries expelled from their territory. It continued in this fashion until there was an eruption of another internecine war among the Yoruba, leading the Abẹokuta people to take the offensive side against Ibadan, who they considered a threat because of their military competence. To prevent Ibadan from lording over them at will, the Abẹokuta indigenes, led by their king, aligned with the British government of Lagos, and the product of their

---

[5] Daryll Forde, *The Yoruba Speaking Peoples of South-Western Nigeria* (London: International African Institute, 1951).
[6] Wikipedia, "Abẹokuta," https://en.m.wikipedia.org/wiki/Abẹokuta.

alliance was the recognition of their town as an independent city-state. Even when all other city-states included in the merging of the Southern and Northern protectorate in 1914 were under the political domination and control of the West, Abẹokuta was given a measure of freedom to run its political affairs.

This is where the history of Abẹokuta becomes more significantly attractive. The idea of waging protests against repressive and totalitarian governments evolved from this historical beginning. The events of 1918 provided another important marker inscribing the bold nature of the Ẹgba people in the annals of history. The colonial Europeans had imposed taxation on the people of the city-state, who immediately waged an offensive protest to repel the inherent despotism, which was calculated to bring about the economic deprivation of the people. Consequently, this led to a war called the Adubi War or Ẹgba uprising.[7] The decision of tax imposition was to further frustrate the efforts of the people as the timing was generally ill-informed. Apart from the existing forced labor, the introduction of the new tax disrupted the people's economic plans and exposed their finances to a more daring challenge. Survival was difficult, but for the simple reality that the ethos of Abẹokuta is descriptive of democratic qualities forcing people to exercise their fundamental rights of protest, especially when political decisions threatened their lifestyle, they immediately organized protests to challenge the decision of the colonialists and to force a rethink.

However, the colonial masters appeared to be determined and unwavering. They ensured that the Ẹgba people were faced with equally hostile groups of soldiers, and this inevitably introduced a coercive dimension to the exchange leading to the loss of life and properties of the Abẹokuta people in droves. Although colonial representatives were also killed in an unconnected event, this confrontation triggered the anger of the European imperialists, and they revoked the earlier political independence conferred on the Ẹgba people and therefore began to subject them to similar treatment as other conquered colonies. At the time these Ẹgba people were laying this foundation, no one had a clue that it was merely providing the ground for the emergence of individuals who would show similar strengths when confronted by daring situations. In the twentieth century, from Fela Anikulapo-Kuti to Wole Soyinka, who both made significant contributions in intellectual circles, to historians of immeasurable worth, Abẹokuta ushers into the Nigerian polity a set of respected individuals with invaluable contributions in their various domains. The next segment discusses the rise of the elite class in Abẹokuta.

---

[7] Oluwatoyin Oduntan, "Elite Identity and Power: A Study of Social Change and Leadership among the Ẹgba of Western Nigeria, 1860–1950" (PhD thesis, Dalhousie University, 2002).

Missionary Activities in Abẹokuta

Several types of research on the history of missionaries' activities in West Africa, Southern Nigeria, and even Yorubaland (Falola 2008 and 2014; J. F. Ajayi, 1965; Ekechi, 1972; E. A. Ayandele, 1966) have been carried out by historians of giant intellectual stature, so much so that any further inquiry into the phenomenon may appear tautological, if not needless. However, the absence of informative scholarly works establishing the connections between the presence of missionaries in Abẹokuta and the eventual production of vibrant Pan-Africanists who ruled in their various fields has thus informed the inclusion of this segment. As perhaps anticipated, listing and giving the significant and brave contributions of individuals highlighted above in the developmental process of Yorubaland, and Nigeria generally, may have the reader wondering why the authors decided to delay this part until now. The stylistic import of this is to familiarize you with the immense value and importance of the city through the crop of individuals it produced and then provide you with the background arrangement which has necessitated this. By no means are we suggesting that missionaries are the chief activators of Abẹokuta's potential. At best, this impression would be misleading and, at worst, revisionist.

If one is tempted to make this wild assertion, it would be most logical to consider the fact that Chief Sodeke, upon whose shoulders rests the background and foundation of the growth of the city, was a pre-missionary Yoruba product whose astuteness was instructive in the planning and envisioning of the city-state. The *Encyclopedia Britannica*'s report that Abẹokuta was a walled town dislocates any contrasting opinion about the inherent greatness of the people and city in the period before the incursion of the Europeans.[8] This is established on the conviction that wall making during the period was a security architecture used to fend off invaders and other potential enemies. Linked to this conclusion is the understanding that Sodeke and his early migrants had been forced to seek out alternative survival routes to escape the internal wrangling that engulfed the Old Ọyọ Empire at the time. Again, there is Madam Tinubu, whose involvement in the making of the modern Lagos cannot be overemphasized. She was an unusually courageous woman who used her tact and influence to make and unmake kings, install and depose leaders, and also to spread her economic tentacles. This all happened before the introduction of the European missionaries into the historical record of the people.

However, there is one undeniable reality about the coming of the missionaries: the enablement of Western miscegenation with Abẹokuta's people geometrically increased their chances of adding value to themselves.

---

[8] Oduntan, "Elite Identity."

At this very point, we must be careful about making uninformed conclusions from the submission given above. For example, the fact that the European coming opened to them an opportunity to add value to themselves does not mean that they did not have value in the first place. But because they had been detached from Ọyọ which served as their nucleus of value generation, there was now an obstacle in the way of their rejuvenation and, as such, their isolation was going to come with immense consequences unless such contact as that enabled by the Europeans came into existence. For example, their access to the non-formal education system was no more, and their expertise in metallurgical knowledge would automatically derail, as it would in other aspects of knowledge systems. But surprisingly, the timely emergence of the European missionaries came with more paradoxes. Therefore, it is necessary to consider the activities of the missionaries that helped them activate their potential.

The pioneering efforts of Rev. Henry Townsend, accompanied by Rev. Ajayi Crowther to establish the missionary presence in Abẹokuta and Nigeria at large, remain blazing. For one thing, the two figures combined their energies to install a firm footing for the Christian mission. Beyond the fact that these two individuals contributed immensely toward the establishment of Christianity in the country, their activities that inspired the intellectual rise of the Abẹokuta indigenes will be given priority in this segment. It is our opinion that the interrogation of this will help significantly to link the creativity of Abẹokutans with the structure available in their society. After the primary intention of the colonialists to "civilize" Africans, the introduction of a policy that would facilitate human and intellectual modernization was given rapt attention. Given their commitment to ensure that Africans immediately became a doppelgänger of their European identity, which would, as a result, facilitate more comfortable relationships and enhance smooth administrative running between them, the early missionaries were embarking on activities that would bring Africans up to speed. This was because, ideologically and politically, Abẹokutans—Africans—and the Europeans are two diametrically opposing peoples.

Immediately, the Europeans began to introduce their formal education systems simultaneously with their religion to the people, as these were considered the two most essential instruments in the process of psychological reconfiguration. For reiteration, European allusion and assertion that their preeminent duty was to "civilize" was quickly interpreted as the assignment to make Africans an extension of Europeans, in which case it would be immensely more comfortable to administer all their intentions without recording failures. The urgency for such a paradigmatic shift was observed in the quick introduction of education to the people. This would, among many other things, be advantageous in many ways. Above all is the tendency to ease the communication between the colonizers and the colonized. This is comfortably captured in the words of Agneta Pallinder-Law in her article

"Aborted Modernization in West Africa? The Case of Abẹokuta" where she states that "Western influence, in form of literacy, new technological skills and Christianity, first reached Abẹokuta in the late 1830s through the arrival of Ẹgba liberated slaves from Sierra Leone known as Saro. The first missionaries to visit Abẹokuta did so in 1842, and the first permanent mission was established in 1846 by the Church Missionary Society."[9]

The maiden school introduced by missionaries in Abẹokuta was opened in 1850, which marked the very beginning of people's enrolment into the Western education system. As expected, initially, the people were less receptive to such an establishment. Still, it nonetheless became the beginning of the people's exposure to a better quality education system, which empowered them in all facets of their life engagement. It was so beneficial to both the people and the missionaries that they began to acquire the language of the missionaries, which would thus aid them in enabling a smooth commutation exchange between Africans and Europeans. Credited with this significant change, the missionaries increased their influence on the people and could access them more than they had before. Opening high school successfully is an indication that the tertiary education system would follow suit, and this became the very foundation of the thoroughbred community that gave birth to those outstanding individuals discussed elsewhere in this chapter. Gradually but steadily, people began to enroll in the schools created by the Europeans to get access to their type of education as getting an education was becoming the only access to a decent life. From that point, an elite class in Abẹokuta was created, which led to the systematic laying of a solid foundation for the people of Abẹokuta. It was the sturdy beginning and foundation which helped people like Soyinka to drink from the wellness of the society and its almost inexhaustible potential, which subsequently catapulted them to an enviable position.

To measure the importance of the introduction of schools, for example, we would be compelled to consider the benefits that came to the people following the creation of schools. Education in the city opens up a wide-ranging potential that includes but is not limited to the reduction of Yoruba language to codification. Prior to the introduction of the Western education system in Nigeria and other African countries, the number of African languages is not reduced to writing. It was the singular efforts of freed slaves from Sierra Leone who came to establish their presence in Abẹokuta that led to the codification of the Yoruba language and other notable languages recognized in writing in the country today. Such an intellectual breakthrough is credited to Rev. Ajayi Crowther, who pioneered the writing of the language after he acquired a Western education. Growing from this,

---

[9] Agneta Pallinder-Law, "Aborted Modernization in West Africa? The Case of Abẹokuta," *Journal of African History* XV, no. 1 (1974): 65–82.

the making, printing, and selling of books was the result of the introduction of the Western education system, and Abẹokuta began its journey into the greatness which it is known for in modern times. This does not nullify the fact that such development became the very ground for imbibing the level of democratic ideology, as a complement to the system available in the society before the incursion of the West. The returned slaves, especially Rev. Henry Townsend, got recognition for his education and his demonstration of quality character.

It was his printing press, *Iwe Irohin*, which facilitated further understanding about the language of the Europeans and the indigenous language all the more. Ideologically speaking, all these developments created the very foundation for the education structures that survived even till later times. The introduction of schools to the people automatically made Abẹokuta the headquarters of intellectual exchange and the producer of resourceful individuals. In one way or the other, the parents or members of the same family as the figures listed in the above benefited from these structures and arrangements, which consequently influenced decisions on their children's education. Funmilayọ Ransome-Kuti, who was a vibrant and influential indigene from Abẹokuta, met a robust educational structure and maximized the inherent opportunity to expand her knowledge. It was after she had her education in the European country that she got exposed to the underlying racism in the bloodstream of Europeans and that therefore informed her protest and resistance for which she was eventually recognized. Similar things happened to other products of Abẹokuta. What sums up their issue is that they bank on the innovative brilliance of their hometown.

Apart from the Western education system, another thing that missionaries encouraged in Abẹokuta was vocational skills like carpentry and masonry. It was part of their goals aimed to ensure that the African people had a sound knowledge about some skills, particularly those that would help in further serving the Europeans. Skills acquisition remains one of the most reliable ways in which an individual can improve their life and lead a value-laden lifestyle. As is already established, the introduction of European ideas in Abẹokuta does not symbolize the absence of the people. New skills are introduced, but rather than serving as maiden editions, they complemented those already available among the people. Whatever historical information that claims otherwise would be an apparent subversion of reality. Having clarified this, it is instructive to add that the skills introduced by Europeans opened another round of opportunity for the people to expand their economic or financial power. The Europeans were open to individuals who can showcase their talents through the skills they acquired and would reward them based on their productions. This advantage was absent for those who did not share relative proximity to the Atlantic just as is obtainable in Abẹokuta. The growth of the people economically, however, suggests that more complex politics would emerge and the corresponding need to rise to its demands.

In addition to their skills acquisition program, another significant area where Europeans registered their presence, which turned out to come with immense benefits for the people, was the introduction of Western medical services. Prior to the emergence of these Europeans on the African scene, the medical system was systematically different from what was present among the Europeans. Since the medical system and practice by the pre-missionary Africans were not particularly organized, it became extensively tricky for them to record much success in addressing the medical challenges facing their people. Again, the short provision of medical personnel was another impediment. However, this changed with the coming of missionaries. Father Jean Marie Coquard, for example, doubled as a missionary and a doctor, and he carried out numerous medical operations in Abẹokuta, having established medical care for the people immediately on arrival. In what was eventually spread across the country, the medical system of the Europeans gave Abẹokuta and the people more advantages to at least thrive in various areas and widen their horizons.

The missionaries' activities in Abẹokuta reached their peak when they encouraged innovation in people's agricultural participation. More crops that were hitherto unavailable were introduced and produced in surprising quantities. This made the people expand their economic influence and further unlock their potential. Generally, the efforts and engagement of these people in the process made Abẹokuta the melting pot of agricultural, political, and economic revolution as people engaged in different fields and partook in many endeavors. All these developments combined to help the city-state in many respects. It is no coincidence that the form of leadership system which was popular among the Abẹokuta people was recognized and valued especially. Although the place houses people of different subcultures and varying religious orientations, Abẹokuta experienced unusual tranquility and saw a significant sense of diplomacy. When a town has all these institutions and structures available to it, it helps the community and the people to devise beautiful ways to lead a purposeful life. One common thing that all the indigenes of Abẹokuta show in their character is the quest to explore their environment and expand their knowledge. They celebrate knowledge because it has always been their weapon used to negotiate important advances for themselves at different levels. Is this not what Wole Soyinka became very popular for?

Abẹokuta: Nineteenth and Twentieth Centuries in Brief

Having highlighted various contributions that the presence of missionaries and Europeans generally triggered in Abẹokuta, we consider it equally important to expose what the pre-missionary time was like in the city-state. The political activism of Funmilayọ Ransome-Kuti and her vibrant son, Fela Anikulapo-Kuti, together with the brilliance and intelligence of Wole Soyinka, compels research into the political economy of the Ẹgba/Abẹokuta people to see if there existed some level of relationship between them and their actions against an oppressive government. First, there are three provinces among the Ẹgba people, namely Ẹgba Alake, Ẹgba Gbagura, and Ẹgba Oke Ọna.[10] Interestingly, each of these three provinces has their different towns with separate Obas, who, in turn, recognize the supremacy of Alake. This, therefore, means that the Abẹokuta city-state is made up of a complex political landscape that requires purposeful leadership for the smooth running of their administrative affairs. The first impression this gives is that the indigenes of Abẹokuta, especially those who have already been highlighted, were brought up in a society where the management of heterogeneous ideas is rife and basic. This, therefore, made it necessary for them to develop a broader mindset that would be disposed to resistance or protests on the occasion that leaders underperform.

Therefore, the political economy of Abẹokuta is the one that represents democracy, where power is evenly distributed and was vested in different institutions that are politically responsible for the running of society. It is implied from this conclusion that adequate attention is given to democratic rules and policies, which are all targeted to improve the people and encourage life-changing innovations. When one realizes that the trio mentioned in this thread exclusively vied for the reintroduction of African knowledge systems or epistemic understanding, one may begin to link the organizational structure of Abẹokuta under which they were developed, to their ingenuity. Indeed, Abẹokuta's politics was in this period run by the Ogboni group,[11] which also saw to the designation of the justice system, security architecture, and the arrangement of the electoral process where the overall leader of the community would be decided. The constitution of their membership is predominantly unknown to the public, and this removed the probability of tricking them into averting justice. The society of these Ogboni was so organized that it forestalled the king's influence to corrupt the selection system or processes. This administrative system, which was later kangarooed by the Europeans when they overtook the space, was an outstanding example of modernized structure.

So beautiful was the organizational structure of Abẹokuta that they even had designates who were in charge of commercial engagements. Popularly

---

[10] Lanre Davies, "The Political Economy of the Ẹgba Nation: A Study in Modernization and Diversification, 1830–1960," *African Nebula* 7 (2014): 74–100, 76.
[11] S. O. Biobaku, *The Ẹgba and Their Neighbours, 1842–1872* (Oxford: Clarendon Press, 1957), 5.

called *Parakoyi* (trade chiefs), they duly represent the interests of each town under the provinces and mediate on issues of commercial infringement. Price regulations, market control, and other related activities fall under their jurisdiction, and their collective welfare was handled amicably. They have a single head, which in turn is helped by other *Parakoyis* for the enhancement of good leadership. This level of organization points to an important conclusion and that is the fact that Abẹokuta was evolving beautifully in their pre-missionary era. The idea that civilization or modernization was brought to them is an act of historical revisionism. After this, we conveniently concur with the thematic position of Pallinder-Law about the abortion of the modernization process of the Abẹokuta people. Without being distracted, an environment that has this type of structure has implicitly exposed its citizens to how best to run their political and economic affairs, not denying them the chances of evolution. Therefore, their brains are bound to experience eruption when they are faced with a different reality wherever they found themselves. It is on this basis that the understanding of Soyinka's works and ingenuity relies heavily on the understanding of the society that produced him.

Lanre Davies, quoting Biobaku, explains further the different dimensions of institutions created to oversee the affairs of Abẹokuta and its people when he talks about the security architecture of the society. The native hunters are simultaneously in charge of their security agency as they are burdened with the responsibility of driving thieves and external invaders away at night, also chasing wild animals out of the people's reach to enhance their safety.[12] This social arrangement enabled their youths to become active members in the development of the society as they could be recruited at a younger age into their military (hunting group) to protect lives and properties, and at a later stage, be conscripted into the commercial groups where more knowledge and understanding about handling the economic activity of the society would then be introduced to them in preparation for future leadership roles. At the latter end of their lives, they are qualified to become a member of the Ogboni society or occupy other leadership roles in the society where they offer their wealth of experience to oversee the affairs of Abẹokuta. The reality that they established this level of consciousness in the management of themselves brings them out as outstanding in politics and other related matters. There were not many civilizations in the world with this level of maturity and tactfulness in the nineteenth century.

At this point, it is not out of line to establish the intricate connection between the personalities of Fela Anikulapo-Kuti, Funmilayọ Ransome-Kuti, Wole Soyinka, and one of the foremost indigenes of Ẹgba whose actions at some point in his existence share compelling similarities with

---

[12] Davies, "The Political Economy," 77.

the one demonstrated by Wole Soyinka, who in the mid-twentieth century, confronted the Southwest government over their intention to usurp power unjustly. During the nineteenth century, a man in Ẹgba named Lisabi emerged as a revolutionary who devised the courageous measures through which the people would be freed from the suzerainty of the Old Ọyọ Empire. The dominance of Ọyọ had seen to the relegation of the people's economic power as they were excessively taxed by the proxy leaders, identified as Ajẹlẹ, representing the Ọyọ Kingdom in administrating political duties on the vassal states. Lisabi methodically empowered the people after winning their hearts through the establishment of a scheme called Aaro where collective efforts were made to rescue the people in whatever area they were lacking. Consequently, he, alongside his team members, torpedoed the Ọyọ supremacy and put an abrupt end to their domination of the Ẹgba people. Wole Soyinka could be referred to as the contemporary Lisabi for his many efforts to challenge uneven domination in Nigeria.

The economic model adopted in the city-state during the nineteenth century is illustrative of its transactional capacity. Prior to the coming of the Europeans, the available literature confirms that the people had conducted businesses where they exchanged goods as needed and necessary. Abẹokuta's people conducted financial engagements that saw to the regulation of their economic activities, which therefore inspired the transformation identifiable within the city. Apart from the opportunity which was ushered into play by the availability of different provinces, making the exchange of their items possible, bonds were strengthened through communication. This, therefore, enabled the exchange of ideas and crops among different people leading to an opportunity for transformation. Various crops, therefore, were exchanged, which included cash crops and other variables. Twentieth-century Abẹokuta thus expanded the available opportunities by increasing the articles of trade, which covered dealing in agricultural products that were popular among Yoruba people as well as those introduced by the Europeans. What remains important, however, is that people in Ẹgba, particularly their leaders, cashed in on this opportunity by imposing commercial taxes, which were subsequently used in running the affairs of the state. Our takeaway from this issue is that both the nineteenth and twentieth centuries, for the Ẹgba or Abẹokuta people generally, were filled with impressive historical narrative.

Attaining this level of coordination was an important factor that attracted various individuals to consider having something to do with Abẹokuta. For example, the freed slaves from Sierra Leone who took their refuge in Abẹokuta did so because it was economically and politically thriving. The fact that their political sovereignty was not challenged by the early Europeans who had already conquered different settlements and places is a pointer to their modernization. In fact, in what would be discovered eventually, when comparative study became paramount, the development of Europe followed this model and system, and this, therefore, frowns at attempts to generalize that Africans were uncivilized people. Since Lisabi organized the people to comb the hegemony of Ọyọ, the internal disparity and contradictions which have hitherto weakened their resolve were attended to and settled for good. Ẹgba people, after their freedom from Ọyọ and the coincidence of defeat, which subdued the political and economic influence of Ọyọ sequel to their subjugation by the Fulani expansionists, encouraged them to register more triumph in domestic and external wars. Between 1835 and 1850, the relative success they recorded in wars prompted them and added significance to their existence.

Suddenly, migrants began to consider Abẹokuta as their target refugee settlement, while returnees from captivity found a new love for the city-state. Without restricting anyone, the city began to grow in numerical strength and, as such, became difficult to challenge in warring encounters. The European government did not harness Abẹokuta until 1918, years after the amalgamation of the Southern and Northern protectorate of Nigeria. This reiterates the intimidating profile of Abẹokuta's arrival into the twentieth century. The Ẹgba United Board of Management (EUBM) was created in 1865, and it remains one of such of its type[13] in the majority of the places ever colonized. It was representative of their intellectualism and astuteness. The EUBM was developed as a response to the need for cooperation between the people who had acquired education and the native technocrats to collaborate and produce modern ideologies that could be used to run the affairs of the state following the dictates of the time. This historical reference does not seek to recast the various things which have been done by the Ẹgba people; instead, it is aimed at exposing the relationship between the productive Abẹokuta and the emergence of valuable people, one of whom is Soyinka.

The EUBM later transformed into EUG, the Ẹgba Union Government, which was saddled with similar responsibilities. However, the constitution of membership was improved, but their general source of income was still largely the imposition of tax and customs duty on goods that were Abẹokuta bound. Although it was created at the tail end of the nineteenth century, it marked the new beginning in the economic and political situations of the country. For example, rules and regulations guiding the agricultural and economic engagement of the people were improved by the time they entered into the new century. The early period of the twentieth century saw people bringing agricultural revolution to Abẹokuta, and its influence was becoming more widespread than before. Over the advice or encouragement of the Europeans, new crops that would secure their interests financially were introduced, and several Abẹokuta farmers

---

[13] Biobaku, *The Ẹgba and Their Neighbours*.

embraced it. They, therefore, began to produce more crops to be exported, and this continued to bring them more financial gains. This exponential growth in both economic and political activities, however, gave the people more pressure than was there before, although it was a pressure that brings about a level of development.

For example, increased agricultural awareness and production means additional demand for a standard transportation system, which, as at the time when Abẹokuta was experiencing this level of growth, was not available. Again, this forced the parties involved, which was the colonial government and the successful indigenes, to introduce the railway system in the 1900s. This was, however, to be complemented by the construction of roads by the EUG, the introduction of vehicles to the environment to facilitate mobility and easy transportation of goods. Attaining this level of great development means that more merchants were fighting their way through to Abẹokuta. People who understood the cardinal position of the city-state to economic development were persuaded to visit it. The introduction of the EUG, therefore, ushered in spiraling success, which again made the place the cynosure of all eyes. More and more, the city-state grew in influence, and it never fell short of employing good philosophical ideas for the management of their affairs. As Abẹokuta became more prosperous, it accommodated more people and provided a good sense of inclusion to all.

From all indications, the greatness that follows Abẹokuta is not spontaneous or sudden, as most narratives would establish. The success attached to the town is a product of sequential growth that comes with pain and anguish in moderate proportions. The fact that the place was exceedingly successful as a collective in the twentieth century validates the assumption that the previous century laid down the foundation. For example, it is generally known that the first woman to drive an automobile in Nigeria came from the city-state, which would have been impossible if those accomplishments were not made in the infrastructural domain. The complex politics that those in Abẹokuta were introduced to and the strong communal philosophy used in overseeing affairs of the complex setting all serve as instruments of education to the people who grew up in the environment. The knowledge of democracy was not alien to Wole Soyinka because, as claimed in *Aké: The Years of Childhood*, the city-state was founded on strong philosophical conventions that taught the people about civilization from the viewing lens of Africans and imbibed into them the culture of togetherness which informed their life orientation.

There was no doubt about the future which the twentieth century would bring to the Abẹokuta people just like other parts of the country after it was merged forcefully in 1914. Signs of this irresistible end were well-laid in the final decade of the nineteenth century, when Europeans showed unprecedented aggression in subduing the people politically and economically. The eventual political design was a noticeable departure from the systemic organization, which was very popular among the Abẹokuta people. For example, we witnessed the ideological maturity in the indigenes of Abẹokuta when they organized EUBM using an admirable philosophy in the management of the group. This includes how they tend to their internal contradictions and broker peace in a culturally heterogeneous society. The elite class is powerful, and this did not take away the fundamental rights of the subaltern. Attaining economic heights was not especially dependent on one's inheritance. People with impressive plans to catapult themselves to another level made it without any obstruction or deliberate antagonism from the elite class. Such a great sense of organization showed once again when the group morphed into EUG, created from the necessity to harness the resources and knowledge of the Western-educated Western indigenes who would pilot the political and economic affairs of the people.

This inclusion, however, was threatened immediately they entered into the new century. These changes, however, are predominantly ideological rather than physical at the initial stage. The African people and their European counterparts differ in matters of ideology. While Europeans only began the quest for gender equality around the nineteenth century, the Yoruba people had maintained a considerable sense of gender equality as this was the very reason for the transformation of both genders as found in Abẹokuta in the nineteenth century and before it. Men and women performed their different but complementary roles, where they both contributed to the geometrical expansion of society. However, the colonizers did not only come to exploit the people's natural and human resources; their social philosophies had unavoidably gone with them to their colonies. As such, the preference shown for the males in leadership duties was unpretentious. The paradigm of representation began to shift from the early period of the twentieth century, which again marked another significant threshold in the history of the people. However, rather than clip the thriving wings of Abẹokutans and stop them from making impressive accomplishments and contributions to better their lives, it seems to have aided it further.

The new century began on a suspicious note as fundamental ideas used to structure Yoruba society were starting to experience an unprecedented negative shift. For example, the introduction of a tax for the women, which came in 1918, raised important questions about the valuation of the female gender and their fortune under the new administrators. It was unambiguous that Western interest was not particularly concerned about the social values and virtues which were respected by the people before their invasion. Although they introduced an indirect rule, they were the ones dictating the content of the ruling, and any negating party did not escape their disciplinary actions, which in most cases were hostile and not hospitable. The change was noticeable, but not many people were courageous enough to channel their annoyance the right way. Indeed, there was no particular way to show grievances other than to protest actions that are considered anti-masses.

In this sense, therefore, the Europeans were going to have a smooth-running because the people had been so physically and psychologically tormented that to consider raising their heads against any show of oppression was then unlikely. Dredging up their economic achievements through heavy tax was a way to secure more finances from the people, according to the calculations of the colonizers. This activated the people's worry and immediately changed not only their ability to make contributions to society but also their resolve to continue to hold the stake they had.

While the new development was received with repressed annoyance, another underlying issue which perhaps was unbearable, rose inevitably. The denial of economic participation through the new tax invariably led to the steady exclusion from leadership roles which they used to take. This means that the women who were important stakeholders in the previous structure were now dispensable, and their influence could be eradicated if not ridiculed outright. However, it would not be received in a similar fashion to that shown earlier. It was used as the basis for staging a protest against the initial decision. The lack of political representation portends danger, and the most effective way to contain this was to demonstrate their annoyance through coordination into formidable groups, which would offer them the opportunity to register their displeasure and provoke desirable changes. The formation of the Abẹokuta Ladies Club, in 1944, was tasked with the duty to harness females' influence to organize protest actions to challenge policies that are continually taking away their economic strength. As the influence of this group continued to grow, the voice of the women began to reach a wider audience and their yearnings projected to a productive stage.

Led by Funmilayọ Ransome-Kuti, the women protested tax inflation. They expressed their desire for flat tax after the repeated use of brutal force to confiscate the goods of the market women. The women were exposed to horrible economic measures and therefore needed serious attempts at financial and economic survival. However, to challenge the powerful British leaders, women needed to arrange themselves in formidable units so that their grievances could be given a more united voice. Under the leadership of Funmilayọ Ransome-Kuti, the plans were executed in a grand style, which brought about the rapid growth in the people's interests. Arrested and detained, Funmilayọ's resolve did not waver, and she became rather strong amid increasing threats. The British government believed erroneously that the best way to contain the growing influence of the women's union was to take their leaders into custody, but this, however, produced what they never envisaged. The women took to protesting and endured the pains that came with it but eventually, their yearnings were crowned with success as the British government revoked policies that aided the confiscation of their goods. Without a doubt, the collective activism of the women—led by this courageous woman—brought about desirable outcomes.

It was only Abẹokuta that clinically preserved its territorial integrity, chasing away the Europeans from taking hold of their city-state until 1914. And to a reasonable extent, they survived another four years before the British began to show more force in taking over their sovereign integrity. It was therefore not coincidental that the desire for independence and democratic process virtually in every spectrum of Abẹokuta indigenes was not ahistorical. What their women achieved in terms of leadership in the twentieth century admirably complemented what the women accomplished during the previous century. As we have already established, the contribution of Funmilayọ in the reclamation of the territorial integrity of Abẹokuta was a continuation of efforts put in place by the preceding generation. She was perhaps influenced by the impressive feats of Madam Tinubu of the previous century, who personally influenced the direction of Lagos politics and partook heavily in the Ogun political structure. She was understood to appropriately consolidate the political power she had by being the wife of the king and negotiating her economic power with potential allies who wanted to use her position as a stepping stone to achieving their own life goals. Her death, however, opened the way for an equally vibrant successor, Iyalode Miniya Jojolola, who ruled with obvious vibrancy.[14]

After her death too (c.1928), women's political representation again declined as the position was not filled accordingly. The women's movement created by Funmilayọ however, has morphed into Abẹokuta Women's Union (AWU), and they showed their capacity to be amenable to the dictates of contemporary national politics, even though their mandate was trimmed to align with native politics. From being an elite club associated with people of higher social class, the group began to incorporate market women in their bid to have more comprehensive coverage. On the ground that women in this setting would add values to the group, especially in the aspect of reaching the interior part of the community, their inclusion was necessary and eventually weaponized to achieve the known agenda. The constitution of membership, which extended to the market women, helped Funmilayọ to push her anti-European agenda, which she believed would encourage the inculcation of African values and cultural traditions. We will recall that she dropped her Christian name in favor of the African one after having contact with the British in her overseas education; therefore, she began the movement by introducing a moderate dose of African systems traditions even in the making of the AWU group. She employed the Yoruba language instead of English, and recognized traditional and native dress as the standard ones during the gathering of the market women. This increased her popularity and expanded her influence.

---

[14] Biobaku, *The Egba and Their Neighbours*.

Some events which occurred outside Africa, particularly the Second World War, had significant impact on the activism struggles of the Abẹokuta women. Britain had lost much economic power in the process and therefore decided to shift the burden on them to their respective colonies to which Nigeria generally, and Abẹokuta mainly, was one. Suddenly, Abẹokuta's women were forced to face food shortages and increased tax, and the police, which had grown powerful under the British in the period, became too power drunk. The confiscation of the women's goods became very pronounced, limiting their chances of economic transformation. Since one of the popular tools in the hands of the women was a protest, Funmilayọ experienced no difficulty in attracting women in their quest to challenge the government. Alake, the king during the period, had become an accomplice to the British government and ruled with uncommon brutality. However, the women were not in the habit of cowing to intimidation. The hatred which the people had for the colonial government had fermented, and this led to the attraction of more women in unprecedented numbers coming to protest and challenge the nauseating policy and the confiscation of their food products. Again, Funmilayọ, alongside her group, recorded success by forcing the authority to rescind their law on the confiscation of the people's food. With this and many more events, the twentieth century in Abẹokuta was another epoch of innovation and transformation in the people's history.

Abẹokuta: The Rise of an Elite

Arguably, Abẹokuta is home to the most accomplished public figures ranging from political technocrats, business tycoons, intellectuals, and purposeful scientists who have made not only names for themselves in their different walks of life, but also made an indelible impact that has changed the course of history for the people in their collective. The input of indigenes of Abẹokuta transcends the African continent, and it is a domestic understanding among Nigerians that their influence in the shaping of the country, Nigeria, is unmatched. It remains incredibly difficult to find another city in the country which has produced more or equal numbers of individuals with outstanding characteristics and contributions to life in the various career paths they have chosen. Right from the foundational period of the city in the eighteenth century to date, people who make significant contributions to the advancement of their collective welfare cannot be found in similar numbers as in Abẹokuta. Surprisingly, this city seems to surpass its record as each century passes. For example, the records that Abẹokuta indigenes made in the nineteenth century dwarfed the ones made before, ditto the ones accomplished in the twentieth century, which was expressly higher than what is recorded in the century before it. In what follows, individuals with outstanding contributions from Abẹokuta are considered.

Funmilayọ Ransome-Kuti

Funmilayọ Ransome-Kuti (1900–1978) was born in Abẹokuta in present-day Ogun State, Nigeria, where she began her academic journey that saw her attaining a higher education degree after her academic activity in Nigeria.[15] Exposed to the systematic racism that dominates the sociopolitical lifestyle of English people while she was there for her studies, she became one of the first Afrocentric intellectuals to reject Eurocentrism and its philosophy. She started her resistance to their dominance by exorcising the Christian name, Frances Abigail, that was given to her at birth. Funmilayọ's aversion to anything totalitarian in nature comes readily in her rejection of ideas and values associated with supremacist ideologues. It would later become undeniable that the repudiation of Western influence, which was the cornerstone of her son's (Fela) musical popularity, had its foundation laid by the actions of his mother. Becoming more informed and politically inclined, Funmilayọ was one of the pioneering African revolutionaries who challenged hegemonic structures and, on several occasions, defeated them hands-down. The creation of the maiden female group, Abẹokuta Women's Union, was very instructive in projecting her protest culture. Because of the foundations she laid for the liberation of women, many literary scholars allude to her as the pioneer feminist in Africa.

Fighting against political oppression, holding leaders responsible for their inaccuracies, calling out personalities that fail to live up to their social responsibility brought about Funmilayọ's fame, and she became instantly known for valiant actions that are not only emancipatory but are also crucial to the people's development. One cannot but marvel at the precocious activities and courageous engagements of Funmilayọ Ransome-Kuti, who single-handedly mobilized the battalion of 10,000 women to confront the then Alake and forced his instantaneous but temporary abdication of power. Like a wildfire, Ransome-Kuti's fame and influence on women was widespread, and her identity immediately commanded maximum respect when mentioned. Accordingly, she remains one of the most versatile products coming from Abẹokuta, whose indelible marks would always remain in the hearts of the people, regardless of the era. As if this was not enough, she personally undertook the protest for women's enfranchisement. Her efforts and commitment are scary, for she established herself confidently in a society that was tending toward patriarchy ever since the invasion by the European expansionists. She was not identified for exemplar contributions on a platter of gold. Funmilayọ Ransome-Kuti was one of the proverbial foot soldiers who used their vitality and ruggedness to fight for the country's

---

[15] UNESCO, "Funmilayọ Ransome-Kuti and the Women's Union of Abẹokuta," *UNESCO Series on Women in African History*, 2014.

independence. For these exceptional and beautiful characteristics, she was eventually recognized as a member of the international peace and women's rights movements.

Madam Efunroye Tinubu

Not to be overshadowed by any female personality produced by Abẹokuta is another woman of valor, Madam Efunroye Tinubu (c. 1810–87),[16] Madam Tinubu was one of the most significant members of the nineteenth-century Yoruba world. She was an aristocrat who engaged in slave trading prior to the coming of the Europeans. Slavery during this time was not chiefly for extensive commercial purposes, such as in the colonial times. Slavery was then dependent on victories in wars where the victorious took prisoners of war for hegemonic reasons. On this account, Madam Tinubu had slaves whom she kept for warring expeditions and agricultural purposes. Her marriage to exiled Ọba Adele opened the platform for making economic growth in an exponential capacity. When she moved with him to Badagry, she used her husband's connections to establish her business tentacles, which eventually spread and became more popular. This was when she began to trade in slaves, salt, and tobacco[17] since the people now established a strong contact with the European merchants. When the tides of leadership turned around, and fortune once again smiled on her husband over his re-installation as the Lagos king, Madam Tinubu maximized the potential to establish her influence.

The ascension of Madam Tinubu into political and economic dominance was far from being a coincidence; in fact, she was very strategic and deliberate in her involvement. The reincarnation of her economic power in Ẹgbaland was the product of her power of negotiation and diplomacy. For example, her support for Oluwole to succeed her dead husband was very pragmatic and tactical for her contribution to the ascension of the former won her opportunities to expand her influence in politics and economics. She demonstrated similar tactfulness when she influenced the installation of Akitoye as the king that succeeded Oluwole, and this once again proved immensely productive. For one, her business tentacles spread exponentially, and she became an excellent figure in the administration of Lagos politics and Ẹgba internal affairs. There was no woman prior to this time who would have made similar accomplishments in the political activities of the people. There is continuous difficulty in finding a man with matching influence. Even when confronted with massive challenges, the equanimity with which

---

[16] UNESCO, "Funmilayọ Ransome-Kuti."
[17] UNESCO, "Funmilayọ Ransome-Kuti."

Tinubu handled them was truthfully unmatched. For example, after falling out of favor with King Kosoko, who manipulated Akintoye to become the king, Tinubu deployed her economic power and political influence to launch counterattacks.

Fela Anikulapo-Kuti

One cannot but marvel at the level at which Abẹokuta continues to be productive in the making and remaking of an elite class that has foreboding influence in the nation's development. While the ones highlighted above are figures during the nineteenth century and early twentieth century, individuals with imposing impact in the making of the country also surfaced from the same town in the postcolonial era. Fela Anikulapo-Kuti was one of these people, and his influence generally speaks to the sociopolitical structuration of the country. Born in October 1938, Fela Anikulapo-Kuti was an inventor of a musical genre that transcends into the twenty-first century, years after his demise. A son to the female activist that doubled as the pioneer of feminist struggle in the country, Fela was innovative, creative, philosophical, and prescient, and his ideas, which were rooted in criticism and protest against oppressive governments, made him immediately popular. Because of his unwavering commitment to the collective freedom and welfare of the people, Fela experienced maximum brutality from the government and endured the pains that accompany being a revolutionary. He was uncompromising and deliberate in his engagement of the government every time there was a show of power, especially when it was needless. Fela Anikulapo-Kuti went to extreme lengths in his pursuance of collective freedom as he put his life on the line on many occasions.

Being the inventor of Afrobeat, Fela became the cardinal point of social and political discussion as people, intellectuals included, increased their interest in the engagement of his revolutionary songs to understand the sociology of thought that created a man such as him in the country that was beleaguered by visionless leaders. Whatever was against the African identity was taken especially personally by Fela as he challenged the supremacist ideologues for their racist prejudices and efforts to sabotage African development, calling them out aggressively in his songs and public comments as he was particularly interested in the redemption of African identity through music. He became very active, using music as the instrument to reach his widespread audience for the sole purpose of inspiring them into actions to tackle various challenges. The ability of Fela to conscript social ills into his music was top-notch as he, at a point in time, constituted a threat to the government who declared him a potential enemy who must be crushed. Detained, subjugated, denied freedom, Fela Anikulapo-Kuti went through a humiliating process in his efforts to establish real democracy through music. Fela's creativity soon enough became the cynosure of all eyes as he was eventually adopted as the masses jury. He, too, was a product of Abẹokuta, and a close relative of Wole Soyinka.

Ebenezer Obey

This icon is another product of Abẹokuta with immeasurable contributions to music, just like the previous candidate. His versatility was arguably unmatched, and his dedication to music generally was second to none. Born in 1942, Ebenezer Obey introduced another brand of music to the Nigerian music industry. Just like every story of success, he experienced challenges and made valuable choices that gave him the eventual triumph. Obey began his musical career on a strong footing to the extent that he was immediately successful in his art as he attracted an audience who were interested in his songs. Abẹokuta must have been the reason behind their creativity, given the flexibility of the man when performing. Again, he was a pioneer in this musical brand and quickly joined the ranks of Abẹokuta indigenes who have made indelible marks. Although he started his tutelage under his first master, Fatai Rolling Dollars, around the 1950s and upon what can be referred to as graduation, he, however, came to public limelight and stardom after introducing the Yoruba brand of music to his style. The introduction of this system challenged the status quo and won for him additional respect from the people who became fond of his music. It was practically difficult to mention the juju brand of Nigerian music without mentioning the contributions of Ebenezer Obey.

If one has to measure the intellectual productions of Ebenezer Obey by counting the number of works that he has been able to produce, one would be confronted with a seemingly never-ending list. Obey has produced songs that deal with the ills in Nigerian society; he has made songs that speak to the political reality of the country. He has also dedicated his artistic ingenuity to systematically reveal the moral decadence of society and the need for an instant turnaround. This is not forgetting the fact that Ebenezer Obey is a practicing Christian whose thematic preoccupation most of the time reveals the decay inherent in, or that has engulfed society. A quick observation of Obey's music will show that he is aware of the corruption in the political terrain of the country and was evaluating it by employing music as a medium to confront the system. There are many albums to his credit, and the majority of them continue to reverberate the concerns of the masses and even Africans in general. Ebenezer Obey and Fela Anikulapo-Kuti are musical icons who simultaneously function as an elite in their own right. In contemporary times, their songs continue to be relevant because they are filled with themes and issues that transcend a generation. Because of their evident efforts, they have changed the face of music through their creativity.

Chief Oluṣẹgun Ọbasanjọ

Chief Olusẹgun Ọbasanjọ is another versatile product coming from Abẹokuta, who has made an indelible imprint on the political terrain of the country and Africa at large. Born in March 1937, Ọbasanjọ had led Nigeria both as a military officer and a democratic candidate. Considering the significant contributions he has made toward the retention of the Nigerian identity, it is safe to say that he is a nationalist with a high degree of patriotism on whose account the country has pulled numerous strings of progress and development. Ọbasanjọ's formative education was provided in Abẹokuta, where he developed an interest in an engineering career, which he chose after joining the Nigerian Army. Ọbasanjọ underwent rigorous training and experience to rise to the level of Major General in the military and was very instrumental toward the resolution of the separatist agenda of the Biafran secessionists. They pounced on the Nigerian government for separation during the early period of Nigeria's independence. It was Oluṣẹgun Ọbasanjọ who the separatists surrendered to, marking the end of the uprisings that lasted for thirty months. He was made the head of military operations in 1975, and this, therefore, qualified him as the most senior officer to take charge of the nation's administrative position after the assassination of the one occupying a higher rank, General Muritala Muhammed, in a coup d'état. His introduction as the new Nigerian leader under the military came with significant advantages for the country's education and economy.

Ọbasanjọ's greatness, like other indigenes of Abẹokuta, did not come on a platter of gold. There were times of trials and travails in the process of his greatness. During his time as a military head, Ọbasanjọ was committed to democratic rules and ensured that he became instrumental in the return to democracy by seeing to the organization of electoral reform and processes that brought Shehu Shagari into the 1979 general elections. Ọbasanjọ retired to Ọta where he enjoyed his statesmanship and eventually contributed immensely toward the forging of peace in Africa generally. Suddenly in 1993, however, General Sani Abacha seized power after the annulment of a democratic election that saw the emergence of Moshood Kashimawo Abiọla as the winner and events began to take a different form. Because Ọbasanjọ was critical of Abacha and the latter was a hard-heated military head, he arrested Ọbasanjọ in 1995. He convicted him as being a member of an impending coup. This, therefore, became the climax of Ọbasanjọ's political and social journey as his end was looming, having been apprehended by the despotic Abacha. As fate would have it, however, Ọbasanjọ survived the incident and was freed after the sudden death of the military dictator.

Chief Moshood Abiọla

Chief Moshood Abiọla, yet again, is another versatile son that Abẹokuta has produced. The reason for his inclusion under the elite class raised by Abẹokuta is predominantly because of his political and economic achievements. This is another illustrious indigene of Abẹokuta who has made very significant efforts for the advancement of their economic condition, following his economic transformation, becoming a known philanthropist. Abiọla contested for the presidency in the 1993 general elections, which he won by an impressive margin. However, his mandate was denied by the then military dictator, General Ibrahim Babangida, who cited election perfidy as the reason. This denial, however, provided some measure of advantage for Abiọla on many grounds. For example, he was immediately seen as a symbol of the country's modern democracy by his admirers in both international and local territories. Like everyone cited in this thread, he also drank from the wisdom and innovative supply of Abẹokuta since he had his formative education there.

These people are beneficiaries of the good tidings of Abẹokuta, which has managed to produce important actors in the country's history. Madam Tinubu functioned as a successful businesswoman and a well-respected kingmaker in Lagos for a protracted period while Funmilayọ Ransome-Kuti was an irrepressible voice in the political terrain of the country where she made significant contributions to the advancement of the country generally. There is Fela Anikulapo-Kuti whose name sends shivers to the spines of military dictators and all the establishment that was anti-Africa in nature. This is not forgetting the influence of Ebenezer Obey, another pioneer in African juju music whose innovation and invention in that regard are magnificent. Politically also, we have General Olusẹgun Ọbasanjọ, whose historical rise in the country remains a point of attraction and commentary to historians, and there also was Chief Moshood Abiọla, aka MKO, whose legal ascent to Nigerian leadership was denied but not forgotten. All the people who are from the innovative making of Abẹokuta are by no means represented here, but those who are included lead us to something important about the town.

Conclusion: Abẹokuta as a Melting Pot of Innovations

The preceding narrative seeks to dissolve the experience of Wole Soyinka into the historical world of Abẹokuta, which represents a pastiche of different events, all of which are appropriately managed for the collective progress of the people. Incredible as it appears, Abẹokuta had a relatable beginning descriptive of every great nation of the world in its radical experience and the transformation of their challenges that eventually brought unprecedented rapid development to the people of the country. The products of the city-state in recent history and their exponential rise grounded in their astuteness and outstanding characteristics in different fields are beautiful attestations to the greatness of the city whose political organization and economic understanding remain very crucial to the collective advancement of the groups they are identified with. From their emergence as a city-state to the current evolution as parts of the British legacy collectively identified as Nigeria, it is challenging to come across any group of people who produce more valuable material in terms of human resources. From what has already been implied, there is an intricate connection between the city and the making of successful and great individuals with extraordinary impact in their various endeavors.

Princess Sara Forbes Bonetta, Madam Tinubu, Funmilayọ Ransome-Kuti, Fela Anikulapo-Kuti, Chief Isaac Delanọ, Chief Moshood Kashimawo Olawale Abiọla, Chief Olusẹgun Ọbasanjọ, Chief Ernest Shonekan, Professor Saburi Biobaku, Professor Thomas Adeoye Lambo, Alhaji Dauda Adegbenro, Ṣegun Ọdẹgbami, Wole Soyinka, and others are names that have made contributions that redefined the African identity and the world's perception about Yoruba simply because of the coverage of their influence. The city has produced important warriors with abilities in the field; it has made roughly three presidents in the postcolonial Nigerian environment, one of which spent about twelve years in power altogether, another who served as an interim president, and the third who democratically won the seat of power but was militarily denied. This is not including the domestic fact that the city has produced freedom fighters who spearheaded liberation movements that forced the country toward a new direction. Given the inexhaustible contributions that Abẹokuta has made to the development of Nigerian society through its production of ideas-filled individuals, there is no contention about the fact that the place is blessed beyond what can be scientifically measured. Although Abẹokuta did not rise to have its own empire as did the Old Ọyọ in previous generations, neither did it arise to become the military base to rescue the Yoruba race against external aggressions as did Ibadan. However, the fact that it produced capable individuals involved in the process of nation-building cannot be overemphasized.

Therefore, when Wole Soyinka alludes to the heterogeneous cultural traditions in Abẹokuta and the display of uncommon equanimity in the administration of peace despite their inherent difference, he is referring to the city as one that espouses great ideological values in tolerating people regardless of their cultural identity and spiritual conviction. For example, Wole gets used to his grandfather, whose cultural knowledge was exploited to widen Soyinka's experience, which in the end influenced the ways he sees the world. No doubt, his Christian parents would principally have become an impediment to this, perhaps if they were given to religious extremism. Soyinka artfully recounts the experience as he was being introduced to the patterns of life and carefully gives the impression that his eventual vastness and intellectual versatility are productive of his childhood experience, which shaped his perception about life. Hurriedly, several critics have concluded that Soyinka is obscure, and sometimes his linguistic system is even a demonstration of complexity. Without factoring in the background experiences that shaped his perception and restructured his life philosophy, comments such as these would continue to occupy the academic community. The fact that his classical biography, *Aké: The Years of Childhood*, is expressed from the point of view of a child affirms the assumption that childhood experience, to a small extent, shapes the mindset and the ideological convictions of humans.

The ingenuity of Soyinka sprang from the innovative brilliance, which has become identical to Abẹokuta. Rather than enhance modernization as many revisionist narratives usually claim, the coming of missionaries instead complemented what was already on the ground for the city has demonstrated an uncommon sense of coordination, commendable capacity for the management of relationships regardless of their complexity, beautiful records of self-development which are unmatched even in many European countries from which the British set sail. Therefore, there is something significant deeply connecting the people and the city's progression from its creation. There is enough evidence to show that the people are modeling their outstanding characteristics in line with their ancestral heritage as characters in the contemporary time are nothing short of an archetype of the previous generations who were successful on every front. For this reason, there is difficulty in finding a town or city-state which has produced as many influential individuals as Abẹokuta has comfortably done. At least, its relevance in Yoruba history and Nigeria as well has spanned three centuries now, and it continues to grow stronger.

Except for those whose area of social influence is the Christian or European cultural praxis, cultural protest manifesting in the abolition of Eurocentric culture dominates the lives of Abẹokuta indigenes. Fela Anikulapo-Kuti dropped his Western name, Funmilayọ Ransome-Kuti did the same thing, and Wole Soyinka followed suit, all in their attempt to promote African identity and denounce the European image which has been imposed on them. All these individuals protest Eurocentric hegemony in most civilized ways. Soyinka confirms in his memoir that Abẹokuta flourishes very impressively even though it houses people with variegated cultural and religious identity. His introduction to the cultural undercurrent of the Yoruba people, especially the one that dwells on the administrative system of the people prior to the overtaking of the Europeans, reshaped his perception about the Yoruba and his works emphasize the importance of cultural rejuvenation in most cases. Knowing the political importance of Ogboni through his grandfather, Soyinka then incubated the plan to become a cultural activist through his intellectual productions as he knew that African history was just a victim of the European power play which sought to reduce its impact and coverage or to diminish its influence through negative narratives.

Without understanding the various cultural undercurrents and the corresponding political system used to administer the affairs of Abẹokuta, or getting familiar with the complex religious beliefs that are available in the city-state, therefore, forcing it to become a center of endeavor, it would be challenging to have a fair grasp of what Soyinka represents, and neither will his biography, *Aké: The Years of Childhood*, make any sense.

4

Collective Traditions, Childhood, and Rites of Passage

A Life of Collective Traditions and Realities

Change was impossible to predict. A tempo, a mood would have settled over the house, over guests, relations, casual visitors, poor relations, 'cousins,' strays all recognized within a tangible pattern of feeling and then it would happen! A small event or, more frequently, nothing happened at all, nothing that I could notice much less grasp and suddenly it all changed! The familiar faces looked and acted differently. Features appeared where they had not been, vanished where before they had become inseparable from our existence. Every human being with whom we came in contact, Tinu and I, would CHANGE! Even Tinu changed, and I began to wonder if I also changed, without knowing it, the same as everybody else.

Wole Soyinka[1]

Four unique specialties set Wole Soyinka apart as an outstanding, world-class scholar. First, he is a cultural transnationalist who has used his intellectual ingenuity to showcase Yoruba culture within a framework of comparative literature. Second, he is an exceptionally gifted artist and a scholar who is not only proficient in all aspects of stagecraft but also all genres of literature. Also, he is a political activist who has put his stagecraft in the service of a dynamic national reimagination. Finally, continuing in his role as a political activist, he proffers policy and developmental options as alternatives to corrupt, impotent leadership and governance of postcolonial nation-states.

---

[1] Wole Soyinka, *Aké: The Years of Childhood* (Ibadan: Bookcraft, 2014), 130.

Wole Soyinka is a living, global icon of scholarship, human rights, and civil activism. He has combined a literary career filled with astounding accomplishments with a legendary, lifelong fight against corruption, colonialism, and imperialism. This book conveys the multifaceted contribution of a man whose living legacy transcends internal politics in Nigeria and Africa. It provides students, scholars, or casual readers with a clear and concise introduction to interpreting and understanding Soyinka's life and works, the impact of which is global in reach and historic in significance.

Born in Nigeria in 1934, Wole Soyinka's literary gifts did not escape the notice of his early teachers. He earned some of his earliest literary prizes while still a student at Abẹokuta Grammar School. He completed his formal education at Government College, Ibadan; University College, Ibadan; and Leeds University, UK. Soyinka's meteoric ascent to heroism, celebrity, and fame began during his undergraduate years at Nigeria's University College, Ibadan (now the University of Ibadan). Along with several other classmates including Olumuyiwa Awẹ, Ralph Opara, Aig-Imoukhuede, and Pius Olegbe, Soyinka formed the Pyrates Confraternity in 1953. The group adopted the motto "Sworn enemies of all Convention." The Pyrates Confraternity soon drew the interest of many other students in part because it promoted "seadogism," or the struggle against injustice.[2]

According to Tunde Adeniran, the Pyrates Confraternity had three main goals: "(i) to abolish conventions; (ii) to revive the age of chivalry; and (iii) to end tribalism and elitism."[3] Its members felt adherence to academic conventions stunted an individual's ingenuity and intellectual possibilities. Institutions of higher learning had lost sight of their real purpose. They were created as places where students were supposed to create new knowledge, which demanded challenging and sometimes rejecting existing scholarship. The group embraced a tradition of chivalry in its effort to join the pursuits of intellectual and moral excellence. The pursuit of intellectual distinction and moral improvement meant little in the face of injustice. It felt that tribalism, expressed as uncritical loyalty, undermined intellect and reason and led people to act blindly in the interest of loyalty to their ethnic group or a desire to be accepted. Tribalism is a pervasive human instinct that has, in its darkest forms, led to continued social inequalities, the elevation of corrupt leaders, and even genocide. Elitism masquerading as meritocracy imbues unqualified and unmerited individuals with privileges while ignoring the more deserving. Soyinka and his peers hoped their attack on the forces arrayed against intellectual, moral, social, and economic freedom on campus would serve as a beacon for the broader struggle in Nigerian society, politics, and culture.[4]

---

[2] Tunde Adeniran, *The Politics of Wole Soyinka* (Ibadan: Fountain Publications, 1994), 43.
[3] Adeniran, *The Politics of Wole Soyinka*.
[4] Adeniran, *The Politics of Wole Soyinka*.

Over the years, Soyinka has remained committed to using his art for larger social and political change. After a brief spell for graduate study at Leeds University in West Yorkshire, United Kingdom, Soyinka returned to Nigeria in 1960, armed with a simple but sophisticated and powerful combination of written words and dramaturgy. He skillfully deployed this arsenal on behalf of civil action against the burgeoning crop of corrupt politicians in the Nigerian First Republic. In his battle against the ruthless Nigerian state apparatus, Soyinka ingeniously deployed his precociousness, professional and artistic skill as a performer and writer of poetry, fiction, nonfiction, and drama to lampoon the corruption and chaos of the western regional government of Nigeria. In 1965, Soyinka demonstrated his audacity as a political activist when he broke into the studio of Radio Nigeria and brandished a gun. He forced the host to swap Premier Samuel Akintọla's recorded speech for a famous manifesto demanding the premier's resignation.

Soyinka's international acclaim came two decades later—belatedly to those who saw him as a hero and undeservedly to his critics who viewed him as a rascal. Long before the Nobel Prize, when in his thirties, Soyinka's international renown began with the *New Statesman*'s John Whiting Award for 1966–67. He was the Overseas Fellow at Churchill College, University of Cambridge in 1973–74, where he wrote the widely acclaimed *Death and the King's Horseman*. He was awarded the George Benson Medal of the Royal Society of Literature and the UNESCO Medal of Arts. In 1986, he became the third African and the only Nigerian thus far to win any Nobel Prize.

His accomplishment ranks him as one of a total of 919 individuals (865 male winners and 54 women) and 24 organizations to become Nobel laureates between 1901 and 2019. He is one of only 114 Nobel laureates in literature and the third African and first West African to receive such recognition. His possession of the intellectual acumen to attain the Nobel summit is but one facet in his seemingly multifaceted but straightforward, complex, and controversial persona. To look only through the lens of scholarship and literary creativity offers a somewhat myopic view of the life and works of Wole Soyinka.

Soyinka's Long Journey to Becoming the Voice and Conscience of African Humanity

Wole Soyinka began his long walk to becoming an iconic figure in global politics during his undergraduate years in the 1950s. During the era of decolonization, Soyinka shifted and widened the themes of his political activism and civil action from anti-imperialism and anti-colonialism to include the causes of human rights, anti-corruption, and good governance, especially as it applied to African political leaders. Because of his massive all-around literary talent, Wole Soyinka is like the proverbial elephant in a crowd of blind people: He means different things to different people depending on the part they touch. In other words, there are so many different aspects of Soyinka's works, life, and politics to explore within his rich corpus of biographical material that, despite all the specialty articles, books, and critiques already written, much remains. Wole Soyinka, Nobel laureate, is a truly global icon of scholarship, human rights, and civil action.

The intricate tapestry of Soyinka's life and work is rooted, intertwined, and woven in a complex fabric of childhood experiences that resonated throughout his adolescence and into his adulthood. Researching and writing about Soyinka is, therefore, akin to searching for the proverbial needle in the hayfield of Soyinka's life and works or for the philosopher's stone to read, interpret, and understand his significance and contribution. An example of his political, cultural, and economic syncretism highlights the need to pursue multiple paths to assess his work and influence. A small, intimate ceremony marking the dedication of the first motor lorry in Iṣara, Node—organized by Soyinka's friend's father, a pioneering Nigerian entrepreneur of the colonial era and proud owner of the lorry—included "*etutu* rituals performed by Jagun, a Christian blessing by Pa Josiah, and a Qur'anic reading by the Imam."[5] Hence, we believe the simple, but by no means easy guiding thesis for a study that seeks to read, interpret, and understand Soyinka's life and works (what he has previously called a "race retrieval project"[6]) is rooted in his anti-imperialist social background, in his privileged comprehensive and holistic mix of African traditions and Western liberal upbringing, and in the enriched and vibrant sociopolitical milieu of post-Second World War Nigerian nationalism and decolonization geopolitics.

Given the richness of both Wole Soyinka's natural heritage and his nurturing cultural environments, we found him to be an insightful classic "subject," or rather a child developmental psychologist's experimental specimen for the controversy regarding which is more dominant and determinant in an individual's personality: nature or nurture, that is, the role of genetic heritage or the environment in shaping one's growth and development. In his memoir, *Aké: The Years of Childhood*, Soyinka recalled his childhood induction to local, national, and international politics of gender inequalities, racism, and the culture war of supremacy between the African and the European traditions. Born in the period of the Great Depression in 1934 and growing up during the Second World War, Soyinka is a product

---

[5] Wole Soyinka, *Isara: A Voyage Around Essay* (Ibadan: Fountain Publications, 1989), 3.
[6] Biodun Jeyifo, "Introduction," in *Conversations with Wole Soyinka*, ed. Biodun Jeyifo (Jackson: University Press of Mississippi, 2001), ix.

of the African "collective reality" of colonialism and imperialism.[7] More significantly, he is also a product of collective African traditions, including a confusing nexus of cultural issues of gender inequality, communal obligations and responsibilities, and the burdens of surrogate parenting and "extended family that acknowledged no limits" on the newly educated elites, all of whom he named and grouped as the "*ex-Ilés*."[8]

The Incomprehensible Irrationality of Adults Bewitched the Little Wole Soyinka

As a child, Soyinka could not comprehend the irrationality of adults. For example, he had to prepare and fortify his mind for a transition from his childhood years to his adolescence, characterized by the sheer nausea of sharing everything with more than a dozen bedwetting children of relatives to the untold inconveniences of a constant, uninvited stream of market women from Işara, his father's town, who, without notice, used his parents' house at Aké as a way station. They dropped in at night with their merchandise as they traveled to and from the market. He lived under the incessant fear of corporal punishment and spent years agonizing over the inexplicable irrationality of his mother's objection to children wearing shoes.

Indeed, Soyinka, whose parents could afford to buy shoes for him and his siblings, remained baffled by the ludicrous principle of "Children do not wear shoes" that applied to not only him and his siblings, but also to numerous other children and wards in his home.[9] His mother, alias "the Wild Christian," would not allow any children, even those who came with shoes from Soyinka's apparently poor, extended family to wear their shoes. He grew to resent the illogical requirements of adults. For example, he felt it ludicrous that adults who do not prostrate to God expected children to prostrate to greet them. Confronted by the chiefs at the Odẹmọ's royal court who asked Soyinka to prostrate to greet the king, he retorted, "If I don't prostrate myself to God, why should I prostrate to you? You are just a man like my father, aren't you?"[10]

Overall, the irrationality of adults and their concept of discipline marveled Soyinka as he contemplated the unimaginable adolescent life in a high

---

[7] James Markham, "Soyinka, Nigerian Dramatist, Wins Nobel Literature Prize," October 17, 1986, https://www.nytimes.com/1986/10/17/books/soyinka-nigerian-dramatist-wins-nobel-literature-prize.html?searchResultPosition=4.
[8] Soyinka, *Isara*, quote on 43 and *ex-Ilés* on vii.
[9] Soyinka, *Aké*, 312.
[10] Soyinka, *Aké*, 178.

school whose principal was an international Scoutmaster but would neither allow boys to have pockets in their pants nor to wear shoes or underpants. Thus, in his last words in *Aké*, Wole Soyinka wrote, "I sighed, feeling the oppressive weight of my years. It was time to commence the mental shifts for admittance to yet another irrational world of adults and their discipline."[11]

From childhood, Wole Soyinka had been engulfed with feelings of the "oppressive weight" of the "collective reality" of Africans and their "*collective* tradition."[12] Because Soyinka "believes that justice is the first condition of humanity," he immersed himself in his art and remains resolutely committed to using his literary works and political activism as a voice of the oppressed.[13] In the first press conference that Soyinka attended in Paris after the announcement of the Nobel award, he declared that he regarded it as an acknowledgment of not only his lifelong efforts to use literature and art as activism but also a repudiation of "centuries of denigration and ignorance" of African literary traditions and heritage.[14]

Several aspects of Soyinka's life and work overlap, and it is difficult to separate his intellectual life from his lifelong political activism. Writing about Soyinka does not fit neatly into a conventional historical chronicle of events. Our attempt to structure Soyinka's life and works into clearly delimited chapters are analogous to separating the seven hues of the rainbow. Therefore, this book will adopt a thematic approach to Soyinka's life and work, focusing on what Biọdun Jeyifo has described as the "collective tradition of modern African literature" that has inspired and sustained Soyinka's "advocacy and solicitude" on behalf of the African literary enterprise in the wake of struggles for independence from the grasp and legacy of colonialism.[15]

What's Soyinka Like? Is He a Provenance of the Crucible of the Ages and a Man of Destiny?

Soyinka is both an enigma and a man of destiny. Ngũgĩ wa Thiong'o, in one of the essays honoring Soyinka at eighty, concluded that Soyinka was

---

[11] Soyinka, *Aké*, 319.
[12] First quote ibid.; and second and third Jeyifo, "Introduction," ix, emphasis added.
[13] Bayo Onanuga, et al., "Soyinka Tells His Exile Story," in *Conversations with Wole Soyinka*, ed. Biọdun Jeyifo (Jackson: University Press of Mississippi, 2001), 198.
[14] Markham, "Soyinka, Nigerian Dramatist."
[15] Jeyifo, "Introduction," xiii.

the Byronic hero, or even better, a renaissance figure, dashing, defiant and daring. His writings plays, poems, memoirs, and novels carry one banner: the man dies in him who keeps silent in the face of tyranny. As a writer and public intellectual who has voiced his concerns over major happenings in the different parts of the continent over the last fifty years and more, he has become the moral and democratic conscience of Africa.[16]

In "The Finest Hour" speech to the House of Commons, Winston Churchill talked about walking with destiny.[17] Similarly, Wole Soyinka seemed to have been just as certain as Churchill that he, too, had chosen to walk with rather than in spite of destiny. Indisputably, his difficult childhood years, which might have broken most people, in fact prepared him for the journey. Hence, to borrow Roy Jenkins's description of Churchill, Soyinka is also a deeply "faceted, idiosyncratic, and unpredictable" nature.[18] Soyinka's imagining of himself as a "man of destiny" helped him transcend provincial and self-interested loyalties to class and tribe.[19]

Wole Soyinka's experiences at the Government College and his relationship with Rev. A. O. Ransome-Kuti, the principal of Abẹokuta Grammar School, lay at the root of his detribalized personality and radicalism. Later in life, Soyinka said that Ransome-Kuti reminded him very much of Winston Churchill. No history of human rights activism would be complete without due recognition of Soyinka's life and works. In a trilogy of memoirs, Soyinka revealed his transition from a dutiful choirboy to a revolutionary young adult. It does not require any profound psychoanalysis of his impressionable experiences during childhood to recognize their powerful cultural impact and influence on his life. In particular, both the multifarious Ijẹbu and Ẹgba royal traditions and his association with colonial expatriates and the emerging Western-educated Nigerian nationalists' elite profoundly influenced Soyinka. His provenance provides an important key to comprehending the foundation, the growth, and the propelling force of his whole career and enigmatic character. For the purpose of this book, we have distilled Wole Soyinka's life and works into five thematic areas: scholarship, relationships, beliefs and values, governance and nation-building, and political activism.[20]

---

[16] Ngugi wa Thiong'o, "The Conscience of Africa," in *Crucible of the Ages: Essays in Honour of Wole Soyinka at 80*, ed. Ivor Agyeman-Duah and Ogochukwu Promise (Ibadan: Bookcraft, 2014), 7.
[17] Winston Churchill, "Finest Hour," https://winstonchurchill.org/resources/speeches/1940-the-finest-hour/their-finest-hour/.
[18] Roy Jenkins, *Churchill* (London: Pan Macmillan Ltd., 2001), 3.
[19] Jenkins, *Churchill*.
[20] Soyinka, *Aké* and Wole Soyinka, *Ibadan: The Penkelemes Years* (Ibadan: Bookcraft, 2014).

"This world is only the negative of the world to come"

We attempt here to not only unravel the legendary and mysterious Wole Soyinka's life but also proffer a practical guide to understanding his complex literary works and political activism. We borrow and then invert a metaphor from the subtitle of Terry Plunkett Hallowell's review of Longfellow's verse: "this world is only the negative of the world to come."[21] Soyinka's lifelong preoccupation with issues of humanity and social justice could be seen as the developed photograph, the world to come. His provenance—his childhood experiences and adolescent dreams—represent the photographic negative that composes the final image. As a child, Soyinka had always been fascinated by the irrational ways of the world of adults. The adolescence he spent at the Government College Ibadan allowed him to nurture, experiment with, and practice his art. The motto of Swanston House, his first residence hall at the Government College, was "justice and fairness."

In his book on the politics of Wole Soyinka, Tunde Adeniran describes this period as one of warring tensions within the young Soyinka, who was "dangerously inquisitive, cautious and reflective, demonstrative of youthful boisterousness and histrionic talents, reclusive, ... [but] apt to giv[e] free rein to his creative urges."[22] Soyinka, who grew up a Christian, began to renounce the Christian concept of God while at the Government College. His childhood was deeply influenced by his father's circle of friends who passionately debated the excesses of power in colonial Lagos, to which he made connections within and outside of his schoolyard. As he grew into manhood, dealing with bullies and finding his own way at school, he also witnessed disturbing acts of racially motivated bigotry, inequality, and state violence against his fellow Nigerians beyond the college. Soyinka "guessed that the place would mark him for life," and it did.[23]

In *The 8th Habit: From Effectiveness to Greatness*, a sequel to the popular lifestyle guide, *The 7 Habits of Highly Effective People*, Stephen Covey professes, "We [humans] are a product of our decisions, not our conditions."[24] Soyinka's life extends Covey's observation. Soyinka, indeed, is more than a product of his decisions and his conditions. He is a product of his *society*, his *times*, and his *chosen responses and reactions to the conditions of his society*. Adeniran has rightly observed that,

---

[21] Terry Plunkett Hallowell, "Longfellow's Verse: 'This World Is Only the Negative of the World to Come,'" *Kennebec: A Portfolio of Maine Writing* 14 (1990): 64–5.
[22] Adeniran, *The Politics of Wole Soyinka*, 33.
[23] Soyinka, *Ibadan*, 19–20, quote on 20.
[24] Stephen R. Covey, *The 8th Habit: From Effectiveness to Greatness* (London: Simon & Schuster, 2004), 179.

Soyinka's personage locates him in many 'worlds.' He is black, he is African, and he is a human being. To be a black man and an African requires black and African consciousness, an involvement in the type of literary creativity through which creative actions are processed for effect through written word.[25]

Scholars, including Adeniran, note how Soyinka's writings reflect his life and his overriding commitment to social change. Soyinka does not apologize that his art can "arouse enthusiastic support or bitter opposition"—and sometimes both conflicting emotions at once.[26] Hence, Wole Soyinka warns his readers that he is "a by-product of the *penkelemes* [peculiar mess]" of Nigerian culture, politics, and society.[27]

The Young Adult: The Making of a Revolutionary

Tell me not, in mournful numbers,
Life is but an empty dream!
For the soul is dead that slumbers,
And things are not what they seem.

Life is real! Life is earnest!
And the grave is not its goal;
Dust thou art, to dust returnest,
Was not spoken of the soul.

Lives of great men all remind us
We can make our lives sublime,
And, departing, leave behind us
Footprints on the sands of time;

Let us, then, be up and doing,
With a heart for any fate;
Still achieving, still pursuing,
Learn to labor and to wait.[28]

---

[25] Adeniran, *The Politics of Wole Soyinka*, 49–50.
[26] Eldred Durosimi Jones, *The Writings of Wole Soyinka* (London: Heinemann Educational Books Ltd., 1973), 10–11, quoted in Adeniran, *The Politics of Wole Soyinka*, 50.
[27] Soyinka, *Ibadan*, x.
[28] Henry Wadsworth Longfellow and H. J. Bruce, *A Psalm of Life* (Satara: Columbian Press, 1878).

Soyinka's extraordinary political activism expresses the spirit of Longfellow's poem. One of Longfellow's precepts for revolutionaries is that they "can make their lives sublime."[29] Soyinka's organizational skills and underground network enabled him to survive for more than sixty years on the frontline of change in civil society and governmentalism. In those sixty years, he has survived a great number of daring confrontations with colonial authorities, including the "do-or-die" Nigerian politicians, and the draconian and diabolical Nigerian military. He has issued statements to the press while imprisoned in maximum security prisons, and he operated a radio station during the notorious Abacha's regime. If Shakespeare was right to counsel that "ambition should be made of sterner stuff,"[30] what stuff is Wole Soyinka made of? What drives him? What makes him tick? What lessons could human rights activists learn from Soyinka's life and works?

We will, in the rest of this chapter, among other things, explore how Soyinka evolved from his puritanical Christian upbringing to a lifelong preoccupation with a fight against colonialism, imperialism, racism, and social injustice. He has promoted a global discourse on good governance. The state's many attempts to silence him, paradoxically, served to promote Soyinka's cause but also fed the creation of myths about him that have continued to make him a legend.

Man's Inhumanity to Man: The Making of a Radicalized Brash Octogenarian

Wole Soyinka owed his opportune position, and consequently his part in Nigerian politics, to the time and place of his birth. As a relative of the Alake of Abẹokuta and the Ọdẹmọ of Iṣara and as the son of a schoolmaster, he had access to and connections with a network of powerful people in Nigeria since the 1940s. Indeed, he came of age in the postwar era of nationalist movements against racial discrimination, colonialism, and imperialism. As a teenager at the Government College, he sometimes skipped classes and traveled to Lagos where he could hear firebrands like Michael Imodu denounce the massacre of Iva Valley miners or watch Hubert Ogunde's *Bread and Bullets*, a play about the coal miners' strike. He witnessed the colonial government ban the play and throw Ogunde in jail for what it felt was incendiary art.[31] Thus, from his secondary school days to his

---

[29] Longfellow, "A Psalm of Life" (1839).
[30] William Shakespeare, "Julius Caesar," *Complete Works of Shakespeare*, Act 3, Scene 2, lines 91–94.
[31] Soyinka, *Ibadan*, 19–20.

undergraduate years at the University College, Ibadan, and Leeds University, United Kingdom, Wole Soyinka has been an active part of the cohort of nationalists who have been fighting for Nigeria's independence. He was the Master of Ceremony on Independence Day in 1960.

Soyinka's student years in Britain provided a unique opportunity to experience the invidious nature of both direct and indirect (or what has now been recognized as institutional) racism. In his memoir *Ibadan*, Soyinka, speaking of himself in the third person, described Great Britain as "a racist battleground that he [Soyinka] skirted with progressive skill, but he could never totally evade the anti-personnel mines that littered the landscape, from the working-men's pubs and public transport, to the restaurants and hotels of Chelsea or Belgravia."[32] Soyinka never missed any opportunity to exhibit his proficiency in "progressive skill" when combatting racism. For example, he simply drank the leftover half of an opened bottle of wine when a customs officer proposed to charge him duty on the extra half bottle over his entitled duty free one bottle. He left the officer after amusing himself with a sarcastic paraphrase of Winston Churchill: "I may get drunk, but later I shall be sober, while you, sir, will always be a racist."[33] In his poem "Telephone Conversation," Soyinka vividly expresses his anger at a white landlady's racism and racial discrimination.[34]

Although raising the Nigerian independence flag struck a deadly blow to colonialism and imperialism, it also silenced many of Soyinka's contemporaries fighting in the movements against alien rule. Soyinka himself simply changed gears, widening the scope of his mission to include the universal cause of human rights and responsible governance. He never relented in his effort to fight corruption in public places anywhere in the world. Given the wave of campaigning for integrity and accountability among private and public officials worldwide, the World Bank has even adopted good governance as a condition for a financial rescue of an ailing or failing economy. It seems the world is catching up with Wole Soyinka.

The seed of the dogged principle or uncompromising philosophy of "the man dies in all who keep silent in the face of tyranny" continued to drive Wole Soyinka's life and works. That seed was sown and rooted in his childhood upbringing and his independent adolescence.[35] Wole Soyinka revealed Apataganga as a place that, "he felt, *defined him in some unchangeable way.*"[36] Though he has witnessed his Aunt Beere lead "women to war," cause the Alake of Abẹokuta to scatter, denounce a British District

---

[32] Soyinka, *Ibadan*, 31.
[33] Soyinka, *Ibadan*, 38.
[34] Wole Soyinka, "Telephone Conversation," in *The Penguin Book of Modern African Poetry*, ed. Gerald Moore and Ulli Beier (London: Penguin, 1963), 187.
[35] Wole Soyinka, *The Man Died: Prison Notes of Wole Soyinka* (Ibadan: Bookcraft, 2014), 3.
[36] Soyinka, *Ibadan*, 18–19. Emphasis added.

Officer for "us[ing] ... the 'yellow' Japs as guinea-pigs for the atomic bomb, rather than their fellow white Germans," Soyinka believed he only truly "understood *conflict*" in his experiences at Apataganga.[37]

Ẹlẹmi Eṣu: Soyinka and the Fear of Being Possessed

Ironically, one significant factor that accounted for Soyinka's survival was his aversion to using violence to effect political change. He is aware of his vulnerability to "emotional explosions," what Daniel Goleman has coined as "neural hijackings."[38] The aphorism "Man, know thyself" is often credited to Luxor Temple in ancient Egypt. There are two parts of the ancient temple: "The External Temple, where the beginners were allowed to enter, and the Internal Temple where a person was only allowed to enter after proven worthy and ready to acquire more knowledge." One of the proverbs in the External Temple is "the body is the house of God." That is why it is said: "Man, know thyself." In the Internal Temple, one of the many proverbs is "Man, know thyself, and you are going to know the gods."

In his memoirs, *Aké: The Years of Childhood* and *Ibadan: The Penkelemes Years*, Soyinka shares two episodes of his self-knowledge and self-awareness of his vulnerability to being possessed by what Wild Christian, his mother, has labelled "*ẹmi eṣu*."[39] In the first episode, adults teased Wole as a weakling and challenged him to box his little brother Dipo. Dipo enthusiastically squared up against his brother, "leap[ing] from side to side in a war-dance all his own creation."[40] Amused, the young Wole did nothing, entranced by his brother's war dance. Suddenly, his brother flew at him and knocked Soyinka down. Ears ringing, Soyinka lay on the ground. He recalled, "I remembered nothing, only a storm of rage in my veins."[41] Soyinka recalled that his mother prayed for him against *ẹmi eṣu* and warned him, "It was so easy to be possessed by the devil."[42] Soyinka wondered if he was indeed possessed, especially when he recalled periods when he blacked out and could remember nothing, like in the fight with his brother. The second "blackout" episode occurred in Egypt. In his response to police interrogation after he broke into the radio station in Ibadan to seize the premier's recorded broadcast, Soyinka explained to

---

[37] Soyinka, *Ibadan*, 18–19.
[38] Soyinka, *Ibadan*, 18–19. For detailed information on emotional explosions, see chapter 2, "Anatomy of an Emotional Hijacking," in Daniel Goleman, *Emotional Intelligence: Why It Can Matter More Than IQ* (London: Bloomsbury Publishing Plc, 1996), 13–29.
[39] Soyinka, *Aké*, 146.
[40] Soyinka, *Aké*, 144.
[41] Soyinka, *Aké*.
[42] Soyinka, *Aké*, 146.

the interrogating officer why he never involved himself in violent rebellion, though he did believe that violence was sometimes called for to effect social change. He mentioned, however, that at times he felt violence welling up in him, as if he were "*possessed!*"[43]

Psychologists have found evidence of emotional explosions akin to moments of being possessed. Daniel Goleman, in his classic book *Emotional Intelligence: Why It Can Matter More Than IQ*, called these emotional explosions neural hijackings:

> At those moments, evidence suggests, a center in the limbic brain proclaims an emergency, recruiting the rest of the brain to its urgent agenda. The hijacking occurs in an instant, triggering this reaction crucial moments before the neocortex, the thinking brain, has had chance fully [to know] what is happening, let alone decide if it is a good idea. The hallmark of such hijack is that once the moment passes, those so possessed have the sense of not knowing what came over them.[44]

There is no doubt that Soyinka's fears of being possessed circumscribed his willingness to use violence in civil disobedience and political action against the colonial administration and the corrupt civil and military juntas in post-independence Nigeria. Consequently, rather than employ violent resistance, Soyinka resorted to the instrumental power of literature. His deadly weapon was his pen. Adeniran notes that Soyinka's writing, including his novels, plays, and poetry

> suggest a peculiar concern for the creation of a just socio-political order based on morals and laws that evolve out of a collective tradition and reinforced by freedom and facilities for the origination, fruition, and expression of ideas. They look back into the past to predict our future sometimes in the tone of Virgil's deterministic fatality that we are warned, very seriously, to watch out![45]

The Revolutionary Artiste as a Global Icon and a Vanguard Conscience of Civil Society

As a global icon and a vanguard conscience of civil society, Wole Soyinka "believes that justice is the first condition of humanity,"[46] and he believes

---

[43] Soyinka, *Ibadan*, 386.
[44] Goleman, *Emotional Intelligence*, 14.
[45] Adeniran, *The Politics of Wole Soyinka*, 107.
[46] Onanuga, "Soyinka Tells His Exile Story," 198.

that "[t]he man dies in all who keep silent in the face of tyranny."[47] To promote the cause of humanity and good governance in post-independence Nigeria, Soyinka had against all the odds, boldly put his *person and pen*, that is, his life and literary works, on the line to confront the authorities of both the Nigerian civil and military governments. Soyinka spent twenty-seven months between 1967 and 1969 in solitary confinement for alleged collusion or complicity with the secessionists during the Nigerian civil war. In 1998, President Sani Abacha sentenced Soyinka to death, in absentia.

Soyinka often expresses opinions about inhumane conditions and tyranny in all parts of the world. In reaction to Donald Trump's ascension as the 45th President of the United States of America, Soyinka penned a lengthy editorial decrying what he believed was a "travesty of collective choice."[48] Soyinka was in the United States in the months preceding the 2016 elections, and he witnessed Trump's campaigning firsthand:

> I watched his face, its body language, listened to his uncouth, racist language, his imbecilic harangues, the insults to other peoples, other races, especially the Hispanics, Africans, and Afro-Americans, even citing once I was told Nigeria as an instance of the burdensome occupation of global space. This is how it begins, how humanity ends up with Cambodia, with Rwanda, with Da'esh. We are watching a Hitlerite phenomenon.[49]

Soyinka wrote the piece in response to incessant pressure on social media for him to fulfill his promise to destroy his US Green Card if Donald Trump won the 2016 American presidential election. At an education conference at the University of Johannesburg, South Africa, the BBC reported that Soyinka did destroy his US Green Card on December 1, 2016.[50]

For decades, Soyinka quietly refused to travel to a few countries in protest over human rights abuses. For example, he refused to travel to Spain when it fell under the illegitimate leadership of Francisco Franco. He refused to travel to China after Tiananmen Square; to South Africa for "her astonishing display of xenophobia, most notably against Nigerians"; and to Cuba, even though Fidel Castro personally decorated him with the Felix Valera Medal of Honor because Soyinka "found the execution of those ill-fated adventurers who tried to escape on a raft excessive, not forgetting the

---

[47] Soyinka, *The Man Died*, 3.
[48] Wole Soyinka, "Red Card, Green Card: Notes Towards the Management of Hysteria by Wole Soyinka," http://saharareporters.com/2016/11/12/red-card-green-card-notes-towards-management-hysteria-wole-soyinka.
[49] Soyinka, "Red Card, Green Card."
[50] Adeniran, *The Politics of Wole Soyinka*, 138–9.

shooting down of a hijacked plane."[51] He found the acts of the adventurers condemnable, but the punishment did not fit their crime.

Given Soyinka's literary and intellectual achievements, in addition to his heritage, he could have quickly become part of the Nigerian elite. He could have taken a high-paying, high-status political or corporate position. Instead, he chose to be a "philosopher-king": "Soyinka opted for the roles of agents'[52] provocateur, opinion mobilizer, the icon of intellectual opposition and political sensitizer."[53] He chose to challenge power from the outside and make it accountable to the people.

---

[51] Adeniran, *The Politics of Wole Soyinka*, 138–9.
[52] Adeniran, *The Politics of Wole Soyinka*, 138–9.
[53] Adeniran, *The Politics of Wole Soyinka*, 138–9.

5

Nobel Laureate: Literary Scholarship and Nation-building

Language study however involves, as we all know, the study of a people's history and culture
WOLE SOYINKA, "RED CARD, GREEN CARD," 2016[1]

Soyinka and the Nobel Prize

To many people today, Soyinka's 1986 Nobel Prize in Literature is the greatest definer of Wole Soyinka's genius and scholarship. The Swedish Academy's stated goal for the award when it founded the prize in 1786 was to promote the "purity, strength, and sublimity of the Swedish language."[2] Hence, Tim Parks wonders, "Was this compatible with choosing the finest oeuvre of 'an idealist tendency' from anywhere in the world?"[3] Interestingly, Soyinka was already well known throughout Sweden because his poetry was first translated into the Swedish language during the 1960s.[4]

---

[1] Wole Soyinka, "Red Card, Green Card: Notes Towards the Management of Hysteria," http://saharareporters.com/2016/11/12.
[2] Quoted in a review article, Tim Parks, "What's Wrong with the Nobel Prize in Literature?" *The New York Review of Books, NYR Daily*, October 6, 2011, https://www.nybooks.com/daily/2011/10/06/why-nobel-prize-literature-silly/.
[3] Parks, "The Nobel Prize."
[4] Kwame Anthony Appiah, "A Master of His Trade," in *Crucible of the Ages: Essays in Honour of Wole Soyinka*, ed. Ivor Agyeman-Duah and Ogochukwu Promise (Ibadan: Bookcraft, 2014), 106.

But, Soyinka has neither written in Swedish nor promoted the "purity, strength, and sublimity of the Swedish language."[5]

So, what could be the root of the attribution of Nobel Prize in Literature to a non-Swede, or even writers who do not speak Swedish, or who have not the least capability to promote the purity, strength, and sublimity of the Swedish language? The explanation is metaphorically rooted in the barter system. In places where money was scarce, barter might be described as exchange resulting from *a double coincidence of wants*: The Swedish Academy was in search of "an honorable formula, [that is] some simple, rapid, and broadly acceptable criteria,"[6] and serendipitously stumbled on a formula for the award of Nobel Prize in Literature. Lo and behold, the lives and works of writers such as Wole Soyinka met the Academy's ingenuous formula.

From his student days at Ibadan and Leeds in the 1950s, Soyinka had been a "sworn enemy of convention."[7] He was a lone global voice for the "stolen voices,"[8] the oppressed voiceless who Frantz Fanon captioned in his book as *The Wretched of the Earth*.[9] Thus, Tim Parks leaves us with what might have been the only mutual coincidence of interests between the Swedish Academy and Soyinka's scholarship. The Swedish Academy had over the years affiliated with activist writers and began to see human rights activism as a complement to its mission. Consequently, the Swedish Academy found an outstanding candidate in Wole Soyinka. Arguably, either the poems or novels of many other writers such as Chinua Achebe, Pepper Clark, or Ngũgĩ wa Thiong'o were also well qualified for the Nobel Prize.

Indeed, Kwame Anthony Appiah praised Soyinka, but noted the outstanding literary achievements of other African writers, particularly Achebe. Appiah opined that it is not always the art but the context and reception that matter more: "one of the reasons why certain people never get the prize is because they have bad politics by the Academy's standards."[10] Appiah stressed, however, that Soyinka's multifaceted talents as not only a novelist but also a playwright, poet, memoirist, and even actor complement and enrich his political activism.[11] In corroboration of this view, Sefi Atta

---

[5] Parks, "The Nobel Prize."
[6] Parks, "The Nobel Prize."
[7] Kọle Omotoso, *Achebe or Soyinka: A Study in Contrasts* (London: Hans Zell Publishers, 1996; reprint, Ibadan: Bookcraft, 2009), xxvi.
[8] See Wole Soyinka, *The Deceptive Silence of Stolen Voices* (Ibadan: Spectrum Books, (2003) 2005).
[9] See Frantz Fanon, *The Wretched of the Earth*, trans. Constance Farrington (New York: Grove Press, (1961) 1963).
[10] Appiah, "A Master of His Trade," 106.
[11] Appiah, "A Master of His Trade," 105.

echoes Appiah: "Soyinka set a precedence of possibility. His life's work is the study of power on a national scale and as if his works are not enough, he himself steps in to redress power imbalance, which, to my mind, is the noblest form of artistic expression."[12]

Other scholars and intellectuals, such as Rosa Figueiredo describe Soyinka's works as "the drama of existence."[13] Nicholas Westcott notes that Soyinka:

> used his status in the cause of principles he held dear, principles that were neither 'African' nor 'British' nor 'western,' but universal, in practice as much a part of traditional Yoruba culture as anywhere else. He brought to all this a righteous anger and an ability to articulate it, together with a wry humor that turned even dramatic events, such as his own flight from the country to avoid arrest, into a narrative that is at once exciting, moving and comic.[14]

Margaret Busby aptly captures Soyinka's wry humor and comic narratives:

> Soyinka is a self-acknowledged by-product of the 'penkelemens' [peculiar mess] of Nigerian politics, in possession of 'an over-acute, remedial sense of right and wrong, of what is just and unjust.' His commitment to freedom and human rights has earned him imprisonment (by Gowon), exile (by Babangida and Abacha), a death sentence in absentia (by Abacha) and

---

[12] Sefi Atta, "Hallo Sefi," in *Crucible of the Ages: Essays in Honour of Wole Soyinka at 80*, ed. Ivor Agyeman-Duah and Ogochukwu Promise (Ibadan: Bookcraft, 2014), 14.

[13] Rosa Figueiredo, "The Drama of Existence: Myths and Rituals in Wole Soyinka's Theatre," *International Journal of Arts and Sciences* 4, no. 1 (2011): 105–13.

[14] Nicholas Westcott, "Soyinka's Cultural Antiphonies," in *Crucible of the Ages: Essays in Honour of Wole Soyinka at 80*, ed. Ivor Agyeman-Duah and Ogochukwu Promise (Ibadan: Bookcraft, 2014), 28. For a comprehensive review of the universality of Soyinka's works, see, for example, Chidi Amuta, "The Ideological Content of Soyinka's War Writings," *African Studies Review* 29, no. 3 (1986): 43–54; Msiska Mpalive-Hangson, "The Politics of Identity and the Identity of Politics: The Self as an Agent of Redemption in Wole Soyinka's *Camwood on the Leaves* and *The Strong Breed*," *Journal of African Cultural Studies* 18, no. 2 (2006): 187–96; Dominic Alimbey Derry, "Exploring the Theme of Corruption in Soyinka's *The Road*," *International Journal on Studies in English Language and Literature* 2, no. 8 (2004): 72–84; and Niyi Akingbe, "Writing Violence: Problematizing Nationhood in Wole Soyinka's *A Shuttle in the Crypt*," *IRWLE* 8, no. 2 (2012): 1–26. For a vivid description of Soyinka's political strategy, see Ruth H. Lindeborg, "Is This Guerilla Warfare? The Nature and Strategies of the Political Subject in Wole Soyinka's *Aké*," *Research in African Literatures* 21, no. 4 (1990): 55–69; Robert W. July, "The Artist's Credo: The Political Philosophy of Wole Soyinka," *The Journal of Modern African Studies* 19, no. 3 (1981): 477–98; and Adewale Maja-Pearce, "Punching Holes inside People: Words of Wole Soyinka," *Third World Quarterly* 9, no. 3 (1987): 986–92.

silence (by Ọbasanjọ). Yet, actively aware of the power of both the gun and pen, he remains able to laugh at himself.[15]

The Nobel Prize award is for the body of work rather than a single book. As highlighted in Chapter 1, Wole Soyinka has unique specialties that give him an edge over other activist-writers and set him apart as an outstanding world-class scholar. However great an achievement it might have been to win the Nobel Prize, Wole Soyinka is much larger than the Nobel Prize. If Soyinka is more than the Nobel Prize, what then is the source of his exemplary scholarship? We identify three iconic aspects of Wole Soyinka's ingenious literary scholarship:

1. The writer as culture hero
2. The autobiographical memoirist as a nationalist, anti-imperialist, and global historiographer
3. The playwright, poet, and novelist as the voice of the voiceless.

The Writer as Culture Hero

In 2004, Odia Ofeimun delivered a lecture at the Obafemi Awolowo University, Ile Ife on Soyinka's birthday. Ofeimun's lecture, entitled "Wole Soyinka: The Writer as Culture Hero," drew on the works of Ato Quayson, Bernard Belasco, and A. H. M. Kirk-Greene.[16] Ofeimun reviewed and noted that the concept of culture hero, a concept developed by Bernard Belasco, described:

> one who personified the modal personality representing the core values of culture, not just in terms of what the Yoruba call *omoluabi*, the true child of the family, but one who performed feats that entrenched the values held strongly to heart by the whole society ... The culture hero was, accordingly, very much the hunter adventuring for game or the warrior who made good from war booty and thereafter shared with the paterfamilias.[17]

---

[15] Margaret Busby, "Fragments from a Chest of Memories," in *Crucible of the Ages: Essays in Honour of Wole Soyinka at 80*, ed. Ivor Agyeman-Duah and Ogochukwu Promise (Ibadan: Bookcraft, 2014), 26.

[16] Odia Ofeimun, "Wole Soyinka: The Culture Hero," in *In Search of Ogun: Soyinka in Spite of Nietzsche* (Lagos: Hornbill House, 2014), 113–175. For an understanding of the concept of "culture hero," see Ato Quayson, *Calibrations* (Minneapolis: University of Minnesota Press, 2003); Bernard Belasco, *The Entrepreneur as Culture Hero: Pre-adaptations in Nigerian Economic Development* (New York: Praeger, 1980); and A. H. M. Kirk-Greene, *His Eternity, His Eccentricity, or His Exemplarity: A Further Contribution to the Study of H.E. the African Head of State, African Affairs* 90, no. 359 (1991): 163–87.

[17] Ofeimun, "Wole Soyinka: The Culture Hero," 127–8.

Accordingly, Kirk-Greene viewed the culture hero as "the modern leader, who consciously and quite deliberately reaches back into the history of his people and, by a positive reaffirmation of their cultural dynamic, simultaneously enhances both his stature and his legitimacy."[18] Ofeimun stressed in his lecture that the culture hero helps redefine culture. Ofeimun also noted that Soyinka's principled stance stood in stark contrast against the Nigerian authorities' blatant corruption and violations of human rights. With every word he wrote and every protest he participated in, Soyinka risked his freedom and even his life.[19]

The Autobiographical Memoirist as a Nationalist, Anti-imperialist, and Global Historiographer

Oftentimes, in the making of the history of a nation, its heroic political figures are products of their time. In the making of Nigerian history, Wole Soyinka belongs to the third generation of the Nigerian Western-educated nationalist elites: the first being the cohorts of Herbert Macaulay and the returned freed slaves, who settled in the Lagos Colony between 1860 and the year of Macaulay's demise in 1946, and the second was the cohort of Dr. Nnamdi Azikiwe, who on his return to west Africa from the United States in 1934 led the nationalists' campaign for Nigerian independence in 1960. Soyinka's five volumes of memoirs and eight volumes of intervention speeches, which altogether run to 2,725 pages and more than one million words, are no ordinary memoir but an important legacy of authoritative chronicles of a living history of man's inhumanity to man from a living legend and a global human rights activist.

In an introduction to the *Intervention Series*, Wole Soyinka noted his purpose was "not, in itself, to resurrect debates. Indeed, the opposite is the case. They are intended to act as triggers of memory."[20] In his historical analysis of the origins of Boko Haram, Soyinka declares his position on the status of the Nigerian nation-state and catalogs the developmental

---

[18] Ofeimun, "Wole Soyinka: The Culture Hero," 129.
[19] Ofeimun, "Wole Soyinka: The Culture Hero," 130, 138, 145–7.
[20] Wole Soyinka, *Between Defective Memory and the Public Lie: A Personal Odyssey in the Republic of Liars, Interventions*, vol. 5 (Ibadan: Bookcraft, 2015), 135–6. For an insight into Soyinka's dramas on postcolonial African states see, for example, Tẹjumọla Ọlaniyan, "Dramatizing Postcoloniality: Wole Soyinka and Derek Walcott," *Theatre Journal* 44, no. 4 (1992): 485–99; and Anne Whitehead. "Journeying through Hell: Wole Soyinka, Trauma, and Postcolonial Nigeria," *Studies in the Novel* 40, no. 1/2 (2008): 13–30.

and leadership issues confronting Nigerian post-independence vis-à-vis postcolonial nations:

> My position today is that the Nigerian citizen ... is conscripted to fight the war of darkness, the deprivation of elementary electric power that is crucial to development and basic existence in a modern society. He or she is conscripted to fight the wars of disease, while the new imperators jet off to Europe and Saudi Arabia for their own treatment. He is conscripted to fight the wars of exposure to the elements for lack of affordable shelter, to battle ignorance for lack of functional educational facilities, facilities that have been run aground, deliberately, by one incumbent neo-colonial fascist after another, be such in uniform or mufti. He is compelled to fight the war of personal and collective security, one that has moved from random killings through armed robbery to kidnapping for ransom, in a situation of near total anomie, not forgetting the rounds of religious slaughter. Every citizen has been conscripted into a private vigilante role for bare survival. Most humiliatingly, he has been conscripted into fighting, all over again, the war of liberation, the struggle to have a voice in the direction of his society, how it should be run, towards what destination and in pursuit of what ideals.[21]

Soyinka recounts the anomic state of the Nigerian nation, including, among so many other issues, military coups, venal politicians who hoard the wealth of the nation, and even pedophiles.[22] He issues a warning: "Sooner or later, the chickens come home to roost."[23]

Although Soyinka sees history as a complementary subject to literature, he is first a creative writer. He declares in his foreword to *Ibadan: The Penkelemes Years*,

> Ibadan does not pretend to be anything but faction, that much abused genre which attempts to fictionalize facts and events, the proportion of fact to fiction being totally at the *discretion* of the author. My adoption of the genre stops short of the actual *invention* of facts or events, however, or the deliberate distortion of history or character of any known figure.[24]

---

[21] Wole Soyinka, "The Precursors of Boko Haram," in *The Unappeasable Price of Appeasement, Interventions*, vol. 3 (Ibadan: Bookcraft, 2011), 40–1.

[22] Wole Soyinka, "Between Law and Responsibility," in *The Unappeasable Price of Appeasement, Interventions*, 45. Also see Soyinka, *Aké*; and Soyinka, "Between Law and Responsibility," 71–2.

[23] Wole Soyinka, "From Growing Pains to Terminal Disease?" in *The Unappeasable Price of Appeasement, Interventions*, vol. 3 (Ibadan: Bookcraft, 2011), 105, emphasis in original.

[24] Soyinka, *Ibadan*, ix.

He also warned in his note on *Iṣara: A Voyage Around Essay* that, "except in two or three cases, ... [I] eliminate all pretense to factual 'accuracy' in this attempted reconstruction of their [Essay and his friends'] times, thoughts and feelings."[25] Scholars such as Biọdun Jeyifo and others have highlighted some of the liberties Soyinka took in describing the 1964 and 1965 uprisings in Western Nigeria. Indeed, Jeyifo predicts that "many of the incidental and circumstantial facts on which Soyinka bases this account of the Nigerian crisis of the mid-1960s will be challenged, and perhaps refuted by the future accounts of this period of Nigerian history."[26] These issues are not minor errors, but "more substantial questions of authorial taste and judgment ... [in] the extraordinarily moving, eloquent and problematic memoir, *Ibadan* [: *The Penkelemes Years*]."[27] However, in spite of Soyinka's disclaimer and Jeyifo's observed errors of facts and chronology, Soyinka's memoirs, novels, plays, and the *Intervention Series* are a remarkable record of Nigerian history since the 1950s to date. It is this form of chronicle that makes Wole Soyinka an autobiographical memoirist who is a nationalist, anti-imperialist, and a global historiographer.

The Playwright, Poet, and Novelist as the Voice of the Voiceless

In his comparative study and analysis of the works of Chinua Achebe and Wole Soyinka, Kọle Omotoso compares the two literary giants in three areas: Pan-Africanism, the Nigerian nation-state, and what he calls "the ethnic national agenda."[28] Omotoso concludes both men are caught up in the contradictory intersections between the three. Odia Ofeimun echoes Omotoso by highlighting the problems of "what to do with a traditional class and culture that had symbolic power and control over the majority of the people, even in the absence of official instrumental power."[29]

Yes, both Achebe and Soyinka were caught up in contradictions, but Soyinka's opposition to negritude in the 1960s grew out of his belief that a tiger does not need to demonstrate its tigerhood. In his story about Africa

---

[25] Soyinka, *Isara*, viii.
[26] These include among others the "Obitun Dancers" who are ascribed to Ado Ekiti instead of Ondo (77); the NEPU female activist Gambo Sawaba (Gambo "Freedom") who is called Salawa Gambo (227); the Winneba Ideological Institute in Nkrumah's Ghana, which is called Winneba School of Political Science (324), all ibid.
[27] Jeyifo, *Wole Soyinka*, 214.
[28] Omotoso, *Achebe or Soyinka*, xxviii.
[29] Ofeimun, "Wole Soyinka: The Culture Hero."

in *A Dance of the Forests*, Eldred Durosimi Jones has claimed Soyinka remained "universal."[30] Ofeimun argues Soyinka "allows integrity to the particularity of the African story without implying that there is something quintessentially, racially, off the place in its progression. A common notion of knowledge is projected in the play which does not assume that the African world demands a different conception of human nature, human rights and human dignity."[31]

The literary works and various prizes awarded to Chinua Achebe and Wole Soyinka personified and engendered the Nigerian nation-state geopolitics, the encoded Igbo-Yoruba ethnic national agenda and the implicit rivalries, and covert envy and covetous jealousies. Soyinka is however misperceived as a "radical" and an "obscured writer," who would not play "the African game."[32] Chinua Achebe once said, "Well I think he [Soyinka] makes a cult of obscurity, especially in his later work, which to my mind is unnecessary and unfortunate."[33] Omotoso, however, sees obscurity as "the critical and stylistic hallmark of Soyinka's writing."[34] Would anyone consider science textbook authors as making *a cult of obscurity*? Or a psychiatrist using professional jargon *an obscured writer*?

More importantly however, what critics have often overlooked and misunderstood is that Wole Soyinka is always aware of the risks and the danger confronting him and his mission and stance against the rentier state apparatuses. Perceived as the enemy of the state, he therefore artfully crafted and built in to his works and life, the so-called obscurity but ingenious strategic and tactical defensive litigation weaponry against the hostile military and civilian governments and diabolic adversaries.

Biọdun Jeyifo sees a "culturally different and complicated cosmology ... as the source of 'obscurity' in Soyinka."[35] Kọle Omotoso, too, noted obscurity as an ineffective way to describe Soyinka's work.[36] As highlighted in the epigraph to this chapter, "Language study however involves, as we all know, the study of a people's history and culture."[37] Wole Soyinka not only studied the history and culture of the people he writes about, but he considers "dramatic resolution, [as] being closer to [his] real profession."[38]

---

[30] In the essay "Thoughts on the African Novel," *Morning Yet on Creation Day*, quoted in Omotoso, *Achebe or Soyinka: A Study in Contrasts*, xxvi.
[31] Ofeimun, "Wole Soyinka: The Culture Hero," 165.
[32] Omotoso, *Achebe or Soyinka*, first quote on xxv, and second and third on xxii.
[33] Omotoso, *Achebe or Soyinka*.
[34] Omotoso, *Achebe or Soyinka*.
[35] Omotoso, *Achebe or Soyinka*, xxiii.
[36] Omotoso, *Achebe or Soyinka*.
[37] Soyinka, "Red Card, Green Card."
[38] Soyinka, "Red Card, Green Card."

Soyinka, therefore, heroically and professionally cultivates the seemingly obscured and encoded basic tools and jargons of poetry, storytelling, and stagecraft (i.e., hyperbole, melodrama, metaphor, satire, suspense, surprise, creative imagination, visualization, humor, idioms, proverbs, soliloquy, fables, significant objects, demonstration and treatment, plot, characterization, etc.) to create effect and engage his audience. Rosa Figueiredo is more accurate in her perception and assessment of Soyinka when she writes that the "metaphysical awareness on the part of the audience is, for Soyinka, most clearly seen in those performances of 'ritual' theatre where a fundamental anxiety manifests itself in members of the audience over whether or not the protagonist will survive confrontation with the forces of chaos which now exist in the arena of performance space."[39]

Soyinka writes not just to entertain the ọgbẹri (the ordinary lay readers and audience) but also the ọmọ awo (the enlightened and knowledgeable members of the stagecraft profession). In addition, without an adequate background knowledge in the language of ritual theater and in the rhetoric of literature, which is Soyinka's trade and specialty, he is inadvertently obscured to the uninitiated (who the Yoruba would call the ọgbẹri). For example, how could anyone appreciate the Abiku's (the spirit child's or a child who comes back) soliloquy to its dispirited mother without first possessing a grounding in the Yoruba ontology of reincarnation, myths, and superstitions, as well as poverty and infant mortality?[40]

How else could anyone appreciate a "Telephone Conversation" between a prospective black African tenant and a white landlady without being aware of the insidious nature and reality of direct and indirect racism or the systemic, institutional racial practices in 1950s Europe and the Americas? Imagine the humor in Soyinka's sarcastic description of the state of his buttocks, which were darker than the rest of his body as the effect of his native custom of making children sit on the floor![41] In Isara, Soyinka's narrative of how the king, Ọdẹmọ, was elected by open contest between two

---

[39] Rosa Figueiredo, "The Drama of Existence: Myths and Rituals in Wole Soyinka's Theatre," International Journal of Arts and Sciences 4, no. 1 (2011): 105. See also K. Naveen Kumar, "Yoruba Tradition and Culture in Wole Soyinka's 'The Lion and the Jewel,'" Journal of Arts, Science and Commerce 2, no. 3 (2011): 88–97; Abiodun Musa Rasheed, "The Drama and Theatre of Wole Soyinka," Encyclopedia of the Arts 11, no. 3 (2006): 216–29; David Maugham-Brown, "Interpreting and the Interpreters: Wole Soyinka and Practical Criticism," English in Africa 6, no. 2 (1979): 51–62; Lawrence Ogbo Ugwuanyi, "I Am Therefore You Are: An Existentialist Perspective on Wole Soyinka's Writings," UJAH: Unizik Journal of Arts and Humanities 12, no. 2 (2011): 65–90; and Noureini Tidjani-Serpos, "The Postcolonial Condition: The Archeology of African Knowledge: From the Feat of Ogun and Ṣango to the Postcolonial Creativity of Ọbatala," Research in African Literatures 27, no. 1 (1996): 3–18.
[40] See Wole Soyinka, "Abiku," The Penguin Book of Modern African Poetry, ed. Gerald Moore and Ulli Beier (London: Penguin Books, (1963) 1984), 187.
[41] Soyinka, "Abiku," 193.

candidates is more than a story. It is a political statement that the Yoruba have democratic traditions and institutions that predated the advent of European colonialism and their so-called evangelical civilizing agenda and a kingship succession culture that are adaptable to modern political system.

Soyinka also apparently employs the shared and universal human language of freedom, justice, and human rights from his inherited tripod cultures and histories to enlist empathy, projective identification, and a virtual reality between his audience and the characters in his stories.[42] Wade Cudeback, who was a teacher and Soyinka's father's pen pal, arrives on the day of the election of the king. It was also a symbolic gesture of the Soyinkas' dream of the universality of human fellowship.

According to Jane Wilkinson, "[t]he will to challenge the abyss, the continued 'battle not merely for a held idea, but more critically for an integrated survival'"[43] drives Soyinka. His work addresses human beings' "most energetic, deeply combative intentions[,] ... bridging the gulf with visionary hopes."[44] Thus, Soyinka joins the cultural terrains of the Yoruba, and specifically that of the Ijẹgba, with his paternal Ijẹbu and maternal Ẹgba families; Nigerian multiethnic national cultures; and English and African colonial cultures to do literature and stagecraft. In other words, he creates, reconstructs, and proffers dramatic solutions for the post-independence conflicts in Africa and elsewhere.

For example, in *Iṣara: A Voyage Around Essay*, Soyinka makes a hero of Damian, "who wanders into Iṣara from nobody knows where and becomes a solid member of the town."[45] When he allows Baroka, the old traditional chief—and not Lakunle, the modern village teacher—to marry Sidi in *The Lion and the Jewel*. This would seem radical, but, in reality, it could be Soyinka exercising his authorial liberty to infuse originality into his writing by breaking the mode of conventional royal status of heroes and heroines. It could also simply be presumed as Soyinka's promotion of Yoruba democratic tradition that allows the enthronement of a stranger to become king if the stranger were the choice of Ifa divination.

However, what really is obscure in *The Man Died*, *Aké*, *Iṣara*, *Ibadan*, and the *Interventions Series*? After a review of the works of Soyinka and Achebe, Omotoso suggested that Soyinka is much more neutral about any attempt to sponsor the triumph of the past over the present because "those who stick to the old ways sometimes succeed and sometimes fail. But those who wish to combine both ways always fail tragically."[46]

---

[42] Ofeimun, "Wole Soyinka: The Culture Hero," 151–64.
[43] Soyinka, *The Man Died*, 25.
[44] Jane Wilkinson, "Daring the Abyss: The Art of Wole Soyinka," *Africa: Rivista trimestrade di studi e documentazione dell'Istituto italiano per l'Africa e l'Oriente* 41, no. 4 (1988): 611.
[45] Omotoso, *Achebe or Soyinka*, 6.
[46] Omotoso, *Achebe or Soyinka*, 25.

Soyinka's Politics of Nation-building and Citizenship

As we have noted in earlier chapters, the foundation for Soyinka's political philosophies and contributions to Nigeria's nation-building and citizenship was laid not only in his upbringing and the detribalized schools and colleges he attended but also in the context of his times, which include nationalism, anti-imperialism and anti-colonialism radicalism, and the post-Second World War "activist moment."[47] His formative years from 1934 to 1960 coincided with a period when the world went through the unprecedented crises of the Great Depression, the Second World War, and the breakdown of the moral and ideological pillars of imperialism and colonialism as a result of decolonization, particularly the reclamation of the lost and denigrated African dignity and heritage. While citing cases to illustrate Soyinka's contribution to Nigeria's nation-building and citizenship, we look at his political activism under the following four themes:

1. Backgrounds to Soyinka's political philosophies;
2. Soyinka's strategies and tactics for nation-building;
3. Soyinka's activist agenda in literature and drama; and
4. Politics and statesmanship: Soyinka's firebrand political activism.

Backgrounds to Soyinka's Political Philosophies

One of the greatest threats to Nigeria's nationhood, citizenship, and nation-building is the erroneous perception among many Nigerians that all nations were created through natural or artificial means. There is a mythical perception that patriotism and committed citizenship come about by providential proclamation rather than being cultivated by human intervention. This ingrained myth has been a bane to Nigeria's nationhood, citizenship, and nation-building. It was rooted in the overused claim by Obafemi Awolowo that,

> Nigeria is not a nation. It is a mere geographical expression. There are no "Nigerians" in the same sense as there are "English," "Welsh," or "French."

---

[47] For details of the "activist moment," see "The Activist Moment: Nationalism and Radical Politics, 1945–1951," in Toyin Falola and Bola Dauda, *Decolonizing Nigeria, 1945–1960, Politics, Power, and Personalities*, ed. Toyin Falola and Bola Dauda (Austin: Pan African University Press): 105–36.

The word "Nigerian" is merely a distinctive appellation to distinguish those who live within the boundaries of Nigeria from those who do not.[48]

However, Peter Apter affirms that however a nation came into existence, human intervention makes people become citizens of a nation. He wrote, and we quote him at length because his words strike at the essence of demystifying the making of citizenship,

> The populations living within the borders of the states where kings of France, England or Sweden were respective sovereigns, became nations. The French nation, for instance, embraces population groups of varying origins, cultures, and even languages. ... Nineteenth and early twentieth-century Europe saw how in many other instances the process of nation-building set in before nation-state came about. It often transcended existing frontiers, rendering them obsolete, and led ultimately to the formation of new states with new frontiers. ... After the Italians had succeeded in forming a nation-state in 1861, Massimo d'Azeglio, the writer and former prime minister of Piedmont, mindful ... of the conflict between northern and southern Italy, is supposed to have remarked: "We have made Italy: now we have to make Italians." D'Azeglio was thus acutely aware that political unification in the national state did not automatically guarantee the existence of the nation. By contrast, a condition of any organized national movement aspiring to create a nation-state is the existence of at least the first stages of nation-building and a national consciousness.[49]

Three conclusions can be drawn from Apter's observations:

1. European nation-states (and indeed virtually all nation-states including those in the Americas and Asia) were all artificial creations that somehow evolved either through amalgamation, conglomeration, peaceful unification, or violent subjugation or conquest of a group of sovereign ethnic nationalities;

2. Creating a nation-state, as in the amalgamation of northern and southern Italy or the northern and southern Nigerian Protectorates and the Colony of Lagos, is only the first step to making the people who live within the nation-state's borders adopt identities that acknowledge those nation-states, in this case either Italians or Nigerians, respectively; and

---

[48] Many authors have described Nigeria as a mere geographical expression. See, for example, Obafemi Awolowo, *Path to Nigerian Freedom* (London: Faber and Faber Ltd., 1946), 47–8.
[49] Peter Alter, *Nationalism*, 2nd ed. (London: Edward Arnold, 1985), 14–15.

3. Nation-building and citizenship require deliberate human actions to organize and create what Soyinka has labeled as a set of "fundamental protocols of coexistence [of a people who live within the borders] of nation space."[50]

In practical terms, a formulation of fundamental protocols of coexistence would include "requiring only the complete surrender of hegemonic dreams, the ethos of inclusivity, the recognition of religious privacy, community primacy, and the manifested will of the authentic landowners of a designated nation space."[51] According to Soyinka, protocols of coexistence "alone is the route to nationhood. Constitution is only a part of the story."[52] In social science parlance, Soyinka's proffered protocols of coexistence require creating political institutions, shared political culture, and shared political values to promote a vested common socioeconomic interest to bind those who live within the geopolitical borders of a nation. Through the bond, they develop a sense of belonging and a readiness to not only subjugate their individual interests, including religious and ethnic affiliations, to the overriding national interest but also be patriotic enough that they willingly pay the supreme sacrifice to defend their stake in the nation.

Soyinka understands what it takes to create and to build a nation and, subsequently to promote a binding national interest. However, this understanding is rooted in his unique and privileged familial network of political activists and in a rigorous childhood education, which amounts in many ways to subtle forms of indoctrination and brainwashing! As highlighted in Chapter 4, Soyinka had firsthand tutelage in Yoruba cultural values, kingship ruling principles, and diplomacy because both sides of his parents' families had close lineages to the Ọdẹmọ of Iṣara and the Alake of Ẹgbaland and both sides were prominent in the royal courts.

Thus, as a child, Soyinka learned a great deal from listening to nationalist conversations and arguments at the feet of elders who visited his father's home; running errands for his mother, who was a leader among women's groups in the town; spending time with relatives of his maternal grandfather the Reverend J. J. Ransome-Kuti, maternal aunt Funmilayọ Ransome-Kuti, and maternal uncle the Reverend Israel Oludotun Rannsome-Kuti (alias Daodu), all of whom were firebrand nationalists; and spending time at either of the kings' palaces. Rev. I. O. Ransome-Kuti was one of the founders of the Nigerian Union of Teachers. His wife Funmilayọ, in collaboration with Eniola Soyinka (Wole Soyinka's mother), organized and mobilized the women in Abẹokuta to reject the unfair taxation of women. The women's resistance undermined the powerful colonial administrative machinery and

---

[50] For details see, Wole Soyinka, "Between Nation Space and Nationhood," a public lecture delivered at the Obafemi Awolowo Foundation in 2009, 4.
[51] Soyinka, "Between Nation Space," 21.
[52] Soyinka, "Between Nation Space," 18.

led Alake to abdicate the throne in January 1949. Of his mother's influence, James Gibbs writes,

> It was through his mother's shop and her trading that Soyinka was drawn to the centre of the life of the town, and made aware of what was going on there. The Yoruba proverb, "*Oja l'aye, Orun n'ile*" makes the point that "The world is a market, heaven is home." It was in this ... microcosm of the world, with the trades-people singing their wares, and Eniola collecting her debts, that Soyinka was drawn deep into the mainstream of Yoruba life, where he learnt the swirling currents far more acutely than he could have at the Wolf Cub meetings or in the Sunday school. The vivid and wide range of characters he has created owe something to the childhood hours spent in charge of his mother's shop when he was "earthed" in the market, and in the family, she gathered around her.[53]

On his paternal side, Soyinka witnessed how his grandfather and others mobilized the common peasants and market women of Işara to not only oppose bureaucratic colonial selection and imposition of a candidate on the people but also organize the first open democratic election of the Odemo of Işara. On Soyinka's religious influences, Gibbs notes that Soyinka

> derived his particular finely tuned understanding of Pentecostalism partly from his mother. In *Brother Jero* and Lazarus in *The Interpreters*, Soyinka created, with a rare deftness and sureness of touch, memorable portraits from the world of charismatic Christianity. He observed and researched the separatist churches, but perhaps he found at home some of the insights into the enthusiasm which make his portraits of pentecostalists so convincing.[54]

Soyinka's Organizational and Operational Strategies and Tactics for Nation-building

From his childhood at Aké in Abẹokuta and in Işara, Soyinka learned that the success or failure of political activism depends on putting in place a calculated number of solid foundations, including:

a. a well-informed and ideologically grounded leadership that is capable of confronting and engaging ruling authorities in meaningful

---

[53] James Gibbs, "Biography into Autobiography: Wole Soyinka and the Relatives Who Inhabit 'Aké,'" *The Journal of Modern African Studies* 26, no. 3 (1988): 546–7.
[54] Gibbs, "Biography into Autobiography," 546.

dialectic dialogues and that is competent to negotiate for better policy options with the powers that be in government;
b. a sound publicity or "propaganda" machinery;
c. a broad-based grassroots mobilization of people;
d. a network of institutions and operational systems to push ideas and to implement proposals;
e. a well-organized and disciplined team; and
f. a sound and reliable intelligence gathering and coordinating network.

Later in life, Soyinka would put the aforementioned lessons into strategic and tactical use to not only help realize his vision of a humane society and his mission for justice and equality but also to implement his political action. Soyinka drew inspiration and motivation from his childhood introduction in the use of democratic dialectics (i.e., well-articulated logical debates to win arguments and influence people). His Uncle Rev. A. O. Ramsome-Kuti, the principal of Abẹokuta Grammar School, encouraged students to use discourses as an effective weapon to argue their ideas. His uncle even excused students who stole his (uncle's) wife's chicken because the students could make a legal argument to justify their action.[55] Also as a child, Wole Soyinka was never short of role models in the value of a good debate and rhetoric from the adults who frequently engaged in heated arguments with his father.

Thus, Wole Soyinka began pursuing his political activism as a teenager at the Government College, Ibadan. In *Ibadan: The Penkelemes Years*, he recalled his first attempt to get his college to change its house emblem's name from Swan to Kestrel, which he considered superior to the swan: "If Kaye [the house prefect] remained unconvinced, he would suggest the topic to the House prefect for the next House debate: 'Why the Kestrel is a superior emblem to the Swan.' ... When you have a goal, don't beat about the bush. Lead your people directly there, but marshal your arguments in advance and be firm in your conviction."[56] Later as an undergraduate, he and a group of seven students established the Pyrates Confraternity to organize civil actions against colonial rule and imperialism.

Throughout his life, Soyinka never missed an opportunity to engage the authorities in dialogue. For example, as a young research fellow in the 1960s, he held a private meeting with Professor Dike, the University

---

[55] For details of how the students who stole a cockerel defended themselves, see Soyinka, *Aké*, 240–4.
[56] For details, see Soyinka, *Ibadan*, 131–5.

of Ibadan's vice chancellor, to discuss academic freedom in the case of undue interference from the visitor Dr. Nnamdi Azikiwe to impose Dr. Sylvester Anieke as the Chairman of the University Governing Council.[57] Dr. Anieke had once resigned from his position as the "first African to head the University teaching hospital" because he was indicted for fraudulently claiming he had D.Sc. from Toronto.[58] Soyinka also had a long conversation with Modele, Samuel Akintọla's daughter, to persuade her not to allow her father, the Premier of the Western region, to use her for his political self-interest.[59]

Soyinka wanted to live up to his principles and convictions. He believes "the writer's personal integrity very importantly includes within it the sense of social responsibility," and that "[o]nly by remaining true to what the writer believes in can he/she function as the 'conscience' of his/her society."[60] Thus, he took a big risk to go to northern Nigeria, albeit to no avail, to appeal to his academic friends to avoid a civil war. He also went east to meet the Biafran leader Col. Odumegwu Ojukwu to persuade him not to secede: a misadventure that eventually earned him a twenty-seven-month detention in prison.

Indeed, one of the most intriguing—and confusing, controversial, and contradictory—features of Soyinka's political activism is that he does not stop at criticizing governments. Perhaps out of naive optimism for a possibility the government might redeem itself, Soyinka has sometimes worked within the governmental apparatus for change. For example, Soyinka organized the Federal Road Safety Corps (FRSC) in the 1970s and worked with the government to save the 1977 Festival of Arts and Culture of Africa and the Black World (FESTAC '77). Soyinka also risked espionage charges when he went to South America to rescue the famous Ori Olokun. In the mid-1980s, Soyinka made the controversial decision to support the dictator Ibrahim Badamasi Babangida, who "would later annul the federal elections of June 1993 and plunge the nation into its worst period of crisis and military dictatorship in the entire post-independence period."[61]

---

[57] Soyinka, *Ibadan*, 233–8.
[58] For details of Dr. Anieke's scandalous claim of D.Sc. from Toronto, see Soyinka, *Ibadan*, 218–19.
[59] Soyinka, *Ibadan*, 249–54.
[60] Ketu H. Katrak, "Theory and Social Responsibility: Soyinka's Essays," *Black American Literature Forum* 22, no. 3 (1988): 500. For Soyinka's view of the writer's social responsibilities, also see Florence Straton, "Wole Soyinka: A Writer's Social Vision," *Black American Literature Forum* 22, no. 3 (1988): 531–53.
[61] Jeyifo, *Wole Soyinka*, 9–10.

Soyinka's Activist Agenda in Literature and Drama

Five phases characterize Soyinka's use of literature and drama, particularly in promoting Nigeria's nation-building and citizenship and in projecting Pan-Africanism in general. Soyinka's constituency expands beyond the borders of Nigeria. Henry Louis Gates Jr. vividly captured Soyinka's mastery of arts as follows:

> Soyinka is a master of the verbal arts. His English is among the finest and most resonant in any literary tradition, fused seamlessly as it is with the resonances and music of the great lyrical, myth-dense, Yoruba tradition. He bears a relation to the poetics of Africa akin to that which Shakespeare bore to England, Pushkin to Russia, Lorca to Spain, Brecht to Germany, and Joyce to Ireland he is the point of consciousness of its language. And, within the movement for democracy in Black Africa, he is both troublesome, insistent conscience and its most eloquent voice.[62]

The first phase was his earliest, pre-independence conventional dramas: *The Swamp Dwellers* (1958), *The Lion and Jewel* (1958), and *The Invention and Other Tales* (1959). The second phase comprised his two mythopoetic plays: *A Dance of the Forests* (1960) and *The Trials of Brother Jero*, which projected his apprehensions for independence. Biọdun Jeyifo has rightly noted that, "Soyinka has a deep, abiding penchant for mythology, metaphysics and mysticism."[63] Chidi Amuta also noted that, "Soyinka has complicated this [Jeyifo's alleged] ambiguity in his reputation by striving, in his earlier works at least, to proffer mythic 'explanations' and resolutions for social problems which ordinarily belong in the realm of historical reality and empirical human experience."[64]

The third phase was what Jeyifo has called Wole Soyinka's 1965 "satirical revue": *Before the Blackout, Kongi's Harvest, The Road, The Interpreters*, and his long poem *Idanre*.[65] The fourth phase, from 1969 to 1981, comprised

---

[62] Henry Louis Gates Jr., "Wole Soyinka: Mythopoesis and the Agon of Democracy," *Georgia Review* 49, no. 1 (1995): 194.

[63] Biọdun Jeyifo, "Soyinka Demythologised," *Ife Monograph Series in Literature and Criticism* 2, no. 4 (1984): 4.

[64] Chidi Amuta, "The Ideological Content of Soyinka's War Writings," *African Studies Review* 29, no. 3 (1986): 43. See also Randa Abou-bakr, "The Political Prisoner as Antihero: The Prison Poetry of Wole Soyinka and Ahmad Fu'ad Nigm," *Comparative Literature Studies* 46, no. 2 (2009): 261–86.

[65] Jeyifo, *Wole Soyinka*, xxvi.

his prison memoirs and a metamorphosis of his mythopoetic literature into direct civil action and somewhat yellow journalistic historiography. Thus, he wrote *The Man Died*, *Madmen and Specialists*, *Season of Anomy*, *A Shuttle in the Crypt*, *Death and the King's Horseman*, and *Opera Wonyosi*. The fifth phase is 1981 to date. In this final phase, a mature Soyinka went back to the basics in his writing, harnessing the power of storytelling and persuasion in film and music to reach out, connect with, and promote his ideas of nationhood, humanity, and social justice to the common people. For instance, his album *Unlimited Liability* (1981) lampooned the outrageous corruption of the Shagari administration and proved a big success. Since 1981, he has published his memoirs in four volumes: *Aké: The Years of Childhood*; *Iṣara: A Voyage Around Essay*; *Ibadan: The Penkelemes Years*; and *You Must Set Forth at Dawn*. He has also released eight volumes of the *Interventions Series* that represent a kind of political manifesto and shared his philosophy of life.

In an interview with Peter Godwin for the UK *Telegraph* on October 12, 2012, Soyinka shared his motivations for using drama and literature as part of his political activism. He wrote:

> I used my weapon, which was writing, to express my disapproval of the [Biafran] civil war .... These were people who'd been abused, who'd undergone genocide, and who felt completely rejected by the rest of the community, and therefore decided to break away and form a nation of its own .... I was in solitary confinement for 22 months out of the 27 [months I spent in jail], and I was deprived of writing material. So, I had to somehow break through the barriers, smuggle in toilet paper, cigarette paper, scribble a few poems, pass messages outside. I was able to undertake exercises to make sure that I emerged from prison intact mentally.[66]

While imprisoned, Soyinka turned to writing for solace and his sanity.

---

[66] "Wole Soyinka: If Religion Was Taken Away I'd Be Happy." Also see the interviews he had with Anthony Appiah, "An Evening with Wole Soyinka," *Black American Literature Forum* 22, no. 4 (1988): 777–85; and Christiane Fioupou, "Interview of Wole Soyinka in Paris in February 1995," *Présence Africaine*, Nouvelle série, no. 154, 2e Semestre (1996): 87–92.

6

Relationships, Beliefs, and Values

I meet a woman, fall in love with her or we simply find we're compatible; she agrees to live with me; a child comes or does not come in the order of things and that, for me, is marriage by whatever name. Mutual consent. And to be mutually dissolved if it comes to that, with a Muslim-type simplicity at its best. To you that's heresy but, that's the code by which I live. For me, it's the genuine bond, not church or court registry, not even the traditional ties or exchange of vows in any idiom. What people call formal marriage has no meaning for me; it never has. When I see a man and a woman contentedly together, I don't ask for their marriage certificate. It's sufficient for me that they considered themselves married to each other, that they're content to be together, that they accept responsibility for anything they bring into the world, and continue to do so even if the union collapses ...

WOLE SOYINKA, *IBADAN: THE PENKELEMES YEARS*, 2014[1]

Soyinka perceives the functions of creative writers to be all-encompassing writers as visionaries. Far from being an escapist concept, Soyinka regarded committed writers, guided by their vision, as using their craft, as critics use theirs, to contribute towards a society based on principles of justice and equality. ... When metaphysical issues or mythic symbols enable a writer like

---

[1] Wole Soyinka, *Ibadan: The Penkelemes Years* (Ibadan: Bookcraft, 2014), 275–6.

> Soyinka to expose the very root of contemporary problems, the "rotten underbelly of society," such exploration is more radical than the "pseudo-stalinists-leninists and Maoists."
>
> KETU H. KATRAK, "THEORY AND SOCIAL RESPONSIBILITY: SOYINKA'S ESSAYS," 1988[2]

Family and Friends

Wole Soyinka makes history, and his life and works are significant elements in the making of Nigerian, African, and world histories. After all, how else can Soyinka's political clout and classic making of history be more astounding than in the case of Chief Oluṣẹgun Ọbasanjọ, a former Nigerian head of state, who credited Soyinka's protest with disqualifying his (Ọbasanjọ's) candidacy for the post of Secretary General of the United Nations? Nothing portrays the complexities and contradictions of Wole Soyinka's life and works more than his private relationships with family and friends. Our readers can imagine the effrontery of an African child, and a Yoruba child for that matter, who could defy the protocol and ethics of gerontocracy and boldly declare the above epigraph to his parents. More important, Soyinka had the principled honesty—or audacity—to disclose in his published memoir an affair he had with a woman engaged to marry another man. Her family protested, and she eventually returned to her fiancé. He confesses, "There was a woman in my bed when she returned, and there have been other women. Don't look shocked now."[3]

In this chapter, we look at four areas in which Wole Soyinka's relationships with family and friends reflect the postcolonial changing phases of history and sociology of Yoruba family relationships. They also demonstrate how Soyinka, as a Western-educated elite, has confronted, resolved, and liberated or freed himself from the inhibitive cultural dilemmas and contradictory politics of the primordial and subsistence labor-intensive agricultural Yoruba family institution. The four areas are:

1. Family and the dialectics of modern relationships;
2. Beyond anachronism: Sexual morality of geniuses and twentieth-century artistes in perspective;

---

[2] Ketu H. Katrak, "Theory and Social Responsibility: Soyinka's Essays," *Black American Literature Forum* 22, no. 3 (1988): 489–501.

[3] Katrak, "Theory and Social Responsibility," 273–4.

3. Soyinka's family affairs, values, and beliefs about marriage; and
4. Soyinka's relationship with his friends.

Family and the Dialectics of Modern Relationships

Wole Soyinka grew up within what Odia Ofeimun has described as "his [Soyinka's inherited] tripod cultures," that is, a mix of strong Christian upbringing and European values, and an equally strong induction into dialectics of the Yoruba culture and anticolonial nationalism.[4] For example, just as his mother, alias Wild Christian, regularly prayed to exorcize *ẹmi ẹṣu* (evil spirit) from Wole's boisterous mind, so also did Pa Akiode, Wole's grandfather, name Wole as Maren, a shortened form of *maren nijo ebi pona* (may you not be on the road on days when the vampire spirits of Ogun are famished and hungry for blood), and religiously made the necessary offerings to the Yoruba pantheon gods, especially Ogun and Ṣango, to protect Wole from the machinations of evil spirits.

Although Soyinka had given up the dogmas of Christianity, he upheld the shared values and principles of charity of the biblical Good Samaritan, as well as Yoruba cultural humanism. Hence, understanding of Soyinka's works and life, especially his social relationships, must be viewed from the then prevailing and conflicting Christian colonial evangelism and the primordial African nationalist cultural worldviews of his time. Andrew Roberts, in his seminal review of the leadership styles of Adolf Hitler and Winston Churchill, explained why Churchill had to substantially revise the earlier proofs of his book *A History of the English-Speaking Peoples* because

> he wanted the work to reflect the lessons of history better than the first drafts had done .... "We are recording the march of events in what is meant to be a lively, continuous narrative. We are primarily concerned with the social and political changes as they occur, especially with those which left their marks on today." ... As Winston Churchill has rightly implied, conventional dialectics of the top-down hierarchical history and historiography of old kingdoms and empires and of the revolutionary republics, biographies, autobiographies, and memoirs only account for the prowess and diplomatic relations of the monarchs, emperors, or the republican dictators. Thus, relationships, either of family or friends were viewed in terms of official friendly or hostile relationships between

---

[4] Odia Ofeimun, "Wole Soyinka: The Writer as Culture Hero," in *In Search of Ogun: Soyinka In Spite of Nietzsche*, ed., Odia Ofeimun (Lagos: Hornbill, 2014), 160.

one kingdom, empire, or republic and the other. For example, before the two World Wars, the German dynasty's House of Saxe-Coburg and Gotha accounted for most of the old European kingdoms. There existed intermarriage, interfamily royal friendships, and trade and commercial treaties among the British, French, Spanish, Dutch, Russian, and German royal families. Indeed, The House of Windsor in the United Kingdom and Ireland only came into being in 1917, when the name was adopted as the British Royal Family's official name by a proclamation of King George V (r. 1910–1936), replacing the historic name of the German dynasty of The House of Saxe-Coburg-Gotha that was in use between 1901 and 1917.

Thus, European powers that mutually engaged in slavery and trade in human beings later colonized and acquired territories with the "might-is-right principle" on the battlefield or around a conference table, as in the 1884 Berlin Conference for the partition of Africa. There was a clear dichotomy between public and private just as there was a clear line of authority between the king, his subjects, and his official clerks or bureaucrats. Everyone in the kingdom knew their place, and no one crossed the line. Family, the church, and trade guilds were strong and mutually agreed agents for socialization, training for the rite of passage for the ascribed cultural roles and duties.

The post-Second World War liquidation of empires and decolonization of dependent territories instituted a new world order: the top-down or hierarchical operating system for running kingdoms and empires. The relevant parameters or paradigms for running the pre-twentieth-century revolutionary republics had broken down. Consequently, gender and marital relationships had to be redefined. What had been acceptable social norms for gender, race, and relationships at home or at work were no longer politically correct. In addition, as African nationalists sought political independence, they also began to redefine not only how they practiced Christianity and interpreted the gospels, but how to reclaim their traditions and cultural identity.

Sharing the professional hazards of public life, or what Churchill called in *Great Contemporaries* "the grievous inquest of history," with the 1953 Nobel Laureate in Literature, Wole Soyinka has been subjected to revisionist, contemptuous, and aggressive criticism of his achievements and overblown hagiographies from his admirers.[5] Andrew Roberts noted that, "Churchill regularly used to joke that he knew that history would be kind to him because he himself would be writing it."[6] The truth is that history has been kind to Soyinka not only because he is writing it and deriving

---

[5] Winston Churchill, *Great Contemporaries* (London: Readers Union Ltd, 1939).
[6] Roberts, *Hitler and Churchill: Secrets of Leadership* (London: Weidenfeld & Nicolson, 2003), 204.

enormous (and oftentimes ridiculously childish, vile, and vulgar) pleasure in defending himself from his critics and revisionists. More important, the growing industry that has emerged around his intriguing life and works resulted because he *makes history.* One way he makes history is by creating, crafting, and trading on intellectual and political controversies, sometimes in melodramatic ways. We are, therefore, primarily concerned with unraveling how Soyinka, cleverly and in the style of a grand French playboy, avoided bigamy and polygamy while having nine children with four women. He is a "serial monogamist." He married three of the women, and the fourth was a woman with whom he did not have a committed relationship. He had casual sex with her on the night of Nigeria's independence. The dialectics of cultural nationalism have had an impact on Soyinka's worldview of marriage and family relationships.

Beyond Anachronism: Sexual Morality of Geniuses and Twentieth-century Artistes in Perspective

To put the controversies surrounding Soyinka's relationships with women into a proper perspective, we ask two questions: What do biographies and psychoanalysis tell us about the longevity, strength, and the physical, sensual, and sexual energy of geniuses? What does economic history tell us about the stagecraft business and the male artistes' interrelationships with women?

Over the ages, psychologists have studied the behavioral and genotypic characteristics of geniuses. What differentiates geniuses from the rest of us humans is that they have the outstanding ability and capability to outperform in virtually all areas of intelligence. For example, it takes a genius to combine an outstanding excellence as a poet, novelist, writer of nonfiction and of faction (faction being a coined word for the combination of facts and fiction, as demonstrated by Soyinka in his memoir *Ibadan: The Penkelemes Years (1946–1965)* and in *Isara: A Voyage Around Essay*), playwright, recording artiste, producer, and several aspects of stagecraft. Soyinka is a genius with bundles of restless, radical creative energy and imagination that transcend lay people's domesticated ideas and concepts of space, freedom, and responsibilities in relationships.

For example, in their classic book *Buzan's Book of Genius,* Tony Buzan and Raymond Keene identify twenty characteristics of a genius: 1) Vision; 2) Desire; 3) Faith; 4) Commitment; 5) Planning; 6) Persistence; 7) Learning from mistakes; 8) Subject knowledge; 9) Mental literacy; 10) Imagination; 11) Positive attitude; 12) Auto-suggestion; 13) Intuition; 14) Mastermind Group (Real); 15) Mastermind Group (Internal); 16) Truth/Honesty; 17) Facing fears/Courage; 18) Creativity/Flexibility; 19) Love of the task; and

20) Energy (physical/sensual/sexual). Tony Buzan also employs eleven indices to rate the greatest minds of all time. The indices are: 1) Dominance in Field; 2) Active Longevity; 3) Polymath and Versatility; 4) Strength and Energy; 5) IQ (Intelligent Quotient); 6) On-going Influence; 7) Prolificness; 8) Achievement of Main Goal; 9) Universality of Vision; 10) Outstanding originality; and 11) Desire to Create Teaching Avenues or Academies for furthering geniuses' ideas.[7] Besides the aforementioned Buzan's list of incontestably sterling, shared qualities of a genius evident in Soyinka's life and works, Soyinka apparently possesses the quintessential longevity, strength, and energy of a genius.

The ethics of human relations and human rights had been evolving since the era of the Christian Reformation. Before the sixteenth-century Christian Reformation, priests lived with women, taking some of them as common law wives.[8] In Nigeria, pioneering nationalist artistes, including Hubert Ogunde, Haruna Iṣọla, Sunny Ade, and Fela Anikulapo Kuti, were known to have imbibed the subsistent farmers' polygamous economic model as a way of running the stagecraft family business. The epigraph to this chapter not only represented Soyinka's code of what constitutes a marriage, but it represented the twentieth century's worldview of marital relationships.

Today, there are worldwide commonplace but anachronistic public and media (radio, television, tabloid, and social media) extrajudicial trials and condemnations of the 1970s and 1980s notables' licentiousness and pedophilic abuse. In *Decolonizing Nigeria*, we noted "the challenges of writing about Nigeria's living history that is, managing the objective realities of shifting conceptual frameworks, anachronisms, methodologies, and ethical frameworks, and the twists of Nigerian ethnic and religious geopolitics."[9] The history of gender relations is evolving and not beholden to traditional values or religious beliefs. We would like to suggest that it is anachronistic to superimpose today's values on the lives of people in the past.

Wole Soyinka's Family Affairs, Values, and Beliefs about Marriage

Deji Sadiq noted that Soyinka was not a polygamist: "He's never known to have more than one wife at a time. He never married when he was still married

---

[7] Tony Buzan and Raymond Keene, *Buzan's Book of Genius: And How to Unleash Your Own* (London: Stanley Paul, 1994).
[8] Harold Klemp, *The Road to Spiritual Freedom: See a Greater Vision of Life* (Minneapolis: Eckankar, 2016), 265.
[9] Toyin Falola and Bola Dauda, *Decolonizing Nigeria, 1945–1960: Politics, Power, and Personalities* (Austin: Pan African University Press, 2017), 69.

to another woman."[10] In her *Guardian* profile article on Soyinka (November 2, 2002), Maya Jaggi described scholars' assessment of Soyinka's attitudes about women: "feminists in the 1980s found fault with his [Soyinka's] portrayal of women." Various scholars argue Soyinka's women characters fall into a limited range of stereotypes: "maidens, mistresses, and matrons." Other scholars argue that though "[h]e is not a feminist, ... 'but neither is he a misogynist. He is a man who respects women, though he also loves women as a source of pleasure and doesn't find that offensive. His women are earth mothers; he idealizes them as goddesses.'"[11]

Soyinka is a very private person.[12] He resists sharing details of his private life, but he has, however, been exceptionally open about it in his published works. For example, he devoted eleven pages of his second memoir *Ibadan: The Penkelemes Years* to share openly how his first daughter from Lettie, the daughter of a Ghanaian High Court Judge, "was seeded on that day [Nigerian Independence Day, October 1, 1960], not intentionally, but that did happen!"[13]

In *Ibadan: The Penkelemes Years*, Soyinka also confessed that his relationship with his second wife, now Chief Laide Soyinka, "was over" as far back as 1965, twenty years before it was officially ended in 1985. After narrating how his political activism put a lot of stress on their relationship, he felt the relationship was irredeemable after his wife took their three children to the police station at Iyaganku, Ibadan, and left them there. She drove off even as one of them held on to the car door.[14] In a prolonged argument with his parents, Soyinka left no one in doubt about his values and beliefs about conventional Christian marriage. He wrote, "the greatest mistake I ever made was in thinking that I could eventually belong to this Pharisaical tribe called monogamists."[15]

Should Wole Soyinka have married his student? We may as well ask, Should King George V have abdicated the British throne to marry his French mistress? Should Prince Charles, Prince of Wales, have divorced Diana, Princess of Wales, to marry Camilla, Duchess of Cornwall? Should Emmanuel Macron have married his teacher who was twenty-five years his senior? Should Dr. Nnamdi Azikiwe have married a sixteen-year old girl? In each of these marital cases, a classic divergence of opinions exists between the societal norms of who is eligible to marry who on the one hand, and

---

[10] Deji Sadiq, "Meet Prof. Wole Soyinka's Wife and 4 of His Children," Lagos *News*, July 11, 2014.
[11] Maya Jaggi, "Profile: Wole Soyinka," *The Guardian*, November 2, 2002.
[12] Jaggi, "Profile: Wole Soyinka."
[13] Soyinka, *Ibadan*, 266–76, 271.
[14] Soyinka, *Ibadan*, 461.
[15] Soyinka, *Ibadan*, 270–1.

the individual criterion for marriage on the other. While working on this book, there were doubts as to whether or not the French people would hold Emmanuel Macron's marriage with Brigitte Trogneux against him during the presidential election! However, thirty-nine-year-old Emmanuel Macron became the president of France on May 15, 2017. He first met sixty-four-year-old Brigitte Trogneux when she was a married, private school teacher with a daughter of the same age and in the same class when Macron was 15. Like Adefolake Doherty Soyinka's family, Soyinka's third and present wife, Brigitte's family did not immediately approve of the relationship with Macron.

In marital relations, each society and family consider *the dignity and honor* of the tribe, but individuals think of *the love of their heart*. Adefolake Doherty Soyinka says of her relationship with Soyinka:

> There were objections from everywhere except from my sisters and brother who were happy if I was. My parents along with most of my relatives objected, not because of anything, they just felt he was too famous and too accomplished. ... His close friends didn't have a problem with it but also everyone had an opinion. ... More than a quarter of a century later, those opinions didn't count, we are still trudging along. I have enjoyed love because of him.[16]

In an interview for *The Spectator*, Ọmọlolu Kassim asked Chief Laide Soyinka, Soyinka's second wife, about her feelings for Soyinka. She said, "Of course, I love him ... How do you marry somebody you don't love? Indeed, I love him. I admire him. It was this affection between us that led to the marriage. How could I have married someone I don't admire?"[17]

Not much public information exists about Soyinka's brief marriage with Barbara Skeath. Considering his acknowledgment of his love and affection for his second and third wives, it is not beyond the realm of possibility to believe that he had deep feelings for her. Olumide Awẹ argues that "the credit for his [Soyinka's] meteoric rise in the literary world should go to Laide, the 'unsung heroine.'"[18] She is not unsung. In 1972, Soyinka dedicated *The Man Died* to his second wife with the words: "This book is deservedly dedicated to Laide who rejected compromise and demanded justice."[19] Similarly, he

---

[16] Olajumoke Elutade, "Wole Soyinka's Wife Relates Their Love Story," *The News Magazine*, July 21, 2014.

[17] Ọmọlolu Kassim, "First [sic] Wife: Laide Speaks on Romance with Wole Soyinka," *The Spectator*, June 29, 2010.

[18] Quoted in Tope Templer Olaiya, "Soyinka ... The 'Visiting' Husband, 'Absentee' Father, but Dotting [sic] Grandpa," Wordpress Blog, July 11, 2014, https://topetempler.wordpress.com/2014/07/11/soyinka-the-visiting-husband-absentee-father-but-dotting-grandpa/.

[19] Wole Soyinka, *The Man Died: Prison Notes of Wole Soyinka* (Ibadan: Bookcraft, 2014), v.

dedicated *You Must Set Forth at Dawn* to Adefolake with the words: "And to my wife, Adefolake, who, during the season of a deadly dictatorship, demoted me from the designation of Visiting Professor to that of Visiting Spouse, but was still left with only an Invisible Spouse as I was swallowed by my study even during visiting hours."[20]

Although most Britons do not seem to have come to terms with or forgiven King George V and Prince Charles's love affairs, both of the families of Brigitte Trogneux and Adefolake Doherty eventually accepted their daughters' spouses. Obviously, Emmanuel Macron's victory in the presidential election meant that most of the French people did not consider his marriage with his much older teacher a transgression important enough to deny him his public post. There are paramount Obas in Western Nigeria who are married to girls the same age as their granddaughters!

Soyinka and His Friends

There is a growing body of books and articles from his old students, work colleagues, and other associates offering an objective appraisal of Soyinka's private relationships with friends. In *You Must Set Forth at Dawn: A Memoir*, he shared how much he cherished friendship and loyalty. For example, he paid for the body of his friend Femi Johnson to be shipped back to Nigeria from the UK so that he could have a decent funeral at home. In the author's note to readers in his memoir, *Ișara*, Soyinka commented on his father and friends: "IȘARA then is simply a tribute to '*Essay*' and his friends and times."[21]

Adefolake Soyinka, Soyinka's third wife, related how her husband's friends played the matchmaking role in their relationship. She remembers

> I knew he liked me from when I was in the University of Ife, but I was young, and he was so accomplished, so I was kind of worried. After I left Ife and went to do my NYSC (National Youth Service Corps) in Kaduna state, Dr. Biọdun Jeyifo [presumably Wole Soyinka's greatest critic] came to visit me and said Kongi (Prof. Wole Soyinka) had been looking for me. After the service year, Dr. Yẹmi Ogunbiyi, [another friend of Wole Soyinka] who was at *The Guardian* got me a job there and one day, Wole stopped by.[22]

---

[20] Wole Soyinka, *You Must Set Forth at Dawn* (Ibadan: Bookcraft, 2014), ix.
[21] Wole Soyinka, *Isara: A Voyage Around Essay* (Ibadan: Bookcraft, 2014), viii.
[22] Elutade, "Wole Soyinka's Wife."

Soyinka cherishes his relationships with his fellow artistes and academic friends, such as Biọdun Jeyifo, Akin Iṣọla, Ọla Rotimi, and his former students, such as Bọlaji Johnson, Yẹmi Ogunbiyi, and Tẹju Ọlaniyan.

Beliefs and Values: Humanism and African Communalism

In furtherance of our primary objective of how this book could help the understanding of Wole Soyinka's works and life, we shall now focus on four key aspects of Soyinka's beliefs and values. The above epigraph by Ketu Katrak highlights the first two key areas. The third aspect we explore challenges and distinguishes between Soyinka's use of his knowledge of the Yoruba Orişa pantheon as an academic or as a lay psychologist rather than as a conventional Orişa devotee. The final question examines Wole Soyinka's acculturated works and life as they project the voice of Africa echoing Soyinka's precepts of universal humanism. The four areas are, therefore:

1. Soyinka perceives writers as visionaries and vanguards of social justice and equality;
2. Soyinka employs metaphysical issues and mythic symbols as operational tools;
3. Soyinka: An Orişa devotee, a fetish masquerade, or a placebo psychologist?; and
4. Precepts of universal humanism in Soyinka's acculturated works and life.

Soyinka Perceives Writers as Visionaries and Vanguards of Social Justice and Equality

Soyinka imbibes Yoruba culture, which does not draw a line between the respective public and private lives and responsibilities of members of the Yoruba community. Neither are the Yoruba philosophical and cultural worldviews nor thinking processes compartmentalized as they are in Western philosophy and specialized disciplines. Hence, Soyinka does not separate his role as a creative, imaginative visionary writer from that of a political missionary or a radical streetwise social activist. As in the Yoruba trade apprenticeship model, Soyinka does not confine his role as a teacher of literature simply to that of teaching his students to read and interpret narratives, drama, and poetry, but he extends his role to making an artiste of his students. He, therefore, combines the role of a playwright with those of producer, actor, and social activist. Biọdun Jeyifo notes that what distinguishes Soyinka from most writers, artistes, and musicians who have played prominent roles in placing the arts at the forefront of the nation-building, democratic struggles of the last five decades

> is precisely the degree to which he has consistently been prone to taking *political and artistic risks* most other writer-activists and the whole phalanx of radical academics and intellectuals would consider either totally unacceptable or quixotic, even when they applaud the courage and originality underlying such propensity for risk taking.[23]

As a visionary writer, Soyinka appreciates that the reality of human conditions means that a story is often the edited and exaggerated version of truth or figments of one's imagination. Hence he combines fictional writings with nonfiction to craft what he called "faction."[24] Indeed, *Death and the King's Horseman* is a fictional reconstruction of the royal funeral tradition in Yorubaland.[25] Henry Louis Gates Jr. observes that Soyinka based "the tragedy that forms the crux of Soyinka's *oeuvre*, *Death and the King's Horseman* ... [on the death of] Ọba Siyanbola Oladigbolu [the Alaafin, or King of Ọyọ, an ancient city in Nigeria]." Yoruba tradition required that when the king died the king's horseman carry out a suicidal ritual sacrifice. The horseman was also supposed to "lead his Alaafin's favorite horse and dog through the transitional passage to the world of the ancestors."[26] The event immediately captured Soyinka's imagination when he first learned about it as well as similar stories. Intrigued, Soyinka wrote *Isara: A Voyage Around Essay*, *Ibadan: The Penkelemes Years*, and *The Lion and the Jewel*, to mention a few of his works based on Nigerian history.

Stewart Crehan has rightly noted what he terms Soyinka's "spirit of negation."[27] For example, Soyinka reveals his idealized civic duties

---

[23] Biọdun Jeyifo, *Wole Soyinka, Politics, Poetics and Postcolonialism* (New York: Cambridge University, 2004), 6.
[24] Soyinka, *Ibadan*, ix.
[25] For a review of Soyinka's play *Death and the King's Horseman*, see Iva Gilbertova, "Wole Soyinka: Death and the King's Horseman," *BRNO Studies in English* 21, no. 1 (1995): 85–96.
[26] Duro Ladipo's play *Ọba Waja* was inspired by the same event in Yoruba. Henry Louis Gates Jr., "Wole Soyinka: Mythopoesis and the Agon of Democracy," *Georgia Review* 49, no. 1 (1995): 188.
[27] Soyinka has two main literary modes: the tragic and the satiric. His tragic drama and fiction, far from hypostatizing the "uncorrupted individual," present us with a dialectic in which self-realization can only be attained through the experience of disintegration, a journey into and through "the no man's land of transition," involving the "annihilation" or "dissolution of self." This is the tragic side of the negating spirit. The satiric side is less dialectical, more destructive in its contempt for those elites and institutions to which the committed artist finds himself naturally opposed.

through the social critiques of Sagoe, his fictionalized true character in *The Interpreter*. Sagoe encourages his friends Kola and Bandele to stop their incessant criticisms: "You only criticize destructively, why don't you put some concrete proposal, some scheme for improving the country in any way, and then you will see whether we take it up or not."[28] Being a practical Socratic philosopher, or what Ishmael Reed has called "a cultural relativist who uses different literary and dramatic traditions in order to create synthesis," Soyinka metaphorically walks his talk.[29] He believes that "the pursuit of truth is a dialectical process."[30]

No cause for justice is too small or too big for Soyinka to take on. To the lower-class market women, he is an archetype of old England's Robin Hood in his activities against the opportunist pickpocket rogues of Ibadan. He concerned himself with the recklessness of drivers on Nigerian roads and is equally concerned about the prebendal politics, impunity, and abuse of office in public service. For example, in his book *The Road* and at the M'bari Writers and Artists Club and Orisun Theatre—indeed in all his works and life—Soyinka does not separate his academic responsibility as a writer and professor from his everyday responsibility as a member of the society in which he operates as a university professor. Neither does he separate his civic responsibility as a Nigerian from his clarion duties to humanity.

Soyinka pursues his concern for human rights and freedom by directing his civil actions against man's inhumanity to man wherever injustice rears its ugly head, either at home or abroad. He rages unequivocally against the *penkelemes* (peculiar mess) of Samuel Akintola's regime in the old Western region, the infamous apartheid regime in South Africa, Sani Abacha's tyranny in Nigeria, and, most recently, against the election of President Donald Trump in the United States. Jeyifo notes that Soyinka's "native Nigeria, apartheid South Africa before the inauguration of black-led majority rule, Hastings Banda's Malawi, Idi Amin's Uganda, Mobutu's Zaire, and Macias Nguema's Equatorial Guinea ... [represent] the most prominent 'theatres' of his fiercest campaigns."[31]

Soyinka Employs Metaphysical Issues and Mythic Symbols as Operational Tools

Soyinka's literary works and social consciousness are informed and underpinned by the Yoruba's holistic, communal cultural values and

---

[28] Stewart Crehan, "The Spirit of Negation in the Works of Soyinka," *Research in African Literatures* 21, no. 4 (1990): 15–31, 17.
[29] Ishmael Reed, "Soyinka among the Monoculturalists," *Black American Literature Forum* 22, no. 4 (1988): 708.
[30] Crehan, "The Spirit of Negation," 16.
[31] Jeyifo, *Wole Soyinka*, 7.

beliefs within today's complex web of democratic and socioeconomic responsibilities. Among the Yoruba, proverbs act as a Pegasus (i.e., the proverbial or mythical flying horse, a search engine, or thesaurus) to convey the meanings of *words*. When a message is locked, encrypted, or coded, proverbs unlock, decipher, encode, or unravel the meaning in the message *Owe l'ẹsin ọrọ, ti ọrọ ba sọnu, owe lafi n wa a*. Yoruba democratic political culture demands that protesters forewarn rulers of public discontent with protest songs before an uprising *orin ni siwaju ọtẹ* and such protest songs are often woven in riddles. Hence, the Yoruba would say *Bi owe, bi owe, l'alu ilu agidigbo, ọlgbọn ni'jo, ọmọran ni m ọ itum ọ rẹ* Agidigbo is a parable expressed with drums; only the knowledgeable could dance in rhythm to its tune, and only the wise could understand its coded message.[32] Bernth Lindfors is therefore right to say Soyinka is

> challenging the world to discover the meaning of his art, to unravel its mysteries and knit its loose, dangling threads into a harmonious pattern. ... The job was impossible, for many clues had been strewn throughout the text, but it took more than an ordinary literary detective to solve so cerebral a case. The average theatregoer, tired perhaps from standing too long on his toes or from listening to a language he did not perfectly understand, either fell asleep or trudged home yawning. Direct communication never took place.[33]

Soyinka writes in riddles and parables. His works and life seem confusing and complicated for anyone who is not well versed in Yoruba history, politics, socioeconomic conditions, and political culture and customs. Younger Nigerian critics and writers have accused Soyinka of "obscurity" and "ambiguity," and "transforming experience into metaphysical, transhistorical, mystical dimensions."[34] These assessments are rooted either in the lack of a proper grounding in, a misunderstanding of, or both, Soyinka's instrumental philosophy of literature and stagecraft not only as the writer's occupational tools but as the writer's primary vocational responsibility for the social transformation of their society.

Soyinka seeks to not only decolonize the African mindset but also engage in dialectical discourse to modernize any outdated African customs. His works and life are reflected in parables that are encoded and shrouded in Yoruba customs and culture, myths, and symbols. Even more important, he

---

[32] Bola Dauda, "Proverbs," *Encyclopedia of the Yoruba*, ed., Toyin Falola and Akintunde Akinyemi (Bloomington and Indianapolis: Indiana University Press, 2016), 284–5.
[33] Bernth Lindfors, "Wole Soyinka, When Are You Coming Home?" *Yale French Studies* 53 (1976): 202.
[34] Biọdun Jeyifo, *The Truthful Lie: Essays in a Sociology of African Drama* (London: New Beacon Books, 1985), 27.

believes that writers' beliefs, values, and vision are the "conscience" of their society.[35] He uses powerful Yoruba symbols such as *aroko* (coded message as in a soldier raising a white flag to surrender in battle), the ontology of protest songs (the Yoruba believe that *orin ni siwaju ọtẹ* radical protest songs often precede rebellions).[36] Humor, satire, metaphor, gossip, and comedy are coded message that can be best appreciated with background knowledge of the imageries and personalities involved. In Yoruba, coding in conversations or dialogues can be as ordinary as two people using *ara ile ẹ* (that your person) to gossip and disguise the identity of their subject to bystanders. Hence, it is difficult to understand Soyinka's *A Dance of the Forests*, *The Road*, and *Madmen and Specialists* without a sound background knowledge of Yoruba beliefs in reincarnation, retribution as justice, and the roles played by the dead and the pantheon of gods in creation, in a fair dispensation of justice, and in the affairs of the living and the unborn.

Soyinka employed mysteries, metaphysics, and mythology more in his earlier works than is prevalent in his works published after the Nigerian civil war. Brenda Cooper describes Soyinka's transition to using "decolonization as a powerful African cultural position" as "not least of all because he has journeyed from a position bordering on cosmopolitanism to a decolonizing nationalist position."[37] Chidi Amuta, however, implies that it was tactically expedient for Soyinka to change his writing style from mythopoetic to a direct, plain, and down-to-earth dialectic because,

[f]or Soyinka, the war experience meant a temporary abandonment (or sublimation) of myth in quest of a more secular idiom for conveying new social concerns and fresh ideological options. The most pervasive attitude from which his new ideological outlook can be grasped is a certain mood of appreciation which questioned society in all its structural and institutional manifestations.[38]

Amuta describes the pessimism that abounds in some of Soyinka's early works, such as *Madmen and Specialists* "as an act of creative exorcism (for the playwright himself) and a venomous condemnation of a dispensation whose operators he had come to see as thoroughly evil."[39] Indeed, in his prison notes for *The Man Died*, Soyinka wrote, "These men are not merely

---

[35] Katrak, "Theory and Social Responsibility," 500.
[36] Bola Dauda, "Communication, Non-verbal," *Encyclopedia of the Yoruba*, ed., Toyin Falola and Akintunde Akinyemi (Bloomington: Indiana University Press, 2016): 72–3.
[37] Brenda Cooper, "The Two-faced Ogun: Postcolonial Intellectuals and the Positioning of Wole Soyinka," *English in Africa* 22, no. 2 (1995): 54.
[38] Chidi Amuta, "The Ideological Content of Soyinka's War Writings," *African Studies Review* 29, no. 3 (1986): 45.
[39] Amuta, "Soyinka's War Writings," 47.

evil ... They are mindlessness of evil made flesh. One should not ever stumble into their hands but seek the power to destroy them. They are pus, bile, original putrescence of Death in living shapes."[40]

Consequently, Soyinka's published volumes in the *Interventions Series* are no less than political manifestos of his ideal precepts for the good governance of a nation-state. Literally, in his speeches, writings, and civil actions, Soyinka combines theory with practice; he combines ivory tower, sophisticated political philosophy with cowboy, streetwise political gangsterism used for a good cause even though it resembles an Italian, mafia-like, underground intelligence network. Soyinka, however, faces a lot of dilemmas and contradictions in using dramaturgy to create a sustainable philosophical foundation or indigenous ideology for the reclamation of African justice and humanity.

Philosophy is about a search for meaning and making sense of life and situations. Lindfors has rightly warned that "[t]he greatest challenge confronting [a] thinking man is to discover the meaning of life by comprehending the mystery of death."[41] As a corollary, Stewart Crehan remarked that Chinua Achebe, for example, misunderstood Soyinka as "an African writer who chooses not to provide answers to philosophical or social questions in his works, but instead gives his reader 'headaches.'"[42] Soyinka, therefore, is susceptible to an error of "a culpable omission, an ideological refusal to accept the true answers and to say what ought to be said."[43]

Crehan also recalls Ngũgĩ's criticism of Soyinka:

Soyinka's good man is the uncorrupted individual: his liberal humanism leads him to admire an individual's lone act of courage, and thus often ignores the creative struggle of the masses. The ordinary people, workers and peasants, in his plays remain passive watchers on the shore or political comedians on the road. ... Soyinka's plays propagate a false, liberal-humanist consciousness.[44]

Yet characters such as Ẹlẹsin Ọba, the Praise-Singer, and Iyalode in *Death and the King's Horseman*; Sidi in *The Lion and the Jewel*; and Damian (Demiyen), alias Wemuja, in *Isara: A Voyage Around Essay* were hardly "no passive watchers on the shore or political comedians on the road." In *Achebe or Soyinka: A Study in Contrasts*, Kọle Omotoso opined that, unlike Chinua Achebe who "is only interested in defending the Igbo traditional

---

[40] Wole Soyinka, *The Man Died: Prison Notes of Wole Soyinka* (Harmondsworth, England: Penguin, 1975), 228, quoted in Amuta, "Soyinka's War Writings," 47.
[41] Lindfors, "Wole Soyinka, When Are You Coming Home?", 206.
[42] Crehan, "The Spirit of Negation," 15.
[43] Crehan, "The Spirit of Negation," 15.
[44] Quoted in Stewart Crehan, "The Spirit of Negation," 15.

elite in both *Things Fall Apart* and *Arrow of God*[,] ... Wole Soyinka, on the other hand, has been kinder to poor and weak characters in his plays, novels, and autobiographies."[45]

Wole Soyinka is a holistic and universal thinker. According to Brenda Cooper, "[h]olistic thinking is the recognition that global social, political and economic structures and determining systems fundamentally affect human lives and creativity."[46] We concede that Soyinka is sometimes ambivalent, as in his first play *The Lion and the Jewel*, which portrays a fictionalized marital custom of polygamy and old men marrying young girls. Sidi chose to marry Baroka, the old village chief. Soyinka, however, is neither a fundamentalist nationalist, such as Ngũgĩ wa Thiong'o, who has abandoned the use of the English language and opted to write in his native Kikuyu language, nor is he in the group of writers that include Mario Vargas Llosa, Derek Walcott, Salman Rushdie, Isabel Allende, Gabriel Garcia Marquez, Bharati Mukherjee, and a few others, which Timothy Brennan describes as the "Third-World cosmopolitans."[47] According to Cooper, "the cosmopolitans are far more muted and ambiguous in their criticism of the West, far more open to the cultural and political advantages of Western culture than their decolonizing counterparts."[48] Cooper, like Hayden White, finds it impossible to classify Soyinka.

If anything, aside from being a false prophet of liberal-humanist consciousness as Ngũgĩ has implied Wole Soyinka is a pragmatic, social-engineering philosopher or philosophical architect who makes frantic efforts to design a set of sustainable and relevant political institutions, democratic systems, and cultural structures to house equitable human (race and gender) rights in postcolonial Africa, and elsewhere in the world.

Thus, in *The Road*, *A Dance of the Forests*, and *Madmen and Specialists*, Soyinka seems obscure because he is philosophizing—literally thinking aloud. He could not be as direct and clear as he is in *The Lion and the Jewel*, or "much more down-to-earth" as he is in *Kongi's Harvest*, "a biting political satire aimed at exposing the egomaniacal fatuity of modern African leaders," because he, too, does not know.[49] Lindfors admonished Soyinka "to heed his own warning and stop squandering his immense wealth of talent on fashionable theatrical trivialities. He may be rather Africa's greatest playwright, but one suspects he could be even greater if he were more nakedly African."[50]

---

[45] Kọle Omotoso, *Achebe or Soyinka: A Study in Contrasts* (Ibadan: Bookcraft, 2009), 6.
[46] Cooper, "The Two-faced Ogun," 44.
[47] T. Brennan, *Salman Rushdie and the Third World* (London: Macmillan, 1989), viii, quoted in Cooper, "The Two-faced Ogun," 48.
[48] Brennan, *Salman Rushdie*, 53.
[49] Lindfors, "Wole Soyinka, When Are You Coming Home?", 206.
[50] Lindfors, "Wole Soyinka, When Are You Coming Home?", 210. In *African Forum* 1, no. 4 (1966): 53, Wole Soyinka warned that, "the poet insists on mysteries only at the peril of truth."

We, however, want to suggest that, first, being a philosopher, Soyinka is being honest with himself in using his talents to initiate a dialectic discourse for solutions to the issues confronting the postcolonial nation-states. Second, as noted in Chapter 5, being a political activist, diplomacy, and safety, and expediency requires that Soyinka is equivocal and ambiguous to create a legal safety net against litigation. Finally, we also concur with Lindfors who surmised that, "[p]erhaps it would be fair to say that when he [Soyinka] feels philosophical, he turns inward, when political, outward."[51]

Is Wole Soyinka an Oriṣa Devotee, a Fetish Masquerade, or a Placebo Psychologist?

Soyinka's traditional African humanist religious beliefs and cultural values are encapsulated in a response he gave in an interview in 2012 for the UK-based *Telegraph* entitled "If Religion Is Taken Away, I'd Be Happy." Soyinka reflected on his upbringing in both Christian and Yoruba traditions, but "gravitated towards a deeper knowledge of the *Oriṣa* which represents the Yoruba pantheon, very similar in many ways to the Greek pantheon. You have reprobate deities, beneficent deities. I found that more honest than a kind of unicellular deity of either Christianity or Islam."[52] Soyinka used the hero figure of Ogun in his fiction and nonfiction works and in his radical and sometimes rhetorical politics of cultural imperialism, decolonization, and reclamation of African dignity and cultural heritage. Our research has shown that Soyinka could not, in any way, qualify as a devotee of any Yoruba deity. Soyinka is an articulate political activist, and he would use any creative and melodramatic tactics and strategies to create symbolic effect.

However, on many occasions Wole Soyinka inexplicably escaped brushes with death. For example, a stray cutlass almost left him blind, but left an indelible scar on his eye. A thunder bolt of lightning struck his classroom and narrowly missed him. A python that was living in his basement moved up and down between the floors of his apartment building, and in and out of his apartment at the University of Ibadan. Finally, there were several attempts on his life during the civil war and during the Abacha regime. Those narrow escapes from death likely remind Soyinka about the premonition that inspired his grandfather to name him *Maren*, a shortened form of *Maren nijo ebi pona* (May you not be on *the road* in days when the vampire spirits of Ogun are bloodthirsty). His grandfather made sacrifices to Ṣango after the thunder struck Soyinka's classroom.

---

[51] Lindfors, "Wole Soyinka, When Are You Coming Home?", 207.
[52] Godwin Peter, "Wole Soyinka: 'If Religion Was Taken Away I'd Be Happy,'" *Telegraph*, October 12, 2012.

On two occasions, Soyinka called on the spirit of Ogun. On the first occasion, Soyinka was not engaging in an act of devotion. He sacrificed a rooster as a psychological ploy to hypnotize the crew helping with his play *Death and the King's Horseman* rather than to seek help from the gods. On the second occasion, he made an animal sacrifice to make a political statement. The second sacrifice (a ram) occurred in 1986, before a group of Nigerian delegates left for Sweden to attend the Nobel ceremonies. Lawrence Ogbo Ugwuanyi observes "These two instances demonstrate his occasional intervention in the domain of the divine and his attempt to be involved in the humble world of the divine worship. But this nowhere makes Soyinka religious in the deep sense of the term. Indeed, Soyinka has never accepted the authority of the divine beyond this point."[53]

Precepts of Universal Humanism in Soyinka's Acculturated Works and Life

In an interview granted to Humanist International in 1997, Soyinka discussed why he considered himself a humanist: "Humanism for me represents taking the human entity as the center of world perception of social organization and indeed of ethics, deciding in other words what is primarily of the greatest value for humans as opposed to some remote extraterrestrial or ideological authority."[54] Wole Soyinka is a humanist who is convinced that "justice is the first condition of humanity," but more than 400 years of slavery, colonization, imperialism, racial and cultural denigration, and postcolonial corruption and inept leadership have compromised justice and human dignity and identity in Africa and African diasporas.[55] Soyinka's work and life are therefore driven by his search for political and philosophical frameworks to decolonize the African mind, to restore African dignity and identity, and ultimately to "reclaim that humanity by force of arms, if needed."[56]

As Albert Einstein had rightly postulated, "No problem can be solved from the same level of consciousness that created it." Yes, the political and socioeconomic developmental issues confronting the postcolonial nation-states were rooted in the consciousness of the past centuries of "might is right," racial and gender superiority, secrecy in government business, and the

---

[53] Lawrence Ogbo Ugwuanyi, "I Am Therefore You Are: An Existentialist Perspective on Wole Soyinka's Writings," *UJAH: Unizik Journal of Arts and Humanities* 12, no. 2 (2011): 75.
[54] Quoted in Ugwuanyi, "Existentialist Perspective," 69.
[55] Soyinka, *You Must Set Forth*, 37.
[56] Soyinka, *You Must Set Forth*, 38.

absolute powers of monarchs and emperors, etc. However, the establishment of the United Nations (UN) after the Second World War, globalization, knowledge economies, and the advancement of worldwide social media and information technology nullified much of what was regarded as acceptable governance in the colonial era.

Soyinka is aware of the realities of globalization and today's worldviews on democracy and good governance. Hence, he is not a revisionist like Leopold Sedar Senghor, the proponent of negritude, nor nostalgic like Chinua Achebe about all aspects of African customs and traditions. For example, in *The Lion and the Jewel*, Soyinka derided the bride price system as "A savage custom, barbaric, outdated ... unpalatable."[57] He believes it is "a disgrace and humiliation to women, to pay the price would be to buy a heifer off the market stall."[58]

In *Whatever Happened to Justice?* Richard J. Marbury, alias Uncle Eric, prescribes two universal laws for social justice and equity to his niece and nephew in seventeen words: 1) "Do all you have agreed to do; and 2) Do not encroach on other persons or their property."[59] In a similar vein and tenacity, Soyinka engaged his writings, works, and life in pursuit of justice and freedom for the human race. He, however, noted in *The Man Died* that, "[b]ooks and all forms of writing have always been objects of terror to those who seek to suppress truth."[60] He professed that, "The man dies in all who keep silent in the face of tyranny,"[61] and concluded that, "THOSE WHO MAKE PEACEFUL CHANGE IMPOSSIBLE MAKE VIOLENT CHANGE INEVITABLE."[62]

---

[57] Wole Soyinka, *The Lion and the Jewel* (London: Oxford University Press, 1963), 9.
[58] Soyinka, *The Lion and the Jewel*, 9.
[59] Richard J. Maybury, *Whatever Happened to Justice?* (Placerville: Bluestocking Press, 1993), 36.
[60] Soyinka, *The Man Died*, xxv.
[61] Soyinka, *The Man Died*, 3.
[62] Soyinka, *The Man Died*, xxviii. Author's emphasis in original.

PART 3

Literary Works

FIGURE 7.1 *Soyinka in the 1980s. Illustration by Kazeem Oyetunde Ekeolu.*

7

Soyinka's Novels

There have been great societies that did use the wheel, but there have been no societies that did not tell stories.
URSULA KROBER LE GUIN[1]

You need a story to displace a story. Metaphors and stories are far more potent (alas) than ideas; they are also easier to remember and more fun to read. If I have to go after what I call the narrative disciplines, my best tool is a narrative. Ideas come and go, stories stay.
NASSIM NICHOLAS TALEB[2]

Introduction

Literature is an essential aspect of human life, interaction, and scholarship; it is not an art that happens in a vacuum. Writers have tried to use literature to mirror the reality of life. Arthur Schopenhauer carefully analyzed how literature deals with noble matters, especially the riddle of our existence and the psychological flux of society and the human heart, ultimately declaring that literature should carry a message that can be used as a tool for the discernment of some deep moral truth.

---

[1] Ursula Krober Le Guin (1929–2018) was an American author best known for her speculative fiction, including science fiction works set in the Hainish universe, and the Earthsea fantasy series.
[2] Nassim Nicholas Taleb, *The Black Swan: The Impact of the Highly Improbable* (London: Penguin Books, 2007), Prologue, xxvii.

An author is born into a social reality, grows up in it, and reflects it in his or her storytelling. And literature does not only reflect, it refracts. It can be a tool to modify stories that are told in new dimensions. However, literature should be truth, striving for it whether it is the truth of a society, the truth of the author, or the truth of the author's imagination. This search can occasionally be sidelined by postmodernism and post-structuralism. Literature now reflects an author's argument of what life is and what the author perceives truth to be, becoming an argument for what life means to the author, not necessarily what life is in reality. Writers are pushing an agenda of many truths; there is no universal truth, although some writers work to portray the universal conditions of life in their writing.

Literary works are closely connected to the history, philosophy (especially moral values), and culture of a people and their society. Literary deployment of language, whether indigenous or foreign, makes critical and analytical points about human emotions and values. Literature and all forms of art are fundamentally about expressions in the form of abstractions, conceptions, and concrete reality. The perception of life and literature are conjoined twins that are, arguably, inseparable.

Novels, plays, and poetry are not just for teaching moral values. They holistically express aesthetics and imaginatively explore models of life. These models provide an opportunity to consider the thematic concerns of any given piece of literary work, affording the ability to examine the literary styles of writers alongside their patterns of expression. These attributes are literary ways of writing about various perceptions of reality in societies and life in general. Thematic concerns in literary works address elements of social background, psychological makeup, or the writer's spiritual state in relation to nature. In short, literature is often an assessment of and a solution to the challenges of life's absurdities by detailing intersubjective relations and historical occurrences. It is a synthesis of time and space in the rhythm of life. These works do not emerge from nothingness—they are a consequence of expectations that arise in social constellations, individual life stories, and visions and plans for the future.

This understanding of literature can be attributed to the works of all renowned writers: from Shakespeare to Dickens, Orwell, Elliot, Camus, Tutuola, Fagunwa, Achebe, Soyinka, Adichie, and others. Their works were influenced by social realities, often forming criticism and responses to overbearing cultural and historical systems. The social reality of African writers is distinct from that of their Western counterparts. Although human conditions are a constant factor, they are affected by them differently. African writers are influenced by colonialism, the crisis of identity, and the need to promote their cultures against the Euro–American cultures that are projected as standard or ideal cultures.

Most works by African writers deal with cultural appropriation, trying to manage a marriage between their culture and the culture of colonial masters. Their work, which exists in time and space, starts to reflect on and contemplate neocolonialism, political structures in their society, and their adaptation in the global world along with other topics. These are the concerns in works by African literary minds, especially Wole Soyinka.

Wole Soyinka is one of Africa's greatest literary minds. He is famous for his plays and poetry. Some circles do describe him as a mere "novelist." His novels, *The Interpreters* and *Season of Anomy*, are not as popular as his plays, but this chapter will examine the thematic concerns in his novels. We shall consider influences on African literature and the role that African literature plays in the contemporary world. It is also worth examining the literary activities of Soyinka and analyzing commentaries and literary criticism of his work. Recurring themes, like activism, politics, history, friendship, and Soyinka's campaign for Yoruba deity shall also be considered.

African Literature: Influence and Role

Scholars and researchers looking to lay a conceptual foundation require a working definition of the term "literature." As with many terms, it has various definitions. Everyone in literary studies can attempt a functional definition of the term, but it is pertinent to evaluate what literature is. It is often seen as "written material such as poetry, novels, short stories, essays, etc., especially works of imagination characterized by excellence of styles and expression and by general or enduring interest."[3]

This concept of literature eliminates some essential aspects of African literature, leaving one poised to ask what African literature is. According to Eileen Julien, the expression "African literature" means poetry, plays, and novels written by Africans in English and French, and perhaps Portuguese.[4] This may define the American and European understanding of African literature, but its full range lies beyond the works written in the languages of colonial masters.

The African concept of literature includes the oral aspect of life; before colonialism and the adoption of European languages, there were bards, storytellers, scribes, poets, and writers in indigenous languages. African oral literature is an essential part of African existence because our body of knowledge is instantiated in our manner of speaking. However, African oral literature is largely unknown, unrecognized, or ignored outside of the

---

[3] Soile quoted in Anaso George and Eziafa Christopher Nwabudike, "Culture, Language and Evolution of African Literature," *IOSR Journal of Humanities and Social Science (IOSR-JHSS)* 19, no. 4, Ver. III (2014): 81–5.

[4] Eileen Julien, "African Literature," in *Africa*, ed., P. M. Martin and Patrick O'Meara (Bloomington: Indiana University Press, 1995), 295.

continent. Africans themselves are beginning to ignore or overlook oral literature and its importance. For inclusiveness, African literature must be recognized not just as the body of work done by Africans in European languages, but also as a group that includes works of artists in their own indigenous languages, whether written or oral.

As universal practices and ideas across time and space, culture is at the center of every society. It is a determining factor in literature and the reason why oral and written literatures in Africa are inseparable. As anthropologists work to unravel the human past, enormous research is dedicated to exhuming the essence of orality in African epistemology and literature. Essentially, African oral traditions are unadulterated, influencing our displays in market squares, at coronations, and at festivals. African literary scholars have dedicated time and energy to pointing out that African literature did not start at the moment of transcription. In *The Content and Form of Yoruba Ijala*, the author, S. A. Babalola argued that his work is to "help correct the erroneous idea given in many journal articles on African Literature that its beginning coincides with the introduction of literacy to African communities."[5] His work on Yoruba poetry, Ijala, is a proof of the existence of literature, in oral form, in preliterate African societies.

Before colonialism, African literature was located completely within the realm of culture. It was a means of socialization for transmitting the core values of societies from one generation to the next. There is a widespread misconception that African literature consists entirely of folk fables about the tortoise and other animals, but nothing could be farther from the truth; African literature extends far beyond that. Before colonialism and Western education, African literature served social, religious, political, and economic functions that can be seen in the sociocultural rites of different African societies. Generally, literature and arts in precolonial African societies were employed to preserve social mores through criticism of impropriety, wherever it was found. Criticism could be levelled at any stratum of society, whether in the palace or in the home.[6]

In a manner of speaking, "African literature was originally oral, and the most traditional manifestation of this literature is in religious ceremonies."[7] African literature encapsulates the physical and the spiritual realm; oral literature in African societies consisted of ceremonies for divinities such as Ogun, Ifa, Ọbatala, Yemọja, Ṣango, and others. Myths, stories, and legends of great African figures were passed down from generation to generation.

---

[5] S. A. Babalola, *The Content and Form of Yoruba Ijala* (Oxford: Clarendon Press, 1966), v.
[6] Adeoti Gbemi, ed., *Ife Journal of The Institute of Cultural Studies*, no. 10 (2014).
[7] Femi Ojoade, "De Origen Africano, Soy Cubano: African Elements in the Literature of Cuba," in *African Literature Today*, ed., Eldred Durosimi Jones (New York: Africana, 1978), 48.

The model of African oral literature is marked by African phonetic practices, vocabulary, expressions, and tonality. This gives African oral literature its integrity, and even those questioning the validity of demarcation between oral and written literature will concede that the circumstances in which oral literature is delivered deserve careful attention.[8] It is a testament to the power of oral literature's psychological and sociological effects—the philological aspect of oral literature. For example, Wole Soyinka's *Forest of a Thousand Demons* is a translation of D. O. Fagunwa's *Ogboju Ọdẹ Ninu Igbo Irunmalẹ*. Although the translation is a great work by Soyinka, there is a lack of hermeneutics to situate the writer in his original language. The beauty of narrating the travails of brave warriors in the forest is not as well represented in translation as it was in its original language.

For the case of oral literature's inseparability from the rest of African literature, Eileen Julien opines that:

African literature has changed tremendously ... because of several important developments: the ever-increasing numbers of women writers, greater awareness of written and oral production in national languages (such as Yoruba, Poular, and Zulu), and greater critical attention to factors such as the politics of publishing and African literature's multiple audiences. These developments coincide with and have, in fact, helped produce a general shift in literary sensibility away from literature as pure *text,* the dominant paradigm for many years, to literature as an act between parties located within historical, socioeconomic and other contexts. Fiction, plays, and poetry by women from around the continent have been singularly important because they 'complicate' the meaning of works by their literary forefathers, bringing those works into sharper relief, forcing us to see their limits as well as their merits.[9]

The role of colonialism and Western education in African literature is omitted from Julien's consideration. Modern African literature was born from colonialism's imposition of Western educational systems—through slavery and missionaries. Despite this, African oral literatures exerted their own influence on modern literature. Johnathan Peters, focusing on the strength of oral literature and its influence on African literature, writes that:

African literature includes the epic tradition kept alive by the griots, traditional bards who recounted the history of their clans as well as of heroic figures in their region ... oral literatures of West Africa have for

---

[8] Isidore Okpewho, *Myth in Africa* (New York: Cambridge University Press, 1983; 1990).
[9] Julien, "African Literature," 295.

the most part been defined from culture to culture, though a handful of studies treat folklore in general and oral traditions in particular as a national or regional phenomenon. Scholars tend to consider the oral tradition separately from the written body of creative literature, even though the latter has been informed to a great degree by the traditional cultures of which the writers are inheritors.[10]

This summary reiterates that African oral literature informed and laid the foundations for African written literature; African oral literature is as valid and important as its written form.

The works of European ethnologists and anthropologists depicted Africans as brutish savages with no epistemic grasp of issues. African storytelling and poetics were dismissed as unworthy of being called literature. Meanwhile, the evils of slavery, colonization, and religious subjugation roused the souls of many writers who stood against inhumanity, whether they faced it in their fatherland or in the lands where they were shipped.

Africa experienced hardships in its long history that left an impact on its literature. One hardship, which led to many others, was that of colonization. From the sixteenth to nineteenth centuries, millions of Africans were enslaved and shipped to countries around the world. One can rightly say that modern African literature holds a marked idea of self-consciousness that brought about awareness of the predicaments of Africans.[11]

For most African countries, toward the periods of independence, "In the 1950s and 1960s, as nations around the continent moved more or less slowly to achieve decolonization, many Africans took up the pen."[12] The literary journey of these African writers began to separate Africans from the intellectual and sociopolitical lives of Europeans and Americans. This crusade of literary deliverance, rescuing African minds from the shackles of colonialism and mental slavery, made "most African Writers write out of an African experience and out of commitment to an African destiny," and critically for them, that "destiny for which the present is but an apprenticeship."[13]

However, there is the problem of language, which has always challenged African intellectual discourse. Debates ask why African cultures, thoughts, and beliefs are expressed in foreign languages—a notable instance is the

---

[10] Jonathan Peters, "English Language Fiction in West Africa," in *A History of Twentieth Century African Literatures*, ed., O. Owomoyela (Nebraska: University of Nebraska Press, 1993), 9.
[11] L. W. Brown, *The African Heritage and the Harlem Renaissance: A Re-evaluation. African Literature Today*, ed., Eldred Durosimi Jones (New York: Africana, 1998).
[12] Julien, "African Literature."
[13] Chinua Achebe, *Morning Yet on Creation Day* (New York: Anchor Books, 1976), 9.

debate, which started in the 1970s, on the question of African philosophy. Despite these writers having different ethnic backgrounds, English is a common language for discussing their postcolonial nations. The use of English has generated many debates asking how a writer, working in the language of a colonizer, consciously contributes to the sense of nationhood in nation-states where that language is not the mother tongue.

One of the many peculiarities setting African literature apart is the problem of unifying African indigenous beliefs, thoughts, and writing across multiple native languages. It should be noted that "Modern African literatures are a product of the encounter between African and European cultures. Their development has been significantly influenced by the nature of that encounter, and later by colonial expediency and the exigencies of decolonization. An understanding of the linguistic anomaly that is a feature of those literatures thus necessitates an archaeological probing of those events."[14] The flourishing of modern African literature cannot be separated from its encounters with colonialism and Western education. Continuing the debate is fruitless because language is not natural, it is social. This allows the thoughts of particular people to be expressed in the language of others; the important matter is to retain the essence of one's belief system.

For Achebe, it is important not to lose sight of the message of our culture. Achebe's response to the question of language is that "let no one be fooled by fact that we may write in English, for we intend to do unheard of things with it."[15] In Achebe's *There Was a Country: A Personal History of Biafra*, he elucidated his position that:

> to help create a unique and authentic African literary tradition would mean some of us would decide to use the coloniser's tools: his language, altered sufficiently to bear the weight of an African creative aesthetic, infused with elements of the African literary tradition. I borrowed proverbs from our culture and history, colloquialisms and African expressive language from the ancient griots, the worldviews, perspectives, and customs from my Igbo tradition and cosmology, and the sensibilities of everyday people.[16]

Achebe's point was that English is the best way to communicate with African people in general and to transmit the African destiny to the world. This attitude was common with modern African writers, to subsume identity in

---

[14] Oyekan Owomoyela, ed., "The Question of Language in African Literatures," in *A History of Twentieth Century African Literatures* (Nebraska: University of Nebraska Press, 1993), 348.
[15] Achebe, *Morning Yet on Creation Day*, 9.
[16] Chinua Achebe, *There Was a Country: A Personal History of Biafra* (London: Penguin Books, 2012), 55.

an indigenous paradigm while writing in a language that is familiar to the world.

Osita Ezeliora describes the goal of modern African literature best in his paper, *Elegy for the Mystery Cocks: Modern African Literature and the Making of its Classics*. He stated, in the case of Achebe, that:

> Achebe's success as a novelist, and as author of *Things Fall Apart* and *Arrow of God* in particular, it does seem to me, is built on a complex combination of factors that subsume, among others, his continued presence in the search for theoretical paradigms in the construction of the identity and authenticity of Modern Literature; the special genius of Achebe as a novelist who quite early in his career chose to domesticate the English language to cover the sensibility of the African; his dexterous manipulation of plot; his construction of recognisable universal characters that not only transcend topographical spaces, but are also very truthfully localised within Africa's sociocultural ambience.[17]

These factors are not unique to Achebe. Other emerging writers also worked to evangelize the African identity with a foreign language. It was the paradigm for them, and it became the essence of African literature. Vincent Theo corroborates this notion that:

> An African literature whose essence does not reach beyond the life of Africans and does not deal with wider issues of man cannot lay claim to much attention. The point being made here is that the ultimate as far as the Africanity of African literature is concerned is the discussion of general condition through an acute analysis of particular African experiences. This is the contribution of African literature to world literature and also its contribution to the understanding of the human mind, human relationships and problems.[18]

Vincent's general idea is that African literature should not solely concentrate on African predicaments. While writing about the African experience and the theme of self-consciousness, writers should show human conditions in general.

Careful study of writers such as Leopold Sedar Senghor, Chinua Achebe, Wole Soyinka, Chukwuemeka Ike, and Amos Tutuola clearly establishes

---

[17] O. Ezeliona, "Elegy for the Mystery Cocks: Modern African Literature and the Making of Its Classics," in *The Postcolonial Lamp: Essays in Honour of Dan Izevbaye*. ed., A. Raji-Oyelade and Oyeniyi Okunoye (Ibadan: Bookcraft, 2008), 130.

[18] Theo Vincent, "Africanity in Modern African Literature," in *The Arts and Civilization of Black and African Peoples. Black Civilization and Literature*, vol. 3., ed., J. O. Okpaku, A. E. Opubor and B. O. Oloruntimehin(New York: Third Press International, 1986), 42–3.

that their work not only shines light on the sociological milieu of Africans, it also places these milieus in a human condition, not just African conditions. When they write, they analyze the metaphysical, ethical, aesthetic, and epistemological concerns of their people in their relation to humanity—not just in relation to Africanity.

The sustained reflection on African sociocultural ambience is logical. A writer adds the power of imagination to the backdrop of an existing sociocultural setting. The Longinus dictum also applies to African writers, that "in statues we look for the likeness of a man; whereas in literature we look for something transcending the human."[19] While African literature retains the peculiarities and particularities of its Africanity, it should seek to be literature that can describe human conditions. It should not be about African humanity alone, but about universal humanity. African literature can contribute to world literature through this endeavor, instead of isolating itself from the rest of the world.

At the beginning of modern African literature, or the African literary renaissance, the role of African writers was to challenge stereotypes, myths, and the predominant image of Africa, recasting them through prose, poetry, essays, and dramas. The role of African writers is not difficult to define, and it is not far-fetched. The position depends on the health of society; it is the writer's responsibility to point out the ills and shortcomings discovered within society.[20] African writers are often influenced by the pains of their people, and language is an important part of the literary discourse. These are some of the roles played by African literature, and it influences society as society influences African literature.

Short Background of Generations in African Literature

Even modern African literature has eras. The work of Chimamanda Adichie reflects the Nigerian civil war and postwar lives alongside the influx of migration. The works of Achebe deal with colonialism and European ideologies and religion. There is a certain disparity: both write about the African sociocultural ambience at different times. A Rwandan writer from the era before the genocide will write differently than someone from the era after it. Even a single writer can experience a shift in focus over time.

---

[19] T. S. Dorch, *Loginus on Sublime: Classical Literary Criticism*. Trans. T. S. Dorsch (Middlesex: Penguin Books, 1965).
[20] Achebe, *There Was a Country*.

The Chinua Achebe that wrote before the Biafran war created different works from the Chinua Achebe who wrote *Arrow of God* and *Anthills of the Savannah*. In the late 1990s, after the demise of Nigeria's military dictatorship, writers shifted from discussing dictatorship and its denial of human rights; they had focused on the curtailment of literary creativity that brought about the death or exile of writers. Postcolonial writing relates with politics. During the dictatorship and afterwards, African writers resumed seeing themselves "as the essential part of a larger social struggle in the search for absent or dying agencies of democratic change."[21]

One of the early writers from Africa's modern literature is Amos Tutuola, whose *The Palm-Wine Drinkard* occupies a position of influence in the landscape of Nigerian and African literature. His 1952 book made an immense contribution, showcasing the dynamic nature of life. Tutuola's radical work was a bastardization of the English language, mixing old and new. Achebe performed a critical analysis of Tutuola's style, stating that in the book:

> There was no attempt to draw a line between what is permissible and what is not, what is possible and what is not possible, what is new and what is old, a car, a bishop all kinds of things that don't seem to tie in. But in fact what you have is the whole life of the community, not just the community, not just the community of humans but the community of ancestors, the Animal world, of trees, and so on. Everything plays a part.[22]

Tutuola's tradition is uncommon because he created a writing style for himself, not one for others to follow. Although his writing style was not well received, it demonstrated the importance of oral tradition in African literature. Peters believes that Tutuola "demonstrated that the oral tradition was very much alive and that it was possible for an individual writer to draw on a communal source and use it to create works that bear the writer's individual stamp."[23] However, regardless of the oral tradition displayed in Tutuola's *The Palm-Wine Drinkard*, Yoruba writers owe a debt to D. O. Fagunwa for making an indelible imprint on the literary language of his people.

After Tutuola's *The Palm-Wine Drinkard*, writers such as Cyprian Ekwensi and Chinua Achebe gained attention with their novels, *People of the City* and *Things Fall Apart*, respectively. While Ekwensi addressed

---

[21] Ismail Baba Garba, "The Lost Language of Enlightenment: Return to Algadez and the New Nigerian Writing," in *The Postcolonial Lamp: Essays in Honour of Dan Izevbaye*. ed., A. Raji-Oyelade and Oyeniyi Okunoye (Ibadan: Bookcraft, 2008), 375.
[22] Achebe, *There Was a Country*, 57.
[23] Peters, "English Language Fiction," 15.

recurring violence in Nigerian politics, Achebe addressed the lives of Igbo people amid colonial influences. *Things Fall Apart* achieved more success than *People of the City*, which was due to:

> its insight into the culture of the Igbo seen from the point of view of an "inside outsider" (a role he had as an Igbo whose missionary upbringing prevented his participation in traditional rituals), a thorough understanding of narrative organization and style, and a keen observation of and absorption with day-to-day happenings, not through the lenses of the anthropologist, but through the clear sight of one who was involved with and felt at one with his culture while at the same time inculcating Western ideas.[24]

Achebe did not dwell on the attitude of emerging writers, demanding that they continually patronize African institutions and restate the evils of colonialism. He did not focus solely on Africanity; his expansive pen looked into the entirety of society and conjured it up for us.

Many writers followed after Chinua Achebe: Timothy Aluko, Wole Soyinka, Gabriel Okara, Elechi Amadi, Flora Nwapa, Buchi Emecheta, Ben Okri, Femi Osofisan, Kọle Omotoso, and others. The new generation of writers includes Chimamanda Adiche, Lola Shoneyin, Nnedi Okorafor, Teju Cole, and Elnathan John.

The first era—of Tutuola, Achebe, and Ekwensi—is dominated with themes of managing sociocultural dynamism, the forces in which the country and continent had found themselves. Their works exemplify the struggle of man with his society. Later writers, such as Soyinka, Emecheta, and Amadi, became voices of the people. They rejected unconventional ways of governance, religions, and other sociopolitical institutions. Contemporary writers took up the same role of social criticism performed by their predecessors, expressing disdain at the new order of things and using writing to voice opposition to social injustice. An elaborate juxtaposition of their works shows that they were influenced by time and space, history and education, and social awareness of the ever-changing contemporary world in which they found themselves.

Assessing the Man and the Writer, Wole Soyinka

Wole Soyinka is an exceptional, rigorous Nigerian poet, dramatist, satirist, and novelist whose works have gained recognition outside of Africa. His life

---

[24] Peters, "English Language Fiction," 17.

is not merely literary; he is ultimately concerned about society. Soyinka is a fierce critic of religious fundamentalism and terrorism. He also promotes religious tolerance and pluralism. Soyinka is one of his generation's great African literary minds, influencing later generations. Biọdun Jeyifo asserts that:

> Among the "titans" of his generation of Nigerian literary artists, Soyinka's career is the closest conscious approximation we have in African literature to the revolutionary or 'sublime' expressions, as opposed to the conservative or repressive currents, of the long postcolonial tradition of the 'big man' of politics, of trade unionism, of coup making, of popular culture and millenarian religious movements.[25]

He is often characterized as the face of struggle in Nigeria, aiming to lay bare the immediate problems in an extraordinarily difficult time. In most cases, if not all, his work's central idea is the duality of the human personality that has creative and destructive potentials operating simultaneously. Professor Oyinade Ogunba opines that "Soyinka has the reputation in certain circles in Nigeria ... of being the artist par excellence in an ultra-modern, twentieth century sense, a man against the establishment, a firm believer in the absolute freedom of the individual."[26] Soyinka, as described by Ogunba, is a protagonist of the people and an antagonist of the oppressors. Soyinka himself agrees that he is born to struggle and fight, but he suggests that "there comes a moment when age dictates the avoidance of certain forms of engagement."[27]

Soyinka is influenced by elements of his ethnic national culture, such as birth, death, aging, marriage, and rituals. Despite the Nigerian writer's cosmopolitanism and eclectic incorporation of the world's most diverse traditions, his literary corpus is deeply embedded in his indigenous Yoruba roots. His work often involves a syncretism of the old guard with the new. This idea of syncretism forms a major aspect of Soyinka's writing.[28]

Soyinka's syncretism of beliefs and systems explains some of the themes in his writing. Kọle Omotoso believes that "Wole Soyinka insists that the colonial encounter is a mere episode, a catalytic episode only. This catalytic effect of the colonial encounter within the Yoruba society becomes the area

---

[25] Biọdun Jeyifo, *Wole Soyinka: Politics, Poetics and Postcolonialism* (New York: Cambridge University, 2004).
[26] Oyin Ogunba, *The Movement of Transition: A Study of Plays of Wole Soyinka* (Ibadan: Ibadan University Press, 1975), 6.
[27] Wole Soyinka, *You Must Set Forth at Dawn* (New York: Random House, 2006), 13.
[28] P. J. Conradie, "Syncretism in Wole Soyinka's 'The Bacchae of Euripides'," *South African Theatre Journal* 4, no. 1 (1990): 61–74.

of his creative inquiry." One can say Soyinka is a child of two civilizations: the African civilization of his birth, and the Western civilization that he experienced through tongue and culture. It is evident in his works; he often merges views from the two worlds. One thing that cannot be taken from Soyinka is his projection of the Yoruba worldview as the epicenter of any intellectual discourse. This makes it impossible to separate Soyinka the man from Soyinka the writer—his works are dominated by the expressions of his views, ideas, and convictions. They document his interaction with his sociocultural world.

As a writer, Soyinka is considered to have a tough writing style; readers find him difficult to comprehend. Kọle Ọmọtọsọ's brilliant comparative analysis of Achebe and Soyinka explains that readers tend to see Achebe's work as easy to grasp, while Soyinka is difficult to read. Soyinka has been criticized for being obscure, impenetrable, and incomprehensible. Some detractors claim that "Soyinka is not in fact attempting to say anything to anyone. Rather, he is out to demonstrate that he is able to manipulate the English language far better than the owners of the language ... and to also demonstrate his cleverness."[29] Although we have reviewed the debate about the "obscurity" of Soyinka's works and life in Chapter 5, we would, for clarity, like to elaborate here. The debate over Soyinka's use of English is not uncommon for the African literary world. Some critics have concluded that Soyinka's writing style is difficult because he is a difficult human being himself—his difficult character and stubbornness shows in his writing. Jeyifo reiterates that:

> Soyinka criticism in these decades has focused intensively on the alleged "complexity" and "obscurity" of his most important writings, without paying systematic or even sustained attention to one important source of the alleged "complexity" and "obscurity." This is Soyinka's literary avant-gardism, his extensive and defining open and experimental approach to the diverse and contending traditions of formal and linguistic resources available to the postcolonial writer or indeed any writer in our contemporary global civilization. The study is thus conceived in part as a critical response to the influence of critical commentary on Soyinka's works in the last four decades, the purpose being to locate the 'difficulty' and "complexity" of his writings in their appropriate linguistic and cultural sources, and to reorient the study of Soyinka as a writer towards a more systematic engagement of his connections to the historic avant-garde movements of the contemporary world.[30]

---

[29] Kọle Ọmọtọsọ, *Achebe or Soyinka: A Study in Contrasts* (Ibadan: Bookcraft, 2009), 4.
[30] Jeyifo, *Wole Soyinka*.

In considering obscurity and privatization of language, Niyi Osundare likens Soyinka to Ogun, his personal god. Osundare stated that:

> Like Ogun his patron god, Soyinka plies the deep jungle of words where daemonic sentences confuse the reader and frustrate his wanderings and metaphors take on baffling proteanness of the chameleon.[31]

Chinweizu appears to be the harshest critic of Soyinka's literary work, writing style, and the Nobel Prize itself. He stated that:

> I thought that his works and the Nobel Prize deserve each other and for those of us who hold that the Nobel Prize is an undesirable prize in Africa and who also find most of Wole's works unreadable I thought from that position that his getting the Nobel would be a case of the undesirable honouring the unreadable.[32]

Critics frequently noted his difficult writing style because of its challenging lexis and syntax—features that are emphasized and analyzed by Edmund Bamiro in his paper, *Stylistic Functions of "Discollocation" in Soyinka's Novels: A Systemic-functional Analysis*. Bamiro defines collocation as a method in systemic-functional grammar that is an indispensable notion for lexical cohesion, and he finds its opposite in Soyinka's style of writing; the semantic tension present in Soyinka's writing style and use of language is a result of discollocation.[33] Bamiro suggests that discollocation in Soyinka's novels should be seen as ideational metaphors and metaphors for mood. The incongruity of Soyinka's language encourages readers to scrutinize the known state of affairs.

Soyinka is difficult as either a writer or a man, which distinguishes him among his contemporaries. And the inaccessible writing style of his novels prevents them from becoming as successful or as well received as most of his plays and his poems. Their difficulty is why his novels have struggled to resonate with larger audiences.

The argument about Soyinka as a person and writer does not address the thematic concerns in his work; literature is a tool for understanding African society. Eileen Julien writes that "African literature is vast and varied, but there are two impulses or currents in African creative works of which we might make special note: the reclaiming of voice and subjectivity and the

---

[31] Osundare, quoted in Kọle Omotoso's *Achebe or Soyinka*, xxiii, 24.
[32] Chinweizu, Onwuchekwa Jemie, and Ihechukwu Madubuike, *Towards the Decolonization of African Literature* (Washington: Howard University Press, 1983), 21.
[33] Edmund Bamiro, "Stylistic Functions of Discollocation in Soyinka's Novels: A Systemic-functional Analysis," *Theory and Practice in Language Studies* 4, no. 12 (2014): 2492–7.

critique of abusive power."[34] Themes in African literature are vast and varied, but they are not limited to either reclaiming voice and subjectivity or the critique of abusive power—that is a parochial notion.

Critically analyzed themes in African literature can be classified into metaphysical, ethical, and sociopolitical. Metaphysical themes center on issues like death, reincarnation, witchcraft, afterlife, and the pantheon of gods. Ethical themes involve the nature of moral issues such as good, evil, consequentialism, and conduct. However, sociopolitical themes include religion, colonialism, governance, and humanism, among others. Thematic preoccupations in African literature showcase the relation between man and society:

> in drama, novel, poetry or short-story, the writer's dialogue with his physical and human environment comes out as a mirror in which his people and society can see what they look like. Every image painted by a skilful artist is expressed or put into writing/print, becomes public property and leaves itself open for evaluation by those who read and understand the language and expression.[35]

Thematically, African writers have used their works to explain and criticize philosophical issues. Critical assessment of African literature reveals that prose, more than drama or poetry, is employed to itemize and detail the myriad of sociopolitical, ethical, and metaphysical problems that bedevil African societies. African writers have used novels to portray recurring social problems such as corruption, unemployment, prostitution, and the loss of African identity.

Thematic preoccupations in African literature have been an important part of Africa's anti-hegemonic resistance, according to Chima Anyadike. Anyadike notes that Achebe used Okonkwo, the hero of *Things Fall Apart*, to explicate the theme of African reality.[36] Another example of thematic preoccupation in Nigerian literature is the idea of colonialism and the confrontation or clash of systems. There are also feminine thematic concerns, as displayed in Buchi Emecheta's *Joys of Motherhood*, an ironical novel showcasing the plight of women in traditional African society and their struggle to raise children in a highly patriarchal society.

---

[34] Julien, "African Literature," 296.
[35] C. A. Adetuyi, "Thematic Preoccupation of Nigerian Literature: A Critical Approach," *English Linguistics Research* 6, no. 3 (2017): 22–6.
[36] Chima Anyadike, "The Cracks in The Wall and The Colonial Incursion: *Things Fall Apart* and *Arrow of God* as Novels of Resistance," in *The Postcolonial Lamp. Essays in Honour of Dan Izevbaye*, ed., A. Raji-Oyelade and Oyeniyi Okunoye (Ibadan: Bookcraft, 2008).

Soyinka's Novels

Soyinka only wrote three novels: *The Interpreters*, *Season of Anomy*, and *Chronicles of the Happiest People on Earth*. Some also consider his memoirs to be novels. *The Interpreters*, published in 1965, was Soyinka's first novel. It has no main protagonist or central figure but, rather, is a sequence of dramatic scenes and lyric descriptions following a chronological sequence, often accompanied by the flashbacks that are common in most of Soyinka's works. Obi Maduakor noted that *The Interpreters* has no continuous, firmly established storyline.[37] Soyinka adopted a labyrinthine movement of plot.

The narrative of *The Interpreters* shuttles back and forth, arbitrarily shifting focus from the present preoccupations of major characters to examine their past, returning to the present and sometimes jumping into the future. It has several central figures, and Soyinka abruptly shifts from setting to setting and from perspective to perspective. The novel's group of protagonists are the interpreters, university graduates who studied abroad and returned to Nigeria because of the country's independence; many African students returned home from abroad in the 1960s to be a part of the self-governance of independent African countries.

Egbo, Sagoe, Sekoni, Bandele, and Biodun are the central figures in *The Interpreters*. These intellectuals are the interpreters of the new Nigeria, and they are trying to find their way within newly independent Nigeria's political structure, which is dominated by corruption, confusion, and insensitivity. An initial reading of *The Interpreters* supports the Yoruba invective "*ko lori, ko ni'ru*," which insinuates a lack of direction and means that something does not have either head or tail. Despite its lack of central plot and central figure, the novel is held together by the interpreters' gradual movement toward an awareness of their situation that brings Soyinka's aim to life.

Among critics, *The Interpreters* is dubbed a success. *Season of Anomy* is not as well received. For Akwanya Amechi, "Soyinka's *Season of Anomy* is said to have raised great expectations after the success of his first novel, *The Interpreters*. The critics, however, found it largely disappointing."[38] Joseph Obi summarized it as a "definitive reading of militarised state in Africa."[39] Maduakor notes that "Wole Soyinka's *Season of Anomy* is an intensely religious book, both in its preoccupation with moral issues and the strong impact of its ritual undertone."[40]

---

[37] O. Maduakor, *Wole Soyinka: An Introduction to His Writings* (Lagos: Heinemann, 1986).
[38] A. Akwanya, *The Superman as Master Narrative in Wole Soyinka's Season of Anomy*, Sage online publication, 2014.
[39] Joseph Obi, "Art, Ideology, and the Militarized African Postcolony: A Sociological Reading of Wole Soyinka's 'Season of Anomy'," *Neohelicon* 25, no. 2 (1998): 403–15.
[40] Obi Maduakor, *Wole Soyinka: An Introduction to his Writings* (New York: Garland Press, 1986), 7.

The title of the novel, *Season of Anomy* reflects the idea that the nation is violently ruled by corrupt business interests and an army that misuses authority and governmental powers to enrich themselves and retain office at all costs. The military regime is well described in the novel; it is a vivid portrayal of the Nigerian state at a time when it was in cataclysmic destruction caused by the powers that be. The book describes the role that an individual can play to become an agent of change and social transformation. Through the character of Ofeyi, the protagonist, and the Aiyero community, Soyinka depicts the theme of corruption and condemns the mass murders and genocide committed against the Igbos in the North in the 1960s.

Thematic Preoccupations of Soyinka's Novels

In both novels, Soyinka puts forward themes and concerns shared by Nigerian and African people. Soyinka is often accused of writing for the Western world, but he does not shy away from having his characters voice concerns over problems specific to Africans. Some of the themes from Soyinka's novels reoccur in his memoirs, which means that themes from the novels are also present in the life of Soyinka.

Metaphysics of Yoruba Gods

The metaphysical themes of Soyinka's work are readily apparent. Soyinka constantly praises and elevates Ogun as his companion god, from his poem, *Abiku*, to the explanation of incisions made on his ankle by his grandfather. In his final memoir, *You Must Set Forth at Dawn*, he links his strife and tenacity to that of Ogun. Soyinka claims that he has failed to grow old gracefully, a process which started at the "magic figure of forty-nine, seven times seven, the magic number of my companion deity, Ogun."[41]

Ogun is one of many gods in the Yoruba pantheon. He is associated with dogs and Ijala-chanting—Ijala is a genre of oral literature customarily practiced by Ọyọ Yoruba of Western Nigeria.[42] The dog is a traditional hunting animal in Yorubaland, and it is no wonder that "hunters predominate among the worshippers of the god Ogun"; it is connected to the legend that "Ogun in his earthly life was a hunter and that as a god

---

[41] Wole Soyinka, *You Must Set Forth at Dawn* (New York: Random House, 2006), 12–13.
[42] S. A. Babalola, *The Content and Form of Yoruba Ijala* (Oxford: Clarendon Press, 1966).

he is the controller of all iron implements, including guns, cutlasses, and swords."[43] This explains Soyinka's love of hunting. Soyinka, recounting one of his hunting experiences with his friends, narrates how Ojetunji Aboyade is nicknamed "silent gun" and Femi Johnson's nickname is "O.B. Lau Lau." Soyinka devised his own ijala hunting song, which he claimed he "had set to the tune of the spiritual *There's a Man Going Round Taking Names*," and he said he replenished it with new verses during outings, "each addition a giveaway for the result of the day's hunt."[44] He also described his love in this recessional:

> Till I fill it full of lead
> I can hear it simmering gently on the flame
> An Aparo's waiting yonder with my name
> It goes, quaw-awk, quaw-awk, quaw-awk
> It's my game
> It just won't go to bed
> So, don't invite yourself to dinner chez moi
> In this hunting clan, the merrier means fewer
> As our forebears' saying goes
> If a hunter counted his woes,
> He would never invite a friend to dinner, which you are.[45]

The author elevates and celebrates Ogun in correlation with Yoruba worship and admiration for Ogun. In *You must Set Forth at Dawn*, Soyinka constantly explores the mythology of Yoruba gods. He exemplifies this in the book when he writes:

> It was good fortune that I could return home—where the gods were still only in a state of hibernation ... I penetrated east, north, south at will and toured the entire West African coast on the trail of festivals and performing companies, keeping touch with gods and goddesses everywhere and celebrating their seasons ... Like the many faces of Ogun, god of the road, the road was also a violent host. The road and I thus became partners in the quest for an extended self-discovery. I stared into the many faces of death, but most often death just taking its leave, its back indifferently turned on heartbreak and destruction ... Ogun had other plans for me, however.[46]

---

[43] Babalola, *Yoruba Ijala*, 3.
[44] Soyinka, *You Must Set Forth at Dawn*, 23.
[45] Soyinka, *You Must Set Forth at Dawn*, 23.
[46] Soyinka, *You Must Set Forth at Dawn*, 111–12.

These references, and others in his works, are part of Soyinka's elevation and celebration of Yoruba gods, especially Ogun. Critics describe his adoption of Ogun as a personal deity and the proclamations in his works as "ogunian metaphysics." For Soyinka, only Ogun can help achieve transcendence between self and essence.

In *The Interpreters*, the metaphysics of African gods are captured in Kola's canvas of the pantheon. It encapsulates the creation myth and establishes the essence and importance of principal deities in the Yoruba belief system. Soyinka's idea of a companion deity is buttressed by Kola's painting, in which he attributes the traits of each deity to each of his friends. The painting is described as:

> Of the first apostate rolling the boulder down the back of the unsuspecting deity ... and shattering him into fragments which were picked up and pieced together with devotion.[47]

In *The Interpreters*, and many of Soyinka's other works, he presents the importance of gods or deities in the everyday life of a Yoruba person. Isidore Okpewho recognizes this idea of Yoruba mythology inserted in Soyinka's works. He agrees that:

> No doubt that it is becoming increasingly clear to us that the tragic element which Soyinka sees in the African character has been projected largely through his own experience, and that in the end the tormented figure of the Yoruba god, Ogun, which Soyinka has constantly presented to us cannot be separated from the trouble-torn personality of our poet-dramatist.[48]

Repeated depictions of Ogun in Soyinka's novels show the fierceness of the god, using it as a foundational metaphor for individual will and agency. The nature of Ogun ensures that belief in him, or a display of Ogunian traits, will rouse an individual to become a voice of his people. These traits are seen in Soyinka's fierce activism and politics. Ogun's traits provide Soyinka with a rationale for contemporary issues. Biọdun Jeyifo affirms that:

> Soyinka's obsession with the myths and symbolism of Ogun goes to the heart of the centrality of the deity and his significations for the writer's project of self-understanding and self-constitution.[49]

---

[47] Wole Soyinka, *The Interpreters* (New York: Africana Pub. Corp., 1965), 224.
[48] Okpewho, *Myth in Africa*.
[49] Jeyifo, *Wole Soyinka*.

This notion of individual will for change is emphasized in *Season of Anomy*, where it is actualized, as opposed to *The Interpreters*, where the Ogunian agency of will is theorized or abstract. The essence of gods was emphasized among the cocoa farmers in the Aiyero village: Ahime, Ofeyi, and others. Ahime exemplifies characteristics of Ọbatala, while Ofeyi is characterized as Ogun. Ogun is important to the plots of both novels; he is projected as the symbol of complete, original one-ness. Ogun is the grand model that humanity should emulate. In his essay, *Of Africa*, Soyinka asserts that:

> for all seekers after the peace and security of true community, and the space of serenity that enables the quest after truth, pleading for understanding from the Orişa for this transgression of their timeless scorn of proselytizing, we urge yet again the simple path that was travelled from the soil of the Yoruba across the African landmass to contiguous nations, across the hostile oceans to the edge of the world in the Americas—*Go to the Orişa learn from the Orişa and be wise.*[50]

Soyinka is a perennial campaigner for Orişa worship because of its completeness—it is a religious pantheon that has not gone on a crusade of its own. The worship of Orişas survived in Cuba and Bahia in Brazil through slaves that were captured from Africa. Soyinka's notion of Ogun's completion as a model for humanity is unfulfilled in *The Interpreters* because Ogun is distorted when Kola unveils his painting at the end of the novel. It is a metaphor to signify why humanity, especially African humanity, is in disarray: we do not fully depict and exhibit the complete traits of Ogun.

Conflict between Ancient (African) and Modern (Western) Systems

Since the West's arrival in Africa, there have been several clashes of worldviews and systems. This is well grounded in Achebe's *Things Fall Apart*. One such clash is the problem of language. Intellectuals in Africa have debated the way forward; Soyinka is one of those who suggested the adoption of Swahili as the continental language. Another conflict has taken place between Africanization and Westernization.

Westernization, as a program, is set as the universal standard of operation in the world. It is often argued that Westernization is the only valid modernity, although this claim has been debunked by many scholars around the world.

---

[50] Wole Soyinka, *Of Africa* (New Haven: Yale University Press, 2014).

Modernity, as defined by the West, is a parochial concept because modernity is multicultural.[51] Some sociocultural systems came through Westerners, and their system of government, religion, and way of life intermingled with African traditional ways.

In *The Interpreters*, when the protagonists return to Nigeria, they try to acclimate to society. They all refuse to accept the totality of Western systems, values, mores, and ways of living. Western worldviews and systems have merits and demerits, and the protagonists' metaphorical role is about separating wheat from chaff. However, their vague philosophy is that only an indigenous worldview can achieve better things in society. This idea was common among African nationalists in postcolonial Africa—Julius Nyerere and his idea of Ujaama, African Socialism, Leopold Sedar Senghor with Negritude, and Kwame Nkrumah's Consciencism. Soyinka is often critical of such movements; he does not reject them entirely, but he warns against over-romanticizing Africa's past. In Soyinka's view, Africans should not moan about the evils of slavery and colonialism, they should live their negritude like a tiger lives its tigritude. It is a comment that has been taken up by critics. Soyinka's concern is that trying to revive the past will be unsuccessful at overhauling the present.

Another example of tradition and modernity clashing in Soyinka's work is Dehinwa's conflict with her mother and her aunt. Dehinwa's mother does not want her bringing men to her apartment at night, but Dehinwa—whose friends are the interpreters—applies the modern rationale that living in her own apartment has given her independence. Dehinwa's family also opposes the idea of marrying a Hausa man, another clash between traditional and modern. As Dehinwa claims independence, her mother and aunt remind her that she is a part of a group. Whatever affects her also affects the family, and she should not bring shame on the family.[52]

Season of Anomy also involves the theme of Western ways interacting with African indigenous ways. It is exampled in Ofeyi's search for a way of life that he finds in the "models from the European world."[53] For him, this is the best model for incorporating individuals within society. However, the new soon meets the old and the Western meets the African. His idea is well received in Aiyero because it was exactly what they had thought of. Ahime observed that:

> It was a most beneficial thing for us, your coming here all puffed up with your sense of mission. It was good to know that our ways have always been the dream of mankind all through the ages and among people so

---

[51] E. W. Said, *Orientalism* (New York: Vintage Books, 1979).
[52] Soyinka, *The Interpreters*, 169.
[53] Wole Soyinka, *Season of Anomy* (New York: Third Press, 1973), 12.

far apart. People as different in appearance as the cocoa-pod from the yam tuber. Eating and drinking differently, worshipping gods with no common ancestors, and yet ...[54]

This remark identifies the similarities between the Western and the African; some Western methods and systems are applicable in African societies, and vice versa. It also involves the subtheme of connective humanity. The idea is that no matter what racial, geographical, and social disparities exist, we are all connected by our humanity.

Soyinka's first two novels and all his other works preach tolerance. *The Interpreters* and *Season of Anomy* are religious, but they are elevations of African traditional religions. Soyinka never ventures far from his idea of syncretism, which is noticeable in Kola's painting that uses Noah, and later the prophet Lazarus, as Osumare, the rainbow. The Osumare serves as hope for humanity after the biblical flood. Lazarus, later replacing Noah, is a metaphor of redemption and resurrection, represented by the biblical story of Lazarus. Soyinka does not show admiration for Christianity, but he does not denounce it. In his memoir, *Aké*, he appreciates being raised by his mother, Eniola, who is nicknamed "Wild Christian."[55]

Corruption, Change, and Social Transformation

Soyinka's novels capture societies that are bedeviled by corruption, violence, and social disorder. In postcolonial Nigeria, corruption is very rampant at all levels of government. In *The Interpreters*, the characters are seen as agents and characterized in terms of the moral positions that they occupy. The protagonists are young professionals, critical of the current state of affairs, and they interpret the modern scenery. They are pitted against corrupt politicians, self-interested public servants, and snobbish academics.

In *The Interpreters*, corruption is one of many unsettling problems that face society. Corrupt politicians include Sir Derin and Chief Winsala, while the snobbish and hypocritical academics include Professor Oguazor and Ayo Faseyi. The novel is set in the 1960s, which recalls Soyinka's narration in *You Must Set Forth at Dawn*—he describes a university at the epicenter of political conflict, forcing intellectuals to pick sides. A similar atmosphere led Soyinka, allegedly, to hold a radio station at gunpoint to protest against the premier of the western region of Nigeria.[56] Like Soyinka, the interpreters confront the problems and challenges that face politicians and intellectuals

---

[54] Soyinka, *Season of Anomy*, 12.
[55] Wole Soyinka, *Aké: The Years of Childhood* (New York: Vintage International Edition, 1981).
[56] Soyinka, *You Must Set Forth at Dawn*.

in independent Nigeria. The five interpreters must become agents of change to bring about social transformation.

The theme of social transformation is also included in *Season of Anomy*. Soyinka's second novel depicts a society held hostage by a cartel of corrupt individuals. They are disloyal, unpatriotic, dishonest, and unfair. The cartel sees politics as a moneymaking business to profit them and their families. Individuals like Ahime, Zaccheaus, Demakin, and Ofeyi become agents of change and social transformation, resisting the cartel. Their model of rebellion stands against social and moral corruption and challenges the status quo. Egbo in *The Interpreters*, like Soyinka, also challenged "what is" with the response: If I only kneel to God, why should I prostrate to you?[57] The response of Ofeyi and his friends is different from a refusal to prostrate, but it stands against what used to be. Ofeyi is not only an agent of change, he is a beacon of hope for the people of Aiyero village. Ofeyi becomes a champion of the downtrodden standing against the cartel.

Conclusion

African literature has a rich history and its heritage is in its orality. Modern African writers have inculcated an attitude of storytelling that reflects their sociopolitical predicaments and milieus. They do not write for the sake of writing alone; they synthesize art with their own emotions and the emotions of their people. This is shown in Soyinka's works, especially his novels.

Soyinka, as person and as a literary figure, is combative and fierce like his companion deity. His politics and concern for humanity inform the themes of his writings. These thematic concerns are important to the African essence—the metaphysics of Yoruba gods as a representation, as a validity for our belief systems. The conflict between the ancient and the modern is an existential dilemma for Africans, and they are still struggling with it. However, Soyinka's prescription is to take what is good of the ancient and syncretize it with what is good of the modern. Themes of corruption, change, and social transformation are present in almost all of his works. Corruption is a weevil, and if it is not addressed, it will burrow deep into the fabric of society and bring about its death. Soyinka's recommendation is that individual will must stand against corruption, and injustice can bring about social and political transformation.

---

[57] Soyinka, *The Interpreters*, 17.

FIGURE 8.1 *Soyinka working on* The Lion and the Jewel. *Illustration by Kazeem Oyetunde Ekeolu.*

8

Dramatic Oeuvre

All the world's a stage, and all men and women merely players: they have their exits and their entrances; and one man in his time plays many parts, his acts being seven ages.

WILLIAM SHAKESPEARE[1]

Introduction

African literature performs utilitarian functions—it has been described as art for life's sake, as opposed to the Western view of art for art's sake. Over the years, African writers have tailored their art to respond to prevailing situations from their own environments. African literary works reflect the realities of their societies; these observations are visible in modern African drama. The modern African playwright reflects society's positive and negative realities in their plays. Characters, settings, and other dramatic devices are used to reflect social, political, cultural, and economic circumstances.

Some scholars regard drama as the literature that walks. The dramatic statement from Shakespeare's *Macbeth*, that the "world is like a stage where everybody acts and quits," is an Elizabethan definition of typical Western drama. As a literary genre, drama allows artists to fully express their whole being. Everything in drama, including gestures and languages, contributes to the meaning. Drama may be the closest form of artistic expression to real life. A work of literature is not drama until it is acted on stage, which is an essential feature of dramatic expression.

---

[1] Brainy Quotes, "William Shakespeare Quotes," https://www.brainyquote.com/quotes/william_shakespeare_166828.

As a subgenre of literature, drama involves a story that is narrated through actions, not through reported speech, as in prose. According to Greek scholars, drama is a work of imitation; a character in a drama is an aggregate character either of vice or by virtue. The character is an imitator and a reflector, becoming the center and the circumference of the work. The elements of drama, such as plot, action, dialogue, setting, and audience, make it different from other forms of literature—it cannot be realized in the written form, and it should be acted on stage.

Drama has been studied as a form of literature for centuries. According to Johnson, it is a poem written for representation. To the people of Johnson's age, drama was poetic, although it belonged to the stage and involved acting as part of a larger production. These elements have been subsumed under the vague term of "representation," making a place for different forms of drama, such as fable, farce, fantasy, melodrama, tragedy, comedy, and tragic comedy. These forms are well explored by Wole Soyinka in his dramatic literary sojourn.

Soyinka's works have been judged some of the best contemporary drama, not only in African literature, but in all works expressed in English. Soyinka was born in Aké and educated at Ibadan and Leeds. He developed as a creative writer and controversial political activist, beginning to earn headlines in the 1960s. During his undergraduate days at University College London, Soyinka was active as a writer, actor, and student politician. His contemporaries included J. P. Clark, Okigbo, Achebe, Adenugba, and a host of others whose names would fill a bibliography of modern African literary scholarship.

Soyinka's greatness as a scholar, poet, novelist, social commentator, actor, director, playwright, and dramatist constitutes an uncommon battery of intellectual accomplishment. He is not only prolific, but also profound. His ideological positions, postures, styles, and language are uniquely observable. This chapter focuses on his dramatic works, but his entire corpus of dramatic works could be classified into groups or stages of development.

The first stage was his mythical historical plays of the 1960s and 70s. These plays include *The Swamp Dwellers*, *Kongi's Harvest*, *Death and the King's Horseman*, *The Road*, *Lion and the Jewel*, and the Jero plays. These plays combined Yoruba myth and indigenous Yoruba tradition to comment vividly on Nigeria's social and political scene. They focused on leaders within the post-independence community of newly freed African countries. The plays in this category were not only written for the sake of drama, they also continued poetic traditions, working with excessive style and obscure language, amorphous plotlines, and semiotically coded styles of characterization. These distinctive features made the plays into top-notch classics, setting Soyinka apart as a stylistic marker of Africa's dramatic form.

Soyinka's plays in the era after 1970 were more satirical, intended to provoke or prevent change by artistically applying humor. These works denounce society's ills: religious bigotry and fanaticism, a general lack of political vision, economic quagmire, and corrupt practices and incarceration. Soyinka also noted the ironic complexity of the nation's intelligentsia in the coup that dethroned traditional African values in the face of colonialism. *The Dance of the Forest* was written as a satire of Nigeria's independence, in which Soyinka characterized Nigeria as a half-child, doomed to die—the play was presented during the celebration of Nigeria's independence from British colonialism in October 1960.

During this era, Soyinka used resources from African myth. This is seen in his characters, who include a dead man, dead woman, spirits, a living human, and the half-child whose survival was in jeopardy. Soyinka combined and mixed elements of Yoruba ritualistic myth to celebrate history and subtly present a modern theme.

Literary critics and historians have considered Soyinka's *Kongi's Harvest* as a dramatic satire that dwells on the excessive power of the traditional kings. The play presents Ọba Danlola as a trenchant example of a foolishly hedonistic and ostentatious king. Kongi is the satirical culprit, denoting the complexity of intellectuals in the societal aberrations of excess, in every possible sense.

Lion and the Jewel also explores and lampoons the traditional system. The king, who is drunk with power, tumbles, and fumbles down to the temple to seduce and abduct an innocent virgin lady to be his wife. This defies the traditional and modern logic of morality. In the same way, Soyinka presents the character of Lakunle, a schoolteacher who is transparently consumed by the virulent pride that accompanies his status as one of society's educated men. Lakunle also attempts to seduce Sidi, the virgin village girl, to become his wife. With these polarities of characterization, Soyinka condemns the aberration of modernism, appealing for a more sane society via the definition of values, morals, and ethical standards that are the features of traditional African society.

As Soyinka's concerns increased over religious bigotry and fanaticism in post-independence Nigeria, his dramatic focus shifted. Readers and literary observers noticed this trend in plays such as *The Trials of Brother Jero* and *Jero's Metamorphosis*. These plays scrutinize the problem of religious exploitation; self-acclaimed prophets misled the masses to reap economic gains from religious observance in Nigeria's immediate post-independence era. Soyinka established that corruption spread beyond Nigeria's political leadership to take root in supposedly sacred places. Churches and mosques had previously been regarded as places that upheld moral standards, resisting desecration and the taint of corruption.

In the 1980s, Soyinka's plays assumed a more inter-African focus. They critically denounced corruption, tyranny, religious hypocrisy, materialism, and the ultimate destruction of the remaining values and cherished integrity of African plays. Soyinka published *Opera Wonyosi* in 1981, condemning the materialistic attitude of contemporary political and economic classes. The title is satirical and comedic: "o pe ra wọnyọsi" translates as "the dupe buys the wọnyọsi lace." It is a subtle dig at the high-flown social life of Lagos in the 1970s, where the lace material "wọnyọsi" was central to the highly ostentatious dress code of the upper class. Their lifestyle displays the results of corruption and embezzlement, revealing a society that only caters to the bourgeoisie and neglects the proletariat.

Another play in this category is the *Play of Giants*, which is a national concern that addresses a universal audience, with special relevance for African countries. The play is set in the United Nations, projecting a theme of political delusion, and challenging corrupt military leaders in Africa in the 1980s. It marked a turning point in his dramaturgy—his use of elevated language, regarded as literary obscurantism, is coupled with metaphysical conceits to show the ills of a society where men are hedonistic. The play shows the height of corruption in Africa and the loss of humanity among African leaders. It is one of Soyinka's more accessible plays, in terms of language, as opposed to the complex language and structure of *The Road*. These literary and linguistic techniques offer a veiled portrayal of the high levels of decadence in Nigerian society and in Africa at large.

Soyinka's work also includes absurd plays that incorporate postmodern and post-structural tenets. These plays mirror the disorder of the world; they do not have linear plots and they are open to multiple interpretations. Sometimes, the actions are unpredictable and generate personal meanings that are not shared by a universal audience. The works are also psychological and deeply philosophical in nature. This dramatic form is European in nature, but Soyinka's adoption of the technique marks a turning point in the history of African drama. Postmodernism, in African drama, is marked by a shift in focus—writers move from "big issues," such as anti-colonialism, corruption, and political disillusionment, to explore "small issues" such as individual maturation, identity and interest, sexual identity and consciousness, and domestic life. Soyinka presents this thematic shift in his later plays *Alapata Apata* and *The Road*, which are absurd, postmodern, and deconstructive. These plays also reflect contemporary society.

The social, political, economic, religious, and literary commitment of the modern African playwright is reflected in Soyinka's plays. This commitment is the playwright's act of either overtly or covertly discussing the social vices that plague Africa's sociopolitical landscape.

Sociopolitical Commitment in Soyinka's Drama

A writer's commitment is the dedication to his or her duty as the voice of a people. It is the interest a writer pays to his or her surroundings when creating a literary work—the decisions to respond to these issues, whether by portraying them unchallenged in artistic work or by proffering solutions to these potential problems that bedevil society.

Julie Agbasiere[2] identifies two schools of thought in her discussion of sociopolitical commitment in Africa. The first is made up of writers who view themselves as teachers; they task themselves with the responsibility of restoring Africa's past, proving to the West that Africa had a culture before colonialism. The second school is made up of scholars who are more concerned with the writer's function as a "chronicler and visioner."[3] This school believes that pressing sociopolitical ills in society should be closely examined. This school of thought asserts that the writer is obligated to show his or her commitment by reflecting the sociopolitical vices prevalent in their own society.

In *The Writer as Righter*, Niyi Osundare[4] asserts that every writer has social obligations to fulfill in society. This work is not easy. Other individuals in positions of power, such as kings and rulers, can create change instantly. However, the writer can only bring about change through appeal and persuasion. The writer's ability to influence members of society is determined by his or her ability to craft works that persuade others to see things from a different point of view. Osundare asserts that "a real writer has no alternative to being in constant conflict with oppression." The writer in any given society is automatically tasked with a duty to speak out against every form of oppression and subjugation. Es'kia Mphahlele[5] asserts that in African literature, writers exhibit their commitment to the African society, setting, and culture. In the fight against colonial rule, African writers showed their commitment by producing works that glorified African culture and opposed cultural imperialism.

Commitment is an integral aspect of African literature as a whole, and Soyinka, a modern African playwright, expressed his sociopolitical commitment in his dramatic works. According to Agbasiere,[6] sociopolitical commitment manifests itself in two ways. The first is the reflection of the beauty of Africa, African culture, and the African past. The second is the depiction of sociopolitical ills and the realities pervading postcolonial African societies. These aspects of sociopolitical commitment are based on the writer's historical era.

The modern African playwright reflects a certain level of commitment in dramatic works. It is usually reflected through satire, in which the

---

[2] Julie Agbasiere, "African Literature and Social Commitment," in *Major Themes in African Literature*, ed., D. U. Oputa, A. U. Ohaegbu (Nsukka: AP Press, 2000).
[3] Agbasiere, "African Literature," 72.
[4] Niyi Osundare, *The Writer as Righter* (Ibadan: Hope Publications Ltd., 2007).
[5] Es'kia Mphahlele, *Chirundu* (Johannesburg: Ravan Press,1979).
[6] Agbasiere, "African Literature."

playwright exposes the sociopolitical ills and vices bedeviling African society by subjecting them to ridicule; the audience is invited to not only see, but also laugh at the folly of those in power. Various African playwrights from the time of the colonial era have written plays showing their dedication to the matters affecting society around them. These playwrights, including Soyinka, use setting, plot, characterization, and other devices to portray their sociopolitical commitment.

Themes of postcolonial disillusionment and neocolonialism dominate the work of modern African playwrights. Africans fought fiercely for their freedom while under the rule of colonial masters, believing that the leadership of their own kind would improve things significantly. When independence was finally won, they rejoiced, thinking that they could finally enjoy the bounty of the land. Unfortunately, the African leaders turned out to be even worse than their white counterparts. These leaders were irresponsible, selfish, and corrupt. They were only interested in amassing wealth for themselves at the expense of the masses.

One sociopolitical ill challenged by playwrights was the irresponsibility of leaders in power. After the colonial masters were expelled from Africa, Africans hoped and believed that their lot would improve; they were now being ruled by their own kinsmen. Unfortunately, this was not the case. Black leaders were only concerned with amassing wealth and claiming positions of power and authority. Instead of providing basic amenities, the greed of black leaders left the people in an even worse position than they were before.

Postcolonial African society was characterized by feelings of disappointment, betrayal, and disillusionment. The people realized that all their struggles had been in vain, and the leaders they looked up to were nothing more than self-serving opportunists. James Ngugi expresses this disappointment in these words:

> I thought then that tribalism was the biggest problem besetting the new East African countries. I, along with my fellow undergraduates, had much faith in the post-colonial governments. We thought they genuinely wanted to involve the masses in the work of reconstruction. After all, weren't the leaders themselves sons and daughters of peasants and workers?[7]

Africans expected politicians to be genuinely interested in rebuilding society and the economy, which had been severely damaged through colonial rule. People felt kinship with these leaders because they shared the same background and experiences. They were confident that black leaders, who had felt what it was like to be poor and oppressed, would do their best to

---

[7] James Ngugi, "Preface," *The Black Hermit* (Essex: Heinemann, 1968), viii.

ensure equal opportunities for everyone and significant improvement in the economy. Unfortunately, this was not the case. The leaders turned out to be hypocrites and liars who abused the people's trust.

Wole Soyinka reflects this theme of disillusionment in *The Beatification of Area Boy*, set during one of the periods in Nigeria's political history when the military had seized power—it can be inferred from Sanda's statement, "A-ah. But the soldiers say life has improved since they took over power."[8] Despite the military's declaration that they would repair the damage done by civilian politicians, the Nigerian state of affairs only got worse. The Nigerian economy was caught in a downward spiral, and inflation and devaluation became the order of the day. It is reflected in the following excerpt:

> TRADER: Even if to say I did, I fit read. Look, na early morning. I dey prepare for my customers and I wan think small. We currency done fall again, petrol dey scarcity, which is to say, transport fare done double. As for foodstuff and other commodity, even gari wey be poor man diet.[9]

Soyinka uses the character of Trader to comment on the appalling state of Nigeria's economy after the military intervention. Even staple food items, such as the gari that was the last resort of the poor, have become unaffordable. The leaders are only interested in occupying positions of power because of the associated prestige—they do not genuinely care about their citizens, and they are too self-serving to make sacrifices for them.

Religious hypocrisy is a salient issue assailing the African postcolonial era. Religious leaders should be upright, decent individuals in society, but they behaved as nothing more than fraudulent crooks using religion to conceal their dishonest activities. Many religious leaders were exposed as parasites, using their influence to manipulate unsuspecting followers. The sociopolitical commitment of modern African playwrights seeks to condemn religious leaders who use their position to cheat naive Africans out of their possessions. This issue is examined in the Jero plays, consisting of *The Trials of Brother Jero* and *Jero's Metamorphosis*. Soyinka exposes how religious leaders exploit their gullible followers, manipulating them to suit their personal desires.

Brother Jero, the major character of the plays, is a bar-beach prophet who lives by his wits. This is revealed to the audience during Jero's opening monologue in *The Trials of Brother Jero*. He regards his role of religious leadership as a trade, and he will do anything to keep from losing this

---

[8] Wole Soyinka, *The Beatification of the Area* Boy (Ibadan: Spectrum Books, 1999), 15.
[9] Soyinka, *The Beatification of the Area Boy*, 7.

profitable "business." Jero drives away his own teacher to claim his plot of land, establishing a moneymaking venture for himself.

In these plays, Soyinka satirizes the spread of Christianity across Nigeria and gullible followers who blindly obey religious leaders. Jero is a charlatan who views his "calling" as a commercial pursuit:

> JERO: ... I am glad I got here before any customers I mean worshippers well, customers if you like. I always get that feeling every morning that I am a shopkeeper waiting for customers.[10]

Jero only "prophesies" what his followers want to hear. He is aware that by keeping his worshippers hopeful, they will return to him and he will retain his power over them. Jero retains power over Chume by insisting that the latter must not beat his wife. Jero does not prevent Chume from beating his wife out of concern for the household, but because it suits his purposes to keep Chume frustrated and angry. Jero's prophesies are self-serving; he only issues them to attract more followers, which can be inferred from the following excerpt:

> JERO: They begin to arrive. As usual in the same order. This one who always comes earliest, I have prophesied that he will be made a chief in his home town. That is a very safe prophecy. As safe as our most popular prophecy, that a man will live to be eighty. If it doesn't come true ... that man doesn't find out until he's on the other side. So everybody is quite happy. One of my most faithful adherents unfortunately, he can only be present at weekends firmly believes that he is going to be the first Prime Minister of the new Mid-North-East State when it is created. That was a risky prophecy of mine, but I badly needed more worshippers around that time.[11]

Soyinka uses the character of Jero to satirize unscrupulous, self-styled religious leaders who apply underhand tactics to draw unsuspecting individuals into their congregations. Soyinka also condemns those who believe religious leaders without question; some leaders are not as respectable as they claim to be. Through the Jero plays, Soyinka exposes the dubious practices of religious leaders along with the unquestioning trust that Christians place in them. Unquestioning trust allows the followers to be manipulated.

Modern African playwrights also show their sociopolitical commitment by examining war's lingering effects on African society—wars, especially civil

---

[10] Wole Soyinka, *Myth, Literature and the African World* (Cambridge: Cambridge University Press, 1979), 20.
[11] Soyinka, *Myth, Literature*, 25.

wars, are an important aspect of Africa's history. Nigeria's civil war lasted from July 1967 to January 1970. The war was fierce, and its lasting effects have been examined by playwrights. Soyinka examines the lingering effects of the Nigerian Civil war in *The Beatification of Area Boy*. The character Mama Put shows that wars have far-reaching effects that last for years; she has been embittered by the murder of her husband and her brothers. In this excerpt, she expresses bitterness and resentment directed at those who took part in the war and killed her husband:

> SANDA: You'll never get over that war. Not ever. Nobody does ...
> MAMA PUT: Medal! And what would I do with that? Keep your medals and give me back yes, even the mangrove swamps ... And don't remind me of medals! They all got medals. Those who did this thing to us, those who turned our fields of garden eggs and tomatoes into mush, pulp and putrid flesh that's what they got medals! They plundered the livestock, uprooted yams and cassava and what did they plant in their place? The warm bodies of our loved ones. My husband among them. My brothers ... And the pilots didn't care where they dropped their bombs. But that proved only the beginning of the seven plagues.[12]

Sanda's statement that nobody can get over the war can be seen as Soyinka's stand on the issue. He depicts wars as physically and emotionally devastating and destructive. Mama Put still suffers the emotional and psychological effects of the war, even though it is years later. Soyinka asserts that war's devastating effects are not restricted to the conflict; they also affect peaceful times.

The sociopolitical vices of crime and violence are part of African society, and African playwrights reflect these ills in their works. The harsh realities of life in postcolonial Africa can force some inhabitants into a life of crime—a lack of job opportunities and bleak future prospects can lead African youths to pursue lives filled with crime and violence. This is seen in Soyinka's *The Beatification of Area Boy*, where characters resort to criminal activities for survival. The Area Boys, led by Sanda, extort money from anyone who comes to the plaza, claiming that the payment is to "protect" vehicles from vandalism. Sanda, the security guard who leads the Area Boys, describes the various forms of protection:

> SANDA: Well, you do know what insurance is, I expect. The same principle operates with these ... oh, it's embarrassing, I mean ... you're right, it's extortion but, I'm afraid that's what goes on here. Everybody puts up with it, and the police condone it.

---

[12] Soyinka, *The Beatification of the Area Boy*, 21.

FOREIGNER: Could you explain, please? I've not quite caught on.
SANDA: I am sorry; I thought it would be quite clear by now. Comprehensive is always advisable because, then, the safety of your car is absolutely guaranteed. You see, sometimes, you have more than one gang operating. So, if you took Third Party, it exposes you to third party risks. Another gang could come and 'do' your car, and you see, the first gang wouldn't interfere. It's the code they have among themselves. Once a gang leaves a sign on your car which says 'Comprehensive', that's it. All other gangs keep off. Third Party buys you immunity only from the party to whom you paid.[13]

Sanda describes these payments as services that are purchased by the Foreigner, but the fact remains that the Area Boys are practicing extortion. They demand payment from innocent citizens with an implied threat of vandalism, claiming that their activities are condoned by the police.

Anyone who tries to outsmart the gang ends up getting robbed; the Big Man Shopper parks his car outside their jurisdiction and still becomes a victim. His car is parked far from the plaza, but it is still vandalized and valuable items inside it are stolen. Soyinka uses this play to depict gangsters and organized crime that plague society. The Area Boys are presented as a fluid, efficient operation headed by none other than Sanda. Ironically, he is a security guard at the plaza. These "Area Boys" must take desperate measures to survive in a society that has refused to give them any opportunities to improve their lot in life.

The issue of ritual killings is also examined in the play, through the character of the Barber. A conversation between the Barber and the Trader reveals just how low people will stoop to make money:

BARBER: You are the original doubting Thomas. But these things happen, that's all I can tell you. You see all those corpses with their vital organs missing breasts in the case of women, the entire region of the vagina neatly scooped out. And sometimes just the pubic hair is shaved off for their devilish mixture. And pregnant ones with the foetus ripped out. Male corpses without their genitals or eyes. Sometimes they cut out the liver ...
TRADER: And what of hunchbacks? Dat na another favourite for making money. They take out the hunch, sometimes while the man self still dey alive.[14]

---

[13] Soyinka, *The Beatification of the Area Boy*, 39.
[14] Soyinka, *The Beatification of the Area Boy*, 14.

The dialogue reflects the horrors taking place in African society, mostly in search of money. Individuals resort to violent, brutal means to make money by any method, regardless of what is involved. Soyinka shows that human life is not considered valuable in African society. The postcolonial African society is one where people will stop at nothing to improve their economic status, even if it means taking a life.

A Child of Two Worlds: Soyinka as a Multicultural Writer

The works of Soyinka, especially his dramatic texts, can be categorized as world literature. Most of his works hold a wide significance, and they have circulated into the world beyond his country of origin. In past years, world literature texts have primarily been masterpieces of Western European literature, but today it is increasingly seen in a global context that draws from other regions. As a result, readers have access to an unprecedented range of translated works from around the world that pursue aesthetics and thematic emphases that have global or universal appeal instead of a national focus.

Out of over a dozen plays authored by Wole Soyinka, *Death and the King's Horseman* is considered one of the greatest owing to the well-structured introduction to African's thoughts and traditions and how it fuses Yoruba and Western elements with its central theme of cultural responsibility. The text is popular among students and academics interested in learning about literature, especially African drama. The play is inspired by a real-life event that occurred in 1946, during which British colonialists stopped the king's horseman, known as Ẹlẹṣin, from killing himself as tradition required after the death of the king. The text has a universalism of thematic preoccupation that can be related to different world cultures. The play reveals a fusion of cultures, bearing traces and consistent chunks of hybridity, cultural pluralism, and transculturalism. It also addresses issues of colonialism and counter-discourse. In 1986, the Swedish Academy awarded Wole Soyinka the Nobel Prize for Literature, citing *Death and the King's Horseman* and *Dance of the Forests* as demonstrations of Soyinka's ability to create dramas with a universal appeal while combining the Yoruba and European culture without placing one above the other. However,

> Westerners who come to *Death and the King's Horseman* without much knowledge of Yoruba culture and belief are apt to focus on the theme of the clash of cultures. Clearly, two cultures, Yoruba and British, are uneasily occupying the same geographic space, although their emotional and spiritual worlds could not be farther apart. During Acts 2 and 4, for example, the British listen to a tango and orchestral music, while the sound of African

drumming is continually heard in the background. Both communities call their members together during the same evening: The British hold a fancy-dress ball with the prince in attendance, and the Yoruba gather for the ritual suicide of the king's richly robed horseman and the burial of the king and his entourage. Although the differences are interesting to observe, the two communities do not enrich each other, but remain apart.[15]

For instance, Ẹlẹṣin's belief in tradition is so strong that he is willing to die for it; however, Simon and Jane Pilkings do not understand African tradition and culture; thus, they labeled them "nonsense," "barbaric," and "horrible custom." Even when Amusa and Olunde point out the disrespect in their behavior, they still go ahead to put on the sacred masquerade's garments to a costume party and mock the ceremonial dance. Simon, though a Christian, his belief appears to be inconsequential to him. He ridicules Joseph for his belief in the holy water, mocks Ẹlẹṣin, disrespects his culture, and calls him an "old pagan."

Simon does not understand or respect Ẹlẹṣin's culture, and he uses his authority to interfere only because he does not want to be embarrassed while the prince is visiting. It is tempting, therefore, to see Simon as the cause of Ẹlẹṣin's not fulfilling his duty, to see the clash of cultures as the force that moves the universe off its course. But in an Author's Note that accompanies the play, Soyinka indicates his displeasure with this reading, which he calls "facile." For Soyinka, Simon's inability to understand is clearly present, but the focus of the play is on what happens to the universe when duty goes unfulfilled. Simon is simply an instrument, or a "catalytic incident merely." Those who understand Yoruba belief can easily see the metaphysical confrontation in the play. For most Westerners, however, the recognizable conflict is between two religions, two races, two communities, and two cultures.[16]

Death and the King's Horseman is set in Oyo, a town in the western part of Nigeria, in 1943 or 1944. The location of the play is crucial for understanding the two worlds that Soyinka presents. During the nineteenth century, Nigeria became a British colony where colonial officers maintained order and guarded the small population of white Europeans who lived in the country. These Europeans and the Africans, the Yoruba people, lived in opposite worlds, with each group fighting to keep alive its traditional way of life in their different communities, one not mingling with the other.

Wole Soyinka omits glossaries in *Death and the King's Horseman* to encourage others to learn about other cultures, especially their language,

---

[15] Encyclopaedia, *Death and the King's Horseman*, https://www.encyclopedia.com/arts/educational-magazines/death-and-kings-horseman.
[16] Encyclopaedia, *Death and the King's Horseman*.

which is Yoruba in this case. This has caused some heavy criticisms for the text. Some people claim the lack of glossaries makes the play inaccessible for people unfamiliar with the Yoruba culture and traditions. Also,

> Several critics have commented on the anachronistic situation presented by the play, observing that by the 1940s the failure of the king's horseman to commit ritual suicide would not have rocked the community. Some have found it difficult to accept that the European-educated Olunde would participate in the ritual. Other critics, particularly those in Nigeria, have written that Soyinka has romanticized the Yoruba, presenting them as more unified and tradition-bound than they are. African Marxist critics find that in emphasizing the cultural and religious differences between the British and the Yoruba, the play ignores essential class differences within Nigeria.[17]

The majority of the harsh criticisms leveled against *Death and the King's Horseman* stem from the preconceived notions that Soyinka's plays are influenced by Western culture and that although they are rich in oral traditions, they are not totally African. Yet, for some, the universality of Soyinka's plays, which has earned him international acclaim and generated positive reviews in Europe and North America, indicates that he has abandoned his traditional African values in favor of the Western culture.

Despite all the criticisms, however, Wole Soyinka is a multicultural writer who has neglected neither his culture nor tradition. Rather, he has helped to disseminate African writings so that they may achieve global significance. Even when he borrows from classical Greek drama, he adds a touch of Africanness to project his social commitment.

Dramatist of Multiple Meanings: A Deconstructive Reading of Soyinka's *Alapata Apata*

Wole Soyinka's play *Alapata Apata* depicts the absurdist and postmodern tendencies in his dramaturgy. It is a dramatic and humorous account of Alaba, a butcher who marks his retirement by sitting on a rock attached to his house, doing nothing. Various conflicts that arise are due to his decision.

Although an initial reading of the play projects a simple, humorous dramatization of a butcher's decision to go into retirement, a deconstructive reading uncovers conflicting meanings and paradoxes. Interactions between the butcher and various characters, such as the Teacher, the noblemen and royalty, the General, the Mother, and Daughter initially provoke laughter. A deeper

---

[17] Encyclopaedia, *Death and the King's Horseman*.

look reveals a chain of meanings that appear different from the established consensus developed from a surface reading of the text. A deconstructive reading of the text can foreground these contradictory meanings.

The play presents binary opposites that include work and leisure, power and powerlessness, elites and commoners, education and illiteracy, and the opposition of order and disorder. Alaba, the main character in the play, embodies the opposites of work and leisure. His retirement foregrounds this opposition and simultaneously subverts it. Even though leisure appears to be privileged in the play, Alaba still works in retirement. It initially appears as though he will exclusively drink palm wine, eat, and sleep, but the progression of the story finds him unwittingly generating fear and respect in Daanielebo and other members of his society. He also holds court on the rock, giving advice to those who request it. Alaba's retirement is just as active as his career as a butcher; a subliminal message from the play may be that one can never really rest for as long as one lives.

The binary oppositions of the ruling class and common man are represented by Daanielebo, the General, Alaba, and the King and his chiefs. A popular conception is that the common man is oppressed and exploited by elites, which appears to be the case during Alaba's encounter with the King and the royal entourage. The chiefs try to force Alaba back to work, attempting to punish him for making himself a chief without the King's consent. However, these same men hurry back to Alaba when they hear exaggerated accounts of his exploits scaring off the General and Daanielebo.

Alaba is eventually made a chief, much to his chagrin, becoming a member of the ruling class and subverting the binary opposites of ruling class and common man. The event establishes that leadership is not restricted to a select few elites; anybody can become part of the ruling class. An instance of supplement is also visible—Alaba, who was once one of the masses, joins society's elite class and shows that the roles are intertwined; today's common man could be a member of tomorrow's ruling class. The other characters, who are indirectly responsible for Alaba's increase in social status, also foreground an element of supplement. Without followers, there can be no leaders, just as without the common man, there can be no elite. Alaba rises to the position of chief because other members of his class spread rumors. It shows that the masses can elevate anyone to a position of prominence, regardless of background.

The idea of elites and commoners is closely related to the binary opposites of power and powerlessness, represented by Daanielebo and Alaba. Daanielebo intends to intimidate Alaba into leaving his position on the rock, but Daanielebo is frightened by Alaba's son and flees the compound. This scene, which initially provokes laughter, subverts the concept of privileging power over powerlessness. It suggests that the powerless are never truly without power, they merely underestimate the value of their power. When Daanielebo panics, Alaba does not even understand what is happening.

After Daanielebo has left, with his medicine man in tow, Alaba finally turns and sees his son. The encounter foregrounds the deconstructive term "supplement." The scene suggests that every situation of powerlessness contains an element of power. The key is to discover this power and learn how to use it—in Alaba's case, it is done unwittingly.

The confrontation with Daanielebo also suggests that power is simply a construct of the mind. Alaba's son is a harmless boy who becomes the feared "daemon of the rock" because his face is painted. The boy has no supernatural powers, but Daanielebo attributes supernatural power to him. The boy attains a status that is powerful enough to send his father's would-be oppressors running in terror.

Derrida argues that logocentric or phonocentric words (either written or spoken) are never truly present in a text—the meaning of a word is provided by its difference from other words; it is contaminated with their meaning. This contamination results in the meaning of a word becoming qualified by the word preceding it and modified by the word that follows. It results in a continuous and subtle deferral of meaning. Derrida coined the term "differance," a combination of the meanings "to differ" and "to defer," as a way of illustrating this concept. This unreliability of language, due to its instability, can also be found in *Alapata Apata*. Baby Picasso's mistake, with the accents on the sign "Aba Alapata Apata" leads to a variety of interpretations made by the other characters.

The Major mistakes Alaba's home for "Aba Alapata," which means quarry. The Trader and her Friend interpret the "Alapata" in the sign to mean the chieftaincy title of Alapata. Alaba himself reads it as Alapata, meaning butcher. We see the unreliability of language as the word "Alapata," intended to mean "butcher," becomes tainted by interpretations of "chief" and "quarry." The contamination ends up diverting the Major and his troops. It also incites the chiefs to punish Alaba when they believe that he has tried to give himself a chieftaincy title. We see different meanings within the expression "Aba Alaba Alapata," and this multiplicity of meanings creates various conflicts in the play.

The concept of dissemination, the uncontrollable plurality of meaning in language, is also evident in the play. Meaning is continually moving along a chain of signifiers; it cannot be tied down to a fixed term. In the play, it is apparent in the expression Aba Alaba Alapata. In this context, the expression should mean "butcher's hamlet," but it is taken to mean "where they split rocks" and as a chieftaincy title. The word Alapata is the problematic component of the expression, giving rise to a multiplicity of interpretations.

A deconstructive reading of *Alapata Apata* yields many contradictory and conflicting messages that involve dissemination, the subversion of binary opposites, and the metaphysics of difference. It incorporates the terms "logocentrism," "phonocentrism," and "differance," which are all characteristics of Soyinka's recent plays. Another Soyinka play, *The Road*, can also be categorized as an absurdist play with absurd situations. The text has no linear plot; it is a jigsaw puzzle and a play of obscuration that involves metaphoric projections such as the spiderweb and the Professor's unattainable quest. In his book *The Movement of Transition*, Oyin Ogunba describes the play as a celebration of Nigeria's decadence—starting from the early days of religious fanaticism and transitioning to political delusion and economic quagmire, treated with invective and satire.

Common Tenets Visible in Soyinka's Plays

Most of Wole Soyinka's plays are set in Yorubaland, dealing with the metaphysical issues that spring from Yoruba belief. They normally include:

1. The celebration of the Ogun festival.
2. Frequent use of ironic titles.
3. Incorporation of elements from Western dramatic tradition, such as Greek tragedy.
4. Adherence to a unity of time and place.
5. Natural dialogue and situations.
6. An avoidance of logical endings, offering a multiplicity of meanings.

Conclusion

Soyinka is a social realist and socialist realistic writer. This refers to his reflection of society in literary works—in social realism, the writer's work is a searchlight that exposes the ills and vices of the surrounding society. It can be accomplished by presenting these ills to the reader without proffering any solution. In *The Trials of Brother Jero*, Soyinka satirizes the hypocrisy of religious leaders and the gullibility of their followers without suggesting any solutions for the problem experienced by society. He simply reflects Lagos from the early-to-mid 1960s to foreground societal ills from that point in time. On the other hand, socialist realism can perform a refraction of society, where social and political ills are presented to the reader along with suggestions for correcting them.

Modern African drama, just like other genres of African literature, portrays commitment to varying issues in the continent. Modern African playwrights do not write in isolation; they are influenced by the issues facing their society at the time of their writing. In Africa, the writer views it as his duty to be an instrument of change in society, and one can find a reflection of African society in literary works. This is the case with Soyinka's drama. The playwright does not write plays merely for entertainment—they write to expose and condemn problems in society.

The commitment of the modern African playwright is usually portrayed through thematic preoccupations visible in the play. These themes revolve around corruption, crime, violence, and other sociopolitical evils present in African society. The concepts of social and socialist realism are important in discussing the commitment of modern African playwrights such as Soyinka. Although social realism reflects society, socialist realism attempts to proffer solutions to the sociopolitical problems that it faces.

9

Soyinka's Poetry

In all the categories of Soyinka's poetry [and published works], we see an attempt even though unacknowledged, to use poetry [literature] as a vehicle for delivering political messages. Sometimes it is dense, at times it is light even with metrical virtuosity. When it is combative it remains graceful.
TUNDE ADENIRAN, THE POLITICS OF WOLE SOYINKA, 1994[1]

I worry less about advertised and sensational risks, more about the more vicious hidden one. I worry less about terrorism than about diabetes ... This may not be too interesting except that it is exactly what other people do not do. ... Half the time I am intellectual, the other half I am a no-nonsense practitioner. I am no non-sense and practical in academic matters, and intellectual when it comes to practice. ... Half the time I am shallow, the other half I want to avoid shallowness in the context of risks and returns. My aestheticism makes me put poetry before prose, Greeks before Romans, dignity before elegance, elegance before culture, culture before erudition, erudition before knowledge, knowledge before intellect, and intellect before truth. But only for matters that are Black Swan free. Our tendency is to be very rational, except when it comes to the Black Swan.
NASSIM NICHOLAS TALEB[2]

---

[1] Tunde Adeniran, *The Politics of Wole Soyinka* (Ibadan: Fountain Publications, 1994), 95.
[2] Nassim Nicholas Taleb, *The Black Swan: The Impact of Highly Improbable* (London: Penguin Books, 2007), 296.

Introduction

The poetry of Wole Soyinka is no different from any of his other creative endeavors; it allows curious observers to experience the writer's vision, philosophies, and creative peculiarities. Getting acquainted with Soyinka's poetry does not provide automatic entry into his world; it is essential to have a solid understanding of the culture that he works with. However, his poetry is a useful entry point.

In literary style and extraordinary scope of genres, and in dramaturgy, Wole Soyinka is not only an outlier but akin to Taleb's metaphorical "Black Swan."[3] Unlike many of his contemporaries, regardless of their infrequent cross-genre adventures, Soyinka's greatness does not come from any single work or field. He is as skilled in drama as in his essays and poetry, deploying his unique energies and ingenuity. Soyinka's productive output contains patterns for accessing and assessing his works; one can work from the general to the specific regardless of genre constraints. Soyinka's approach and artistic philosophy create echoes that can be found in virtually all his works. Critics and scholars can identify recurrent motifs and ideologies in his works. An engagement with Soyinka's poetry requires a recognition of this overarching philosophy, even when the goal is to identify the presence of others. To achieve an essential knowledge of Soyinka's poetry, we must grapple with his approach to art in general, and to poetry in specific.

Soyinka's approach has been given many labels: visionary,[4] mythopoeic,[5] reconstructive, revolutionary, Euro-assimilationist, and shamanist. These labels and others receive discursive dominance depending on context and the specific component of the Soyinka oeuvre being addressed. It is almost impossible to fit Soyinka into any single box; any attempt to weave preconceived critical or theoretical assumptions through his works will yield an array of (unforeseen) possibilities.

Any Soyinka's work is like a prism, dispersing a broad spectrum of complex colors after a strip of investigative light passes through it. His works yield rich meanings when set against established philosophies and critical principles, although some critics have levelled charges of obscurantism when considering Soyinka's work.[6] As an alternative, one can approach Soyinka's work with flexible assumptions, applying notions that are fluid enough to

---

[3] Ibid.
[4] Thomas R. Knipp, "Irony, Tragedy, and Myth: The Poetry of Wole Soyinka," *World Literature Written in English* 21, no. 1 (1982): 5–26.
[5] Mary T. David, "The Theme of Regeneration in Selected Works of Wole Soyinka," *Black American Literary Forum* 22, no. 4 (1988): 645–61.
[6] Critics like Jemie, Madubuike, and, most especially, Chinweizu, have spoken of the obscurantist of Soyinka's works—these three are the most vocal of Soyinka's critics, even though their opinions are well shared by a lot of others.

adapt and accommodate the shifting, transitory currents discoverable in different texts. This approach requires a flexible frame of understanding whose principles can tease out possible meanings without undue coercion. Forces can be traced from text to text that display intertextuality, recurring ideologies that are reinforced by an overall consistent posture. The entire Soyinka oeuvre can be investigated for interconnecting chemistries pointing toward a coherent, single ideological impetus from the author himself.

The other option is to read Soyinka selectively. This would extract selective texts from Soyinka's body of work to test specific principles, hoping that the findings are comprehensive enough to account for other texts. The critical reader would have to seek out currents of ideology in single texts, using them as a basis for intertextual connections. These ideologies could be aesthetic, philosophical, or notional; each of these categories has subthemes that offer further delineation. A constructive unification of these themes can categorize Soyinka's broad works for greater accessibility.

A level of obvious complexity is present in Soyinka's works. Complexity does not necessarily mean obscurantism, despite the claims of critics. A work can incorporate or create a network of paradigms to communicate meaning, which requires the identification of the network's presence, carefully unknotting its latticework before meaning can be deduced. Describing this type of complexity as obscurantism is overreach.

The idea of accessibility refers to the ease of locating Soyinka's ideologies in and across his texts. His essay-lectures, drama works, plays, and autobiographic works have varying degrees of accessibility. His poetry defies clean categorization; the poetry of Soyinka before independence differs from that which came after independence. These differences still offer channels toward instructive reconciliation—such reconciliation is possible because the same ideological strands run through the works, however different in temper and maturity. Despite the changes in time, context, form, and content of each poem, the currents that sustain the agency of the poems are fuelled by an identifiable source.

This source is collected in Soyinka's social vision. There have been many explanations for this: many have examined ritual symbols, myth motifs, and dramaturgy in Soyinka's works to explain his vision and approach to literature, explaining how it must serve the human condition;[7] others have engaged Soyinka's concept of the Fourth Stage;[8] and some have

---

[7] See Biọdun Jeyifo's chapter on "Ritual, Anti-Ritual, and the Festival Complex in Soyinka's Dramatic Parables" in *Wole Soyinka: Politics, Poetics, and Postcolonialism* (Cambridge: Cambridge University Press, 2003); see also Knipp, "Irony, Tragedy, and Myth," 5–26. See also, Stanley Macebuh, "Poetics and the Mythic Imagination," *Transition* 50 (1975): 79–84.

[8] Ibironke Olabode, "Fourth Stage: Wole Soyinka and the Social Character of Ibadan," *History Compass* 13, no. 11 (2015): 541–9.

investigated the socialist impulse in Soyinka's works directly.[9] Soyinka's pedagogy, regardless of format, is generally engineered for society, or for social direction. No matter which form of myth he is using, or what approach to literature has been crafted by his imagination, the end result is society. Macebuh has asserted that Soyinka's exercise of his mythic imagination develops robust ways of reinventing and redirecting contemporary African life.[10] The dimensions that myths—as African history[11]—take in Soyinka's hands reveal human nature: they show how actions and the concept of choice serve as illuminators, signifying the psychic conditioning of average Africans faced with difficult choices and how they affect the social fabric.

Soyinka's use of myth to investigate and reflect current conditions is rooted in his preoccupation with African life. His imagination is essentially mythopoeic; this mythopoeic force is a primary reason for the myth that is both legacy and medium in Soyinka's artistic world. There is a vibrant connection between myth and Soyinka's appraisal of social behavior. Distilling these into a single equation can account for the various poetic manifestations of Soyinka's vision, which is influenced by personal experiences. Those experiences are anchored on the conditions of Soyinka's inhabited spaces, making this equation possible:

Social function + Visionary reconstruction = Social direction

Soyinka believes in the poet's social function from ideation to execution. It means that the poet's tools must be saturated with profound social consciousness. His application of these tools reflects a consideration of society as dominant in the creative scheme. With this consideration in mind, he applies his tools to execute the duty of the social poet—this duty involves the ends to which his vision and vessels are directed, reconsidering the course of society. The poet, regardless of aesthetics, personal ideas, or preferences, must be socially relevant and committed. Beyond that, the method of social commitment must be implicated in the process.

---

[9] Odun T. Balogun, "Wole Soyinka and the Literary Aesthetic of African Socialism," *Black American Literature Forum* 22, no. 3 (1988): 503–530. See also, Abiọla Irele, "The Season of a Mind: Wole Soyinka and the Nigerian Crisis," in *The African Experience in Literature and Ideology* (Exeter: Heinemann, 1981), 198–211.

[10] Macebuh, "Poetics and the Mythic Imagination."

[11] The relation between myth and history is complementary, recording the narratives of reality in the material sense and revealing the influence of the social behaviors that make up those narratives. History is the combination of actions, motives, and influences, and it is stored in cultural memory for retrieval and reuse by subsequent generations. Myths are born from these processes of retrieval, making them history in their own sense.

Soyinka's position on poetry can be gleaned from his poems. Although his poetry is expansive, a single equation runs through it.

On Pretexts and Intertexts in Shaping Textuality

Evidence of Soyinka's mythopoeic imagination can be found within his poetry. It can be seen in the way that he harnesses his mythic heritage, the Yoruba worldview, in a Universalist manner. Yoruba heritage is deployed to assume Universalist functions and to account for universal human conundrums. Soyinka himself has experienced two separate cultures through his scholarship; he has admitted to approaching his Yoruba culture in synecdochic terms with that of Africa. By successfully accounting for the complexities of modern existence, Soyinka turns myths into tools of engagement.

Myths are not strung up by Soyinka to popularize or glamorize their source culture; negritude ideology and its proponents have been criticized by Soyinka for using this approach. The distinction is in the instrumentality: in Soyinka's hands, myths are deployed as paradigms for explaining, comprehending, and assessing contemporary patterns and behaviors through principles and organizing philosophies. This, combined with the absence of loudness, "shoutiness," or showy self-promotion, distinguishes Soyinka from the negritude writers and the way that many of the pretextual mythic motifs are used in first- and second-generation poetry. Negritude essentially demarcates cultural awareness and re-arrival through the modern poetry of Soyinka and Senghor (and his cohorts). This is problematic for Soyinka when such effort "declaims on the African reality but fails to produce it."[12]

The production of poetry is a process of revival that reinvigorates the medium of advocacy in fresh ways, achieved through a remediated poetic form of engagement with the human condition, especially the psychical. Patterns of modern behavior that point to dominant metaphysical and metapsychical ancestral legacies can be detected through this process. Soyinka's criticism of Senghor is that he shies away from this activity, failing to achieve an animist awareness that can transform the details of experience into paradigms of universal conditioning.

This process sits at the center of African poetry's legacy.[13] Soyinka's example shows that it is never enough to declaim the symbols and strengths of cultural Africa; they must be recreated and put to use in new ways.

---

[12] Okpure O. Obuke, "The Poetry of Wole Soyinka and J. P. Clark: A Comparative Analysis," *World Literature Today* 52, no. 2 (1978): 216–23.
[13] This point is made in Soyinka's essay, "And After the Narcissist," where he criticized the negritude ideology.

They should speak for themselves and for those within whose circles they thrive, whether they be attitudes, social laws, liminal realities, quandaries, or the crisscrossing vicissitudes that affect human life. It may be an overgeneralization, but a case can be made for Macebuh's claims about Soyinka's relationship to myth: "Indeed, there is a profound sense in which it might be said that the chaotic nature of social behavior in our time is the single most important justification for Soyinka's meditations on myth."[14] This claim is ambitious, but it is true that Soyinka's reliance on pretextual influences provides conceptual provisions that allow him to engage with modern humanity and our current circumstances.

Pretexts are elements, legacies, features, and rich symbols of the past that are consciously cultivated by writers—Africans—to set their works in context. They also allow writers to achieve other objectives such as representation, glorification, popularization, and reorientation. Soyinka's poetry has always included Yoruba cultural significations, but it is executed in ways that embody the African existence for Universalist reception. Some have said that this is the result of Soyinka's hybridized consciousness, much like any other Westernized African writer. His hybridization has also led to accusations of leveraging his intertextual references as signs of Euro-assimilationist tendencies. Soyinka's systematic deployment of the Ogun÷Obatala binary, working Yoruba myths into conceptual poetic frames and principles, is a potent case in point. Soyinka's patron is Ogun, the Yoruba god of creativity, and Ogun's deployment in Soyinka's poetry is substantial.

As the god of creativity and destruction, Ogun's radical impulses and contradicting oppositional forces are often referenced as a frame of inquiry for the psychological polarity that manifests in the average person. Polar opposites of good and evil, destruction and creation, and warmongering and peacemaking are associated with Ogun; it is not far-fetched to assert that this knowledge has provoked Ogun's distinctive employment as a critical frame of psychical evaluation. Ogun is often manifested in seven ways—as god of iron and metallurgy, explorer, artisan, hunter, god of war, guardian of the road, and the creative essence[15]—using the god's dual nature to visibly render the contradictions inherent in Africans and all humans.

Human actions condition the environment and characterize the spirit of the age, which means that postcolonial chaos is a consequence of conflicting inner personalities as it gestures toward imprints of the mythical. Soyinka views his Yoruba heritage in synecdochic terms with African culture, and his Yoruba mythic interventions are rife with continental relevance. The polar nature of Ogun manifests, in several degrees, as the average modern Yoruba person who must execute actions in line with the parallels of Ogun and

---

[14] Macebuh, "Poetics and the Mythic Imagination," 80.
[15] See Tanure Ojaide, "Two Worlds: Influences on the Poetry of Soyinka," *Black American Literature Forum* 22, no. 4 (1988): 767–76.

Ọbatala. Soyinka, in expounding his argument, explains that understanding the essences of these gods will aid the conception of neurotic balances or the peculiarities of modern existence.

Ọbatala and Ogun are polar opposites—one is the god of "spiritual complacency," and the other is the god of the "tragic dare." To cite a practical example, the renowned Yoruba tolerance of other cultures, and especially tolerance for the Western world's culture, spirituality, and politics, can be considered a manifestation of this ancestral psychic framework, even as this tolerance threatens the organicity of its inner and outer self-coherence, as it does in the god's own mythic history. Ojaide believes that such mythic explanations of modern behaviors also accommodate Ogun, which is self-evidently true in acts that defy the social order, whose mythic influence plays out in the extremes of actions or expressions of conflicting personhood; it ultimately gives life to a modern Ogun archetype. It is not the accuracy of the claims that matter here, but the fact that Soyinka's engagement with pretexts are not solely for cosmetic or curatorial purposes. Soyinka has deployed the pretext motifs of Ogun as internal and immanently constitutive structures to the import and export of his poetry.

In *Ogun Abibiman* and *Idanre and Other Poems* we see Soyinka weave these mythic essences into the texture of his poetry. The reader's receipt and conception of significance and messages in the poems are influenced by their ability to see patterns of mythic and ritual deployments. Ogun is heavily and covertly stitched into the nucleus of these poems, but Soyinka provides room for other gods such as Orişa nla, Şango, Ọrunmila and Eşu in *Idanre*. *Idanre* is divided into the "Idanre poems," which are further divided into seven sections, and a host of others. This collection of poems, about thirty-six in number, subdivided into six sections, is heavily invested with Yoruba mythology. Even though there are personal reflections, and his audience is universal, Soyinka invests his abstraction of the human experience with metaphysical qualities, reinvigorating native heritage through Yoruba mythic history.

Many of his poems, like "Abiku," "Dawn," and "Idanre," owe a great deal of their textuality to the myths used by Soyinka. "Death in the Dawn" is another such poem; the mythic is silenced to the extent where it is invoked through the cockerel smashed on the windscreen and the man dead in the smash. The occurrences take place on a road said to be guarded by Ogun, Guardian of the Road, who also destroys in an ironic, polarizing sense. Soyinka beseeches the man to rise at dawn, but what lies ahead when "dawn's lone trumpeter," the cockerel itself, is destroyed? This inquiry is Soyinka's way of rejecting the negatives of technology, which is a very modern conundrum, while channeling the contrasting essence of his patron-deity and his culture's mythic heritage surrounding the road.

Soyinka's pretextual fascination is not limited to the ritualistic. Cultural ethos, expressions, and values are the bedrock of Soyinka's poem "Koko Oloro." Its propitiatory tone, which beseeches natural elements and forces for aid in its supplication, reflects the implorations that initiates and even average Yoruba people often make toward the gods—especially the act of using enticing materials to enhance their requests.

Another such poem is "Dedication," which harvests the details of Yoruba naming ceremonies. Edibles, farm produce, and other items are powerful cultural symbols used to usher a newborn into the world. In Yoruba culture, these items are highly symbolic; they are used in prophetic measures. "Abiku" is another poem that invokes the ritual and sociocultural nuances of the Yoruba. It reflects the life of Abiku, a child who moves between the world of the living and the dead, dying and returning, never fully here or there. The myth of the Abiku is applied by Soyinka to situate Yoruba concerns within the larger context of human experience.

Soyinka's relationship with Yoruba pretexts is observed in the way his poem differs from another poem titled "Abiku," written by J. P. Clark. The reality of the Abiku, the Ogbanje who dies and returns to cause suffering for parents, is illustrated by Clark. Soyinka's version goes further: his preoccupation with the concept of life and death examines how the Yoruba worldview accounts for these developments and the Abiku's implications for the Yoruba consciousness of existence. Soyinka's poet persona speaks directly as an Abiku, compared to Clark's presentation using a third-person voice, which shows Soyinka's proximity to the concept of the Abiku myth. It extends from a belief or idea to become a universal consideration of rebirth and death. The insinuations and references to the Yoruba worldview, practices, and rituals connected to the Abiku are all marshaled into a unified paradigm.

Soyinka's poems are influenced by aspects of traditional orality. The lyrical strength of poems in *Idanre* and *Ogun Abibiman* bear strong resemblance to Yoruba oral poetry. Rhetorical devices deployed in Yoruba poetic tradition, such as rhythmic rendition of prayers or supplication, or rhythmic speech, repetition, invocation, wordplay, and even praise poetry (*oriki*) can be found in Soyinka's work. Boasts and authorial braggadocio that are specific to African poetic forms are rendered in poems like "Abiku".

The satiric quality of Soyinka's poetry, and his general approach to ridiculing society's vices, is influenced by Yoruba forms of satirism. One such form is the use of the masquerade as a satiric tool, where a spiritualized entity upholds accepted mores by clowning and ridiculing those who have committed social offenses. Poems in *A Shuttle in the Crypt*, written during his incarceration, embody satirical strains—Soyinka applied a lens to the corrupting influence of power while struggling in solitary confinement. The lyrical, dramatic, and meditative qualities of his poems bear heavy echoes of his cultural awareness.

Soyinka's ability to meld present reality with his cultural heritage has given him a balanced view of subjects. His work lacks the preoccupation that would allow the past to overshadow the present or vice versa. His pretextual influences coalesce with his intertextual influences, reinforcing his poetic vision. Soyinka's use of ritual motifs, mythic history, and cultural symbols are driven by a vision of engaging with the universal principles that undergird modern attitudes and affairs.

Political estrangement and other afflictions that have plagued post-independence Nigeria, redirecting the trajectory of the newly independent nation, are brought into the center of Soyinka's poetry. Societal conditions have always fed literary direction and textual orientation; for this reason, Soyinka has depicted situations that have led critics to claim that he has a philosophy of pessimism. However, he is recounting the modern postcolonial situation as he sees it. In his essay, "The Writer in an African State," Soyinka asserts that the African writer must rise to the demands of the time, deducting usable and salvageable legacies from the recurrent cycle of human stupidity.[16] Soyinka expresses this duty of the poet in relation to his material reality. It is a cyclical vortex that stresses the human will in an endless abyss, facing dilemmas caused by a disrupted past, ruinous present, and future that has been aborted before it is even conceived.

Soyinka's Fourth Stage comes to mind—not only does its synthesized approach to poetry unify pretexts and intertexts, it also opens up the mind to Soyinka's vision of moving beyond mere antiquarian benefits. His fascination with the past collects keepsakes that permit a holistic engagement with culture in its present dimensions. Intertexts, in this sense, are stimuli emanating from the environment as social currents, conditions, or the endless cycles of stupidity that influence Soyinka's poetic form and content.

Political history, national chaos, and human quandaries have all been identified as momentous influences on art. Soyinka has seen the chemistry of ritual, mythic, and cultural heritage connected to modern conditions; this essential alchemy produces the required instruments of revolution. Many of his poems, such as "Death in the Dawn," follow this pattern. He assumes a critical posture toward technology while drawing on the myth of Ogun, the god with conflicting essences. Technology is both an aid for existence and a source of destruction, similar to the way Ogun signifies the duality of creativity and destruction. This motif is interwoven with the other ironic performance of the Ogun essence, enabling death on a road where he is meant to be a protector.

On Ideology and Activism

The highly interconnected nature of Soyinka's philosophies about art, and the direction it must take in society, mean that any discussion of his artistic

---

[16] Wole Soyinka, "The Writer in an African State," *Transition* 31, no. 6 (1967): 11–13.

work will involve a discussion of his ideology and activism. Soyinka's incarceration shifted his sensibilities as a writer closer to the realm of the activist, which may have led Ojaide to state that Soyinka's imprisonment altered his voice and viewpoint—we do not see Soyinka merely as an observer, as in his poems prior to *A Shuttle in the Crypt*, we see him as a participant, witness, or victim. Ojaide's remark about Soyinka's imprisonment affecting his activism is accurate; Soyinka increased the tenor of his protest, which is what his revolutionary vision is about.

The satiric impulse found in "Telephone Conversation" differs from the poems in *Shuttle*. Soyinka's incarceration moved him closer to his vision, which Balogun called "a decisive shift in his political alignment."[17] Independence and post-independence realities contributed to the robustness of his political ideology. His return from Europe created space for a hybridized poetic influence emphasizing his aesthetic peculiarities. Just as imprisonment amplified his personal voice, postcolonial Nigeria amplified his social commitments beyond their original dimensions.

Soyinka did not sacrifice aesthetics for his ideology; his experiences provided new ideas for channeling his vision. He transitioned from being the kind of artist concerned with instrumentalizing a hybridized reality—that of a culturally conscious African writer exposed to Western aesthetics—to become a committed artist. This transformation left defining echoes in his prison notes and poetry, as well as in the essay "The Writer in an African State." His new consciousness, brought about by the jarring postcolonial reality, advocated for visionary reconstruction. It promoted an Afrocentric literary aesthetic that was driven by vision and implicated in its home affairs.

Soyinka's vision was supported by action—he held a media broadcaster at gunpoint and his pursuit of peace led to imprisonment under charges of conspiring with the enemy—and this action took center stage in his poetry. His decision to take over a broadcaster so that he could play a prerecorded message was a compulsive and calculated act, utterly creative as well as daring. When considering the Ogun aesthetics, it seems that Soyinka's understanding of how poetry should work in the hands of the African writer has arisen from a revolutionary spring that overflows with the essence of the god of the dare. Soyinka carried this revolutionary ideology into poems in *Shuttle*, where he dared the powers-that-be, the hegemonic neocolonial structures, with his creative poetry.

Soyinka's life of activism inflected his poetry. He headed or participated in political groups such as the National Democratic Organization, National Liberation Council of Nigeria, and Pro-National Conference Organization. He also served as chairman of the Democratic Front for a People's Federation. The poems in *Shuttle*, mostly written during his imprisonment, attend to

---

[17] Balogun "Literary Aesthetics," 507.

the realities of that incarceration; they oscillate between meditations on his predicament, those of his fellow inmates, and the failings of the warped prison system as a miniature version of the nation-state, which was moving in the wrong direction. Jeff Thomson correctly identified the word "shuttle" in the title being used as a metaphor for poetic witnessing and cultural chronicling.[18] The meditative tone of Soyinka's poems in that collection are due to the author's centrality within the situation, witnessing and analyzing his reality and its root causes, attempting to construct ideological methods of contesting reality's demands. These are acts of chronicling, a self-aware task that can be a method of engagement and birth, as a product of rumination.

The prison poems signify that the prison is Soyinka's own shuttle for reclaiming his psyche from the deadly grip of the Gowon government and its apparatuses of control. The totality of his experience in the shuttle challenged him to generate new ways of dealing with cultural and national quandaries, encouraging him to discover ways that the poetic process can be used to shield and protect. In "Procession," one of that collection's poems, Soyinka addresses the metaphoric possibilities of the shuttle as a means of witnessing and recording the evils of perverted power. It is a safe space that Soyinka is forced to construct, inhabit, and rely on.

Soyinka's lived reality, and his attempts to process it in *Shuttle*, offered a chance to criticize government programs, such as the prison itself. In "Live Burial," he indicts the prison system and the state ideology behind it. The collection is divided into seven sections. One of them, "Phases of Peril," considers state violence, which Soyinka vehemently opposes. *Shuttle* is a political statement of cultivated angst and resolute ideology. This angst is sustained in "To the Madmen over the Wall," where his voice assumes defiance. His spirit of camaraderie is awakened by his unpalatable experiences and the stress imposed on his spirit.

In the poem, the metaphor of speaking in "foreign tongues," having "dared the infinite" and "journeyed back," establishes that the "human heart may hold only so much despair" before confronting its tormentors. There is a noticeable shift in his tone, perception, and ideology, which shows how the prison experience will modify and birth Soyinka's visions for literature and revolutionary reconstruction, along with the vision for social direction that has been identified with him over time. The poem is a nudge to the spirit, revealing that the prison and the shuttle are both places of birthing and experiencing, recording and provoking, and places of stress as well as reaction. "Conversation at Night with a Cockroach," just like "October 66," concerns itself with political violence in the nation. Soyinka drew attention to the 1966 pogrom, identifying with the Igbos of Southern Nigeria in

---

[18] Jeff Thomson, "The Politics of the Shuttle: Soyinka's Poetic Space," *Research in African Literatures* 27, no. 2 (1996): 94–101.

opposing government violence that had characterized the political sphere since Independence—it was a far cry from what had been expected after transitioning from the colonial government.

It is bewildering that Soyinka was the subject of relentless controversies, accusing him of being a thorough Euro-assimilationist, unduly exalting the West through his use of language, and projecting himself as held spellbound by some unacceptable version of philosophical pessimism. These were all employed as the ideological forebears of controversial allegations against present-day creative writers accused of Eurocentrism, stereotyping Africa for greater glory, and the ever-present ideological anchor: poverty-porn in postmodernist African literature.

Soyinka's socialist ideology has been questioned because of his personal aesthetics. Balogun has asserted that Soyinka's commitment to advancing African socialism, which occurs in works such as *The Man Died*, *A Play of Giants*, and *Opera Wonyosi*, should be dismissed and reinterpreted as subtle Eurocentric crusades. Critics claimed that continuous cultivation of European mythology, which divided the African front through narratives of personal salvation and communal deliverance as a result of messianic or individualistic efforts, perpetually diluted his socialist messages to the point of obscurity.

Balogun chose examples from Soyinka's prose and dramatic works. But the socialist impulse and Afrocentric fidelity to social awakening and communal progress is present in his poetry: it exists through Soyinka's recording and sanctioning of ugly realities. Soyinka creates ways to deliver these messages in theory and form that can be found in many of his works, especially *The Man Died*. Similar ideas serve as the foundation for *A Shuttle in the Crypt*, if not many of his poems. *The Man Died* and the majority of the poems in the *Shuttle* were written in prison, and others were written with Soyinka's prison experiences in mind.

The atrophy of foresight, unchecked subjectivism, and prescriptive criticism have made detractors brand Soyinka with ill-fitting ideological labels, such as Anglo-modernist.[19] An extensive list of his alleged transgressions include obscurantism, fidelity to a Hopkinisian massacre of the English language's syntax and semantics and Greco-Roman mythology, the use of Shakespearean lexical items and other such archaisms, disconnection from his audience, turgidity, and unreadability.[20] The last two charges characterize many negative opinions of Soyinka's poetry and literature in general.

---

[19] Bernth Lindfors, "Beating the White Man at His Own Game: Nigerian Reactions to the 1986 Nobel Prize in Literature," *Black American Literature Forum* 22, no. 3 (1988): 475–88.

[20] See Lindfors, "Nigerian Reflections"; see also Chinweizu, Onwuchekwa Jemie, Ihechukwu Madubuike, *Toward the Decolonization of African Literature* (Washington: Howard University Press, 1983).

One cannot deny the complexity of Soyinka's work, or that it may be difficult for some readers. However, complexity is not the same as inaccessibility, and textual allusions or idiosyncratic use of mythic history on a universal basis are not the same as unreadability; none of these are Euro-assimilationist. Prescriptive criticism attempts to box Soyinka's work, including poetry, into these categories. The foundations of these ostensibly critical approaches rest on specific ideas for what Soyinka should write and how he should write it, or what African literature should be. Besides setting the boundaries of the acceptable, prescriptive criticism is only good for exclusion.

African literature, which espouses literary ideologies and includes authorial dispositions, cannot be collapsed into a monolithic whole. There is no one way to write African poetry. There is no single way in which it can be written. The inability of Soyinka's critics to extract or effectively deduce Soyinka's social commentary through the mythic has enabled their prescriptive criticisms. And this is not their only shortcoming.

Those who accuse Soyinka of Eurocentrism—claiming that he makes unnecessary allusions to Greek or other Euro-cultural symbols—on the basis of comparative disposition forget two things: First, Soyinka is well acquainted with his native culture, to the point where he generates a reconstructed vision of literature through the mythopoeic. His reference to Dionysus, for example, is not born of fascination or cultural kowtowing. It comes from a mind that seeks universal parallels to address African issues with global sensibilities. Second, the Western-trained African writer already exists in a state of consciousness where parallels are drawn by default, especially when thinking in one language and writing in another draws in two different worlds.

The best example of this criticism is the literary tussle between Soyinka and the Bolekaja critics (the trio of Madubuike, Chinweizu, and Jemie, grouped under a name translated as "come down, let's fight"), which came to a head after Soyinka received the Nobel Prize in 1986. Both sides engaged in literary mudslinging and disparaging comments, and other literary heavyweights shared their own thoughts on the matter. In one exchange, Soyinka compared the Bolekaja troika to that of the Chichidodo, a loathsome and hypocritical figure. In Ayi Kwei Armah's *The Beautyful Ones Are Not Yet Born*, Chichidodo is a character that detests faeces while feasting on the worms that have made the faeces home.

Soyinka wrote a scathing essay,[21] with the full wrath of his intertextual logic, that dismissed the Bolekaja trio and their creative enterprise as "stuck

---

[21] The essay titled "Ethics and Aesthetics of Chichidodo" by Wole Soyinka was published in *The Guardian* in 1985.

in a latrine bucket."[22] He drove home his point by describing their continuous attempts at criticism as a kind of sickness "too far gone for ministration."[23] He concluded that "a centre of pus substitutes for grey matter in their head and they have never made friends with the word 'integrity.'"[24]

Soyinka responded to several of Chinweizu's criticisms that had been published as essays, including "That Nobel Prize Brouhaha" and "Pan Africanism and the Nobel Prize." To understand Chinweizu's stance and the allegations leveled against Soyinka and his poetry, a short excerpt from Chinweizu's essay is pertinent:

> I am not one of those who stand in uncomprehending awe before Soyinka's literary works ... Maybe, if [the] works were even harder to make sense of, and even more pandering to Graeco-Roman mythology, they might have edged out the hard-to-decipher species the French nouveau-roman which got the Swedish Academy's nod. As for all the heartaching in some circles, I don't see why any self-respecting African who understands the cultural role of the Nobel Prize, would lust for a moment for the damn thing.[25]

In the same essay, Chinweizu referred to the Nobel Prize and Soyinka's works as a case of "the undesirable honouring the unreadable." Chinweizu considered the Nobel Prize to be "a bewitching instrument for Euroimperialist intellectual hegemony, and the conceit that a gaggle of Swedes, all by themselves, should pronounce on intellectual excellence for the diverse cultures of the whole wide world."[26]

Chinweizu's assumptionist, prescriptive posture toward the yardstick of global literary excellence and what it should be are a display of his aesthetically and ideologically defined concerns. Chinweizu's views encapsulate the extent and nature of the charges levelled against Soyinka's works. Another excerpt provides additional detail:

> The jokers in the literary community are that small coterie who fancy themselves as seers, shamans, or pathfinders on some mystic 'Fourth Stage,' and who go about claiming that their heads are buzzing with prophetic and priestly 'visions' ... those who refuse to write what even their friends would be eager to read, those drunk on private visions which

---

[22] Soyinka, "Chichidodo."
[23] Soyinka, "Chichidodo."
[24] Soyinka, "Chichidodo."
[25] See Chinweizu's essay, "That Nobel Prize Brouhaha," published in *The Guardian*, November 3, 1985. Or Bernth Lindfors, "Africa and the Nobel Prize," *World Literature Today* 62, no. 2 (1988): 222–224.
[26] Chinweizu, "That Nobel Prize Brouhaha," 222.

they find great difficulty in communicating to bystanders they make it difficult for the public to either accept writing as valuable work or see the career of a writer as anything but a lunatic pact with needless poverty.[27]

The significance of Chinweizu's addition to Soyinka's list of crimes is that it condemns the alleged absence of social commitment, devoid of communal gain and seeking to exalt the individual. He implies that Soyinka's ideological representations in text privilege the centralization of individual salvation, portraying messianic individuals who shoulder the community's burden and carry them to the Promised Land.

Chinweizu, and others in that school of thought, reject endeavors that bestow heroic status on an individual who becomes worthy of respect, reverence, and honored status. They accuse Soyinka of perpetuating literary mysticism on philosophical and aesthetic grounds—successful mystification efforts will "yield great psychological gains to their propagators"[28] and elevate them to the status of cultural heroes. Soyinka has been compared to a literary shaman and a literary Napoleon; one expects tributes and increased authority from propagandist use of literary powers, and the other expects fearful, unquestioning obedience through the mystification of his person performed by his creative works.

Not only is Soyinka accused of having no worthwhile social commitment in his poetry, he has also been accused of offering a strange type of poetry that is pessimistic, pretentiously messianic, and self-serving. This criticism becomes even more dubious when considering the logic behind these charges and the reality of Soyinka's mythopoeic relationship with poetry. The nucleus of the critics' argument is that contemporary poetry should derive genuine inspiration from oral tradition instead of being divorced from it. Soyinka's poetry draws legitimately from oral tradition and elsewhere. (The real question is what "genuine" inspiration means, and how these critics have measured ingenuity in relation to mere extraction from the source culture.) It would seem that critics have confused or substituted complex and idiosyncratic use of language with the absence of social commitment; there is a difference between means and ends.

Soyinka's poetic ends have always been a revolutionized social direction, but the means that he uses to achieve them have been personal, difficult, and challenging—this has not meant a divorce from oral tradition. Is the "legitimate" inspiration desired by critics one that is defined by the qualities of "easy" and "simple"? And is the easy and simple aesthetic socially relevant by default if the opposite is treated as a deviation? Must poets

---

[27] See Chinweizu's essay, "Pan-Africanism and the Nobel Prize," originally published in *The Guardian*, April 13, 1986.
[28] Chinweizu, "Pan-Africanism."

rehash the substance of oral tradition as it exists in native culture? Soyinka does the opposite of that, not only using myth but interrogating it. Yes, the language of myth is simple,[29] but Soyinka's usage is not in total fidelity to its primordial state: Soyinka's deployment of myth is revolutionary, reconstructive, and mythopoeic. Despite this, his detractors have clung to personal definitions of social commitment.

Liberal nationalists and Marxists have described Soyinka as a threat to African nationalism, despite the obvious poetic shift from an aesthetic-oriented Soyinka to a socially conscious one. The same works that critics dismiss have elicited favourable responses from scholars like Molara Ogundipe-Leslie, who refers to obscurantism as daring experiments with language, finding that his inter-cultural explorations attain a transcendent universality. Both Abiọla Irele and Isidore Okpewho have made comments on Soyinka's simultaneous universality and indigeneity.

A confusion of means and ends appears to be the principal culprit behind the charges levelled against Soyinka's poetry and his obvious social commitment. The alleged philosophical pessimism is merely a realistic reflection of present conditions in a postcolonial state. Deployed as the opposite of philosophical pessimism, Soyinka's accurate depiction of the postcolony's moribund condition is itself a means to an end: invoking the revolutionary spirit. To dismiss his philosophy as pessimistic is to accuse him of exalting deprivation, corruption, chaos, and the suppression of human rights in his poetry.

If accessibility, simplicity of language, philosophical optimism, or any of the other implicit expectations of critics are considered to be the default for oral tradition, and African poets must reinforce them to display their Afrocentricity, then the critics have no authority to be the ultimate arbiters of that which is Afrocentric and Eurocentric. As Macebuh has observed, Soyinka is preoccupied with language not as "the index of style, but as a vehicle of mythic meaning."[30] Language has always been a vehicle; Soyinka uses it as a vehicle for a tailored sensibility. It does not show that the nucleus of Afrocentricity, the African-centered vision, has been perverted.

Conclusion

Soyinka's poetry idiosyncratically uses resources to achieve the African literary vision: commitment to the society and its progress. Soyinka's poetry is heavily invested with oral features and predicated on his African cultural

---

[29] Macebuh, "Poetics and the Mythic Imagination."
[30] Macebuh, "Poetics and the Mythic Imagination," 82.

sensibilities. His chosen methods of birthing poems betray an ideational process that is deeply rooted in his culture—as if Soyinka were thinking in Yoruba—but using a delivery process that accommodates all his sensibilities. As an African and a Western-trained African poet, it is as though he speaks to the world. Despite the claims of his critics, this hybridity does not detract from Soyinka's poetry any more than Soyinka's use of mythic language detracts from his presentation of the current human conundrums. His engagement with the present does not hinder his cultivation, engagement, or even criticism of the past.

Soyinka's poetry is full of resources and should be seen as such. These resources allow Soyinka to reach the universal human, transcending the local into the global, and from the global into the metaphysical and back. To understand Soyinka's poetry, one must approach it without a prescriptive notion of mythic language, African oral poetry, or representations of socialist impulse in poetry. One must be ready to discover what it means for poetry to be influenced by visionary reconstruction toward social direction, principally in terms of technique and content, manner and matter, and form and meaning.

FIGURE 10.1 *Fighting for justice. Illustration by Kazeem Oyetunde Ekeolu.*

10

The Politics of Soyinka's Literature

The artist has always functioned in African society as the record of the mores and experience of his society and the voice of vision in his own time.
WOLE SOYINKA[1]

Introduction

Each literary work of art reflects the complex imaginings, experiences, and ideologies of its creator. These reflections can reference the sociopolitical realities of the writer's environment, or they can be an externalization of the writer's personal experience; the relationship between society and literature compels both entities to influence each other. In Africa and around the world, literature is made for society—it often represents the writer's commitment to sociopolitical struggles. However, in the context of literature, politics do not necessarily concern the governance of a country. They can address the maneuvers and conflicts of literature within society, usually involving critics along with the sociocultural and political realities of their environment.

Every artist uses a distinct form and style when presenting ideologies, creating work from their own experience that can develop new experiences for those who encounter it. Mouffe opines that "artistic practices play a role in the constitution and maintenance of a given symbolic order or in its

---

[1] Wole Soyinka, "The Writer in a Modern African State," *Art, Dialogue and Outrage* (1968), ed. Biọdun Jeyifo (Ibadan: New Horn Press, 1988), 20, quoted in Abịọla F. Irele, "The Achievement of Wole Soyinka," *Philosophia Africana* 11, no. 1 (2008): 14. Emphasis in the original.

challenging and this is why they necessarily have a political dimension."[2] In this context, politics concerns the operations of Soyinka's literature in African society, its interaction with critics, and its contribution to the constitution of an African literary and sociopolitical order—it also considers Soyinka's work confronting accepted norms by using deviant techniques and ideologies.

A study of Soyinka's literature can examine the writer's ideologies and the political engagements of his work. We can also consider the complexity of Soyinka's literature in relation to dominant African content, languages, forms, and styles, along with the attendant controversy that surrounds his literature. These factors provide insight into the politics of Soyinka's literature.

Overview of Soyinka's Literature

Soyinka, the first West African to receive a Nobel Prize, is a Nigerian dramatist, essayist, novelist, and poet. His works are enriched by his African heritage, which includes the traditional folklore and religion of the Yoruba people. Obiajuru Maduakor has stated that Soyinka draws creativity from the mythology and culture of his people, providing insights into the worldview and belief system of the Yoruba people.[3] Henry Louis Gates, Jr., states that:

> Soyinka's work largely modernistic tragedies with direct formal ties to Euripides, Shakespeare, Synge, Yeats, Brecht, and Lorca is deeply grounded in Yoruba proverbs and mythology, the densely lyrical and resplendent Yoruba language, and the cryptic mystical poetry of the Ifa Oracle.[4]

In his essay, "The Fourth Stage," Maduakor describes Soyinka's work as an attempt to explain the concept of tragic myth as it is perceived through the Yoruba worldview. Richard M. Ready has interpreted Soyinka's work as an exploration of the tragic element of Yoruba art.[5] And W. Gao views

---

[2] Chantal Mouffe, *Agnostics: Thinking the World Politically* (London: Verso, 2013), 91.
[3] Obiajuru Maduakor, "Soyinka as a Literary Critic," *Research in African Literatures, Special Issue on Criticism and Poetry* 17, no. 1 (1986): 1–38.
[4] Henry Louis Gates, Jr., "Wole Soyinka: Mythopoesis and the Agon of Democracy," *The Georgia Review* 49, no. 1 (1995): 187–94; Stanley W. Lindberg, "Lasting Laurels, Enduring Words," *The Georgia Review* 49, no. 1 (1995): 6–7.
[5] Richard M. Ready, "Through the Intricacies of 'the Fourth Stage' to an Apprehension of Death and the King's Horseman," *Black American Literature Forum* 22, no. 4 (1988): 711–21.

Soyinka's work as a systematic study of Yoruba aesthetics relating to ritual tragedy while examining Ogun, the Yoruba god, as an essential tragedy.[6]

The concept of tragedy in the Yoruba worldview influences Soyinka's drama, *Death and the King's Horseman*. In the author's note attached to the text, he asks the reader to receive the play as an examination of the "Universe of the Yoruba mind."[7] It illustrates the collision of the alien colonial culture with that of the indigenous people, and it examines their varying conceptions of tragedy, honor, tradition, and history. This must have informed the opinion of Carolyn Jones, who wrote that "Soyinka's rethinking of ritual in his essay 'The Fourth Stage' is significant to his concept of tragedy."[8]

Death and the King's Horseman centers on an impending ritual suicide; the act is viewed as a responsibility for the king's horseman to uphold, and he is expected to feel pride and contentment in a task that is so sacred and important. Soyinka has noted that the tragedy is not in the death of the king's horseman—which the character of Mr. Pilkings as representation of the colonial other, might expect—but the tragedy lies in the horseman's reluctance to commit this sacred act. The drama redefines the ideology behind ritualized killings: if death is an interruption of order, then the ritual suicide restores the balance between humans and cosmic forces. Soyinka's handling of traditional rituals is an effort to preserve indigenous identities and culture within a postcolonial nation that has been influenced by alien values and ideals for many years.

One of Soyinka's foremost essays, "After the Narcissist," was published in 1966 and contains his critical reflection on early post-independence African writings.[9] In his essay "From a Common Back Cloth: A reassessment of the African literary image," Soyinka challenges the Eurocentric criticisms of African literature. He notes that the West only finds African work palatable when the writer is imitating the creative form and style of Europeans, or when the work approaches their idea of normalcy.[10]

Soyinka's essays, "The future of West African Writing," published in 1960, and "The Critic and the Society: Barthes, Leftocracy, and other Mythologies" (1981), proffer theoretical concepts to understand the unsettling issues associated with contemporary postcolonial discourses. Ketu H. Katrak has

---

[6] W. Gao, "'The Fourth Stage' and 'Ritual Tragedy' of Wole Soyinka: Death and the King's Horseman for example," *Foreign Literature Studies* 33, no. 3 (2011): 127–34.
[7] W. Gao, "The Fourth Stage".
[8] Carolyn M. Jones, "Rethinking the Tragic Theory/ Rewriting Tragedy: Wole Soyinka's 'Death and the King's Horseman'," *World Literature Written in English* 35, no. 1 (1996): 78–94.
[9] Biọdun Jeyifo, *Wole Soyinka Politics, Poetics and Postcolonialism* (New York: Cambridge University Press, 2004).
[10] Ketu H. Katrak, "Theory and Social Responsibility: Soyinka's Essays," *Black American Literature Forum* 22, no. 3 (1988): 489–501.

noted that these issues include the hegemony of Western theorizations. Katrak also identifies Soyinka's opinions on social responsibility as represented in the essays, noting that Soyinka considers social responsibility to be more than the sole responsibility of the postcolonial writer; it equally involves critics of postcolonial writings.[11]

In "The Writer in an African State," published in 1997, Soyinka examines the delusions of the African writer and the state's contentions with social responsibility and identity. He asserted that African writers were stuck in the past, unable to consider the realities of the present or grasp its opportunities. Soyinka wrote that:

> with the victory of the colonized over the externalized tyrant, the writer submitted his integrity to the monolithic stresses of the time. For this, any manifesto seemed valid; any –ism could be embraced in clean conscience. With few exceptions, the writer directed his energies to enshrining victory, to reaffirming his identification with the aspirations of nationalism and the stabilization of society.[12]

Soyinka saw the African writer's tendency of producing works that pursued ideas with popular appeal was one that would lead to the death of the creative consciousness. To him, there is a striking absence of correlation between African literary works and the realities that produced them, leading him to declare that "the Africa writer needs an urgent release from the fascination of the past." Soyinka felt that African writers should stop using historical events to romanticize Africa's past, and his claims have fueled some conceptions of African literature as constant reminiscences of idealized pictures from Africa's past, hoping for its nostalgic return while denying obvious postcolonial disillusionment.

Soyinka's works have been wielded as tools for sociological reform and political change, referencing the sociopolitical necessities of the African state. Odun Balogun has noted that Soyinka's works are predominantly satires—frequently, they are less linguistically obscure and their accessibility affords them an attendant popularity. Balogun further identifies the writer's *Requiem for a Futurologist* (1983) and *A Play of Giants* (1984) as Soyinka's most popular satires.[13] Little effort is made to conceal the objects of these satires, which is why Balogun identifies *Before the Blackout* (1965) as a collection of Soyinka's most direct satirical presentations, often inspired by incidents from the continent's history.[14]

---

[11] Katrak, "Theory and Social Responsibility."
[12] Wole Soyinka, "The Writer in an African State," *Transition* 75, no. 76 (1997): 350–6.
[13] Odun Balogun, "Wole Soyinka and the Literary Aesthetic of African Socialism," *Black American Literature Forum*, 22, no. 3 (1988): 503–30.
[14] Balogun, "Wole Soyinka and the Literary Aesthetic."

Soyinka uses his satire to reveal the excesses of African politicians; he explores the disillusionment of the postcolonial nation state as part of his revolutionary commitment. Traditional leaders are also targeted alongside national politicians. Soyinka's more serious satirical representations look at several sociopolitical dynamics. The play *Madmen and Specialists* (1970) looks at the interchange of power between political leaders, referred to as madmen and specialists, using the civil war to inflict dehumanizing psychological effects on Nigerians.[15] Soyinka's play *The Trials of Brother Jero* mocks some of the social realities of Nigerian society. He ridicules the state's religious hypocrisy, revealing its folly and possibly rescuing its unsuspecting victims. Matthew Q. Alidza has interpreted the play as an expression of the writer's skepticism toward the Nigerian elite who would replace the British colonizers.[16]

Most of Soyinka's works are considered sociopolitical satires that both ridicule and critique sociological injustices in African society. The play *The Lion and the Jewel*, published in 1962, addresses the conflict of modernism and indigenous African traditions. His works have become direct tools for social protest; his literature reflects his political concerns along with his literary ambitions. Like most of his works, Soyinka's *The Lion and the Jewel* also incorporates his cultural heritage and understanding of Yoruba aesthetics.

Setting aside the writer's social responsibility of indicting corruption in society, Soyinka's other works, including *A Dance of the Forests*, reveal his understanding of traditional Yoruba mythology. Neloufer de Mel notes that *A Dance of the Forests*, published during the throes of independence, was a disturbing interruption of the season's festivities. She states that:

> The play was a deliberate intervention at the time of Nigerian Independence which went against the grain of celebration to foreshadow and disturbingly evaluate the presence of neo-colonialism in the newly "liberated" African continent.[17]

De Mel also acknowledged the incorporation of traditional folklore, writing that:

> the play was a vehicle through which Soyinka legitimized the Yoruba myth of Ogun for contemporaneous existence (and in doing so engaged in the prime de-colonizing move of rehabilitating indigenous epistemes

---

[15] Balogun, "Wole Soyinka and the Literary Aesthetic."
[16] Matthew Q. Alizda, "A Reading of Soyinka's *The Road* in the Light of Roland Barthes' Theory of the Semic Code and Symbolic Code," *Elixir Literature* 49 (2012): 10124–7.
[17] Neloufer de Mel, "Myth as History: Wole Soyinka's A Dance of the Forests," *Wasafiri* 9, no. 18 (1993): 27–33.

from the negativity assigned them by the colonizer), by dramatizing what he saw as its central dictate.[18]

Soyinka's literary works are dedicated to his social responsibilities: awakening Africa's consciousness to confront neocolonialism and political imperialism, and defending African culture by legitimizing homegrown cultural epistemes that were demonized over time by ignorant colonizers. His literary works continue to reflect political and cultural commitment, supporting Green's opinion that Soyinka's literary works are a blend of past, present, and future.[19] Soyinka's commitment to past and present is displayed in his constant expression and adaptation of traditional folklore, and his political farces often address the future by exposing and correcting society's sociopolitical ills.

In addition to his work as a dramatist and playwright, Soyinka has written and published celebrated prose, including *The Interpreters* in 1965, which was a deviant text published in early postcolonial Nigeria. It explores the disillusionment of postcolonial Nigeria and the deep-rooted cultural hegemony left by the recently departed colonizers. Sola Adeyemi has opined that Soyinka's *The Interpreters* narrates the unfolding confusion of African elites managing religious and political affairs in the newly independent Nigeria.[20] It implies that the country's homegrown political and religious systems, which were abandoned under the colonizers, might have reduced the social intolerance that marked the era. Soyinka was concerned about the new Nigerian state's future, connecting it with the country's colonial past. It reinforces Green's conception of plays that have temporality and the tendency to blend past, present, and future to analyze society.

Soyinka is also a poet. His poem *A Shuttle in the Crypt*, published in 1972, is described by Akingbe as a recounting of the writer's time in prison, which upholds the author's social responsibility to expose society's political shortcomings and other relevant issues. Akingbe describes the text as "a retrospective anthology, uncovering the brutality and high-handedness of the military administration of General Yakubu Gowon in silencing dissent opinions."[21] This pattern is found in all Soyinka's literary works; they tend

---

[18] De Mel, "Myth as History," 27.
[19] Laurence Jabulani Fraser Green, "Assailing 'As': A Study of Wole Soyinka's Drama." Thesis Submitted to the School of Graduate Studies, Department of English, McMaster University, Ontario, Canada, 1989.
[20] Sola Adeyemi, et al., "Interpreting the Interpreters: The Narratives of the Post-colony in Wole Soyinka's *The Interpreters*," Cross Cultures 168 (2013): 29–38; and Bernth Lindfors and Geoffrey V. Davis, *African Literature and Beyond: A Florilegium* (Amsterdam: Rodopi, 2013), 168.
[21] Niyi Akingbe, "Writing Violence: Problematizing Nationhood in Wole Soyinka's *A Shuttle in the Crypt*," *Tydskrif vir Letterkunde* 50, no. 2 (2013): 124–47, 124.

to criticize Africa's political affairs and the actions of influential social and religious groups.

Criticisms and Controversies

Since the inception of Soyinka's literature, and its introduction to Nigeria's literary scene, controversy and criticism have called the writer's African authenticity into question. Willfried F. Feuser has noted that several Nigerian critics have accused Soyinka's literature of promoting British Euro-modernism and serving as a tool for sustained British imperialism.[22] Soyinka's works have been identified as un-African from a formalistic perspective, which has become an established ideological position. Biọdun Jeyifo corroborates this notion, explaining that Soyinka's literature has been accused of expressing "Europhile intellectualism."[23]

Critics who oppose Soyinka's literature claim that its Euro-modernist content and ideology are toxic to the African literary space. Attacks on the form and language of his work are used to level charges of literary obscurantism in his literature, and these claims are given weight by Soyinka's formal presentation of poetry and his adaptation of Western classic drama. Balogun has emphatically stated that most of Soyinka's literature is inaccessible to the average reader, further advancing claims of obscurantism. For Balogun, Soyinka's infusion of linguistic and textual elements promotes an obvious complexity.

In Soyinka's defense, he has asserted that he does not deliberately set out to confuse his readers; he made the claim in an interview with Agetua that was cited by Balogun.[24] Without intending to castigate Soyinka's work, Anyokwu stated the following after attempting to analyze *A Dance of the Forests*:

> Even when we try to piece together the sophisticated "plotless plot" of the play, we still come up against a formidable phalanx of the play's opacity, its linguistic obscurantism which makes the play's overall meaning difficult.[25]

---

[22] Willfried F. Feuser, "Wole Soyinka: The Problem of Authenticity," *Black American Literature Forum*, 22, no. 3 (1988): 555–75.
[23] Biọdun Jeyifo, *Art, Dialogue, and Outrage* (Ibadan: New Horn Press Limited, 1988).
[24] Balogun, "Wole Soyinka and the Literary Aesthetic," 503–530.
[25] Christopher Anyokwu, "Ode to Chaos and Amnesia: Fractured Narrative and Heteroglossia as Postcolonial Othering in Wole Soyinka's 'A Dance of the Forests'," *Nordic Journal of African Studies* 21, no. 1 (2012): 34–48.

Soyinka's critics question his ideologies, values, language, style, and content, along with his literature's relevance for the ordinary African environment. Soyinka has proven that he can simplify his work to make it more accessible, considering that some of his literary comedies, such as *Lion and the Jewel*, are more approachable for the ordinary reader. However, Balogun suggests that Soyinka must believe that such simplification would be equivalent to a depletion of art and an act of condescension toward his readers.[26] This theory supports Soyinka's belief that literature should be an avenue for educating society.[27]

Negative criticism of Soyinka's literature can be traced to the article by Chinweizu, Onwuchekwa Jemie, and Ihechukwu Madubuike, "Towards the Decolonization of African Literature," published in the December 1974 issue of the journal *Okike*, edited by Chinua Achebe.[28] These critics became known as Bolekaja critics, from the label that preceded their criticism of Soyinka's literature—they challenged the form of Euro-modernist literary works emanating from Africa, seeming to place the focus and blame on Soyinka's literature as a facilitator of Western imperialism. From the critics' point of view, Soyinka's Europhilic literature was a setback to the Pan African struggle for a legitimized African literature. They suggested that African writers should incorporate devices from African literary aesthetics and oral tradition in more diverse ways.[29]

Soyinka's refusal to endorse Leopold Sedar Senghor's negritude initiative invited skepticism about the African-ness of his literary products. Negritude, in its most basic sense, asserts blackness and creates awareness of one's African heritage;[30] Soyinka perceived it as an "inherently invalid doctrine."[31] For him, the true mark of African-ness in literature is not the forceful assertion of self, but rather an indifferent awareness and acceptance of self. His opinion stems from his view that early African writings were imitations of European literary traditions, or they were written to meet and exceed European expectations of primitive and exotic literature, not for self-assertion.[32] This opinion must have influenced this critical opinion;

---

[26] Balogun, "Wole Soyinka and the Literary Aesthetic."
[27] Balogun, "Wole Soyinka and the Literary Aesthetic."
[28] Feuser, "Wole Soyinka: The Problem of Authenticity."
[29] Bernth Lindfors, "Beating the White Man at His Own Game: Nigerian Reactions to the 1986 Nobel Prize in Literature," *Black American Literature Forum* 22, no. 3 (1988): 475–88.
[30] Victor C. Ariole, "Negritude and Tigritude: An Analysis of Language Content for Development Purposes," *Contemporary Experiences: Journal of African Humanities* 1, no. 1 (2013).
[31] Maduakor, "Soyinka as a Literary Critic," 3.
[32] Bernth Lindfors and Martin Banham, "The Beginning of a Nigerian Literature in English," *Review of English* 3 (1962).

And if we speak of negritude in a more acceptable broader sense, Chinua Achebe is a more "African" writer than Senghor. The duiker will not paint "duiker" on his beautiful back to proclaim his duikeritude; you'll know him by his elegant leap. The less self-conscious the African is, and the more innately his individual qualities appear in his writing, the more seriously he will be taken as an artist of exciting dignity ... Senghor seems to be so artistically expatriate ... (and he and poets like him) are a definite retrogressive pseudo-romantic influence on a healthy development of West African writing.[33]

Soyinka espouses a universal, holistic approach to literature. Bandyopadhyay has observed that Soyinka reaches out to the rest of the world through his art.[34] With his emphasis on the complementarity of cultures and the synthesis of human knowledge, it is clear why Soyinka would view the negritude concept as a barrier to Africa's creative growth. Povey corroborates Soyinka's opinion, explaining that the concept soon became restrictive, dictating appropriate themes and attitudes for African writers.

Soyinka clearly challenges the restrictions of negritude in his advocacy for the embrace of universal knowledge, incorporating a multiplicity of cultural tensions into his work.[35] Ojaide unintentionally supported the notion of universality, writing:

Soyinka's essays and creative work reveal a voracious reader of Western literatures. Soyinka is an exception to the typical African intellectual whom Chinua Achebe describes as reading a few uninspiring British novels. His passion for drama brought him into contact with Greek and European dramatists. References to Antigone, the Stygian mysteries, and Lethe are part of the classical culture underlying his work. The Greek dramatists (Sophocles, Euripides, and Aeschylus) would particularly have appealed to the Yoruba-raised poet because of their similar attitude toward gods and tragedy. Hence his equating Yoruba gods to Greek gods and his references to Dionysus and Prometheus are not surprising. Here is a ready synthesis of African and European cultures in which the local is universalized and the universal simultaneously localized.[36]

---

[33] Lindfors and Banham, "The Beginning of a Nigerian Literature," 90.
[34] Kajal Bandyopadhyay, "Tension and Synthesis in Wole Soyinka's Plays," University of Dhaka, 2012.
[35] John F. Povey, "Contemporary West African Writing in English (1966)," *World Literature Today* 63, no. 2 (1989): 258–63.
[36] Tanure Ojaide, "Two Worlds: Influences on the Poetry of Wole Soyinka," *Black American Literature Forum* 22, no. 4 (1988): 767–76.

Maduakor has also noted that negritude was restrictive and narcissistic, exercising control over literary expression, and he considers the movement to be a ploy to restrain the natural dispositions of a writer—it confines the creative mind within thematic and ideological impositions that are the bane of literary creativity. Soyinka, cited in Maduakor's work, asserts that the creative mind should not be legislated.[37]

Soyinka's literature is a product of his traditional Yoruba epistemologies and folklore, enriched with mythologies, rituals, and songs. His dramatic presentations involve dance, masquerade, and pantomime. Nkengasong has implied that Soyinka's literary works, such as *A Dance of the Forests*, tend to receive more attention from his African critics than other works that are devoid of these devices.[38] A majority of his works incorporate a wide range of literary art forms from around the world, giving him the appearance of an African literary renegade.

The school of critics led by Chinweizu has accused Soyinka's work of involving "old fashioned, craggy, unmusical language, obscure and inaccessible diction, a plethora of imported imagery and a divorce from African oral poetic tradition."[39] The final charge is unexpected, given the folklore and oral tradition of the Yoruba people that inspired Soyinka's works.

Chinweizu's claims of Eurocentric affiliation are challenged by Makau, who has asserted that Soyinka's use of Yoruba deities provides a traditional background for his works—he exhibits an obsession with the personality of Ogun, who seems to make an appearance in most of his works. Makau has suggested that Soyinka's use of Ogun embodies a universality of Greek gods, appropriating their values to present the Yoruba god.[40] Chinweizu and his associates, referencing Soyinka's *Idanre*, stated the following to support their claims of literary opacity and ambiguity:

> The imagery is imprecise and opaque and lacking in evocative power. All we can decipher is the names of the various deities: Ogun, Ṣango, Ajantala, Esu, Ọrunmila Orinshala. But in this narrative poem it is never clear who does what to whom and with what consequences. It is often difficult to tell who the many pronouns he, she, we, us refer to. We are shut off from the experience on both the intellectual and emotional levels. The language is a formidable barrier, and even after you have hacked

---

[37] Maduakor, "Soyinka as a Literary Critic."
[38] John Nkemngong Nkengasong, "Samuel Beckett, Wole Soyinka, and the Theatre of Desolate Reality," *Journal of African Literature and Culture* 1 (2005).
[39] Maduakor, "Soyinka as a Literary Critic," 32.
[40] Kitata Makau, "Narrative Techniques in Wole Soyinka's *The Interpreters*," Thesis Submitted to University of Nairobi (University of Nairobi Library, 2000).

your way through it, you still cannot understand, what, if anything, is supposed to be going on.[41]

Soyinka has used the term "selective eclecticism" to defend his unique literary approach and to describe his attempt at universalism.[42] He has referred to his critics as "Neo-Tarzanists," viewing their charges of literary obscurantism as an inability to appreciate the beauty of diversity inherent in his literature.[43] Soyinka's literature is an attempt to appreciate the universality of knowledge, and he has stated that his critics fail to:

> appreciate the kind of exploration which I am making into points of departure as well as meeting points between the African and European literary and artistic traditions, quite unabashedly exploiting various complementarities or contradictions in my work.[44]

Soyinka does not deny the influence of European literary traditions; he views them as literary resources worthy of exploration. In his opinion, literature and writing are a "combination of various pressures."[45] Great literature requires the artist to think outside the box of the ordinary, exposing themselves to a combination of external and internal pressures so that they can find the right approach to social responsibility. This explains why Soyinka incorporates Euro-modernist literary traditions in his production of "great literature."

In the article, "Towards the Decolonization of African Literature," many individuals harshly criticized the 1986 decision to award the Nobel Prize to Soyinka. One such critic is Olatunji Dare; Feuser has noted that Dare challenged the choice of Soyinka for the Nobel Prize and stated the following:

> Perhaps this was their way of rewarding Professor Wole Soyinka for putting his great talents so unstintingly to the service of his Euro-modern masters in particular and Western imperialism in general. The Nobel citation, his acceptance speech, and the way he flaunted his half-white head of hair instead of covering it up with a cap are proof enough of his well-known blancophilia.[46]

---

[41] Chinweizu, Onwuchekwa Jemie and Ihechwuku Madubuike, "Towards the Decolonization of African Literature," *Transition* 48 (1972), 42.
[42] Bandyopadhyay, "Tension and Synthesis," 5.
[43] Bandyopadhyay, "Tension and Synthesis," 5.
[44] Bandyopadhyay, "Tension and Synthesis."
[45] Bandyopadhyay, "Tension and Synthesis," 4.
[46] Dare Olatunji, "More Matters Arising," *The Guardian*, 1986, 9.

These remarks are a little too personal to pass for constructive criticism; by creating a tension between a "true" African appearance and a Western-inspired one, the critic has politicized the writer's appearance. Soyinka's work was dismissed as a tool for Western imperialism, and his originality was called into question. It was clearly an attempt to undermine Soyinka's achievements, exhibiting a more general skepticism of Africa's creative talent.

Soyinka has also been criticized by a group among the Ibadan-Ife leftist critics, known as the Marxist school, led by Biọdun Jeyifo and Femi Osofisan. They tend to evaluate works from the Marxist's perspective of historical materialism, a concept that views the growth and development of human society as the interplay of material forces. Karl Marx rejected the idea of intangible factors, such as supernatural forces, playing decisive roles in the course of human history and development.[47] Nigerian adherents of the Marxist school of thought expect works of art to represent tangible processes of social development at play in the society at the time of their production.[48]

Nigerian critics from the Marxist school hold that any work existing independently of historical materialism's laws is not realistic—such art is likely guilty of being falsified, romanticized, mystified, and mythicized. This is relevant because, according to Obi, Soyinka's view of history and art is rooted in Yoruba mythology.[49] Soyinka's use of myth in representing human experiences has made him an easy target for the Nigerian Marxist critics. In the opinion of the Marxists, as recorded by Maduakor, "Every utterance of the Nigerian Marxists echoes the view that Soyinka's perception of history is static, mythic, and therefore unrealistic."[50]

Balogun has observed that despite Soyinka's commitment to Nigeria's sociopolitical development, and his revolutionary approach to society, Marxist critics are quick to criticize his literature. Balogun also notes that some of their accusations recount a long line of sins in Soyinka's wake:

> His is a feudalist mentality upholding a hegemonic, reactionary view of African history; in him we have a romantic idealist who promotes a reactionary world view with metaphysical mystification and befogging mythology; he is a bourgeois intellectual whose social analysis is uninformed by scientific materialist dialectics; he is a cynic peddling a pessimistic philosophy of human history, a chronic individualist that

---

[47] Sreekumar Nellickappilly, "Aspects of Western Philosophy," National Programme on Technology Enhanced Learning (NPTEL), 2014.
[48] Maduakor, "Soyinka as a Literary Critic."
[49] Joseph E. Obi, "Art, Ideology, and the Militarized African Postcolony: A Sociological Reading of Wole Soyinka's Season of Anomy," *Neohelicon* 25, no. 2 (1998): 403–15.
[50] Maduakor, "Soyinka as a Literary Critic."

sees periodic salvation in man's history of cyclic futility only in terms of the heroic acts of lonely messianic individuals; he is a socially irrelevant writer who alienates his would-be audience by consciously cultivating linguistic obscurantism.[51]

Another one of these critics is the playwright Femi Osofisan, who also ridicules Soyinka's use of mysticism and myth as an act of indifference to the "logic of historical contradictions in the dialectics of flux."[52] Additional criticism has been made by Omafume Onoge, G. G. Darah, and Jeyifo—in an analysis of *Death and the King's Horseman*, Jeyifo applies the theory of historical materialism to declare that the play is unable to accurately depict the differences between conflicting groups and social classes in the indigenous society. To Jeyifo, this is a misrepresentation and misinterpretation of indigenous society, but he does not conclude that Soyinka is completely ignorant of the materialist processes of history. Jeyifo ultimately finds that Soyinka's mystification of the natural conceals class struggles.[53] It is safe to say that dogmatic Marxists neither acknowledge nor recommend myth-inspired and -informed literature.

Marxist aversion to Soyinka's work is reciprocated by Soyinka himself. He has declared that "since I'm not a Marxist, I do not spout Marxist rhetoric."[54] Balogun notes that in a foreword to the play *Opera Wonyosi* (1977) Soyinka divides his leftist critics into two distinct groups: the "the mouthers and opportunists" and "the genuine but theoretically obsessed."[55] Balogun has suggested that Soyinka does not consider the former group to be worthy of note. Soyinka exhaustively recounted the weaknesses of the latter group in an inaugural lecture titled "The Critic and Society: Barthes, leftocracy and other mythologies" at the University of Ife in 1982.[56] In his opinion, the second group of critics was constrained by the ideology of Marxism, a school of thought that can lead to literary unproductivity—the inability to recognize the socialist function of a literary work, or its potential to lead a revolution, regardless of its mythical inspiration.

In a later analysis of Soyinka's works, Jeyifo relaxes his antagonism to state the following:

Soyinka is the greatest mythopoeist in contemporary African literature and as such the scale of values and referents within which his works are

---

[51] Balogun, "Wole Soyinka and the Literary Aesthetic," 503–30.
[52] Maduakor, "Soyinka as a Literary Critic," 30.
[53] Maduakor, "Soyinka as a Literary Critic."
[54] Wole Soyinka, *Art, Dialogue, and Outrage: Essays on Literature and Culture* (Ibadan: New Horn Press Publishers, 1988), 114.
[55] Balogun, "Wole Soyinka and the Literary Aesthetic."
[56] Balogun, "Wole Soyinka and the Literary Aesthetic."

conceived embrace the cosmic framework of man's terrestrial existence ... Soyinka's mythopoeisis has a personal, idiosyncratic dimension as well as a matrixed, cultural source.[57]

Soyinka has been subjected to critical appraisal that implies a distinction and defiance to conformity in his work. The Nobel Prize that he received consolidates and reaffirms his exceptional appropriation of African mythology, along with his distinct intellectualism.

Ideology and Impact on Soyinka's Literature

Ideology can be viewed as a body of principles, belief systems, and philosophies that belong to an individual or group. Ideology is usually expressed through action, and some of those actions are represented in the work of the group or people who adhere to it. The African writer is propelled by an ideology, or series of ideologies, that are reflected in art, framing their opinions and coloring the lens of their creative work. Close reading of a literary creation will reveal the writer's opinions and beliefs on sociological, psychological, and political issues.

Soyinka's literature and theater are impacted by individual ideologies. One of his deepest convictions is the efficacy and relevance of socialism for a nation's growth and development. He has opined that socialism is the most "human form of government for a country like Nigeria."[58] Victor Banjo and Alele, cited in Balogun, note that a conversation with Soyinka revealed his view that socialism was "the only chance for Nigeria."[59] The revolutionary undertone of the writer's works is usually grounded in his convictions of humanist socialism.

Socialism, in the basic sense, refers to an economic or political system emphasizing the relationship between the state, the individual, and society. It promotes social equality, the distribution of resources and income—based on contributions to and ownership of capital—and a collective form of decision making. Socialists view the individual not as an autonomous being, but rather as one who is defined in relation to others.[60]

Soyinka was not enthusiastic about the arrival of Nigeria's independence. His work *A Dance of the Forests*, which was published to celebrate the attainment of independence, was more of a prediction, warning of the

---

[57] Lindfors, "Beating the White Man at His Own Game."
[58] Katrak, "Theory and Social Responsibility," 9.
[59] Balogun, "Wole Soyinka and the Literary Aesthetic," 507.
[60] George Esenwein, "Socialism," *New Dictionary of the History of Ideas* (New York: Charles Scribner's Sons, 2005): 2227–35.

possible outcomes that could befall the nation-state if leaders did not make conscious efforts to renounce ethnic histories of corruption, dishonesty, and exploitation. Soyinka saw wars, hardship, and disorder as the likely outcome if these negative ethnic patterns continued. These predictions, included in many of his works, drew controversy that saw him accused of espousing philosophical pessimism. Soyinka countered these charges by stating that his work was only a representation of objective reality.

Soyinka was imprisoned for two years due to his active participation and involvement in political issues facing the country. His incarceration pushed his ideological stance away from nationalism toward African socialism. Balogun has observed that most of Soyinka's literature reasserts the author's socialist commitment by unambiguously infusing a socialist orientation and revolutionary stance for Africa. Balogun has also noted that Soyinka cannot be called a socialist writer, but instead seems more vested in nationalist writings where Soyinka advocates the "bourgeois philosophy of pure art."[61] By the mid-1960s and the dawn of postcolonial disillusionment, exasperated by the country's flawed political leadership, Soyinka embraced socialist ideals; his literary works soon began to reflect them.

"The writer in an African State" is considered to be the work marking Soyinka's dramatic shift from his "bourgeois philosophy of pure art" to focus more on "Afrocentric aesthetics of literature."[62] Balogun notes that *The Man Died* fully celebrates Soyinka's socialist ideologies and his socialist aspirations for the country. Soyinka uses the work to illustrate the experiences of his imprisonment and arrest, including situational reports that detail the factors culminating in the civil war. In his autobiography, Soyinka suggests a socialist system for Nigeria's redemption.[63]

Balogun has examined Soyinka's mythopoeic imagination as part of the ideological influences contributing to Soyinka's literature.[64] Balogun finds the works to be inspired by Yoruba cultural mythology, which is a resistance to the assimilation and acculturation driven by colonialism; works centered on Soyinka's mythopoeic imagination have been recognized by critics as ones that have been designed to retrieve the culture and race of the African people. Soyinka's infusion of myth and ritual is a unique way of blending African aesthetics and ideology—Balogun has stated:

> Soyinka, like other African writers, has been dedicated to a positive affirmation of African culture. In the face of the denial of validity to African culture by white supremacists, the affirmation of authenticity is

---

[61] Balogun, "Wole Soyinka and the Literary Aesthetic," 506.
[62] Balogun, "Wole Soyinka and the Literary Aesthetic," 507.
[63] Balogun, "Wole Soyinka and the Literary Aesthetic."
[64] Balogun, "Wole Soyinka and the Literary Aesthetic."

positive, revolutionary. What is even more significant is the way Soyinka goes about the task of validating African culture.[65]

Several critics have identified similarities between Soyinka's attempt to recover race through myth and ritual and the negritude ideology that he criticized. Soyinka's infusions of ritual and myth, as well as Senghor's negritude, are attempts to recover Africa's essence and aesthetics after colonialism and slavery's deep-rooted traumas. Soyinka's aversion to negritude is not tied to the ideology's objective, but to the approach employed by the Negritudists. Therefore, to clarify the differences in their various approaches, Balogun wrote:

> The negritude-inspired parade of emotionality and closeness to nature whose peak was the emergence of cultural troupes that thrilled world audiences with bare-breasted virgins and erotic dances has since been recognized as an historical error. Soyinka's approach is to delve into culture, reexamine it, identify its positive essence, and appropriate it into African literature just as Western literature has been enriched by Greek, Latin, and Judaeo-Christian cultures.[66]

Soyinka's cultural mythologies and African aesthetics impact and frame his literary works, as represented in *A Dance of the Forests*, while Soyinka's endorsement of socialist ideology influences his revolutionary works.

The Political Engagements of Soyinka's Literature

Nigeria's turbulent political history shows why Soyinka, a writer who believes in the social responsibility of literature, has written and published literary works that challenge the political ideologies and practices of the postcolonial African state. It reaffirms the idea of a strong nexus existing between art and politics in society. In an interview with John Agetua, cited in Jeyifo's *Wole Soyinka: Politics, Poetics, and Postcolonialism*, Soyinka stated:

> A book if necessary should be a hammer, a hand grenade which you detonate under a stagnant way of looking at the world ... we haven't begun actually using words to punch holes inside people ... but let's do

---

[65] Balogun, "Wole Soyinka and the Literary Aesthetic," 518.
[66] Balogun, "Wole Soyinka and the Literary Aesthetic," 518.

our best to use words and style, when we have the opportunities, to arrest the ears of normally complacent people, we must make sure we explode something inside them which is parallel of the sordidness which they ignore outside.[67]

Soyinka is confident that literature can address society's important issues, engaging the nation politically and addressing those who would steer the ship of state. Maduakor has noted that after the publication of the essay "The Writer in a Modern African State," Soyinka's literary works, especially the plays, took on political tones. Although it uses symbols and mystical references, *A Dance of the Forests* explores corruption in Africa's past while indicting the visionless political space of postcolonial Nigeria. The characters of Adenibi, the court historian, Mulieru, and Mata Karibu depict high levels of corruption and a disregard for the interests of others.[68] Maduakor has observed that the play explores the tragic future of newly independent Africa, and Jeyifo has stated that the play was:

> written and produced as part of the Nigerian independence celebration in 1960, appropriate to the historic task of forging a nation out of diverse people and communities that the celebrations symbolically entailed, the central action of the play revolves around a gathering of tribes at which the festivities intended to celebrate the glorious past and the hopeful future of the assembled tribe turns into an unanticipated encounter with evils in past and present life of the community. [69]

Soyinka begs all of Africa to avoid repeating its past mistakes by presenting his fears for Africa's future. The political engagements of his work are not restricted to the Nigerian state; they encompass all of Africa.

Kongi's Harvest explores political power in contemporary Nigeria, covertly implying that the nation's politics are built on the vestiges of tradition. Soyinka's work represents the political realities of Africa; as stated by Maduakor, the play "marks the beginning of open political commentary in Soyinka's dramatic career."[70] Soyinka's works, such as *Madmen and Specialists*, *A Play of Giants*, *A Shuttle in the Crypt*, *Season of Anomy*, and *Opera Wonyosi*, have harbored strong political opinions.[71] They are proof of his commitment to alleviating social injustices on the African continent.

---

[67] Biọdun Jeyifo, *Wole Soyinka Politics*, 89.
[68] Maduakor, "The Political Content of Wole Soyinka's Plays," *Journal of Commonwealth Literature* 28, no. 1 (1993): 82–96.
[69] Jeyifo, *Wole Soyinka Politics*, 120
[70] Maduakor, "The Political Content of Wole Soyinka's Plays."
[71] Maduakor, "The Political Content of Wole Soyinka's Plays."

Maduakor observes that *Madmen and Specialists* explores a new aspect of the political system: the military.[72] In Nigeria and other parts of Africa, the corruption characterizing the "democratic" system fueled social and political instability that led to the proliferation of military regimes along with political brutality and social anarchy.

Kongi's Harvest can be considered a reflection of the contemporary military government's activities and brutality.[73] The discussion of military dictatorship continues in works such as *Jero's Metamorphosis*, in which the character of Jero returns to wear a military uniform and receive many accolades; he is also seen giving out military ranks arbitrarily. The play reflects the writer's opinion of how easily military ranks can be gained in a Nigerian context. Soyinka also uses the character of Jero to condemn the Nigerian military's moral fiber.

Opera Wonyosi continues the writer's commitment to examining the military government. The characters of Inspector Brown, Colonel Moses, Captain Macheath, and Emperor Boky represent the army; as in *Jero's Metamorphosis*, the military's moral character is examined using the character of Macheath, who becomes a bandit after retiring from the army. While others are in active service, Macheath begins a life of crime and violence and builds strong ties with people in the upper echelons of power. Macheath's connections allow him to avoid a death sentence while the other officers, who are equally corrupt, also avoid penalties by remaining in service.[74] The events imply that the uniform disguises the military's true character. Maduakor has noted that Soyinka makes connections between the play and Nigeria's reality:

> Soyinka demonstrates in this bitter satire that, whether in the barracks or on the highways, crime was a lucrative profession in the oil boom Nigeria of the 1970s. Each of Macheath's colleagues inspector Brown, Col. Moses, Emperor Boky, and their civilian accomplice Chief Anikura is an enemy of the people because each is equally guilty of every crime that Macheath has been charged with.[75]

King Baabu (2002) and *A Play of Giants* (1984) also consider the actions of military leaders in African regimes. *King Baabu* examines the military regime of the Nigerian state, and *A Play of Giants* addresses the entire African

---

[72] Maduakor, "The Political Content of Wole Soyinka's Plays."
[73] Kayode Afolayan, "Wole Soyinka's A Play of Giants and King Baabu: The Crises between Ideology and (Social) Vision," *Tydskrif Vir Letterkunde* 54, no. 1 (2017): 158–69.
[74] Afolayan, "Wole Soyinka's A Play of Giants."
[75] Maduakor, "The Political Content of Wole Soyinka's Plays."

continent. Soyinka connects real-life situations with the characters in his plays. In *A Play of Giants*, he uses four characters to satirize the condition of tyranny in the continent. Field Marshal Kamini of Bugara represents Field Marshal El Hadji and Dr. Idi Amin of Uganda, and Benefacio Gunema, Emperor Kasco, and General Barra Toboum represent Macias Nguema of Equatorial Guinea, Jean-Baptiste Bokassa of the Central African Republic, and Mobutu Sese Seko of Congo, respectively.[76] Through the play, Soyinka recognizes government injustices against artists around the world—Byron Kadawa, who was the leader of the Uganda National Troupe at the Festival of Black and African Arts in 1977, was murdered by the government of Idi Amin.[77]

King Baabu uses four characters to examine the nature of corruption in the Nigerian state, represented by the fictive nation of Gautu. The following generals represent Nigerian military leaders: Generals Uzi, Potipoo, Rajinda, and Basha Bash represent Generals Muhammadu Buhari, Sani Abacha, Abdusalam Abubakar, and Ibrahim Babangida, respectively.[78] The play reflects Nigeria's tumultuous atmosphere on June 12, 1993, when the presidential election was annulled after it was believed to have been in favor of Alhaji Moshood Abiọla. After the annulment, and after Soyinka's criticism of the government's decision, Soyinka was accused of orchestrating bombings and charged with treason.[79] The writer's description of Abacha paints a horrifying picture of power's intoxication and the pervasive incivility of a military regime.

Afolayan has observed that in both plays, the characters of Kamini and Basha shed light on military expressions of profanity and the talkative nature of the military despite their poor grasp of language and their incompetence in economic and political affairs.[80] In these plays and other works, it is apparent that Soyinka's work mirrors the political realities of the African government while serving as a mediator between the government and the people.

Conclusion

This chapter has explored the relationship between Soyinka's literature and African society, examining how it reflects several ideological and sociopolitical factors along with their controversies. The literature

---

[76] Afolayan, "Wole Soyinka's A Play of Giants."
[77] Afolayan, "Wole Soyinka's A Play of Giants."
[78] Afolayan, "Wole Soyinka's A Play of Giants."
[79] Afolayan, "Wole Soyinka's A Play of Giants."
[80] Afolayan, "Wole Soyinka's A Play of Giants."

was created in a continent fraught with the complexities of colonial imposition and postcolonial disillusionment; an examination of the political engagements of Soyinka's works can reveal socialist aspirations and ideologies along with a revolutionary commitment to the continent's political affairs.

PART 4

Legacies and Conclusion

11

Soyinka's Contribution to Literature

> *Soyinka wrote prodigiously in all literary forms and genres. ... and more portentously, Soyinka occupies his distinct place within the "quartet"* [Achebe, Soyinka, Okigbo, and J.P. Clark] *on account of his propensity for taking very daring* **artistic** *and* **political** [emphasis original] *risks in furtherance of his deepest political and ethical convictions, risks which often entailed considerable peril to himself and also profoundly challenged, but at the same time complexly re-inscribed the determinate elitism of his generation of writers. The articulation between the political and artistic risks is one of the most fascinating and complex aspects of Soyinka's career.*
>
> BIODUN JEYIFO[1]

Introduction

Wole Soyinka's stature as a writer of international repute is already confirmed; this luxury permits his profile to serve and remain a source of inspiration across the board: across generations, nations, and disciplines or other socially defined categories. That—at least in contemporary times or since the debate about his death and its overreach—the author, the corporeal space he inhabits, and his texts are seen and projected as infinitely

---

[1] Biọdun Jeyifo, *Wole Soyinka: Politics, Poetics, and Postcolonialism* (Cambridge: Cambridge University Press, 2004), 5.

reactive to one another in a tripartite transaction where the one influences the others in extensive measures, it has become increasingly commonplace to see the author in his work and the work in its author, ditto his influences, both as a creator and the created. While not a provincial requirement, this is especially characteristic of Third World writers burdened with the yoke of representation, contesting coloniality and engaging the shifting states of postcoloniality regardless of aesthetic commitments or preferences.

The importance of the above is that aesthetic control on the part of writers' manifest ideological commitment. To translate this in simple terms: there exists a systematic process of inclusivity between aesthetic ideology and notional ideology, with the one simply aiding the other in its struggle. This position contradicts accusations levelled against aesthetically driven works of many African writers, especially like Soyinka and those of his generation accused of being Euro-assimilationist. Accusations that made serious and seemingly tidy claims that largely failed to account for the complex relationship between Western-trained African intellectuals and African traditional symbols; that failed to accommodate the reality of these aesthetics as tools of analysis acquired during the process of self-exiling, and with which the process of complete return home is initiated and negotiated. These tools might exist outside African culture, just as averred by Thomas Knipp,[2] but they are channels paving the way for the returned African to reconnect with a past almost made a relic by the condition of coloniality, to contest this condition and its after-effects in the collective psyche, and mount a process of synthesizing the old and the modern Africa, and Africa and the world, especially in ways where none is foreground or background but equally constitutive of the final product of representation.

This crucial oversight by critics that failed to find the Western-trained African intellectual located both within and outside the African tradition enough to see it from within and without, so that (particularly in the case of Soyinka) they are able to criticize undue defensive positions taken in contest of coloniality or in celebration of Africanity, made it such that the benefits of these tools and the consciousness behind them were missed entirely or mislabelled. On the one hand, they were labelled Euro-assimilationist; on the other, they are instigators of the literature of vision, the type of literature which Soyinka defines as "a creative concern which conceptualizes or extends actuality behind the purely narrative, making it reveal realities beyond the immediately attainable, a concern which upsets orthodox acceptances in an effort to free society of historical or other superstitions."[3] This type of literature manifests in various unorthodox ways, and it is this defiance of

---

[2] Thomas R. Knipp, "Irony, Tragedy, and Myth: The Poetry of Wole Soyinka," *World Literature Written in English* 2, no. 1 (1982): 5–26.

[3] Wole Soyinka, *Myth, Literature, and the African World* (Cambridge: Cambridge University, 1966), 66.

routine that rubs off wrongly on critics, provoking contexts of criticisms and criticisms of contexts. Both signify the role of contexts and contests in the making of a writer and possible ways of influence. Wole Soyinka is made by and has made contexts and contests: his African roots have suggested possible ways to chart his creative destination, and by idiosyncratically taking the unusual road—a condition with dual implications—amassing a number of detractors and criticisms, and by that automatically generating several levels of contestations. He has not only cleared a new path in a familiar precinct, but has made way for others who share, at the very least, a similar conviction.

Soyinka is that African writer suggesting ways of return even to the alienated writer, regardless of degrees of alienation or those who look within from without, those educated in the West, employing aspects of Western logic, or writing with a hybridized consciousness, without losing fidelity to the motherland, which remains the dominant subject of their creative endeavors. For the continental writer, through and through, Soyinka is suggesting new ways through which the old can be continually revisited and how each revisitation can be made anew. Soyinka's concern is with the endless levels of innovation at all possible stages of creative imagination to the moment the collective consciousness is influenced to create the literature of vision. Ultimately, Soyinka's influences are not isolated or readily identifiable the way stars can be identified against the blank curtain of a dark sky; his influences are interwoven, only to be read and identified in a cluster of tightly woven details, each of which speaks for itself and then for the others. To attempt to put it simply, for the matter itself readily defies any such attempt, Soyinka's influences on the trade through which he has made his name are implicated in the contexts that he has brought to light and the ways he has gone about doing so, and the contestations of those ways and the contexts of those contestations. For this obvious complex reason, to begin an engagement with Soyinka and his composite and multimodal manner of influences, perhaps, requires setting him within a particular frame, one made from the culture from which he has harvested a lot of symbols, and one which would throw up the necessary image and details essential to the subject of this chapter. To do this, we start with the image of Soyinka as a source whose Yoruba equivalent is *orisun*.

"Orisun," Soyinkan Imperative, and Visionary Reconstruction

In relation to sources and origins, whose Yoruba lexical equivalent is "orisun," there is a fitting idiomatic reference deployed by the Yoruba, in correct context of course, that serves in the capacity of an appropriate reminder of the essentialism of a source or one's source. The reference works in several fashions, applying itself as a cautionary reminder, a subtle lecture about humble beginnings, or a prudent take on the importance of appreciating one's heritage, history, or resource place. But the general fundamental message is the essentialism of a source of a thing; this essentialism is made more principal by the enduring and abiding force for which a source is recognized and reverenced, eliciting the generic reference "orisun ti ko gbọdọ gbẹ" (lit., the source that must not dry). Two crucial things are implicated in that idiom that are vital to this approach to Soyinka: one is a general recognition of the enduring and generative energies of the source by the Yoruba, which make a source identifiable as a source; the other is the part and paths humans must take to ensure a source remains a source.

Like the proverbial orisun that never dries, Nigeria is never devoid of formidable energies whose weight and import echo across time and space, meaning Nigeria is a source, providing necessary impetus for creative and ideological transitions. The connection between national events and literature is well defined in the domain of sociology, history, and literature, and lends credence to the position of society and its events defining the form and focus of both great and poor literature. These energies, in the typical nature of the orisun as a center of generative force, are forever in transit, in a state of perpetuity, making their marks and marking their presence in and through time, even when their form demands some sort of grounding. Their origin requires a point of inception, and they must be locatable temporally and in space. However, because they are constituted of this orisun-type of generative force, one regenerative and, therefore, perpetual, they are motile: they mark their (re)generative peculiarities by leaving traces of their existence and by reconstituting themselves in ways evocative of a traceable trajectory. For clarity's sake, an example is fitting at this point: it is commonplace for the Yoruba, and perhaps many of the world's cultures, to trace the origin of any corporeal thing by consciously outlining a map of growth of the thing itself (whatever technology they use in doing so notwithstanding). This means the corporeal thing itself is a source unto itself and its own source. This thought finds some degree of resonance within Western philosophy too. Western theoreticians, proponents of Transformational-generative Grammar or post-structuralists in particular, might explain this through the Trace concept, a philosophy that accounts for the presence of the essence (that is, history of being and transition) of a thing in another. Therefore, attempts at investigating a thing can lead to the discovery of a network of events outlining the history of its past life, a history that justifies its current standing and presence in the way an explorer relates to a map. In Nigerian history since the Amalgamation by Frederick Lugard in 1914, there have been energies—and we use this in the sense in which humans are (frames of) energies, just as science, mythology, biology, theories and other forms of knowledge have repeatedly told us—that have acted in the capacities of an "orisun," producing knowledge and influencing bodies of knowledge.

These humans are, in a non-far-fetched way, what could be called living synoptic mirrors because they evocatively (even if briefly) remind us of the nexus between the Yoruba view of what makes a source and these energies spoken thereof. Wole Soyinka belongs, without any iota of doubt, to this category: 31 plays, 3 novels, 8 poetry collections, 3 short stories, 5 memoirs, and 13 notable essays, among many other creative works that simply and vehemently defy neat categories, are enough to set one apart through the ages. What any portraiture of Wole Soyinka through his body of works immediately and conclusively instructs is that he towers above and is larger than any holistic attempt at textual profiling.

Is Wole Soyinka some sort of orisun or just the product of one? This question can only be adequately attempted (with the mission of arriving at a logical conclusion) by engaging the Soyinka oeuvre. One would then hope to make connections, outline networks, and draw maps that must suggest the trans-generational, trans-national, trans-temporal, and enduring signatures or influences of Soyinka. Appreciating or simply detecting these influences must take into consideration expressions that betray earlier sources of inspiration shaped creatively to bear current contextual implications. Accordingly, as a product of a source, Soyinka must have retraced his steps to retrieve the past and its legacies to creatively locate it in the present without accentuating or causing the sort of temporal friction that hints at chronological incompatibility. As a source himself, he must have been responsible for the germination and production of certain currents that have shaped contemporary literature as we have it.

The act of cultural relocation or retrieval is well associated with Soyinka. Many scholars have described the presence of a self-conscious concern with myth in Soyinka's body of work.[4] Knipp for instance identifies a level of reciprocity between his reliance on myth and his poetry. But it is not only to poetry that Soyinka has devoted his fascination with myth and ritual for practical and instructive literary purpose—instructive because the rationale behind Soyinka's literary output is a certain kind of social commitment. His drama and satires, even his essays, are testifiers to this rich and healthy engagement. In rendering visible the inner workings of Soyinka's philosophy of literature in drama, Biọdun Jeyifo presents ritual as "persuasively invoked

---

[4] Knipp, "Irony, Tragedy, and Myth." See also, Biọdun Jeyifo's extensive take on this aspect on Soyinka in "Ritual, Anti-Ritual, and the Festival Complex in Soyinka's Dramatic Parables," in his *Wole Soyinka: Politics, Poetics, and Postcolonialism* (Cambridge: Cambridge University Press, 2003); see also Frances Harding, "Soyinka and Power: Language and Imagery in Madmen and Specialists," *African Languages and Cultures* 4, no. 1 (1991): 87–98.

as a revitalizing and revolutionizing source for contemporary drama and theatre,"[5] laying emphasis on Soyinka's use of ritual to push revolution and the discourse or vision of revolution. In his essays and books, such as *Myth, Literature and the African World* or "Drama and the Idioms of Liberation," Soyinka aptly presents ritual as liberating. How is ritual liberating? It is all contained in the vision of Soyinka. This vision has led to labels such as Soyinka's theater being called "The theatre of Ritual Vision."[6] This vision, which is an idiosyncratic reconstruction of available material for social conditioning, is well expressed in his plays, an example of which is *Madmen and Specialist*, one of the plays written after his incarceration. Written for the stage, he consciously incorporated an open confrontational relationship between the audience and the actors in a way that mimicked the Yoruba Egungun ritual performances, a dramatic form where there are no boundaries between performers who embody the spirit of ancestors and the audience who welcome and celebrate these ancestral spirits. Here, Soyinka's now popular concept of the Fourth Stage thrives, striving for a social reorientation of the audience through the incorporation of myth and ritual for sensitization and awareness.

Because the play itself is anchored on disruption and chaos, Soyinka effectively anticipated the involvement of the audience in the reality of the play so as to effectuate the transition from fictional world to reality, where the audience can be stoked to proper responses. The disruption in the play in turn moves from the reality of the play into that of the audience, collapsing both fictional visions with those of reality. This is exactly what Soyinka's Fourth Stage embodies, the stage of liminality, where the human soul is stressed and where all forces of consciousness, living, dead, ancestral, and unborn are thrown. Harding, writing on the play, talks about the absence of resolution at the end and of relief, which heightens the involvement of the audience.[7] The absence of fixed demarcations between audience and performers in terms of the reality, performance, and dialogue falls in line with the Egungun performances in which any type of resolution achieved at the end is collective, leading to a collapse between the worlds of the imaginative, fictive, spiritualized/mythic, and corporeal, a condition which is often discomforting to performer-spectators and a condition which plays to the strength of Soyinka's vision.

The collapse of the divide as it occurs in the traditional dramatic forms of the Egungun ritual creates a sense of immediacy, which is what Soyinka aimed for, and the implicit references to the setting of the Egungun ritual, in terms of acrobatics, rendering of songs, staccato dialogues and words, endless

---

[5] Jeyifo, "Ritual, Anti-Ritual," 125.
[6] Jeyifo, "Ritual, Anti-Ritual," 125.
[7] Harding, "Soyinka and Power."

song and dance, all indicate Soyinka's literary vision—the type that breaks boundaries, revises or creatively deploys old forms, and sits at the center of his mythopoeic approach. According to Harding, such deployments to aid the enactment of the theme of abuse of power and unchecked authority, especially in ways that are more dance and kinetic than words and verbal form, reveal Soyinka's continued interest and engagement with the world mythopoeically. Ritual symbols, mythopoeic engagement with the world and the use of the masquerade, this time explicitly, can be found in Soyinka's other works like *The Road* and *Death and the King's Horseman*. Soyinka's use of ritual motifs and symbols for historicizing and historical purposes in his plays is experimental, esoteric, and referential to the cultural dynamics of the Yoruba and African mystical life. For this reason, Soyinka has often been called a mythopoeic creator.[8]

His relationship with myth is often dual: on one end, he deploys existing myth in a creative fashion to address a contemporary issue; on the other, he works contemporary experiences into patterns. These patterns often are reinforced by his use of myth-derived images.[9] In the end, he becomes employer and creator of myth, attracting, subsequently, tags of being mythic and mythopoeic. Herein, thus, lies the first indicator of Soyinka as source and product. This is in particular true for two reasons: Soyinka's self-declared instrumental relationship with myth is as vocal as his social commitment, as seen in the succeeding quote: "one of the social functions of literature: the visionary reconstruction of the past for the purposes of a social direction."[10] Soyinka's comment here is as revealing as it is instructive: it is an attempt to redirect current literary projection and lay sustainable patterns for future ones. Soyinka's firm belief in the social commitment of African writers is well established through his works and his essayistic (essay-lectures inclusive) pedagogies.

His ambitious experiment with literature, specifically his drama, is almost of an imperative kind, driven by a pedagogic approach that is at once experimental, idiosyncratic, revisionist, revolutionary, and almost prescriptive. A cautious reading of his works, principally *Death and the King's Horseman*, *Season of Anomy*, *The Bacchae of Euripides*, *A Play of Giants*, and *The Road*, reveals a responsive and responding Soyinka— to historical events, socioeconomic conditions, and collective crisis of consciousness and material reality. *Madmen and Specialists*, written and staged at the Commonwealth Arts Festival after his imprisonment during the Civil War, responds emphatically to the war, as seen in the estranged

---

[8] Harding, "Soyinka and Power." See also, Mary T. David, "The Theme of Regeneration in Selected Works of Wole Soyinka," *Black American Literary Forum* 22, no. 4 (1988): 645–61.
[9] Knipp, "Irony, Tragedy, and Myth."
[10] Wole Soyinka, *Myth, Literature*, ix.

filial relationship between a father and son caused by psychological war wounds. *Death and the King's Horseman* follows suit, capitalizing on and revolutionizing the culturally devastating consequences of the Western/colonialist-African contact on African cultures during colonialism for the purpose of social reorientation; it reenacts a revised historical event. Many of such instances, even his prison poetry and notes—culminating in the memoir *The Man Died*—are creative responses to human experience and conditions. It is as if Soyinka was both a diagnostician and a medium—a good example being his Independence play, *A Dance of the Forest*, which harnessed rich ritual symbols of reincarnation and regeneration to commemorate the Independence as well as warn the post-Independence body politic of the dangers of failed leadership.

Of course African writers and poets of the first generation had laid groundwork for this sort of literary direction, covertly prescribing pathways to take through various ideologically-driven works, works espousing Negritudian and overtly Pan-African sentiments, ways Africans could "be" against the colonial-white gaze—ways Africans took as the defensive route. The first generation of writers and poets merely sought to celebrate and assert their preferences for African culture, without much criticism. To correct stereotypical images and counter assumptions about Africa through effusive vocalizations and praise was a major strategy of this generation. Of course, also owing to their reliance on cultural symbols of Africa to pursue and effect positive views of Africa and its history, these ones could be referred to in some sense as mythopoeic. They cultivated and wove these myths into their art.

The "Soyinkan imperative" that sets him apart enough to be considered a chief influence in the literature of the continent resides in the complex strategies with which his mission as a revolutionary reconstructivist is enacted in his works without falling into the fault for which he had criticized negritude and those of his generation who took up the nationalist mantle. His criticism of negritude in his essay "And After the Narcissist" perhaps is a sufficient illumination of the Soyinkan way of social analysis in literature for collective redirection. Soyinka did not merely use or appropriate these myths and ritual symbols in his works, he participated in them by revising them on idiosyncratic terms, critically analyzing them and their philosophies or assumptions to cause a major shift in focus and in use. In *A Dance of the Forest* is contained Soyinka's metaphorical criticism of the historical and cultural past of Africa, toward sensitizing the present, especially the independent nation of the need to be on guard and to abstain from uncritical appreciation of African past—which was one of his pet peeves against the Negritude movement. Soyinka's mythopoeic relationship with the ritual past here is twofold: critical and revisionist. Deployment of ritual motifs, such as the dance of welcome for the spirits and the self-discovery for the mortals to relive crimes, abound in the play and are recreated in ways that have resonant literal significances so that they too hold messages that would challenge the fabric of social orientation and material reality.

Knowing Soyinka to be fond of such reconstruction, it is no surprise he would criticize negritude and then move on to complexly but effectively show how to engage with the past. By using the metaphoric duiker or its skeleton to symbolize effortless and genuine greatness, and that of the tiger—a notion often mistakenly interpreted as the creation of a counter-ideology to negritude in the form of tigritude—Soyinka asserts his commitment to a symbolic way of representation: one that is subtle but potent, complex in its significations but that never misses its mark and is fully in tune with its purpose, that is, one which is not a foreground or a background to anything but just *is*. Soyinka's point in Kampala 1962, where he made the reference to the tiger and in Berlin where he clarifies his position, is a refutation of the strategy that the cultural nationalist movement was taking, which was about showing the greatness of African culture, history, and tradition to a West that had demonized it rather than allowing the greatness of Africa to speak for itself. To allow African history and culture to speak for itself in present times and in ways that would resonate with the currents of the modern world is what framed Soyinka's mythopoeic relationship with literature. His works present multiple ways to generations after him and even his peers on how literature can be a means of broad-spectrum social analysis, one critical of itself and its subject. More so, Soyinka was educating a continent on how its literature should be.

Soyinka's imperative is instructive in that it sought to allow the African past and its rich cultural heritage to flourish in the present without following in the uncritical and defensive pattern peculiar to many postcolonial works, especially of negritude. Soyinka's shift from a nationalist stance preoccupied with African aesthetics to that of a socially committed artist would fully come into effect in the mid-1960s,[11] a period which required such transitions, owing to the multiple failed directions the African post-colonies and their governments began to take and his own social realities after returning from England. Still, both aesthetic and social consciousness have equal berth within Soyinka and provided ample space for Soyinka to deploy pre-textual signs, resources from his cultural heritage, in such a manner that the entire Soyinkan imperative, which for the sake of summary could be called a reconstructive visionary approach, could chart pathways for other coming generations to follow. Soyinka's imperative, resounding enough both at home and abroad, elicited responses from various corners—

---

[11] Odun T. Balogun, "Wole Soyinka and the Literary Aesthetic of African Socialism," *Black American Literature Forum* 22, no. 3 (1988): 503–30.

some mere acknowledging, some commending,[12] while others outrightly criticizing it—that serve as a litmus test for the extent of its reach. Leslie-Ogundipe's reference to Soyinka's creative preoccupation with existential themes with universal applications, transcendent and particularly relevant, described his aesthetic preferences as the tools with which Soyinka makes the world his audience. Isidore Okpewho commented on how Soyinka's aesthetic deployments are inherently reflective of the "mythic foundations of creative activity" and how his works holistically emphasize present reality and the kinds of realities that must be aspired to, to help in social structuring.

How Soyinka does the aforementioned is emphatically reliant on his reconstructive cultivation. His use of the Ogun motif in his essays and works remain resonant for this reason. Thus, it is easy, as has been done by some scholars, to identify recurrent aesthetic trends in some of Soyinka's works and group them based on their target audience: Wright, for instance, groups Soyinka's plays into four categories: The early plays, which he calls those in the naturalistic idiom, for their accessibility to Western audiences; the ritualistic plays, those heavily reliant on African mythico-ritual order and also universal; also the ritualistic plays' heavily experimental and based on Soyinkan idiom; and the revues, which Wright tags the shot-gun satires.[13] Running through these several manifestations of the Soyinkan imperative is a potent ideological strand, which is the voice of conscience. In imploring African writers, Soyinka, directly and otherwise, states in many of his essays and interviews like "The Writer in an African State"[14] that the voice of conscience must be resolute in an African writer and his works.

The "Voice of Conscience" speaks to the grooming of a dissenting and objectivist impulse, one that is by default revolutionary and visionary—since both are often mutually inclusive. Soyinka's reconstructive approach is visionary not only because of its objectivist temper—objectivist because the cultivation of the legacies of the past to address the present is often borne of a certain kind of dissatisfaction with the status quo—or humanistic approach, but because of its regenerative impulse. Another illuminating statement that would shed light on Soyinka's instrumentalist relationship with myth is in his book of essay-lectures *Myth, Literature and the African World*, where he talks about his concern to render into expressive vehicles myth and ritual

---

[12] Molara Leslie-Ogundipe, "Reflections on the 1986 Nobel Prize," *The Guardian*, October 27, 1986: 9. See also Isidore Okpewho, "The Mystic Essence," *The African Guardian*, October 30, 1986. Also see Molara Ogundipe-Leslie, "A Comment on Ogun Abibiman," *Critical Perspectives on Wole Soyinka*, ed., James Gibbs (Washington: Three Continents, 1980), 198–199. See also Julius Nyerere, *Ujamaa: Essays on Socialism* (London: Oxford University Press, 1968); and Oyin Ogunba, *The Movement of Transition* (Ibadan: Ibadan University Press, 1975).
[13] See Derek Wright, *Wole Soyinka Revisited* (New York: Twayne Publishers, 1993).
[14] Wole Soyinka, "The Writer in an African State," *Transition* 31, no. 6 (1967): 11–13.

for the purpose of conveying and addressing the self-apprehension of the African socio-sphere.

A work like *Death and the King's Horseman* is an apt example of his visionary reconstruction, wherein Soyinka creatively deployed ritual and past mytho-cultural legacies to convey and reinstate values lost or buried during and after the European encounter. A popular reading of the work highlights the negative values of aristocracy and classism: why must the Ẹlẹṣin Ọba be made to die in order to continue to serve his dead King, and why must he be made royalty for a short period before he dies, as if such honor were to keep him compliant—which in reality it was—when in essence his servitude continues in the afterlife? These questions frame general perception of the drama text; but, on another hand, is Soyinka's attack on a post-independence culture of irresponsibility, where social responsibilities are skirted, especially after obtaining benefits from the incentives attached to such offices? The Ẹlẹṣin Ọba's ordeal, in the context of its social-cultural framing, is a recreation of the philosophy of social sacrifice that attaches to roles of headship, which follows in the Yoruba principle of communally charged "ẹbọ" (sacrifice). The atonement, either for collective or personal reasons, is the tip of the spear that leads the entire community to the home of the gods, and as such must be seen in that headship role. The underlying principle of the Ẹlẹṣin Ọba narrative would be that of responsibility to collective ethos and social duty. Soyinka's use of reconstructed historical events, which are in some sense myths—after all, history in the present is, to some extent, a reconstructed fact shaped by the demands of contemporary reality—is visionary as it does not only account for the place of myth in shaping current orientation but also tries to chart social direction through reinstating genuine values. These values extend beyond the debates of class struggles and European incursion in the natural trajectory of African history and culture.

This approach by Soyinka boosts his regenerative capacities to recreate extant mythologies and ritual forms to re-chart social direction. He states that "secular imagination recreates existing mythologies [and] since even the most esoteric world of symbols, ethics, and values must originate somewhere, the authentic images of African reality give such writers a decisive imaginative liberation,"[15] and so the reconstructivist energy of Soyinka as a product of a source is pushed to the fore of his creative enterprise. More so, in the same breadth, his source-nature or regenerative capacity as a source of creation is given ample amplification. If the symbols, ethics, and values that constitute the reconstruction originate from someplace whence they can be retrieved, the retriever must share essential relationship with this source—if

---

[15] Soyinka, "The Writer in an African State," 121.

not originate from it—to be naturally acquainted for effective utilitarian reconstruction. By so doing, the retriever comes full circle as a source. This assertion naturally directs us toward another reason why Soyinka's profile as a source and product is germane to the discussion at hand. Soyinka was not merely forging new ways of engaging the discourse of postcoloniality but was also instructive of how to navigate its direction.

This other reason is well stated by Knipp: Soyinka's visionary reconstruction of myth in his body of work contributes to the development of contemporary mythic patterns.[16] Visionary reconstruction, as exemplified by the reconstructed historical ritual detail in the Ẹlẹṣin Ọba story for instance, is an example of the process and substance of historical retrieval being subjected to the modifying effects of contemporariness. Soyinka's acceptance of a decisive creative imagination in dealing with even the most esoteric of images and symbols speaks to the grooming of a mythopoeic presence and how such presence is being woven into the fabric of social thought. This is so that contemporary appraisal of the past in relation to the present can have a distinct and refreshing character, and such character or characteristics can be threaded into dominant perspectives or patterns of consideration and comprehension that frame themes to be found in contemporary African literature. Eventually, these patterns become some sort of contemporary mythic pattern. Past legacies are being retrieved from a colonial-induced state of fixity into the present to create a present-past or as Knipp puts it a "useable past." This carves room for prophetic visions and possible future trajectories.

Soyinka's contribution to the milling of myth for visionary pronouncements or as myth-engineered vehicles for aesthetic and social commitment is expressly visible in the continuous deployment of the mythological and ritual values of the African culture in contemporary narratives, from the plainly literary to those of the Afrofuturistic. In fact, in a rather complex way, Soyinka's mythopoeic use of old legends, mythic narratives, ritual symbols, and esoteric African motifs in his literary works in a reconstructed manner can be said to have anticipated certain aspects of the present dimensions and direction of the Afrofuturistic discourse in African literature. Although rather more complex, the nucleus of Soyinka's relationship to myth can be said to be instructionally concerned about return and reconnection to the past, exorcising Western gaze that has led to a disharmony between indigenous ways of feeling and Western ways of rationalizing those feelings and that corners the African into a defensive position, and a synthesizing of the modern and the creatively retrieved past for present reorientation and production of possible African counter-futures.

---

[16] Knipp, "Irony, Tragedy, and Myth."

Recasting African experiences, reconstituting African history without the effects of Western displacement, and anticipating African-centered futures are the fundamental principles behind Afrofuturism as an aesthetic category and ideological component of the general agenda of returning agency to the African. We see this sort of revolutionary incorporation of the past into the present in works like the *Interpreters*, which basically lends itself to the flexibility and distortion of temporality. David, critically revisiting the story, puts it categorically as "time past stepping in and out of time present."[17] Soyinka's mythico-ritual experiments with African temporality also play out in other ambitious dramas of his such as *A Dance of the Forest*, *The Road*, and *Madmen and Specialists*. This temporal maneuvering to accommodate the past in a present for appropriate resituating of African past sits at the heart of the Afrofuturist enterprise, which has as one of its major philosophies the portrayal of the non-linearity of African time.

Thus, following Afrofuturist principles where literatures are considered avenues that provide alternate means of retrieving the past, Soyinka, who is not an Afrofuturist writer per se, can be said to have anticipated and appropriated contemporary Afrofuturist ideals in his works. The deployment of ritual motifs, symbols of sacrifice, mythic elements, and reconstructed historical details of regeneration and resurrection in a work like the *Interpreters* connects with the tenets of present dimensions of Afrofuturism, which in essence identifies histories of the past, present and future, that deny the epistemology, knowledge, and place of Blacks (continental and diasporic) and reweave counter histories that make connections between the three temporal junctures for African agency. In addition, Soyinka's Fourth Stage, which is the meeting point of the past, present, and future, ties with the emphasis on multidimensionality by Afrofuturism. For summary purposes, Afrofuturism is about reimagining the future to eliminate whitewashed versions and envisioning of alternatives to the present, all in the bid to centralize black concerns and life.

Kodwo Eshun's definition of Afrofuturism, even though it privileges diasporic Blacks, is apt for it essentially captures it as "a program for recovering the histories of counter-futures"[18] created by hostile forces to the black experience. The use of science tropes, cultural symbols, mythologies, fantasy, and magic realism are all means to an end. Sekoni's building of the first power station in the *Interpreters* connects to Afrofuturist claims of bridging the technology divide promoted by whitewashed visions of Africa and Blacks in general. This feat itself locates the African away from the dominant discursive notions of Africans as projected by current

---

[17] David, "The Theme of Regeneration."
[18] Eshun Kodwo, "Further Considerations of Afrofuturism," *The New Centennial Review* 3, no. 2 (2003): 287–302.

envisioning of the future which equates Africa and African future with doom. And because Soyinka carefully links the enactment of this will to previous visions where Sekoni sees the sea as his ally in overturning his creative setbacks. Thus, seeing built bridges and hospitals and ways he could harness power to transform his society—power he has been deprived of by the colonialists—the visions no longer remain mythic or fantasies but are possible counter-futures. Although, Sekoni's visions of what he is capable of achieving is Soyinka's way of implicating possible futures in the present, thereby collapsing the future (that is the realm of the unborn) in the present (realm of the living); and when Sekoni would eventually die, his present is first aborted with the destruction of the power plant, which then destroys his dreams and, hence, his future. The stress of will is all the more emphasized, which is a dominant manifestation of the chaos akin to the Fourth Stage, the realm of chaotic liminality, foolishness, and strife.

However, for the reason that Soyinka does not emphatically engage with the flowering of this possibility into the future, if we consider the actions of the corrupt that truncate this possible future and the dream of Sekoni—the same thing he does in *Madmen and Specialists* refusing to resolve the tension brought about by the emplacement of the past (effects of the war and the war in general) in the present and the collapse of African temporality (eliminating the divide between performer's fictive world and that of the spectators' non-fictive reality) as it obtains in African ritual—we cannot entirely call Soyinka an Afrofuturist, most especially because his preoccupation is with the nature of the current social direction in relation to the past, while the futuristic takes tertiary status. We also see Soyinka's *A Play of Giants* challenging the reconstruction of the sociocultural consciousness of the people by bearing a reconstructed past on them and leaving them in the present to envision the possibilities of their futures. It would seem Soyinka leaves the future open-ended and that his concern is with the African past and how it could provoke possible present alternatives.

Nevertheless, the influence of Soyinka's preoccupation in fighting ruinous imaginaries of African heritage by cultivating African cultural legacies from a state of temporal stagnancy in the past to disrupt and challenge hegemonic present visions and future imaginaries, especially with mythologized and mythopoeticized strategies, moving back and forth through time, space, and cultures to revolutionize the trajectory of Africa sociocultural presence, can be seen in many contemporary Afrofuturist works that move away from depictions of African past as a forgotten relic and future as catastrophic or that eliminates the presence of Africa in the projection of future world histories. Writers like Nnedi Okoroafor, Wale Talabi, Derine Norman, Leslie Nneka Arimah and a host of others are predominantly Afrofuturist, reenacting, reconstituting, and revising African myths, rituals, and past life to resituate African past in the present with the hope of carving a central space for the African in the futures already imagined by the West (global) futures industry. After all, even in his Nobel Prize speech, the reliance on his African cultural heritage to fashion a cultural crossroads between Alfred Nobel and Ogun, the patron oriṣa of creativity and the arts, to reach both a global and home audience, took center stage.

The literary direction of Soyinka's works, being products of particular sources—African cultural legacies and an idiosyncratic milling of its symbols into universal motifs—laid pathways and ushered possible directions for subsequent African writers to follow, making him into a source of imperatives, visions, and of counter-revolutionary directions to coming generations.

Aesthetic Vision and Social Commitment: Soyinka's Fourth Stage

Certainly, Soyinka's social commitment has been the debate of a lifetime, owing to the complexity with which his grievances are spun into literary texts and the intolerance with which it is received in certain quarters. Yet, it is Soyinka's level and manner of social commitment that is resonant enough to be seen as a source of influence to the general body of African literature, and to generalize to some extent, world literature. (At the very least, a Nobel Prize win is a testament of a kind to the universal usefulness of a writer's oeuvre.) Even though Soyinka was not the only of his generation performing the social task, his voice was audible and creatively ingenious enough that it carved a path away from the usual status quo.

Soyinka's mode of social commitment is enough to fill several volumes, as the mode a particular genre takes differs from how each text separates itself from those of the same generic category. Thus, to know, engage, and approach Soyinka through his work, one must be selective. By being selective, one can then hope the investigative endeavor presents channels through which, at the very least, the activistic Soyinka of the political essays can be appreciated through engaging the visionary reconstructivist Soyinka of the plays, or that echoes of the Soyinka of the shot-gun satires can be reconciled with the mythopoeic Soyinka. Of course, this is not positing the presence of a clear-cut separation between the authorial versions—they are, after all, projections of a single-source character. But by approaching Soyinka this way one first establishes pathways toward appreciating the composite relationships between textual and contextual Soyinka; secondly, one can think of the various textual "Soyinkas" as productions/archetypes, as each contains a life force of its own, the type often set up as capable of bringing into existence a series of reactions with contextual implications.

Thirdly, one can think of the textual and contextual Soyinka in distinctive but interconnected terms.

A practical example is Soyinka's autobiographical *Ibadan*. In it we discover the formation, process, and the relative peaking of the political sensitization of Soyinka. The Soyinka the reader encounters in *Ibadan* is the transitioning one, a far cry from the Soyinka who authors and contours this textual-Soyinka for the readers. His return to the city of Ibadan from England after a period of five years of self-exile is recorded in this narrative, as well as the transformations he undergoes as a result of this arrival, which culminate in his theoretical and conscious renewal, enough for him to derive new visions. Soyinka describes a place in Ibadan, Apata, as a force that had defined him in unchangeable ways, so much so that he longed to return there, a place where he had been schooled and which he had identified as having schooled him in the complexity of conflict. Ibadan rekindled and animated forces in Soyinka that were uniquely Ibadan, even if the vision would transcend spatial limitations. For this purpose, Soyinka would confess that it was Ibadan that turned him into an adult.[19]

The instantaneous and visible manifestations of history are evidently dramatized in the narratives of the transformation of spaces,[20] argues Olabode Ibironke, because spaces are not only instrumental in revealing the histories of political transformations and sociocultural transitions, they shelter forces, spirits, matter, and chemistries that shape the visions of those who inhabit them. Hence, the social character of any place, which is always unique to it, provides impetus for the provocation of conditions necessary and potent enough to induce and alter whatever is doable, conceivable, and thinkable. The "adult Soyinka" here is the one whose understanding of the realities of postcolonial Nigeria is shaped by his experiences in a specific setting, and who would go on to produce works shaped by the motions of that space; after all the political history of a nation affects the formal properties of the literature of that nation, either directly in form of traditions or in form of personal visions that are eventually embraced by others—which is the case with Soyinka.

The periods of transition of Nigeria from colonialism to self-rule coincided with the process of transition brought about by his return home. More so, it was in Ibadan (both the place and the narrative), while still grasping for a firm grip on the shifting reality of postcolonial Nigeria, that Soyinka would lay hold of a resolute "contemporary theatre vision or statement of being."[21] It is no wonder that the realities of society are powerful enough to shape a

---

[19] Wole Soyinka, *Ibadan: The Penkelemes Years: A Memoir: 1946–1965* (London: Methuen, 1994), 16.
[20] Olabode Ibironke, "Fourth Stage: Wole Soyinka and the Social Character of Ibadan," *History Compass* 13, no. 11 (2015): 541–9.
[21] Soyinka, "Ibadan," 97.

writer's aesthetic choices and social vision. The transition from anxiety of what to expect upon disembarking from the plane to puzzlement as to the changes and motions of the newly independent nation, and befuddlement about his incarceration and how his home could be his prison came to a head when his father, upon visiting him in prison, welcomed him home.

Ibadan teaches us two things that connect with the train of thought pursued to this point: one, textual-Soyinka differs from one text to another, and to duly appreciate the influences of Soyinka to the art, one must treat each text-based Soyinka as a result of certain conditions that are specific to times and places which are junctures in the life cycle of the contextual and living Soyinka. The second instruction is more urgent: the experiences of Soyinka from text to text are unique enough to leave different manner and modes of social influences. After all, it was in Ibadan, used here as a placeholder for both narrative and space, that Soyinka was able to connect both an aesthetic vision and social imperative together into the concept of the Fourth Stage.

To Soyinka, the Fourth Stage is the "vortex of archetypes and the home of the tragic spirit."[22] The multidimensionality of African space is such that there is a space for ancestors, which is the past; the present belongs to the living; the future to the unborn. The three categories of forces, to Soyinka, are governed by the same ritual rules as demonstrated in his play written for the social-political condition of Nigerian independence, *A Dance of the Forest*. The deities, the living, and the unborn are all thrust into the same situation, obeying the same laws, suffering the same agonies, and deploying the same intelligence for ritual[23]—all these for a plunge into the immeasurable gulf of transition. This gulf for transition is as sociopolitically defined as much as it bears a strong metaphysical presence. For this reason, it is possible for Soyinka to project the dismal political and sociocultural realities in postcolonial Nigeria in mythic dimensions. Soyinka's immeasurable gulf of transition of all forces resonate with the political reality of Nigeria's transition from the condition of colonialism to self-rule and Soyinka's jarring experiences upon his return home and his growth into the "adult."

Owing to the endless nature of transitions, especially of the kind experienced by Nigeria, the immeasurability of the Fourth Stage is so well defined that it is indeed the home of the tragic spirit; it accurately symbolizes the unending changes of undesirable substance or nature, the endless cyclical motions of debauchery and social irresponsibility and the rifts they cause in postcolonial history. The Fourth Stage for Soyinka is the space of rude awakening and awareness, where the mythic and the realistic are jumbled together, and the forces of such consequences are forever interlocked in the

---

[22] Soyinka, *Myth, Literature*, 140.
[23] Soyinka, *Myth, Literature*.

psyche. It is why it is a vortex; the disruptions by human foolishness, the possible dystopic futures, the interrupted past which becomes the "prison house of history"[24] and what Olabode Ibironke calls the "paradoxes of existence"[25] that cause all forms of disillusionment to collide in the Fourth Stage. The Fourth Stage then is the being moreness wherein postcolonial writers and their imaginations are thrust and whence they produce works that speak to the conditions of past, present, and possible futures that have birthed the disruptive motions that are presently overwhelming.

Soyinka's conception of the Fourth Stage is so germane to African literature because it harnesses perfectly what he had tried to achieve with his visionary reconstruction and his social direction, without one superimposing itself over the other. It fits perfectly into the frame of postcolonial theorizing, the kinds that are being deployed to explain the material realities as well as the sociocultural states of postcolonies and postcolonial writers. Even though it is taken as a dramatic concept, its applicability is wide. As a result of its far-reaching influence, enough works have been carried out on the significance of the Fourth Stage as an ingenious addition to conceptualizations around dramatic literature and theater.

With the Fourth Stage, Soyinka is able to activate his social commitment the more in a way that he can bring his mythopoeic sensibilities to bear and explain the fabric of African social reality, which is always caught in a process of continuity, just in the way the Fourth Stage is. Performativity in African drama and theater is implicated in Soyinka's conception of this liminal state, because performativity ties to identity construction, boundary crossing, and the violation of boundaries. Shifts of identities by characters or performers are initiated with the aim of legitimizing all the claims performance makes in the process of enacting itself. This process requires believability on the part of the social audience owing to the transitions that are constantly unfolded in the processes of being of the characters. This is because the rationality behind dramaturgy or characterization is hinged on the presentation of a request that the world accepts as real the impressions thrown up before their presence. Like the average living person who acts as himself and hopes, implicitly or explicitly, as the case may be, that his person is considered one with the characteristics his actions conveys, and that the actions he executes are not in discord with the range of possibilities derivable from the frame of personality he has put up. The borderline is that there is a synergy between his reality as processed by others and what he does with that reality. Soyinka's Fourth Stage merges both audience and characters by fusing both performance as enactment and the nuances of those performances as received by the audience. Beneath all this chaos of

---

[24] Ibironke, "Fourth Stage."
[25] Ibironke, "Fourth Stage."

self-determinacy, which is the realm of the modernist, is the aim toward self-definition. Navigating this fusion of different ends of the identity spectrum, of being perpetually self-aware, of constructing and deconstructing identity, of being trapped in unbroken transitions, of being caught in the chthonic realm where the human will is stressed, is the African trapped in a vortex of war between personal definition and collective or socially charged tensions. This implicates postcoloniality and the conditions inherent in the postcolonial or postmodern world, which is often the aftermath of the collision of the abruptly truncated past, the stagnant present, and an abortive future.

Soyinka's concept as a result transcends the theatrical or rituals and myths of drama into a broad literary concept. Its affordances in explaining the social African caught in a battle of conflicting binaries: rational and irrational; destructive and constructive; revolutionary and narrow-minded. These categories are embodied by Soyinka's characters, for regardless of whichever categories they fall into, they are perpetually defined by the conflicts between tradition, modernism, and postmodernism, or the contests between colonial imprints, African legacies, and neo-imperialism. Hence, the place of Soyinka's myth and ritual in his drama is not as a background element to emphasize a point but as an integral part of the narrative to cast a socially relevant commentary on the dilemma of the postcolonial world where all sorts of identities and realms clash.

That the Fourth Stage is the realm of unending transitions means the Soyinka ideology that must be reproduced in each work must necessarily be one caught in endless motions of awareness—and since spatial conditions determine the formal properties of literature, such as themes, plots, characters, the overbearing ideology, which must be the stamp of the author's consciousness—reflects the endless motions of influences and transitory phases the author has passed through to get to that point. For these reasons, enough works have established the distinctively independent versions of Soyinka readers can encounter from work to work,[26] which when screened in a composite manner, leads to a holistic view of the single essence behind the various authorial personas.

Conclusion

It is an almost impossible task to try and compress Soyinka into one essay; to attempt to extricate moments of influences from a larger pool of influences is another level of task, as they are all intricately interwoven, so much so that any attempt to start at one particular point as the basis reveals

---

[26] See Knipp, "Irony, Tragedy, and Myth," 5–26. See also Balogun, "Literary Aesthetic."

something that must come before. Ordinarily one would ask in relation to Soyinka, what comes first: his vision at reconstructing the use of the past or the currents of the present? Or is it his imperative about what the means of reconstruction must be, or is it the agency of the Fourth Stage? Not minding the levels of sub-questions that can be generated from each of the existing questions, what the afore-stated does is to open the eyes to the multilayered form of Soyinka's contributions to literature, even though some would readily and insularly ascribe his importance to drama. As revealed, Soyinka's influence influences itself in a way that defies easy extraction; therefore, it is not enough to say this is where Soyinka is great. A single concept such as the Fourth Stage stretches and covers every other conceptual framework he has engineered or presented as paradigms of revolutionizing the subject of change for generations of writers and critics. (By merely providing critics with what to criticize, Soyinka has presented himself as an influential force. Also, by continuing the tradition of literary activism, he is representing the impulse of the realm of transition that seeks to liberate itself from the prison of history.) Yet the Fourth Stage, as apt, encompassing, and effective as it is, owes its impetus to a lot of his later articulations in essays, poetry, drama, and narratives, his experiments with ritual and myths, and his conscious social awareness about the state and nature of the postcolony and the duties of leaders and the postcolonial writers. The nature of this intricacy has allowed for the form of the essay such that it tries to follow a progressive thought structure without too many distractions in form of sub-segments, especially considering the nature of the subject's notion about transition being unending and progressive. If one thing has been established, it is that Soyinka is a source of revelation, a stream from a larger cultural source. And yet this stream acts like a tributary, feeding a larger tradition: postcolonial, postmodernist, and all that comes after that. Summarily, his source leads to other sources that have come before him and will come after.

FIGURE 12.1 *Writing in the 1990s.* Illustration by Kazeem Oyetunde Ekeolu.

12

Soyinka's Literary Achievements and the Use of Language

I keep reminding people that I have a very large constituency which extends beyond Nigerian borders: I tend to see even Nigerian problems in the context of my vision of Africa. This has been with me for a long time, ever since my student days, when I was so focused on South Africa, that my early play dealt with apartheid.
WOLE SOYINKA ON IDENTITY, 1992[1]

Introduction: Soyinka's Personal and Literary Background

As already noted in Chapter 1, Akinwande Oluwole Soyinka, generally known as just Wole Soyinka, was born on July 13, 1934, in Abẹokuta, Nigeria. He is the second child of his parents, Samuel Ayodele and Grace Eniola Soyinka.[2] His childhood and adolescence were spent in Abẹokuta, Lagos, and Ibadan, respectively. He is a Yoruba from south western Nigeria. Among the schools he attended was the Government College Ibadan (1946–1950), a place that would be considered his first exposure to writing and literary achievements, since as observed by Jeyifo, Soyinka began writing and winning prizes for his art while at the Government College. Between 1950

---

[1] Wole Soyinka, "Wole Soyinka on 'Identity:' A Conversation with Ulli Beier, 1992," reprinted in Jeyifo, *Conversations with Wole Soyinka*, 179.
[2] Salsabeel Kassem, "Wole Soyinka, Bibliotheca Alexandrina," http://www.britannica.com/EBchecked/topic/557228/Wole-Soyinka.

and 1952, Soyinka took up a job as an inventory clerk at a pharmaceutical store owned by the government, but while at it, some of his stories were read on national radio.[3] From 1952 to 1954, he went on to the University College Ibadan where he continued to hone his creative writing skills. He also participated in drama and played lead roles, and he also edited the school publication *The Eagle*, before proceeding to the University of Leeds in England in 1954 where he graduated with honors in 1957.[4]

Having expressed an affinity to the creative arts while in England, Soyinka continued his production of literature and commenced work on two plays, *The Swamp Dwellers* and *The Lion and the Jewel*. The latter, as noted by Gibbs, was read by Anne Piper in Sloane Square on behalf of the Royal Court.[5] Jeyifo also states that Soyinka also worked in the Royal Court Theatre in London as a Play Reader. And he directed a Nigerian group in the performance of his play *The Swamp Dwellers*. Also, in 1959, Soyinka is noted to have directed some of his works in an "Evening" in the Royal Theatre, including songs, poetry, and a play, *The Invention*, which is reflexive of the writer's aversion to apartheid and racism and his interest in Black American writings. In that same year, Soyinka also wrote a song titled "Long Time Bwana," which reflected the opinions and feelings of the Kenyan people with reference to the colonial violence of the British against the people of Kenya.[6]

Soyinka returned home in 1960 to direct his plays, write, and do research.[7] In the same year, he completed a radio play with the title, *Camwood on the Leaves*,[8] while Gibbs also notes *The Tortoise* as another of the radio plays. He also acknowledges a television play known as *The Father's Burden* as well as a stage play known as *The Trials of Brother Jero*.[9] Soyinka also organized a group of theater performers known as "The 1960 Masks" and went ahead to produce the play *A Dance of the Forests*, which was later published in 1963. The play was a satirical representation of the newly independent nation with its romanticized yet erroneous notions of the past while also predicting the future to be no better if conscious efforts are not made to prevent a repeat of the past. In 1964, Soyinka formed a new theater group known as the The Orisun Theatre Company and produces his play *The Lion and the Jewel* in the English and Yoruba languages.

---

[3] Biọdun Jeyifo, *Wole Soyinka: Politics, Poetics, and Postcolonialism* (Cambridge: Cambridge University Press, 2004).
[4] Gibbs, *Wole Soyinka* (London: Macmillan Publishers Ltd., London, 1986).
[5] Gibbs, *Wole Soyinka*.
[6] Gibbs, *Wole Soyinka*.
[7] Gibbs, *Wole Soyinka*.
[8] Jeyifo, *Poetics and Postcolonialism*.
[9] Gibbs, *Wole Soyinka*.

However, from the early 1960s, Soyinka's literary reputation began to grow internationally—his publication of several other plays, prose texts, poetry as well as the production of his plays in theaters contributed to that. In the early years succeeding independence, Soyinka involved himself in the publication of radio and television plays, some productive, some others have forgotten. In 1961, he expanded his location to several cities across the globe. Gibbs observes that Soyinka began to attend conferences around the world like in Italy and America while his poems were published in Sweden.[10] He also participated in the making of a film reflecting the cultural heritage of the Nigerian people, "Culture in Transition," with Soyinka as the presenter.[11]

In subsequent years, Soyinka began to tackle the political affairs of the nation using his literature. Therefore, in 1965, he produced *Before the Blackout*, a political satire that explores the unrest in western Nigeria at the time. He also released and premiered the play *Kongi's Harvest* in Lagos. Soyinka also staged the play *The Road* in affiliation to the Commonwealth Arts Festival in London, and at the festival, he read his poem *Idanre*. And in that same year, he published his novel *The Interpreters*.[12]

In 1967, Jeyifo notes that Soyinka published *Kongi's Harvest*, *Idanre*, and other poems early in the year. His plays *The Trials of Brother Jero* and *The Strong Breed* were involved in an off-Broadway production at the Greenwich Mews Theater in New York City.[13] Gibbs also observed that Soyinka seemed to concentrate on the production of poetry and essays in the early months of 1967. His works included *Massacre October "66"* and *For Her Who Rejoiced*, while his critical essays that included *And After the Narcissist? Of Power and Change* and *The Fourth Stage* were also submitted for publication. Aside from Soyinka's input on political affairs using his literature, Gibbs notes that he had a strong contribution and influence on the press. However, with the political unrest in the country and Soyinka's involvement in an attempt to stop an impending civil war, he was rearrested in August 1967 and detained without trial.[14]

Following an ongoing production of his play *Kongi's Harvest*, Soyinka took over the production giving it an anti-Gowon/anti-military angle. However, in 1968, Jeyifo notes that the writer translated D. O. Fagunwa's Yoruba hunter's saga originally known as *Ogboju Ọdẹ Ninu Igbo Irunmalẹ*, while his play *Kongi's Harvest* was produced by Negro Ensemble Company at St. Mark's Theater, New York.[15] Soyinka's detention without trial

---

[10] Gibbs, *Wole Soyinka*.
[11] Gibbs, *Wole Soyinka*.
[12] Jeyifo, *Poetics and Postcolonialism*.
[13] Jeyifo, *Poetics and Postcolonialism*.
[14] Gibbs, *Wole Soyinka*.
[15] Jeyifo, *Poetics and Postcolonialism*.

continued until October in 1969; before then the writer was held in solitary confinement in Kaduna Prison where he wrote poetry with a "quill and cell manufactured 'ink' between the lines of printed books."[16] Following this incarceration, Soyinka published the prose *The Man Died* in 1972, which is a testament to his experiences while in prison. Upon his release, Gibbs notes that Soyinka quickly took up the position of director of a drama school at Ibadan and also published three of his plays and poems that he produced from his experience and time in prison.[17]

By 1970, Soyinka saw to the establishment of the Department of Theatre Arts in the University of Ibadan. He accepted an invitation to perform at the Eugene O'Neill Center, at Waterford, Connecticut, USA, and as stated by Gibbs, went with the incomplete work on *Madmen and Specialists*. He also started an acting group and equally played the role of *Kongi* from his play *Kongi's Harvest* in Calpenny Films' production of his play. After these events, Gibbs and Jeyifo agree that Soyinka left Nigeria for a self-imposed exile, which took him to several places around the world. However, while away, he published several essays and gave many lectures. He also published a compilation of African poetry, *A Shuttle in the Crypt* (1972), *The Man Died* (1971) his prose text *Season of Anomy* (1973), and other plays that include: *Jero's Metamorphosis* (1973), *Camwood on the Leaves* (1973), *The Bacchae of Euripides* (1973), which was also produced by the National Theatre at the Old Vic, London. Also, while in exile, Soyinka was appointed Visiting Professor of English at the University of Sheffield and overseas fellow at Churchill College, Cambridge University.[18]

Having spent most of his self-imposed exile in Europe, in 1974 Soyinka settled in Accra where he took on the responsibility as an editor of *Transition*, a top intellectual magazine at the time. The publication was employed for revolutionary movements against some tyrants in Africa, namely Francisco Macias Nguema, Jean-Bedel Bokassa, and Idi Amin. Soyinka also joined forces with the South African poet Dennis Brutus in the formation and inauguration of the Union of Writers of African People of which Soyinka was elected the secretary.[19]

The year 1975 saw the overthrow of Yakubu Gowon in a coup orchestrated by Murtala Muhammed who eventually took over as head of state. Soyinka returned home and took up the position of Professor of Comparative Literature at the University of Ife. He also published his drama *Death and the King's Horseman* (1975). However, the following year brought with it the assassination of Murtala Muhammed, a clear

---

[16] Gibbs, *Wole Soyinka*, 9.
[17] Gibbs, *Wole Soyinka*.
[18] Jeyifo, *Poetics and Postcolonialism*.
[19] Gibbs, *Wole Soyinka*.

indication of the sustained political unrest in the country. However, Murtala Muhammed was succeeded by General Oluṣẹgun Ọbasanjọ as the Head of State. In that same year, Soyinka published the works "Myth, Literature and the African World" and "Ogun Abibiman." In 1977, he produced the play *Opera Wonyosi*, an adaptation of Bertolt Brecht's *Threepenny Opera* and John Gay's *Beggars*, which was first performed in October 1977. The play addresses the tyranny in Africa as well as the effects of the oil boom in Nigeria. Given the restiveness in the country at the time, the writer's plans for the play's performance in Lagos were thwarted.

According to Gibbs, Soyinka brought together a new group which he called "Guerrilla Theatre Unit" from the University of Ife Theatre. He, as a writer, did not desist from his efforts at political revolution; therefore, he is stated to have written playlets that were aimed at being performed in car parks, the marketplaces, and the streets. These playlets addressed the inherent corruption in the country, as well as all the existing ills in society at the time. Some of these playlets include: *Before the Blowout*, which focused on the crookedness and charlatanism of some characters in his work *Opera Wonyosi*.[20] In that same year, 1977, Soyinka also participated in the administration of the Second Black and African Festival of Arts and Culture (Festac) held in January.[21]

In 1979, Soyinka directed and featured in the play *The Biko Inquest*, which is an edited version of the proceedings from the South African courts on the death of Steve Biko, a leader of the black consciousness movement at the time.[22] The play exposed the injustice, inhumanity, and brutality in South Africa. However, such a demonstration was equally necessary in Nigerian society given the unrest and almost identical brutality there. Toward the end of 1979, Soyinka was granted an opportunity to direct his play *Death and the King's Horseman* in Chicago at the Goodman Theater, and with the success of that production, the play was moved to the Kennedy Center in Washington DC. This also raised the reputation of Soyinka in the American theater.

In December 1980, Soyinka delivered an inaugural lecture on the topic "The Critic and Society: Barthes, Leftocracy and Other Mythologies."[23] The lecture has maintained a high level of relevance, especially with reference to the writer's eventual controversies and debates. Also, in connection to the profiteering and fraudulent activities surrounding the importation of rice at the time, Soyinka wrote a play titled *Rice Unlimited* in an attempt to protest against the socioeconomic conditions of the country. In 1982, Soyinka

---

[20] Jeyifo, *Poetics and Postcolonialism*.
[21] Jeyifo, *Poetics and Postcolonialism*.
[22] Gibbs, *Wole Soyinka*, and Jeyifo, *Poetics and Postcolonialism*.
[23] Gibbs, *Wole Soyinka*.

published his autobiography, *Aké*, in his hometown of Abęokuta in a place called Aké; the work focuses on the initial eleven years of the author's life. As a personal account, the writer addresses several issues concerning the claims of a Euro-modernist style and preference in his literature.[24]

During the launch of his autobiography, Jeyifo notes that Soyinka used it as an avenue to address the government of Shehu Shagari, pointing out the evils and inhumanity of his administration.[25] Also, in March and April 1982, Soyinka presented his radio play *Camwood on the Leaves* at the National Theater in Lagos and delivered a lecture with the title "Shakespeare and the Living Dramatist" at Stratford on Avon in England.[26] The writer also went ahead to write the play *Die Still, Dr Godspeed*, which was broadcast on the African service of the BBC. He also wrote and directed the play *Requiem for a Futurologist*, a full-length play and stage version of *Die Still, Dr Godspeed*. Also, in attacking the shocking corruption and maladministration of the government at the time, Soyinka released songs on an album titled "Unlimited Liability Company" that was broadcast and sold aggressively in the weeks prior to the August elections of 1983.[27]

In 1984, his film that recorded the events of the 1983 elections with the title, "Blues for a Prodigal" was released, and by the end of the year, Yale Repertory Theater produced his play, *A Play of Giants*. In the same year, the play was published. In 1986, Soyinka was awarded a Nobel Prize in Literature, which was announced by the Swedish Academy.[28] However, the writer's literary achievements did not end there. In 1987, his work *Death and the King's Horseman* was produced at the Lincoln Center in New York. In 1988, a collection of his essays on literature and culture was published, and in 1991, a radio play titled *A Scourge of Hyacinths* was broadcast on BBC radio. Also in 1992, the stage version was premiered in Sienna, Italy.[29] The play explores the political hypocrisy and corruption that had for so long held the nation captive.

In 1993, amid the civil agitation and political unrest in the country, Soyinka premiered and published the play *The Beautification of an Area Boy* at the West Yorkshire Playhouse in Leeds. The following year, he published a memoir titled *Ibadan: The "Penkelemes" Years A Memoir 1945–1965*. Forced into exile in 1996 by the Abacha regime and the heightened military intimidation in the country, he published the essay, "Open Sore of a Continent: A Personal Narrative of Nigeria's Crisis." In 1998, following

---

[24] Gibbs, *Wole Soyinka*.
[25] Jeyifo, *Poetics and Postcolonialism*.
[26] Gibbs, *Wole Soyinka*.
[27] Jeyifo, *Poetics and Postcolonialism*.
[28] Gibbs, *Wole Soyinka*.
[29] Jeyifo, *Poetics and Postcolonialism*.

the unexpected death of Abacha in June, Soyinka returned from his four-year exile, and in 1999, he published a collection of poems under the title "Outsiders" and also published "The Burden of Memory, the Muse of Forgiveness."[30] By the year 2000, the writer already had a trail of literary achievements in his wake.

In the year 2000, Soyinka published the essay "The Credo of Being and Nothingness," and in the following year, he wrote the play *King Baabu*, which also premiered in Lagos that year.[31] In 2004, he wrote an essay titled "Climate of Fear? The Quest of Dignity in a Dehumanized World." In 2006, another set of his autobiography titled *You Must Set Forth at Dawn, A Memoir* was released. In 2009, Soyinka received The Academy of Achievement Golden Plate Award in the United States. In 2011, he wrote the play *Alapata Apata* and won the Obafemi Awolowo Leadership Award in 2012. In 2013, he also won the Anisfield Wolf Book Award and the International Humanist Award from the international humanist and ethical union as well as the British Humanist Association in 2014.[32] The writer's list of achievements continues to go on.

Examining Soyinka's Literary Achievements

Having explored chronologically Soyinka's life and literary history, it is imperative to examine the significance and controversies associated with some of the writer's literary awards and achievements. This will shed light on the extent and gravity of his literary journey as well as its implications for the global perception of African scholars. As far back as 1967, Euba is of the opinion that, given Soyinka's human investment and extraordinary creativity, he has received a myriad number of literary awards and honors. Among this long list of awards is the John Whiting Drama Prize, which he received with Tom Stoppard in 1967,[33] he was honored with a Jock Campbell-New Statesman Literary Award, London in 1968.[34]

As earlier stated, in 1986, Soyinka was awarded the Nobel Prize for Literature by the Swedish Academy. Mustapha considers this award the most important award the writer had received especially since he is the first

---

[30] Jeyifo, *Poetics and Postcolonialism*.
[31] Celucien L. Joseph, "Wole Soyinka: Chronology and Selected Bibliography," *The Journal of Pan African Studies*, 8, no. 5 (2015): 190–5.
[32] Joseph, "Wole Soyinka: Chronology."
[33] Femi Euba, *Wole Soyinka* in *Postcolonial African Writers: A Bio-bibliographical Critical Source Book*, ed., Siga Fatima Jagne and Pushpa Parekh (New York: Routledge, 2012), 438–54.
[34] Jeyifo, *Poetics and Postcolonialism*.

West African to have received it.[35] The Nobel Prize in Literature is among the most prestigious awards given on merit to the most remarkable literary scholars. To buttress this notion, Meyers is of the opinion that

> The Nobel is the longest running literary prize, has the greatest éclat. It has a dignified royal ceremony in Stockholm on December 10 (the anniversary of Alfred Nobel's death), grants the largest amount of money ($1.3 million) as at the time of publication, and generates the most publicity to the winner.[36]

However, Meyers questions the merit of the Nobel award as well as the objectivity of the Swedish Academy. In his opinion, the academy is often blinded by a list of factors that have so far caused the award to be given to mediocrities. These factors include: race, geography, politics, and gender. This is not to imply that Soyinka is undeserving of the Nobel award. In fact, as the case maybe, being a black man in the early years of black consciousness movements, to be granted such an award could imply nothing but merit. However, Meyers has a different opinion on the award of the Nobel Prize given to Soyinka. In his opinion,

> When an African was due for the award in 1986, tribal politics influenced the decision. It was given to Wole Soyinka from the dominant Yoruba tribe of Nigeria, who'd been imprisoned for political reasons and sentenced to death, instead of the better writer, Chinua Achebe, a minority Ibo who's supported Biafran independence during the civil war.[37]

Aside from Meyers, Soyinka's Nobel Prize has equally attracted a lot of controversy from the Nigerian literary community. His work has generated a lot of buzz with reference to authenticity and African loyalty. Oguntayo is of the opinion that Naiwu Osahon one of Nigeria's pioneer pornographers accuses the writer's work of being un-African.[38] As we have noted in Chapter 10, while in reference to his Nobel award, Dare Olatunji chided the Swedish Nobel academy for awarding the writer, while also stating most vindictively the following:

---

[35] Kara Mustapha, "The Inferior Sex: A third World Feminist Approach to Wole Soyinka's *The Lion and the Jewel*," *International Periodicals for the Languages, Literature and History of Turkish or Turkic* 10, no. 16 (2015): 847–62.
[36] Jeffrey Meyers, "The Literary Politics of the Nobel Prize," *The Antioch Review* 65, no. 2 (2007): 214–23, 214.
[37] Meyers, "Politics of the Nobel Prize," 220.
[38] Ademola Oguntayo, *The Legion of Critics* (Lagos, African Concord, 1986).

Perhaps this was their way of rewarding Professor Wole Soyinka for putting his great talents so unstintingly to the service of his Euro-modern masters in particular and Western imperialism in general. The Nobel citation, his acceptance speech, and the way he flaunted his half-white head of hair instead of covering it up with a cap are proof enough of his well-known blancophilia.[39]

Olatunji's opinion about Soyinka's award of the Nobel Prize can be considered merely vindictive and biased. By implying that Soyinka is at best an agent of Western imperialism denies or rather understates the writer's political activism and efforts at righting the wrongs inherent in African society. Olatunji's opinion is illegitimate, because aside from Soyinka's experimentation with literary techniques, as well as Jeyifo's claims of his political and artistic risks, he still draws deeply from the epistemological resources of his Yoruba heritage while also adopting the global diversity of various literary and artistic traditions to enrich and distinguish his literature. To top it all off, King is of the opinion that Soyinka's literature has created awareness for African literature. He also believes Soyinka's work to be centered on an African worldview and goes still further to consider him one of the "best dramatists of our time."[40]

The distinctiveness of Soyinka's literature is a product of many influences; according to Ojaide these come from two perspectives: the indigenous as well as the foreign. However, they both have an impact on the writer's language, style, and technique as well as the ideologies and concepts he espouses. To Ojaide, this combination of African and foreign literary and artistic tradition has led to the writer's creation of a "personal authenticity."[41]

Soyinka has, however, shown immense interest in Yoruba folk traditions, and therefore received a Rockefeller Foundation research fellowship to study Yoruba folk drama.[42] This knowledge has so far impacted Soyinka's plays and poetry by way of his infusion of proverbs, dialogue and chant-like rhythms, myth, and the Yoruba worldview.[43] To put it succinctly, cited in Gibbs, Soyinka notes that "The Yoruba aesthetic matrix is the fount of my own creative inspiration."[44]

---

[39] Olatunji Dare, "More Matters Arising," *The Guardian*, 1986, 9.
[40] Bruce King, "Wole Soyinka and the Nobel Prize for Literature," *The Sewane Review* 96, no. 2 (1988): 339–45.
[41] Tanure Ojaide, "Two Worlds: Influences on the Poetry of Wole Soyinka," *Black American Literature Forum* 22, no. 4 (1988): 767–76.
[42] Gibbs, *Wole Soyinka*.
[43] Ojaide, "Two Worlds."
[44] James Gibbs, ed. *Critical Perspectives on Wole Soyinka* (Washington: Three Continents, 1980), 4.

Bandyopadhayay also notes that Soyinka employs the use of Yoruba myths and cosmologies in the composition of his plays; he also bases his tragic works on the mythologies of the Yoruba people, which oftentimes combines the historical and contemporary realities with his own personal modern views to several issues.[45] To corroborate this notion, Ojaide goes ahead to state that

> Soyinka makes use of Yoruba myths, superstitions, and beliefs in his poetry. There are references to Yoruba gods and what they represent, beliefs about the presence of ancestors who receive offerings from the living to protect them, and 'the same child who dies and returns again and again to plague the mother.'[46]

Therefore, Soyinka's adoption and appropriation of the epistemological resources of Yoruba culture must have colored Balogun's opinion on the writer when he stated that Soyinka has dedicated his literature to a revolutionary validation and reaffirmation of the culture of the African people.[47] As part of affirming and validating the African cultural epistemologies, Soyinka's literature is also influenced by the Yoruba concept of tragedy which, therefore, justifies Gates's opinion in the following statement:

> Soyinka embeds his tragic agon in the densely metaphorical world of mythopoesis, structured in a language that is startling for the originality and aptness of its metaphors. We can best see this by analyzing the tragedy that forms the crux of Soyinka's oeuvre, *Death and the King's Horseman*, referred to so specifically by the Swedish Academy in its citation honoring Soyinka's works.[48]

Also, as noted by King, the writer's literature is organized by imageries, symbols, and the Ogun mythology. Soyinka's works reflect the personal and religious significance of the Ogun god to the Yoruba people. Therefore, with the constant appearance of the Ogun in several of his works, Soyinka legitimizes the Yoruba myth of Ogun. This, therefore, counteracts the claims that the writer's works are inauthentic and are solely aimed at promoting the imperialism of the West. Therefore, it can be stated that the Swedish

---

[45] Kajal Bandyopadhayay, *Tension and Synthesis in Wole Soyinka's Plays* (Dhaka: University of Dhaka, 2012), 5.
[46] Ojaide, "Two Worlds."
[47] Odun Balogun, "Wole Soyinka and the Literary Aesthetic of African Socialism," *Black American Literature Forum* no. 22, no. 3 (1988): 503–30.
[48] Henry Louis Gates Jr., "Wole Soyinka: Mythopoesis and the Agon of Democracy," *The Georgia Review* 49, no. 1 (1995): 187–94, 188.

Academy's choice of a Nobel laureate in 1986 was well deserved, and to consolidate this opinion, Gates asserts that, "Soyinka is one of the few creative writers in the world who could have as justifiably been awarded the Nobel Peace Prize as that for Literature."[49]

However, at the Nobel Prize banquet on December 10, 1986, Soyinka draws a connection between Ogun and the creativity that led him to be so honored. To reaffirm his legitimization of the Ogun deity and the Yoruba traditions of his people, he accords Ogun the credit of his creativity and referred to Ogun as his creative muse and "the god of creativity and destruction, of the lyric and metallurgy." Using his speech, the writer reemphasizes the deity's creative ability and discretion by implying that Ogun had predestined that moment and that deity is also the source of Alfred Nobel's ingenuity, which is why Soyinka stated the following in his speech:

> This deity anticipated your scientist Alfred Nobel at the very beginning of time by clearing a path through primordial chaos, dynamiting his way through the core of earth to open a route for his fellow deities, who sought to be reunited with us mortals.[50]

However, given the global popularity and recognition associated with the Nobel Prize, the selection of Soyinka for the award in 1986 had immense implications for African literature. The award created awareness for African literature and placed African writing on the global map. Soyinka, recognizing the implication of the award on African literature, stated the following as the only reason for his acceptance of the award. Cited in Jeyifo, the laureate goes ahead to state that

> I have not been able to accept the prize on a personal level ... I accept it as a tribute to the heritage of African literature, which is very little known in the West. I regard it as a statement of respect and acknowledgment of the long years and centuries of denigration and ignorance of the heritage which all of us have been trying to build. It's on that level that I accept it.[51]

However, it is worthy of note that in the same year, Soyinka was also awarded the Agip Prize for literature.[52]

---

[49] Gates Jr., "Mythopoesis," 187.
[50] Wole Soyinka, "Nobel Prize Banquet Speech, 10 December 1986," *Black American Literature Forum* 22, no. 3 (1988): 447–8.
[51] Jeyifo, *Poetics and Postcolonialism*.
[52] Molefi Kete Asante, *The History of Africa: The Quest for Eternal Harmony* (New York: Routledge, 2014).

Long after Soyinka's award of the Nobel Prize, he was also awarded "The Academy of Achievement Golden Plate Award" in the United States in the year 2009. The Academy is an American academy of achievement, which was established with the aim to encourage young people and give them the opportunity to meet with real life achievers, such as Soyinka. Since 1961 the award has been given to only twenty-five awardees, considered to be exceptional men and women of great accomplishments in diverse fields of endeavor.[53] This award is a prestigious award and has so far been given to remarkable persons since its inception, one of whom is the Nobel Laureate Wole Soyinka. This, therefore, throws weight behind his literary achievements.

In 1990, Soyinka was awarded the Benson Medal from the Royal Society of Literature in the United Kingdom. Founded in 1916 by A. C. Benson, it is aimed at honoring writers who produce "Meritorious works in poetry, fiction, history, and belle letters."[54] So far, the medal has only been awarded to remarkable persons who have done extraordinary work in literature. However, to pass for meritorious works in literature, Soyinka has been able to remain productive even though the Nigerian government at the time had made several attempts at silencing and repressing his efforts at eliminating injustice and exposing societal ills and various mal-administrations of various governments. He has used his literature to instruct, to ridicule, and to expose so many covert evils in the postcolonial Nigerian society. Gates, therefore, lends credence to this opinion by stating:

> It is true, of course, that since 1986 Soyinka has also published dozens of essays addressing immediate political crises in Nigeria. It was these essays and his statements to the Nigerian and international press that led to his being forced into exile late last year. Soyinka can be readily defined as one of Nigeria's (and black Africa's) proto-agonists.[55]

Therefore, for one to be forced into exile for political reasons, such a person must have aggravated the government in power. This, therefore, validates the opinion that Soyinka's literature has had immense impact on the sociopolitical realities of the African nation which then justifies the Benson medal from the Royal Society of Literature.

Also, in 2013, Soyinka was awarded the Anisfield-Wolf Lifetime Achievement Award given by the Anisfield Wolf Book Awards and sponsored

---

[53] Academy of Achievement, "Golden Plate Awardees," https://www.achievement.org/our-history/golden-plate-awards/.
[54] Royal Society of Literature, "The Benson Medal," https://rsliterature.org/award/the-benson-medal/.
[55] Gates Jr., "Mythopoesis," 188.

by the Cleveland Foundation. The award was established in 1935 by Edith Anisfield Wolf in 1935 in honor of her father, John Anisfield, and her husband, Eugene Wolf, as a reflection and representation of the family's commitment to social justice. The awards take into consideration publications and books that have impacted the conception and understanding of human diversity and racism. As noted by Gates and cited in Crosley, "the 2013 Anisfield Wolf winners are exemplars who broaden our vision of race and diversity."[56] However, the Anisfield Wolf award had initially been given to Soyinka in the year 1983 for his autobiography *Aké: The Years of Childhood*.

In 2017, he was awarded the Europe Theatre Prize, which was first awarded in 1987. This prize is meant for the personality in theater who has encouraged "understanding and the exchange of knowledge between peoples."[57] While announcing the award, the general secretary of Europe Theatre Prize, Alessandro Martinez, stated that the author had won the special prize category as a result of his ability to serve "as a proponent of an ideal bridge between Europe and Africa in a deeply delicate period for the present and the future of our continent."[58] Martinez's claims of Soyinka's contribution to society are not far-fetched. The writer's literature has often been accused of having a series of Western influences, and this is usually in an attempt to undermine his creative ingenuity and loyalty to his African background. However, in his defense, Soyinka refers to his critics as Neo-Tarzanists and goes ahead to state that his work has become a bridge between European literary and artistic traditions and the African literary traditions, while also implying his inclination to universalism and the complementarity of literary cultures as against restrictive approaches suggested by his critics. To put it succinctly, Soyinka opines that his critics do not

> appreciate the kind of exploration which I am making into points of departure as well as meeting points between the African and European literary and artistic traditions, quite unabashedly exploiting various complementarities or contradictions in my work.[59]

As we have noted in Chapter 10, Ojaide, however, recognizes the universality of Soyinka's literature and his ability to appropriate and appreciate a multitude of cultures, hence aiding the understanding and

---

[56] Hilary Crosley, "Nobel Laureate Wole Soyinka wins Anisfield-Wolf Book Award,", https://www.theroot.com/nobel-laureate-wole-soyinka-wins-anisfield-wolf-book-awards-1790896125/amp.
[57] Kunle Ajibade, "Wole Soyinka Wins the Europe Theater Prize," https://www.pmnewsnigeria.com/2017/12/12/wole-soyinka-wins-europe-theater-prize/.
[58] Ajibade, "The Europe Theater Prize."
[59] Bandyopadhyay, *Tension and Synthesis*.

exchange of knowledge between people, which is why we would like, at the risk of repetition, to recall Ojaide who has described Soyinka's literature thus:

> Soyinka's essays and creative work reveal a voracious reader of Western literatures. Soyinka is an exception to the typical African intellectual whom Chinua Achebe describes as reading a few uninspiring British novels. His passion for drama brought him into contact with Greek and European dramatists. References to Antigone, the Stygian mysteries, and Lethe are part of the classical culture underlying his work. The Greek dramatists (Sophocles, Euripides, and Aeschylus) would particularly have appealed to the Yoruba-raised poet because of their similar attitude toward gods and tragedy. Hence his equating Yoruba gods to Greek gods and his references to Dionysus and Prometheus are not surprising. Here is a ready synthesis of African and European cultures in which the local is universalized and the universal simultaneously localized.[60]

Aside from literary awards, Soyinka has accumulated a wealth of honors from several institutions in different parts of the world and also has so far invested and thrived in academia. In the year 1962, Jeyifo states that Soyinka was appointed a lecturer in the University of Ife, but very typically, the writer resigned to protest against the university's alignment with the infamous Samuel Ladoke Akintola.[61] He was also appointed as head of the drama school at the premiere University of Ibadan in 1967, but as a result of his arrest in August in connection to his agitations to call off the war that same year, he was unable to take up the offer.[62] Also, in 1972, the University of Leeds awarded Soyinka a Honoris Causa Doctorate.[63] However, during his self-imposed exile from 1973 to 1976, the writer was a visiting professor in the University of Sheffield and an overseas fellow in the University of Cambridge at Churchill College. He was also a visiting professor at the University of Ghana, Legon in the Institute of African Studies. He also took up the position of lecturer of comparative literature at the University of Ife and eventually became the head of department in Dramatic Arts.[64] In 1981 amid the political agitation and a series of satirical revues staged by Soyinka, the writer was also appointed as a visiting Professor to Yale University.

---

[60] Ojaide, "Two Worlds."
[61] Jeyifo, *Poetics and Postcolonialism*.
[62] Jeyifo, *Poetics and Postcolonialism*.
[63] Centre for African Studies (LUCAS), "Honorary Degree," Leeds African Studies Bulletin 19 (1973): 1–7.
[64] Euba, *Postcolonial African Writers*, 438–54.

To buttress the above notion, Euba is of the opinion that Soyinka has served in the capacity of visiting lecturer in several universities across the globe, such as Harvard and Emory University. He has equally served as a distinguished scholar in residence at Duke University in the year 2008 and also in New York University (NYU) at the Institute of African American Affairs.[65] The list continues on. In 1993, Soyinka was given an honorary doctorate at Harvard University, while in 2002 he was also given an honorary doctorate at Princeton University. Most recently in 2017, Soyinka joined the University of Johannesburg in South Africa as a distinguished professor in the faculty of humanities.[66] Also in 2018, the University of Ibadan named its arts theater after him while the Federal University of Agriculture Abẹokuta (FUUNAB) conferred on him an Honorary Doctorate of Letters.[67]

Wole Soyinka and the Use of Language

Soyinka's career of well over fifty years has consisted of writing and publishing novels, poetry, essays, and drama in the English language. Though his accomplishments are many and are highly praised, he is best known as a playwright. His drama has been inspired by some Western writers, such as J. M. Synge, an Irish playwright, but it is mostly a reflection of traditional African theater as well as Yoruba culture, mythology, music, and dance.[68] Also of note, Soyinka's work has reflected his experiences in politics and as an incarcerated exile from Nigeria. Soyinka was an exile during the Nigerian Civil War, and was imprisoned after he was charged for colluding with the Biafrans. Then in 1997, Soyinka was in exile again and was even sentenced to die for "antimilitary activities" a sentence which, thankfully, was dismissed.[69] In summary, Soyinka's work is infused with his deeply profound cultural and personal experiences that have resonated with audiences for decades.

Soyinka is renowned for his effortless wielding of literary tools like indigenous plotting, flashback, and symbolism that form great texture and

---

[65] Euba, *Postcolonial African Writers*.
[66] Retrieved from https://www.uj.ac.za/newandevents/pages/nobel-laureate-prize-winner-wole-soyinka-joins-uj.aspx.
[67] Seyi Babs, "26th Convocation Ceremony FUNAAB to Honour Prof. Wole Soyinka, Prof. Toyin Falola" (2018). Retrieved from https://community.unaab.edu.ng/blog/2018/11/15/26th-convocation-ceeremony-funaab-to-honour-prof-wole-soyinka-prof-toyin-falola.
[68] The Nobel Prize, "Wole Soyinka Biographical," https://www.nobelprize.org/prizes/literature/1986/soyinka/biographical/.
[69] Poetry Foundation, "Wole Soyinka," *Poetry Foundation*, n.d., https://www.poetryfoundation.org/poets/wole-soyinka.

nuance to his plays. But, of course, in all of his works, he is commended for his humor, use of irony and satire, poetic phrasing, reflective nature, and assignment of characters to specific language patterns (dependent on their moral disposition and place in society). For all of these reasons, Soyinka won the Nobel Prize in Literature in 1986, and he was the first West African to be given this distinction.[70]

Some have mistaken Soyinka's more humorous or satirical work as evidence of his indifference to the trials of Africa and specifically Nigeria, but this is far from the truth.[71] While he may have written about some of the sinister realities in Africa and Nigeria in a satirical style, his intentions have always been profound and intellectual, and there is always a moral behind the satire (usually having to do with an assessment of Africa's and Nigeria's realities after slavery and colonialism).[72] For instance, *The Lion and the Jewel* (first performed in 1959) is regarded as a play lighter in tone, but Soyinka uses this tone to parody schoolteachers who are Westernized. His other plays, lighter in tone, such as *The Trials of Brother Jero* (first performed in 1960) and *Jero's Metamorphosis* (1973) also serve to parody, only this time the parody is about the fat and conniving priests of African churches who trick their gullible parishes.[73] Soyinka's satirical writing style in these works and others clearly convey his awareness of how humor and irony are effective methods of jabbing at hypocrisy and political dysfunction in Nigerian society much to the chagrin of critics and authoritarian leaders. Perhaps this awareness is best articulated by the character Konu in Soyinka's play *The Detainee*: "I had to learn that tyrants cannot afford a sense of humor. It's the weapon they fear most."[74]

As F. Abiọla Irele noted, much of the evaluation of a writer's influence and talent has to do with their ability to use words and mold language masterfully. This is more than style, however. The mastery of language more importantly involves the writer's ability to communicate a particular meaning or message so that the reader or viewer becomes enveloped in the language itself living through the words and their created emotions. It also involves the writer's ability to effectively communicate their philosophy of the world or a specific issue in such a way that they demonstrate that they are not passive or withdrawn in their own self-reflection. Rather, the writer is deliberately inviting the reader or viewer to enter their mind and join in a

---

[70] Amy Tikkanen, "Wole Soyinka: Nigerian Author," *Encyclopaedia Britannica*, n.d., https://www.britannica.com/biography/Wole-Soyinka.
[71] F. Abiọla Irele, "The Achievement of Wole Soyinka," *Philosophia Africana* 11, no. 1 (2008): 11.
[72] Irele, "The Achievement of Wole Soyinka," 12.
[73] Tikannen, "Wole Soyinka."
[74] Irele, "The Achievement of Wole Soyinka," 12.

communal engagement with a philosophy of the world or a specific issue.⁷⁵ Martin Heidegger, a phenomenologist, so eloquently expressed the influence of language, when written or spoken so expertly:

> Language is language, speech. Language speaks. If we let ourselves fall into the abyss denoted by this sentence, we do not go tumbling into emptiness. We fall upwards to a height. Its loftiness opens up a depth. The two span a realm in which we would like to become at home, as to find a residence, a dwelling place for the life of man.⁷⁶

Certainly, then, when studying Soyinka's work closely, it becomes readily apparent that he is not indifferent to African and Nigerian issues at all,⁷⁷ for much of his appeal and brilliance comes from his ability to create a specific African or Nigerian experience, worldview, and engagement for the reader or viewer. This is done through Soyinka's revitalization of the English language so that the English language is actually infiltrated with an African or Nigerian emotion and consciousness.

While Soyinka writes in English, none of his works align with the traditional understanding of "Anglophone": a person or place that primarily speaks English. Soyinka and his work complicate and expand the term because, even though his characters appear to be speaking English on the stage or in the text, this is merely a plot device so that English-speakers can understand the characters. In actuality, the characters are speaking Yoruba to one another. This unusual layering of language creates a new kind of literary meaning and redefinition of what an "Anglophone" work can be. Consequently, Anglophone works do not have to simply refer to works performed in English, with no underlying languages or realities implied. Anglophone works can now refer to two other things. They could refer to works that are written in English but only because English was forced upon the author's or characters' culture.⁷⁸ They could also refer to "what

---

⁷⁵ Irele, "The Achievement of Wole Soyinka," 5–7. As Irele also notes, this sort of execution of language seems to be directly opposed to some forms of modern Western literature that seem to be entirely devoid of meaning or ethos, such as the works of the existentialist writer Samuel Beckett.
⁷⁶ Martin Heidegger, *Poetry, Language, Thought*, trans. Albert Hofstadter (New York: Harper & Row, 1971), 191–192, quoted in Dele Layiwola, "Nigeria – Revisiting Language in Two Wole Soyinka Plays," *The IATC Journal/Revue de l'AICT* 15 (2017), http://www.critical-stages.org/15/nigeria-revisiting-language-in-two-wole-soyinka-plays/.
⁷⁷ Irele, "The Achievement of Wole Soyinka," 11.
⁷⁸ This is similar to how Irish writers often write in English, rather than Gaelic, according to Biọdun Jeyifo, "This Wole Soyinka Play Showed the Future of English," *BBC*, May 9, 2018, http://www.bbc.com/culture/story/20180509-this-wole-soyinka-play-showed-the-future-of-english.

it means around the world when one is English-speaking in relation to other languages with which English mixes and collides to invent new and expanded communities of speakers of the language at home and abroad."[79] This concept is presented in *Death and the King's Horseman*, for example, when Yoruba idioms and proverbs are recreated in English (in a non-literal manner so that they can be more readily understood by English-speakers). In this way, it is almost as though a new language is created, as there is no way to produce a comprehensive and intelligible word-for-word translation from Yoruba to English.[80]

Thus, Soyinka gave new life to English and infused it with nuanced cultural implications. Anglophone English, therefore, is not necessarily just spoken English; it can also be "an echo chamber in which languages subjugated by English assert important dimensions of their distinctiveness as living languages"[81] or a "third realm of consciousness."[82] The significance of this sort of "rebirth" of English was beautifully articulated by Penelope Gilliat, a prominent critic of London stage performances:

> Every decade or so, it seems to fall to a non-English dramatist to belt new energy into the English tongue ... In the reign of Stage Sixty at the same beloved Victorian Building at Stratford East, a Nigerian named Wole Soyinka has done for our napping language what brigand dramatists from Ireland have done for centuries: booted it awake, rifled its pockets and scattered the loot into the middle of next week.[83]

Soyinka's confronting of the English language demonstrates "diglossia," a linguistic term meaning a juxtaposition of two languages (in Soyinka's case, Yoruba and English). When Soyinka uses English to convey Yoruba idioms, thoughts, or culture, he expresses the internal conflict of a colonized individual—one who struggles to move about seamlessly between two cultures or world visions.[84] Mikhail Bakhtin, a Russian philosopher and critic, said quite aptly that a person who is colonized exists in a logosphere where their natural, inherent way of speaking about the world is challenged by another language forced upon them.[85] Certainly, the "imported language" may not be as comfortable for a colonized individual to use to communicate,

---

[79] Jeyifo, "Wole Soyinka Play."
[80] Jeyifo, "Wole Soyinka Play."
[81] Jeyifo, "Wole Soyinka Play."
[82] Irele, "The Achievement of Wole Soyinka," 8.
[83] Penelope Gilliat, quoted in Jeyifo, "This Wole Soyinka Play Showed the Future of English."
[84] Irele, "The Achievement of Wole Soyinka," 8.
[85] Mikhail Bakhtin, *The Dialogic Imagination: Four Essays*, ed. Michael Holquist, trans. Caryl Emerson and Michael Holquist (Austin: University of Texas Press, 1981), as cited in Irele, "The Achievement of Wole Soyinka," 8.

for they may not feel they can use the language as effortlessly and without rehearsal. The imported language, instead, is used more like a method of crossing between "two realms of experience, two orders of life."[86]

Even with this inevitable conflict, Soyinka allows his reaffirmed identity and inner fortitude to shine through triumphantly in his work. He ingeniously makes his English "sound Yoruba" (hence giving the language new life) by allowing it to reflect the linguistic exuberance and personal enthusiasm of Yoruba. In order to understand this concept, it is important to know that African cultures greatly revere words, and African people tend to pay a great deal of attention to the choice of their words in their own language so that they can convey a deliberately witty or insightful point. But of course, not all African cultures revere words in exactly the same way. Some African cultures use quips and pithy language, while other African cultures practically treat their language and word choice as though they were gifts from gods. Yoruba culture very much so is more like the latter of these two African cultural extremes, and this mentality is very much present in Soyinka's work because it is so exuberant.[87] For instance, Soyinka writes in a way that clearly shows a captivation with words through his use of enunciation and idioms.[88]

Furthermore, the very fact that he writes for stage plays shows a form of oral literature, which of course is incredibly significant in Yoruba culture. Through this sort of oral literature, Soyinka's language—as with Yoruba oral storytelling and myth telling—achieves greater gravitas and more of a ritualistic nature.[89] Soyinka is very much conscious of this, and he said of the significance of words being presented in a religious ceremony: "Language reverts in religious rites to its pristine existence, eschewing the sterile limits of particularization ... and words are taken back to their roots, to their original poetic sources when fusion was total and the movement of words was the very passage of music and the dance of images."[90] He also said of words being spoken in a ritualistic way more generally: "What is transmitted in ritual is essence and response, the residual energies from the protagonist's excursion into the realm of the cosmic will which ... charges the community with new strength for action."[91] Clearly, this sort of "charging of the community with new strength for action" is a powerful example of Soyinka's ethos.

---

[86] Irele, "The Achievement of Wole Soyinka," 8.
[87] Irele, "The Achievement of Wole Soyinka," 8.
[88] Irele, "The Achievement of Wole Soyinka," 9–10.
[89] Irele, "The Achievement of Wole Soyinka," 9.
[90] Wole Soyinka, *Myth, Literature and the African World* (Cambridge, UK: Cambridge University Press, 1976), 147, quoted in Layiwola, "Nigeria – Revisiting Language in Two Wole Soyinka Plays."
[91] Soyinka, *Myth, Literature and the African World*, 34, quoted in Irele, "The Achievement of Wole Soyinka," 9.

It is in this way that Soyinka really does bring new life to English. He does not submit in fear or despair to the fact that he must migrate between "the English brain" and "the Yoruba brain." In fact, it is Soyinka's relationship to both languages that makes his writing so impactful and creative. Soyinka also does not imply to Yoruba readers or viewers that all hope is lost for them. Rather, he uses the virtues of both languages—the liveliness of Yoruba and the "robustness" of English[92]—to acquaint his audience with the complications of colonization and also show his audience the strengths of the colonized people, whom he sees as those who continue to fight and find creativity and identity in a new form of expression. As Soyinka himself said of colonized black people's assertion of their autonomy through new language use: For Africans, English became "a new medium of communication" that embodied "a new organic series of mores, social goals, relationships, [and] universal awareness all of which go into the creation of a new culture ... Black people twisted the linguistic blade in the hands of the traditional cultural castrator and carved new concepts into the flesh of white supremacy."[93] Irele has also added that the intermingling of Yoruba and English (that Soyinka demonstrates so richly) allows for African people "to overcome the disabling stresses of [their] historical condition and to transcend them in a new vision of life."[94]

Conclusion

So far, this work has chronologically examined the life and achievements of Wole Soyinka as a creative writer, political activist and academic. It has also analyzed the politics of his Nobel Prize award in 1986 while also examining the political implications of his award to the Nigerian literary community. With the countless achievements and endeavors of the writer thus examined in this work, this critical appraisal is, therefore, of the opinion that the writer has invested immensely in the literary culture of the African continent and has also impacted the political situation in the country at different times and in different political eras. The profundity of Soyinka's use of English in genres of literature is in a class of its own!

---

[92] Irele, "The Achievement of Wole Soyinka," 9–10.
[93] Wole Soyinka, *Art, Dialogue and Outrage: Essays on Literature and Culture* (New York: Pantheon Books, 1993), 88, quoted in Braj B. Kachru, "English as an Asian Language," *Links & Letters 5* (1998): 104–5.
[94] Irele, "The Achievement of Wole Soyinka," 11.

13

Conclusion: Will Soyinka's Works Outlive Him?

Some are born great, some achieve greatness, and some have greatness thrust upon 'em.

WILLIAM SHAKESPEARE[1]

Introduction

History remembers people for diametric reasons and things: heroism, martyrdom, tyranny, altruism, criminality, notoriety, ingenuity, legendary leadership, arts and literature, monumental artifacts and architecture, technological invention and discovery, geographical explorations, outlier and pioneering thoughts and deeds, and many other small or great legacies. History abounds with inexhaustible examples of the unforgettable people in all the fields of human endeavor. While Winston Churchill is remembered for heroism during the Second World War, Adolf Hitler is diametrically remembered for causing the war and for all the atrocities of the war including the gas chambers, the Holocaust, and the loss of millions of lives. Roger Bannister, the British athlete, lingers in human memory for running a mile in less than 4 minutes, and the aviation industry will never forget the Wright Brothers. Over the years, 919 individuals and 24 organizations have been awarded the Nobel Prize. But only a handful of these individuals, such as Albert Einstein, Madam Curie, and Sir Alexander Fleming (and less so his joint awardee collaborators Ernst Boris Chain and Sir Howard Walter Florey), whose works predominantly in the sciences have made remarkable

---

[1] Williams Shakespeare, *Twelfth Night*, Act 2, Scene 5.

impact on humanity remain in human memory for more than a few years. Most have been forgotten within one or two decades after their moments of fame.

Yes, human memory is short, but why are some people remembered or immortalized while others fade away? Could the answer to the mystery be in Eugene Hickok's thesis that, "Time has a way of rewriting history?" While expressing little surprise that most Americans know little or nothing about the idea of federalism and exhibit a stunning ignorance of American history generally, Eugene Hickok remarked, "Time has a way of rewriting history. Years go by and facts become forgotten or distorted, and the context in which events unfold becomes lost in the mists of memory. Aggravating all of this is the work of 'historians' who seek to 'interpret' history unencumbered by any knowledge of or appreciation for what actually might have taken place."[2] Will *time* wipe out Wole Soyinka's works and life from the shores of history? With the passage of time, will the context in which events unfolded in Soyinka's time, and would the facts of what actually happened and informed his literature, activism, and his agenda for African transformation have been forgotten or distorted? In the article "Beating the White Man at His Own Game," Bernth Lindfors raises a big question over the prospect of Wole Soyinka's works and life:

> Some, Chinweizu, already entertain serious doubts about the value of what Soyinka has done. Others may go on acclaiming him even while openly acknowledging they cannot comprehend his works. The real test may come many years from now, when Soyinka is a remote ancestral figure rather than a dynamic, forceful presence influencing contemporary events. Will the works outlive the man? Some past Nobel Prize winners have already been forgotten because their writings spoke only to their contemporaries, not to future generations. Is Soyinka's voice strong and clear enough to echo through the ages?[3]

In this concluding chapter, we review Wole Soyinka's legacies within our subtitle of this book: Literature, Activism, and the African Transformation.

---

[2] Eugene W. Hickok, *Why States? The Challenge of Federalism* (Washington, DC: Heritage Foundation, 2007), 25.

[3] Bernth Lindfors, "Beating the White Man at His Own Game: Nigerian Reactions to the 1986 Nobel Prize in Literature," *Black American Literature Forum* 22, no. 3 (1988): 487. For some critical views on Wole Soyinka's life and works, see, for example, Ali Mazrui, "Wole Soyinka as a Television Critic: A Parable of Deception," *Transition* 54 (1991): 165–77; Willfred F. Feuser, "Wole Soyinka: The Problem of Authenticity," *Black American Literature Forum* 2, no. 3 (1988): 555–75; James Gibbs, "Tear the Painted Masks. Join the Poison Stains: A Preliminary Study of Wole Soyinka's Writings for the Nigerian Press," *Research in African Literatures* 14, no. 1 (1983): 3–44; and Bernth Lindfors, Wole Soyinka, "When are You Coming Home?" *Yale French Studies* 53 (1976): 197–210.

Wole Soyinka, Nobel laureate, is truly a living global icon of scholarship, human rights, and civil action. Three unique specialties set Wole Soyinka apart as an outstanding world-class scholar: 1) he is a cultural transnationalist who has used his intellectual ingenuity to showcase Yoruba culture within a framework of comparative literature; 2) he is an artist and a scholar who is exceptionally gifted in all genres of literature and proficient in all aspects of stagecraft; and 3) he is a political activist who has deployed his stagecraft to the dynamics of national and global re-imagination. Soyinka means different things to different people depending on the part they choose to interrogate. As an all-round guru in all genres of literature, Wole Soyinka is bequeathing a multifaceted living legacy of outstanding scholarship and political activism that transcends the borders of Nigeria and even the African continent. We think Soyinka's legacy is multidimensional, and it is misleading, if not myopic, to consider his legacy solely in terms of the Nobel Prize. In reviewing the outlook for Soyinka's literature, activism, and the African transformation, we draw attention to the following eight areas, among many others, as a telescope for a long view of Soyinka's works and life: 1) the provenance setting for Soyinka's literature; 2) the universal hues of classicism, mythopoeism, and modernism in Soyinka's literature; 3) Yoruba occupational apprenticeship in Soyinka's drama; 4) mafia and maverick activism in Soyinka's literary works; 5) ontology of African culture, orality, and diglossia in Soyinka's literature in English; 6) Soyinka's political activism and the African transformation; 7) African voice of the voiceless: a vanguard of universal humanity and human rights; and 8) an octogenarian model of a healthy lifestyle for longevity.

The Provenance Setting for Soyinka's Literature

Wole Soyinka is a child of destiny; proverbially, he was born in the right place, in the right sociocultural environment, in the right family, and in the right time. In Chapter 4, we interrogate and explain how Wole Soyinka's skills and experiences as a writer and a performing artiste are shrouded in the "collective traditions" and in the collective realities of his Yoruba sociocultural background and upbringing. Soyinka not only imbibed but artfully and professionally cultivated and traded on his childhood's Second World War anti-colonial protest culture and multicultural heritage to inform and drive his mission as a vanguard of human rights, anti-corruption, and the people's voice for responsible governance. Wole Soyinka's life and social activism are of interest to audiences beyond the shores of Nigeria, and indeed beyond the African continent, because the iconic worldwide issues of sleaze, insider trading, corporate false accounting, kleptomaniac political operations, and mafia organized financial crimes (to mention a few of his civil action engagements) reflect not only upon the human condition of the North-South divide and the postcolonial conditions of independent nations, but they also help us locate him as a global figure who in himself has become a discourse in the public sphere of Africa.

In Parts 1 and 2, Introduction and Context, and Historical and Cultural Background respectively, we metaphorically essayed the *setting* for Wole Soyinka's literature. Specifically, Abẹokuta, the city of creativity and innovations and Soyinka's birthplace, was the right place. The Second World War with the catalyst forces of change was the right time for political activism against colonialism, imperialism, racism, and all other forms of oppression and man's inhumanity to man. Soyinka was only a child during the Second World War, a teenager at the time of the British disengagement from its colonies, and a 26-year-old young adult with university degrees at the time of Nigerian independence. These multiple experiences contributed to Soyinka's rise to fame in his chosen career and his political activism. Soyinka was only eighteen years old in 1952 when the colonial administration coopted the first group of Nigerian nationalists in preparation for self-government and independence. He was among the third set of students to be admitted to Nigeria's premier university. Between the ages of thirty and sixty-five (1964–1999), he was a distinguished and respectable contemporary of both the military and civilian Nigerian leaders who emerged at the end of the First Republic. The first group of nationalist leaders was decimated during the January 1966 military coup d'état.

Indeed, Odumegwu Ojukwu, the military governor in the Eastern region, who later declared the Biafran state in 1967, was born on November 4, 1933, and was only a few months older than Soyinka. Yakubu Gowon, who emerged as the Nigerian head of state after the second coup d'état in July 1966, was born on October 19, 1934, hence three months younger than Soyinka. Oluṣẹgun Ọbasanjọ, who served as a military head of state and as a civilian president, was born on May 5, 1937, and was three years younger than Soyinka, while Murtala Muhammed, who became a military head of state after Yakubu Gowon, was born on November 8, 1938, and was four years younger than Soyinka. Bola Ige, Soyinka's friend and classmate at the University College Ibadan, later became the governor of a Western state in 1979. Ige was born on September 13, 1930, and was only four years older than Soyinka. Chinua Achebe was born on November 16, 1930. Almost without exception, these men's parents were privileged Christians and either teachers or colonial federal officials who held posts across Nigeria. For example, Odumegwu Ojukwu was born in Zungeru, and Bola Ige and Yakubu Gowon were born in Zaria. The middle name of Major Chukwuma Nzeogwu, who led the first military coup d'état, is *Kaduna*. He was born in Kaduna. According to Bola Ige, his generation was made up of "detribalized" Nigerians, whose political philosophy of nationalism in West Africa was modeled after Nnamdi Azikiwe's anti-imperialism and anti-colonialism before the incursions of ethnic and national rivalries subverted Pan-Africanism and Nigerian national solidarity within Nigeria and among the other West African colonies.[4]

Borrowing William Shakespeare's words, by accidents of time and place of birth, Wole Soyinka was born great! We have already highlighted Abẹokuta, Soyinka's birthplace, as a city of innovation and creativity. In addition, the tides of decolonization and being one of a few hundred Nigerian university graduates out of a population of about fifty million Nigerians at the time of independence, Soyinka had greatness thrust upon him and his cohort of the educated elite. By accident of time and place Soyinka belongs to the privileged foundation elite members of the independent Nigeria. The University College, Ibadan only produced 450 graduates between 1951 and 1960.[5] From his rebellions against the English dining culture of wearing formal dress with tie to dinner at the University College, Ibadan in the early 1950s, to his protests against the Abacha military regime that earned him a death sentence in 1998, to becoming the first Nigerian Nobel laureate, Soyinka has made history. No mapping of the history of Nigeria would be complete without Soyinka's footprints.

The Universal Hues of Classicism, Mythopoeism, and Modernism in Soyinka's Literature

In Chapter 11, we noted that Wole Soyinka is *a fountain source* of African literature in English, whose Yoruba equivalent is *orisun*. Wole Soyinka belongs without an iota of doubt to the category of humans, in a non-far-fetched way, who could be called living synoptic mirrors because they evocatively (even if briefly) remind us of the nexus between the Yoruba view of what makes a source and these energies spoken thereof: 31 plays, 3 novels, 8 poetry collections, 3 short stories, 5 memoirs, and 13 notable essays, among many other creative works that simply and vehemently defy neat categories, are enough to set one apart through the ages. Given that Wole Soyinka wrote "prodigiously in all the literary forms and genres,"[6] it is therefore not surprising that his literary work is polarized as a universal hue of classicism,

---

[4] Bola Ige, *People, Politics and Politicians of Nigeria (1940–1979)* (Ibadan: Heinemann Educational Books, 1995), 47.
[5] Toyin Falola and Bola Dauda, *Decolonizing Nigeria, 1945–1960: Politics, Power, and Personalities* (Austin: Pan-African University Press, 2017), 412.
[6] Biọdun Jeyifo, *Wole Soyinka: Politics, Poetics, and Postcolonialism* (Cambridge: Cambridge University Press, 2004), 5.

cultural mythopoeism, and modernism. For example, *Death and the King's Horseman*, *A Play of Giants*, *The Bacchae of Euripides: A Communion Rite* are within the realm of the classical— William Shakespeare's historical plays such as *Julius Caesar*, *Macbeth*, etc.—while *A Dance of the Forests* and *Requiem for a Futurologist* are examples of his mythopoeism. *The Trials of Brother Jero*, *Jero's Metamorphosis*, and *Opera Wonyosi* are some of his modernist oeuvre. What any portrayal of Wole Soyinka, through his body of works, immediately and conclusively reveals is that he towers above and is larger than any holistic attempt at textual profiling.

For example, in Chapter 9, we noted that unlike many of his contemporaries, regardless of their infrequent cross-genre adventures, Wole Soyinka's greatness does not come from any single work or field. He is as skilled in drama as in his essays and poetry, deploying his unique energies and ingenuity. Soyinka's productive output contains patterns for accessing and assessing his works; one can work from the general to the specific regardless of genre constraints. Soyinka's approach and artistic philosophy create echoes that can be found in virtually all his works. Critics and scholars can identify recurrent motifs and ideologies in his works. Soyinka's approach has been given many labels: visionary, mythopoeic, reconstructive, revolutionary, Euro-assimilationist, and shamanist. These labels and others receive discursive dominance depending on the context and the specific component of the Soyinka oeuvre being addressed. It is almost impossible to fit Soyinka into any single box; any attempt to weave preconceived critical or theoretical assumptions through his works will yield an array of (unforeseen) possibilities. To achieve an essential knowledge of Soyinka's poetry, we must grapple with his approach to art in general, and to poetry in specific. The poetry of Wole Soyinka is no different from any of his other creative endeavors; it allows curious observers to experience the man's vision, philosophies, and creative peculiarities. Getting acquainted with Soyinka's poetry does not provide automatic entry into his world and into how enduringly his works will pass the test of time; it is essential to have a solid understanding of the culture and the overarching sociopolitical philosophies that he works with. An objective projective imagining of the prospects of Soyinka's works and life requires a recognition of these overarching philosophies, even when the goal is to identify the presence of others.

Soyinka chooses the appropriate literary styles and tools to execute and deliver his chosen agenda. As a literary modernist and at the same time a cultural mythopoetic, Soyinka is always suggesting new ways through which the old can be continually revisited and how each re-visitation can be made anew. Soyinka's concern is with the endless levels of innovation at all possible stages of creative imagination to the moment the collective consciousness is influenced to create the literature of vision. Ultimately, Soyinka's influences are not isolated or readily identifiable the way stars can be identified against the blank curtain of a dark sky; his influences are interwoven, only to be read and identified in a cluster of tightly woven details, each of which speaks for itself and then for the others. To attempt to put it simply, for the matter itself readily defies any such attempt, Soyinka's influences on the trade through which he has made his name are implicated in the contexts that he has brought to light and the ways he has gone about doing so, and the contestations of those ways and the contexts of those contestations. For this obviously complex reason, to begin an engagement with Soyinka and his composite and multimodal manner of influences, perhaps requires setting him within a particular frame, one made from the culture from which he has harvested a lot of symbols, and one which would throw up the necessary image and details essential to the subject of the essay.

In Chapter 5, we noted that what separates Soyinka's literary scholarship from his contemporaries is that Soyinka believes that, "Language study however involves, as we all know, the study of a people's history and culture."[7] Wole Soyinka not only studied the history and culture of the people he writes about, but he considers "dramatic resolution, [as] being closer to [his] real profession."[8] Soyinka, therefore, heroically and professionally cultivates the seemingly obscured and encoded basic tools and jargons of poetry, storytelling, and stagecraft (i.e., hyperbole, melodrama, metaphor, satire, suspense, surprise, creative imagination, visualization, humor, idioms, proverbs, soliloquy, fables, significant objects, demonstration and treatment, plot, characterization, etc.) to create effect and engage his audience. Rosa Figueiredo is quite accurate in her perception and assessment of Soyinka when she writes that the "metaphysical awareness on the part of the audience is, for Soyinka, most clearly seen in those performances of 'ritual' theatre where a fundamental anxiety manifests itself in members of the audience over whether or not the protagonist will survive confrontation with the forces of chaos which now exist in the arena of performance space."[9] Soyinka

---

[7] Wole Soyinka, "Red Card, Green Card: Notes Towards the Management of Hysteria," http://saharareporters.com/2016/11/12.
[8] Soyinka, "Red Card, Green Card."
[9] Rosa Figueiredo, "The Drama of Existence: Myths and Rituals in Wole Soyinka's Theatre," *International Journal of Arts and Sciences* 4, no.1 (2011): 105. See also K. Naveen Kumar, "Yoruba Tradition and Culture in Wole Soyinka's '*The Lion and the Jewel*,'" *Journal of Arts, Science and Commerce* 2, no. 3 (2011): 88–97; Abiodun Musa Rasheed, "The Drama and Theatre of Wole Soyinka," *Encyclopedia of the Arts* 11, no. 3 (2006): 216–29; David Maugham-Brown, "Interpreting and the Interpreters: Wole Soyinka and Practical Criticism," *English in Africa* 6, no. 2 (1979): 51–62; Lawrence Ogbo Ugwuanyi, "I Am Therefore You Are: An Existentialist Perspective on Wole Soyinka's Writings," *UJAH: Unizik Journal of Arts and Humanities* 12, no. 2 (2011): 65–90; and Noureini Tidjani-Serpos, "The Postcolonial Condition: The Archeology of African Knowledge: From the Feat of Ogun and Ṣango to the Postcolonial Creativity of Ọbatala," *Research in African Literatures* 27, no. 1 (1996): 3–18.

writes not just to entertain the *ogbẹri* which literally means the ordinary lay readers and audience, but also for the *ọmọ awo*—the enlightened and knowledgeable members of the stagecraft profession.

Iṣara, Soyinka's narrative of how the king, Ọdẹmọ, was elected in an open contest between two candidates is more than a story. It is a political statement that the Yoruba have democratic traditions and institutions that are adaptable to modern political systems. Soyinka also apparently employs the shared and universal human language of freedom, justice, and human rights from his inherited tripod cultures and histories to enlist empathy, projective identification, and a virtual reality between his audience and the characters in his stories.[10] Wade Cudeback, who was a teacher and Soyinka's father's pen pal, arrives on the day of the election of the king. It was also a symbolic gesture of Soyinka's dream of the universality of human fellowship.

Yoruba Occupational Apprenticeship in Soyinka's Drama

Although Hubert Ogunde, Kola Ogunmola, and Duro Ladipo were forerunners of Théâtre Arts in Nigeria, Wole Soyinka took theater arts to the intellectual level in Nigeria. Modeled after the traditional apprenticeship, Soyinka not only established the Department of Théâtre Arts at the University College, Ibadan solely to teach literary appreciation and critiques and to turn out "academic drama scholars," but he also introduced performance arts, trained artistes and playwrights, established a performance artistes troupe (The Orisun Theatre Company) and produced his play *The Lion and the Jewel* in the English and Yoruba languages. Many of his students became playwrights and dramatists. Obviously, today's Nollywood had benefited from Wole Soyinka's pioneering templates in performance arts in the Nigerian universities. For example, Soyinka's Street or Motor Parks Standup playlets and dramas demonstrated to the amateurish artistes how to start their own drama business. Wole Soyinka will also be remembered for rescuing the 1977 Black and African Festival of Arts and Culture (FESTAC, '77) from a total collapse.

---

[10] "Wole Soyinka: The Writer as Culture Hero," *In Search of Ogun: Soyinka In Spite of Nietzsche*, ed. Odia Ofeimun (Lagos: Hornbill, 2014), 151–64.

Mafia and Maverick Activism in Soyinka's Literary Works

Historians will in future wonder how Wole Soyinka was able to hijack a government radio station; to smuggle out press releases from a maximum security prison; to operate an underground radio station to irritate a military government that had already passed a death sentence on him; to move in and out of the country while the state security agents were hunting for him; and to do a lot of mafia-and-maverick stunts to the annoyance of a military administration! Soyinka confessed his avid belief that tyrants cannot stand the fang of the writers' pen and humor. In his book, *The Man Died*, he wrote, "Books and all forms of writing have always been objects of terror to those who seek to suppress truth."[11] Hence, he skillfully armed himself with a simple but sophisticated combined power of written words and dramaturgy as tools for civil action against the burgeoning crop of corrupt politicians in Nigeria and in Africa at large. To take on the ruthless Nigerian state apparatus, Soyinka ingeniously deployed his precociousness, professional skills and experiences as a performing artist, and his outstanding and all-round talents in all genres of literature (i.e., poetry, fiction and non-fiction, faction, drama) to lampoon the corruption and chaos of the postcolonial African states. Obviously, posterity will find Soyinka's mafia and maverick strategies and tactics for civil disobedience an intriguing case study in how to subvert tyrant intelligence and security apparatuses.

Ontology of African Culture, Orality, and Diglossia in Soyinka's Literature in English

Wole Soyinka like his forerunners, Amos Tutuola and Chinua Achebe is a creator, a courier, and a curator of African literature in English. Soyinka is a chronicler, a memoirist, and a historiographer of African human conditions. With his literary corpus and memoirs, Soyinka elevates oral African philosophies, beliefs, and values. Soyinka championed and aggrandized the cause of oral African literature in English. In Chapter 12, we noted that Soyinka's confronting of the English language demonstrates "diglossia," a linguistic term meaning a juxtaposition of two languages (in Soyinka's case, Yoruba and English). When Soyinka uses English to convey Yoruba idioms, thoughts, or culture, he expresses the internal conflict of a colonized

---

[11] Wole Soyinka, *The Man Died* (Ibadan: Bookcraft, 2014), xxv.

individual—one who struggles to move about seamlessly between two cultures or world visions.

According to Jane Wilkinson, "[t]he will to challenge the abyss, the continued 'battle not merely for a held idea, but more critically for an integrated survival'"[12] drives Soyinka. His work addresses human beings' "most energetic, deeply combative intentions ... bridging the gulf with visionary hopes."[13] Thus, in Chapter 5, we noted that Soyinka joins the cultural terrains of the Yoruba, and specifically that of the Ijẹgba, with his paternal Ijẹbu and maternal Ẹgba families; the Nigerian multiethnic national cultures; and the English and African colonial cultures in both literature and stagecraft. In other words, he creates, reconstructs, and proffers dramatic solutions for the post-independence conflicts in Africa and elsewhere. For example, in *Iṣara: A Voyage Around Essay*, Soyinka makes a hero of Damian, "who wanders into Iṣara from nobody-knows-where and becomes a solid member of the town."[14] This could simply be presumed as Soyinka's promotion of the Yoruba democratic tradition that allows the enthronement of a stranger to become king if the stranger were the choice of Ifa divination. When he allows Baroka, the old traditional chief—and not Lakunle, the modern village teacher—to marry Sidi in *The Lion and the Jewel* it seems radical, but it could be that Soyinka was exercising his authorial liberty to infuse originality into his writing by breaking the mode of conventional royal status of heroes and heroines. After a review of the works of Soyinka and Achebe, Omotoso suggested that Soyinka is much more neutral about any attempt to sponsor the triumph of the past over the present because "those who stick to the old ways sometimes succeed and sometimes fail. But those who wish to combine both ways always fail tragically."[15] With five memoirs; eight volumes of his public speeches, opinions, and oftentimes controversial views and reactions to political issues of the day; more than twenty volumes of historical plays, novels, factions, and books of poetry; and other published academic works, he has bequeathed humanity with invaluable new approaches to historiography and archival methodology.[16] Yes, some of his records are questionable, but they are mostly a great treasury for future historians and researchers. Many students of literature

---

[12] Soyinka, *The Man Died*, 25.
[13] Jane Wilkinson, "Daring the Abyss: The Art of Wole Soyinka," *Africa: Rivista trimestrade di studie documentazione dell'Istituto italiano per l'Africa e l'Oriente* 41, no. 4 (Dicembre 1988): 611.
[14] Omotoso, *Achebe or Soyinka: A Study in Contrasts*, 6.
[15] Omotoso, *Achebe or Soyinka*, 25.
[16] For a review of Soyinka's contribution to historiography see, for example, Glenn Odom, "'The End of Nigerian History:' Wole Soyinka and Yoruba Historiography," *Comparative Drama* 42, no. 2 (2008): 205–29. For a review of his autobiographies, see, for example, Alioune Sow, "Political Intuition and African Autobiographies of Childhood," *Biography* 33, no. 3 (2010): 498–517.

have obtained research degrees on Soyinka's scholarship.[17] In spite of all the social and political controversies and the doubts about authenticity that surround his works and life, we want to think he will be remembered for a long time as a great chronicler, memoirist, and historiographer.

In controversial matters involving Soyinka, it is a difficult and formidable task to disentangle the facts from fictions—and factions. It is a problematic process to sort out the rights and wrongs! For example, when Soyinka worked with the Federal Road Safety Commission, Tunde Adeniran noted that Soyinka was a consummate administrator, demonstrating "a high degree of administrative efficiency, discipline and accountability," traits he also demonstrated as the head of various university departments: "[Soyinka] was the master conceiver and the grand designer of multidimensional programmes of the Commission made operational within political structures and process that were constantly changing."[18] In addition, in an address during a farewell parade to mark Soyinka's stepping down as Chairman of the Governing Council of the FRSC on September 3, 1993, Olu Agunloye praised Soyinka "as [an] originator, designer, typist, driver, patrol man, [and] Executive Chairman."[19] Soyinka served without drawing a salary. However, in certain circumstances, Soyinka was reportedly difficult to work with. In this regard, for example, some of his students were not impressed that he was hardly present at his lectures. In a tribute to him in *Before Our Very Eyes*, Olumuyiwa Awẹ, draws attention to some of the difficulties Soyinka creates for those who work with him.[20]

Soyinka's Political Activism and the African Transformation

In Chapter 10, we noted how Wole Soyinka uses his satire to reveal the excesses of African politicians and interrogated how he explores the disillusionment of the postcolonial nation-state as part of his revolutionary commitment. Most of Soyinka's works are considered sociopolitical satires that both ridicule and critique sociological injustices in African society.

---

[17] See, for example, Chonsi John M. Lunga, "A Critical Analysis of Wole Soyinka as a Dramatist, with Special Reference to his Engagement in Contemporary Issues," MA thesis, University of South Africa, 1994.
[18] Tunde Adeniran, *The Politics of Wole Soyinka* (Ibadan: Fountain Publications, 1994), 147–148.
[19] Olu Agunloye, "A Parade of Honour for Duty, Excellence and Integrity," quoted in Adeniran, *The Politics of Wole Soyinka*, *The Politics of Wole Soyinka* (Ibadan: Fountain Publications, 1994), 148.
[20] See Olumuyiwa Awẹ, "Before My Very Eyes," in *Before Our Very Eyes*, ed., Dapo Adelugba (Ibadan: Spectrum Book, 1987).

The play *The Lion and the Jewel*, published in 1962, addresses the conflict of modernism and indigenous African traditions. His works have become direct tools for social protest; his literature reflects his political concerns along with his literary ambitions. Like most of his works, Soyinka's *The Lion and the Jewel* also incorporates his cultural heritage and understanding of Yoruba aesthetics. Traditional leaders are also targeted alongside national politicians. Soyinka's more serious satirical representations look at several sociopolitical dynamics. The play *Madmen and Specialists* (1970) looks at the interchange of power between political leaders, referred to as madmen and specialists, using the civil war to inflict dehumanizing psychological effects on Nigerians. Soyinka's play *The Trials of Brother Jero* mocks some of the social realities of Nigerian society. He ridicules the state's religious hypocrisy, revealing its folly and possibly rescuing its unsuspecting victims. Setting aside the writer's social responsibility of indicting corruption in society, Soyinka's other works, including *A Dance of the Forests*, reveal his understanding of traditional Yoruba mythology.

The octogenarian Wole Soyinka's life and works are issues rather than events. Soyinka, in all his life, has been engaged in social engineering and reengineering using different genres of literature, including stagecraft to offer alternative public policy options, and to inform (and sometimes to incite) and mobilize civil action. Wole Soyinka views the reclamation of African cultural identity as the social responsibility of an African writer. Hence, his literary works and life of political activism suggest ways of return even to the alienated writer, regardless of degrees of alienation or those who look within from without, those educated in the West, employing aspects of Western logic, or writing with a hybridized consciousness, without losing fidelity to the motherland, which remains the dominant subject of their creative endeavors.

Soyinka is however neither a revisionist nor a fatalist. He is pragmatically idealistic and realistic. He is continually engaged in a constant and never-ending strategic and tactical reinvention of his activism agenda. One unique and creative element of Soyinka's works and political activism is the sheer range of issues with which he continues to engage. While working on this book, we noted that not one week passed without Soyinka being in the news; he often commented on and shared his views on national or international issues regarding human rights. Soyinka's life continues to be full and extraordinary. Every day brings new controversies that spawn reams of paper. For example, Soyinka and the eighty-two-million Naira birthday celebration organized in his name by the Rivers State during Rotimi Amaechi's administration. In November 2017, Soyinka made the news when it was falsely rumored that he objected to his son marrying an Igbo woman and that Soyinka's son Tunlewa married an Igbo woman, Nneka Nwachukwu, who was allegedly ten years older in Atlanta, Georgia. But the truth is that Tunlewa was older than Nneka. As we noted in Chapter 6, it is also remarkable to imagine that Soyinka, who objected to his parent's imposition of marital traditions, would dictate who his son married. The following week, Soyinka was again defending himself in the media for supporting the Buhari administration. The media argued Buhari's administration did not align with Soyinka's typical standard of governance. As Soyinka did on the military execution of Ken Saro-Wiwa during Sani Abacha's regime on November 10, 1995, he called on Nigerian youths to take over the baton and carry on the struggle. He followed this cause with comments on the atrocities of the herdsmen in Nigeria. In September 2020, Soyinka was on the air with an article entitled, "Between 'Dividers-in-Chief' and Dividers-in-Law." While using the opportunity to pass derisive remarks on the United States' President Donald Trump, Soyinka rocked the sinking boat of Nigerian powers that be, challenging Olușẹgun Ọbasanjọ, the former head of state, as "co-architect with other past leaders of the crumbling edifice that is still generously called Nigeria," and to make innuendoes directed at Muhammadu Buhari, the current president, for over-centralization, for lopsided appointments to crucial positions in the civil service and parastatals, and for his inability to provide the basic human requirements for Nigerians. And before the dust could settle, he has engaged in another controversy as to how Ọbatala, the god of creation and fecundity and one of the Yoruba pantheon (Orișas) gods, is more tolerant than the God of Christianity.

Soyinka has strategically continued to widen the scope of his political activism, unlike Dr. Nnamdi Azikiwe, who rose to fame because of his campaign against colonialism and imperialism and for his support for the workers' general strike in 1945. Azikiwe's relevance dwindled immediately after Great Britain granted independence to its colonies. British liquidation of its colonies literally deflated Azikiwe's sole act of anti-colonial political activism. Soyinka, too, played a great role in the struggle for independence and in the success of the workers' general strike in 1964. However, he moved on to other issues. He diversified his political activism agenda. After independence in 1960, Soyinka changed his civic activism from anti-colonialism to other issues, such as anti-apartheid, deaths caused by drivers on Nigerian roads, good governance, anti-vice, and human dignity.[21]

---

[21] For an overview of the various areas of Soyinka's civil actions see, for example, James Gibbs, "The Writer and the Road: Wole Soyinka and Those Who Cause Death by Dangerous Driving," *The Journal of Modern African Studies* 33, no. 3 (1995): 469–98; Lunga, "A Critical Analysis of Wole Soyinka as a Dramatist" ; Adebayo Mosobalaje, "Readers of Wole Soyinka's Political Drama and Theatre," *The African Symposium: An Online Journal of the Educational Research Network* 11, no. 1 (2011): 166–77; Henry Louis Gates, Jr., "Censorship and Justice: On Rushdie and Soyinka," *Research in African Literatures* 21, no. 1 (1990): 137–9; Gates, Jr., "Wole Soyinka, Mythopoesis and the Agon of Democracy," 187–94; F. Odun Balogun, "Wole Soyinka and the Literary Aesthetic of African Socialism," *Black American Literature Forum* 22, no. 3 (1988): 503–30; Dominic Alimbey Derry, "Exploring the Theme of Corruption in the Soyinka's *The Road*," *International Journal on Studies in English Language and Literature* 2, Issue 8 (2004): 72–84; and Amanda Price, "The Theatre of Promiscuity: A Comparative Study of the Dramatic Writings of Wole Soyinka and Howard Barker," PhD thesis, University of Leeds, 1995.

African Voice of the Voiceless: A Vanguard of Universal Humanity and Human Rights

In the 1950s, at the beginning of his chosen mission to fight for human rights, it was easy to dismiss Soyinka as an exuberant youth who presumably would mellow with time. However, as an octogenarian, Soyinka remains the firebrand that he was in his early childhood years. The energy, courage, audacity, and readiness to die for a just and collective cause placed Soyinka's politics and statesmanship in a class of their own. Biọdun Jeyifo has asserted that,

> Soyinka wrote prodigiously in all the literary forms and genres. ... and more portentously, Soyinka occupies his distinct place within the "quartet" [Achebe, Soyinka, Okigbo, and J. P. Clark] on account of his propensity for taking very daring *artistic* and *political* risks in furtherance of his deepest political and ethical convictions, risks which often entailed considerable peril to himself and also profoundly challenged, but at the same time complexly re-inscribed the determinate elitism of his generation of writers. The articulation between the political and the artistic risks is one of the most fascinating and complex aspects of Soyinka's career.[22]

No history of the war against corruption and state terrorism in Nigeria, indeed, of the entirety of Africa and the world at large, would be complete without recognizing Soyinka's powerful and strident voice in his works, such as *Season of Anomy*, *The Man Died*, *The Jero Plays*, *Madmen and Specialists*, *The Road*, *The Lion and the Jewel*, *Death and the King's Horseman*, *A Shuttle in the Crypt*, *A Play of Giants*, *The Open Sore of a Continent: A Personal Narrative of the Nigeria Crisis*, *King Baabu*, *Bacchae of Euripides*, and *Interventions: Between Defective Memory and Public Lie*.[23]

In 1953, Soyinka launched the Pyrates Confraternity to begin his lifelong political activism and crusade against colonialism, conventions, elitism, and the inexcusable complicity of the comprador educated elites.

---

[22] Jeyifo, *Wole Soyinka: Politics, Poetics, and Postcolonialism*, 5.
[23] For a review of Soyinka's works on civil right issues see, for example, Derek Wright, "The Festive Year: Wole Soyinka's Annus Mirabilis," *The Journal of Modern African Studies* 28, no. 3 (1990): 511–19; Derek Wright, "Soyinka's Smoking Shotgun: The Later Satires," *World Literature Today* 66, no. 1 (1992): 27–34; Bruce King, "Wole Soyinka and the Nobel Prize for Literature," *The Sewanee Review* 96, no. 2 (1988): 339–45; and James Gibbs, "Prize and Prejudice: Reactions to the Award of the 1986 Nobel Prize for Literature to Wole Soyinka, Particularly in the British Press," *Black American Literature Forum* 22, no. 3 (1988): 449–65.

Arguably, Soyinka's 1953 student anti-colonialism and imperialism Pyrates Confraternity is now believed in many quarters to be the origin of cultism, drug abuse, and criminality among undergraduates in Nigerian universities, and that sentiment will outlive Soyinka. Professor E. A. Ayandele has categorized Nigerian leaders into four groups: 1) the educated elites as the Deluded Hybrids (the first generation of the educated elites who saw themselves as members of the imperial motherland); 2) the Collaborators (the second generation who collaborated with the colonial powers); 3) the Windsowers (the nationalists who fought for independence and promised life more abundant in postcolonial era); and 4) the New Nigerians (the postcolonial children).[24] In the *African Times*, Ayandele elaborated on these categories:

> The [deluded] educated elite more or less under the influence of the Christian faith, more or less imbued with Christian principles, precepts, are and will be indispensable as a vanguard of the great army of civilization that must be projected upon the ignorant barbarism of heathen Africa whenever the means for such projection shall be arranged.[25]

Ironically, it has been no more than sixty years since neocolonialism replaced colonialism, and globalization replaced imperialism. Apparently, Soyinka's works and life will remain relevant for a long time not only because the issues of humanity he championed are as alive as "Mary Dyer, a Quaker, who was hanged in the 1600s for her membership in an unconventional faith."[26] Four hundred years on, Soyinka is protesting against the death penalty for blasphemy. More important, the so-called New Nigerians whom Ayandele presumed were the long-awaited messiahs who would redeem Nigeria have turned out to be nothing but reincarnated—if slightly improved versions of—Deluded Hybrids, Collaborators, and Windsowers. In Pilkings's line in *Death and the King's Horseman*, Soyinka apocalyptically wrote, "You think you've stamped it all out but it's always lurking under the surface somewhere."[27]

Soyinka is synonymous with the global crusade against corruption and irresponsible leadership and governance. For example, after a comprehensive review of Soyinka's works and life (politics, poetics, and postcolonialism), Biodun Jeyifo concluded that *From Zia with Love*, preceded by *Jero's*

---

[24] E. A. Ayandele, *The Educated Elite in the Nigerian Society* (Ibadan: Ibadan University Press, 1974; reprint, 1979).
[25] *African Times*, July 1, 1880, quoted as epigraph in Ayandele, *The Educated Elite*, 7.
[26] Lindfors, "Beating the White Man at his Own Game," 487.
[27] Lindfors, "Beating the White Man at his Own Game," 487.

Metamorphosis, Opera Wonyosi, and *A Play of Giants*, is Soyinka's ultimate response against the cruelty and corruption of military despots against the Nigerian people:

> The elaborate carnivalesque mode with which the anti-militarism of this play is rendered puts it in the company of [his] earlier plays ... each of which also marshals a combination of dialogue, music, spectacle and plebeian festivity to attack the pretensions to absolute and invincible power by Africa's postcolonial military dictators.[28]

Soyinka's mythopoetic works and his symbolic and melodramatic glorification and revival of the Yoruba pantheon (Orişas) gods, however, may not survive the onslaught of the continued tsunami of Christian Pentecostalism and Islamic fundamentalism that has not only infected the minds of most Nigerians, including intellectuals, but also inadvertently reinforced European cultural imperialism.

It would be pretentious to expect Soyinka's works to convert people to worshippers of any of the Yoruba pantheon (Orişas) gods: Ogun, Şango, or Qbatala. In other words, his earlier works, such as *A Dance of the Forests*, *Death and the King's Horseman*, and *The Lion and the Jewel*, may become dated with time. Similarly, Soyinka's *Intervention* series may become dated because they dealt with issues of the moment. However, Soyinka's post-civil war political satires, such as the *Madmen and Specialists* and *From Zia with Love*, and his prison notes and poems, such as *The Man Died*, *A Shuttle in the Crypt*, and *Poems from Prison*, despite the allegations of obscurity, will outlive him simply because they rekindled clarion calls for civil societal action—in the spirit of Antonio Gramsci and Nelson Mandela—against tyranny and people's inhumanity.

Octogenarian Model of a Healthy Lifestyle for Longevity

In a private correspondence with Bola Dauda, Obafemi Awolowo wrote "Life begins at 70." He felt that at age seventy, a person conquers the "'tyrannies of the flesh,'" which are the source of all vices. It is also an opportunity to act and think more spiritually: "Now that he is more spiritual than before, his mind force should be stronger; he should be more mentally acute in all the things that really matter in life; and should, therefore, be more useful

---

[28] Jeyifo, *Wole Soyinka*, 114.

to society." Though the body may fail, Awolowo cautioned, the decline of old age "can be substantially retarded by rigorous and scientific physical exercise."[29]

With Soyinka, however, it seems life really begins at eighty! At this stage in his life, Soyinka exudes the mental alertness and boldness, and even the physical agility of the "soldier" he was when he confronted colonialism and imperialism in his youth. Soyinka enjoys nature and hunting, but he is neither a teetotaler nor a vegetarian, neither a puritan nor a monk! Soyinka loves wine, women, cigars, and bush meat! What then accounts for his longevity and good health? He has an enlarged prostate, but that is not anything to worry about for an octogenarian. Given the fascination of researchers with the brain of the deceased Albert Einstein, one would not be surprised if Soyinka's greatest legacy turned out to be an attempt by medical historians, geriatricians, archeologists, and anthropologists to study his brain to answer the questions: "What were his flesh, bones, mind, and Soul like?" What was the secret of his youthful age and physic? And more important, what accounts for his youthful energy and the Spartan or the gladiator's audacity to dare put his life and his privileged elitist social standing on the line for what Biọdun Jeyifo has described as *artistic* and *political* risks?[30] Posterity will for a long time remember Wole Soyinka because his works and life have engaged the intractable human issues and the essence of humanity. In other words, there are a many specialist articles and books on different aspects of Wole Soyinka's works, life, and politics, but Soyinka has given humanity a classic literary corpus and a lot of biographical materials with which we could portentously conclude that Soyinka's works will outlive him.

---

[29] All quotations from Chief Obafemi Awolowo to Bola Dauda, in his letter of July 11, 1984, at the occasion of Awolowo's seventy-fifth birthday that same year.
[30] Jeyifo, *Wole Soyinka*, 5.

BIBLIOGRAPHY

Abou-bakr, Randa. "The Political Prisoner as Antihero: The Prison Poetry of Wole Soyinka and Ahmad Fu'ad Nigm." *Comparative Literature Studies* 46, no. 2 (2009): 261–86.
Aboyade, Olabimpe. *Wole Soyinka and Yoruba Oral Tradition in Death and the King's Horseman*. Ibadan: Fountain Publications, 1994.
Abrams, M. H. *A Glossary of Literary Terms*. Chicago: Heinle and Heinle, 1999.
Academy of Achievement. "Wole Soyinka: The Literary Lion." https://www.achievement.org/achiever/wole-soyinka/#interview.
Achebe, Chinua. *Morning Yet on Creation Day*. New York: Anchor Books, 1976.
Achebe, Chinua. *There Was a Country: A Personal History of Biafra*. London: Penguin Books, 2012.
Adeniran, Tunde. *The Politics of Wole Soyinka*. Ibadan: Fountain Publications, 1994.
Adetuyi, Chris A. "Thematic Preoccupation of Nigerian Literature: A Critical Approach." *English Linguistics Research* 6, no. 3 (2017): 22–6.
Adeyemi, S. "Interpreting the Interpreters: The Narratives of the Postcolony in Wole Soyinka's *The Interpreters*." *Cross Cultures* 168 (2013): 29–38.
Afolayan, Kayode. "Wole Soyinka's A Play of Giants and King Baabu: The Crises Between Ideology and (Social) Vision." *Tydskrif Vir Letterkunde* 54, no. 1 (2017): 158–69.
African Times, July 1, 1880, quoted as epigraph in E. A. Ayandele, *The Educated Elite in the Nigerian Society*. Ibadan: Ibadan University Press, 1974.
Agbasiere, J. "African Literature and Social Commitment." In *Major Themes in African Literature*, edited by D. U. Oputa and A. U. Ohaegbu. Nsukka: AP Press, 2000.
Agunloye, Olu. "A Parade of Honour for Duty, Excellence and Integrity." In Tunde Adeniran, *The Politics of Wole Soyinka*. Ibadan: Fountain Publications, 1994.
Agyeman-Duah, Ivor and Ogochukwu Promise, eds. *Crucible of the Ages: Essays in Honour of Wole Soyinka at 80*. Ibadan: Bookcraft, 2014.
Ajibade, Kunle. "Wole Soyinka Wins the Europe Theater Prize." https://www.pmnewsnigeria.com/2017/12/12/wole-soyinka-wins-europe-theater-prize/
Akingbe, Niyi. "Writing Violence: Problematizing Nationhood in Wole Soyinka's *A Shuttle in the Crypt*." *Tydskrif vir Letterkunde* 50, no. 2 (2013): 124–47.
Akwanya, Amechi. *The Superman as Master Narrative in Wole Soyinka's Season of Anomy*. SAGE Open 5 (2014).
Alizda, Matthew Q. "A Reading of Soyinka's *The Road* in the Light of Roland Barthes' Theory of the Semic Code and Symbolic Code." *Elixir Literature* 49 (2012): 10124–7.

Alter, Peter. *Nationalism*. London: Edward Arnold, 1985.
Amuta, Chidi. "The Ideological Content of Soyinka's War Writings." *African Studies Review* 29, no. 3 (1986): 43–54.
Anyadike, Chima. "The Cracks in the Wall and the Colonial Incursion: Things Fall Apart and Arrow of God as Novels of Resistance." In *The Postcolonial Lamp: Essays in Honour of Dan* Izevbaye, edited by Remi Raji and Oyeniyi Okunoye, 279–293. Ibadan: Bookcraft, 1995.
Anyokwu, Christopher. "Ode to Chaos and Amnesia: Fractured Narrative and Heteroglossia as Postcolonial Othering in Wole Soyinka's *A Dance of the Forests*." *Nordic Journal of African Studies* 21, no. 1 (2012): 34–48.
Appiah, Kwame A. "A Master of His Trade." In *Crucible of the Ages: Essays in Honour of Wole Soyinka*, edited by Ivor Agyeman-Duah and Ogochukwu Promise, 106. Ibadan: Bookcraft, 2014.
Appiah, Kwame A. "An Evening with Wole Soyinka." *Black American Literature Forum* 22, no. 4 (1988): 777–85.
Ariole, Victor C. "Negritude and Tigritude: An Analysis of Language Content for Development Purposes." *Contemporary Experiences: Journal of African Humanities* 1, no. 1 (2013).
Asalache, Khadambi. "The Making of a Poet: Wole Soyinka." *Présence Africaine*, Nouvelle série, no. 67, 3e Trimestre (1968): 172–4.
Asante, Molefi Kete. *The History of Africa: The Quest for Eternal Harmony*. New York: Routledge, 2014.
Atta, Sefi. "Hallo Sefi." In *Crucible of the Ages: Essays in Honour of Wole Soyinka at 80*, edited by Ivor Agyeman-Duah and Ogochukwu Promise, 11–8. Ibadan: Bookcraft, 2014.
Awẹ, Olumuyiwa. "Before My Very Eyes." In *Before Our Very Eyes*, edited by Dapo Adelugba. Ibadan: Spectrum, 1987.
Awolowo, Obafemi. *Path to Nigerian Freedom*. London: Faber and Faber Ltd., 1946.
Ayandele, E. A. *The Educated Elite in the Nigerian Society*. Ibadan: Ibadan University Press, 1974.
Babalola, S. A. *The Content and Form of Yoruba Ijala*. Oxford: Clarendon Press, 1966.
Babs, Seyi. "26th Convocation Ceremony FUNAAB to Honour Prof. Wole Soyinka, Prof. Toyin Falola." https://community.unaab.edu.ng/blog/2018/11/15/26th-convocation-ceeremony-funaab-to-honour-prof-wole-soyinka-prof-toyin-falola.
Bakhtin, Mikhail. *The Dialogic Imagination: Four Essays*. Edited by Michael Holquist, trans. Caryl Emerson and Michael Holquist. Austin: University of Texas Press, 1981.
Balogun, T. Odun. "Wole Soyinka and the Literary Aesthetic of African Socialism." *Black American Literature Forum* 22, no. 3, (1988): 503–30.
Bamiro, Edmund. "Stylistic Functions of 'Discollocation' in Soyinka's Novels: A Systemic-functional Analysis." *Theory and Practice in Language Studies* 4, no. 12 (2014): 2492–7.
Bandyopadhyay, Kajal. *Tension and Synthesis in Wole Soyinka's Plays*. Dhaka: University of Dhaka, 2012.
Banham, Martin. "Wole Soyinka: An Appreciation." Leeds African Studies Bulletin. https://lucas.leeds.ac.uk/article/wole-soyinka-an-appreciation-martin-banham/

Barry, P. *Beginning Theory: An Introduction to Literary and Cultural Theory.* 2nd ed.. Manchester: Manchester University Press, 2002.
Barthes, R. "The Death of the Author." In *The Norton Anthology of Theory and Criticism*, edited by V. B. Leitch. New York, W.W Norton and Company Ltd., 1986.
Beier, Ulli. "Wole Soyinka on 'Identity.'" In *Conversations with Wole Soyinka*, edited by Biọdun Jeyifo, 167–81. Jackson: University Press of Mississippi, 2001.
Belasco, Bernard. *The Entrepreneur as Culture Hero: Pre-adaptations in Nigerian Economic Development.* New York: Praeger, 1980.
Bennis, Warren. *Still Surprised: A Memoir of a Life in Leadership.* San Francisco, CA: Jossey-Bass, 2010.
Bertens, H. *Literary Theory: The Basics.* 2nd ed.. London: Routledge, 2001.
Biobaku, S. O. *The Ẹgba and Their Neighbours, 1842–72.* Oxford: Clarendon Press, 1957.
Birch, D. *Language, Literature and Critical Practice.* London: Routledge, 1989.
Brainy Quote. "William Shakespeare Quotes." Xplore. https://www.brainyquote.com/quotes/william_shakespeare_166828.
Brennan, T. *Salman Rushdie and the Third World.* London: Macmillan, 1989.
Britannica. "Abẹokuta." https://www.britannica.com/place/Abẹokuta.
Brodie, Clara. "'The Story We Had to Tell': How Chinua Achebe and Wole Soyinka Reclaimed Nigerian Identity Through Their Writing." *Honors Thesis Collection*, Wellesley College, Paper 89, 2013. https://repository.wellesley.edu/thesiscollection/89.
Brown, L. W. *The African Heritage and the Harlem Renaissance. A Re-evaluation. African Literature Today*, edited by Eldred Durosimi Jones. New York: Africana, 1998.
Brunschwig, Henri. "L'Avenement de l'Afrique Noire." In *West Africa Under Colonial Rule*, edited by M. Crowder. London: Hutchinson, 1968.
Brusby, Margaret. "Fragments from a Chest of Memories." In *Crucible of the Ages: Essays in Honour of Wole Soyinka at 80*, edited by Ivor Asyeman-Duah and Ogochukwu Promise, 19–26. Ibadan: Bookcraft, 2014.
Buzan, Tony and Raymond Keene. *Buzan's Book of Genius: And How to Unleash Your Own.* London: Stanley Paul, 1994.
Celucien, Joseph L. "Wole Soyinka: Chronology and Selected Bibliography." *The Journal of Pan African Studies* 8, no. 5 (2015): 190–5.
Centre for African Studies (LUCAS), "Honorary Degree." July 31, 1973. https://lucas.leeds.ac.uk/article/honorary-degree/.
Chinweizu. "That Nobel Prize Brouhaha." *The Guardian*, 1985.
Chinweizu. "Pan-Africanism and the Nobel Prize." *The Guardian*, 1986.
Chinweizu, Onwuchekwa Jemie and Ihechukwu Madubuike. *Toward the Decolonization of African Literature.* Vol. I, *African Fiction and Poetry and Their Critics.* Washington, DC: Howard University Press, 1983.
Chinweizu, Onwuchekwa Jemie and Ihechukwu Madubuike. "Towards the Decolonization of African Literature." *Transition* 48 (1975): 29–57.
Churchill, Winston. *A History of the English-Speaking Peoples.* London: Cassel and Co., 1956.
Churchill, Winston. *Great Contemporaries.* London: Readers' Union Ltd., 1939.

Churchill, Winston. "Finest Hour." June 18, 1940. https://winstonchurchill.org/resources/speeches/1940-the-finest-hour/their-finest-hour/.
Conradie, P. J. "Syncretism in Wole Soyinka's Play, 'The Bacchae of Euripides'." *South African Journal* 4, no. 6 (1990): 61–74.
Cooper, Brenda. "The Two-Faced Ogun: Postcolonial Intellectuals and the Positioning of Wole Soyinka." *English in Africa* 22, no.2 (1995): 44–69.
Covey, Stephen R. *The 8th Habit: From Effectiveness to Greatness.* London: Simon & Schuster, 2004.
Crehan, Stewart. "The Spirit of Negation in the Works of Soyinka." *Research in African Literatures* 21, no. 4 (1990): 15–31.
Crosley, Hilary. "Nobel Laureate Wole Soyinka wins Anisfield-Wolf Book Award." https://www.theroot.com/nobel-laureate-wole-soyinka-wins-anisfield-wolf-book-awards-1790896125
Dauda, Bola. "Proverbs." *Encyclopedia of the Yoruba*, edited by Toyin Falola and Akintunde Akinyemi, 284–5. Bloomington: Indiana University Press, 2016.
Dauda, Bola. "Communication: Nonverbal." *Encyclopedia of the Yoruba*, edited by Toyin Falola and Akintunde Akinyemi, 72–3. Bloomington: Indiana University Press, 2016.
David, Mary T. "The Theme of Regeneration in Selected Works by Wole Soyinka." *Black American Literary Forum* 22, no. 4 (1988): 645–61.
Davies, Lanre. "The Political Economy of the Ẹgba Nation: A Study in Modernization and Diversification, 1830–960." *African Nebula* 7 (2014): 74–100.
De Mel, Neloufer. "Myth as History: Wole Soyinka's 'A Dance of the Forests'." *Wasafiri* 9, no. 18 (1993): 27–33.
Derry, Dominic Alimbey. "Exploring the Theme of Corruption in Soyinka's The Road." *International Journal on Studies in English Language and Literature* 2, no. 8 (2004): 72–84.
De Vroom, Theresia. *The Many Dimensions of Wole Soyinka.* Archived 5 June 2013 at the Wayback Machine, Vistas, Loyola Marymount University.
Djelloul, Bourahla. "Modernism in James Joyce's Ulysses and Wole Soyinka's The Interpreters: A Comparative Study." MA diss., University M'hamed Bougara at Boumerdes, 2008. http://dlibrary.univ-boumerdes.dz:8080/jspui/bitstream/123456789/4835/1/bourahla.pdf.
Dorsch, T. S. *Longinus on the Sublime: Classical Literary Criticism.* Translated by T. S. Dorsch. Middlesex: Penguin Books, 1965.
Elutade, Olajumoke. "Wole Soyinka's Wife Relates Their Love Story." *The News Magazine*, July 21, 2014.
Esenwein, George. "Socialism." In *New Dictionary of the History of Ideas*, edited by Maryanne C. Horowitz, 2227–35. New York: Charles Scribner's Sons, 2005.
Euba, Femi. "Wole Soyinka." In *Postcolonial African Writers: A Bio-bibliographical Critical Source Book*, edited by Siga Fatima Jagne and Pushpa Parekh, 438–54. New York: Routledge, 2012.
Ezeliona O. "Elegy for the Mystery Cocks: Modern African Literature and the Making of Its Classics." In *The Postcolonial Lamp. Essays in Honour of Dan Izevbaye*, edited by Remi Raji and Oyeniyi Okunoye, 97–135. Ibadan: Bookcraft, 2008.

Falola, Toyin and Bola Dauda, eds. "The Activist Moment: Nationalism and Radical Politics, 1945–51." *Decolonizing Nigeria, 1945–60: Politics, Power, and Personalities*, edited by Toyin Falola and Bola Dauda, 105–36. Austin: Pan African University Press, 2017.
Falola, Toyin and Bola Dauda. *Decolonizing Nigeria, 1945–60: Politics, Power, and Personalities*. Austin: Pan-African University Press, 2017.
Fanon, Frantz. *A Dying Colonialism*. Translated by Haakon Chevalier. New York: Grove Press, 1967.
Fanon, Frantz. *The Wretched of the Earth*. Translated by Constance Farrington. New York: Grove Press, 1961; 1963.
Feuser, Willfred F. "Wole Soyinka: The Problem of Authenticity." *Black American Literature Forum* 22, no. 3 (1988): 555–75.
Figueiredo, Rosa. "The Drama of Existence: Myths and Rituals in Wole Soyinka's Theatre." *International Journal of Arts and Sciences* 4, no. 1 (2011): 105–13.
Finnegan, Ruth. *Oral Literature in Africa*. Nairobi: Oxford University Press, 1970.
Fioupou, Christiane. "Interview of Wole Soyinka in Paris in February 1995." *Présence Africaine*, Nouvelle série, no. 154, 2e Semestre (1996): 87–92.
Forde, Daryll. *The Yoruba Speaking Peoples of South-Western Nigeria*. London: International African Institute, 1951.
Fulghum, Robert. *All I Need to Know I Learned in Kindergarten: Uncommon Thoughts on Common Things*. London: HarperCollins Publishers, 1994.
Gao, W. "'The Fourth Stage' and 'Ritual Tragedy' of Wole Soyinka: Death and the King's Horseman for Example." *Foreign Literature Studies* 33, no. 3 (2011): 127–34.
Garba, Ismail Baba. "The Lost Language of Enlightenment: Return to Algadez and the New Nigerian Writing." In *The Postcolonial Lamp: Essays in Honour of Dan Izevbaye*, edited by Remi Raji and Oyeniyi Okunoye, 375–90. Ibadan: Bookcraft, 2008.
Gates Jr., Henry Louis. "Censorship and Justice: On Rushdie and Soyinka." *Research in African Literatures* 21, no. 1 (1990): 137–39.
Gates Jr., Henry Louis. "Wole Soyinka: Mythopoesis and the Agon of Democracy." *The Georgia Review* 49, no. 1 (1995): 187–94.
Gbemi, Adeoti, ed. Ife Journal of The Institute of Cultural Studies 10 (2014).
George, Anaso and Eziafa Christopher Nwabudike. "Culture, Language and Evolution of African Literature." *IOSR Journal of Humanities And Social Science (IOSR-JHSS)* 19, no. 4, ver. III (2014): 81–5.
Gibbs, James. "The Writer and the Road: Wole Soyinka and Those Who Cause Death by Dangerous Driving." *The Journal of Modern African Studies* 33, no. 3 (1995): 469–98.
Gibbs, James. "Biography into Autobiography: Wole Soyinka and the Relatives Who Inhabit 'Aké.'" *The Journal of Modern African Studies* 26, no. 3 (1988): 546–7.
Gibbs, James, ed. *Critical Perspectives on Wole Soyinka*. Washington: Three Continents, 1980.
Gibbs, James. "Tear the Painted Masks. Join the Poison Stains: A Preliminary Study of Wole Soyinka's Writings for the Nigerian Press." *Research in African Literatures* 14, no. 1 (1983): 3–44.
Gibbs, James. *Wole Soyinka*. London: Macmillan Publishers, 1986.

Gibbs, James. "Prize and Prejudice: Reactions to the Award of the 1986 Nobel Prize for Literature to Wole Soyinka, Particularly in the British Press." *Black American Literature Forum* 22, no. 3 (1988): 449–65.

Gilbertova, Iva. "Wole Soyinka: *Death and the King's Horseman.*" *BRNO Studies in English* 21, no. 1 (1995): 85–96.

Godwin, Peter. "Wole Soyinka: 'If Religion Is Taken Away, I'd Be Happy'." *Telegraph*, October 12, 2012.

Goleman, Daniel. *Emotional Intelligence: Why It Can Matter More Than IQ*. London: Bloomsbury Publishing Plc, 1996.

Green, Laurence Jabulani F. "Assailing 'As': A Study of Wole Soyinka's Drama." A Thesis Submitted to the School of Graduate Studies, Department of English, McMaster University, Ontario, Canada, 1989.

Gulere, Cornelius Wambi. "Foreign Languages: Lessons from the Past, Innovations for the Future." Foreign Languages Conference, 2014.

Harding, Frances. "Soyinka and Power: Language and Imagery in Madmen and Specialists." *African Languages and Cultures* 4, no. 1 (1991): 87–98.

Heidegger, Martin. *Poetry, Language, Thought*, trans. Albert Hofstadter. New York: Harper & Row, 1971, 191–2, quoted in Dele Layiwola, "Nigeria – Revisiting Language in Two Wole Soyinka Plays." *The IATC Journal/Revue de l'AICT* 15 (2017). http://www.critical-stages.org/15/nigeria-revisiting-language-in-two-wole-soyinka-plays/.

Hickok, Eugene W. *Why States? The Challenge of Federalism*. Washington, DC: Heritage Foundation, 2007.

Ige, Bola. *People, Politics and Politicians of Nigeria (1940–79)*. Ibadan: Heinemann Educational Books, 1995.

Ilori, Oluwakẹmi Atanda. "The Theatre of Wole Soyinka: Inside the Liminal World of Myth, Ritual and Postcoloniality." PhD diss., University of Leeds, 2016. http://etheses.whiterose.ac.uk/15733/1/ILORI%2C%20O.A.%20School%20of%20Performance%20%26%20Cultural%20Industries%20PhD%202016.pdf.

International Movie Database. "Kongi's Harvest." *IMDb*, n.d., https://www.imdb.com/title/tt0151243/.

Irele, F. Abiọla. "The Season of a Mind: Wole Soyinka and the Nigerian Crisis." In *The African Experience in Literature and Ideology*. Exeter: Heinemann, 1981.

Irele, F. Abiọla. "The Achievement of Wole Soyinka." *Philosophia Africana* 11, no. 1 (2008): 5–19.

Jaggi, Maya. "Wole Soyinka: Lamenting Nigeria's Peculiar Mess." *World Policy Journal* 11, no. 4 (1994/1995): 55–9.

Jaggi, Maya. "Profile: Wole Soyinka." *The Guardian. Guardian News and Media*, November 2, 2002. https://www.theguardian.com/books/2002/nov/02/theatre.artsfeatures.

Jenkins, Roy. *Churchill*. London: Pan Macmillan Ltd., 2001.

Jeyifo, Biọdun. *The Truthful Lie: Essays in a Sociology of African Drama*. London: New Beacon Books, 1985.

Jeyifo, Biọdun. "Introduction." In *Conversations with Wole Soyinka*, edited by Biọdun Jeyifo, ix. Jackson: University of Mississippi Press, 2001.

Jeyifo, Biọdun. "Soyinka Demythologized." *Ife Monograph Series in Literature and Criticism* 2, no. 4 (1984).

Jeyifo, Biọdun. "This Wole Soyinka Play Showed the Future of English." *BBC*, May 9, 2018. http://www.bbc.com/culture/story/20180509-this-wole-soyinka-play-showed-the-future-of-english.
Jeyifo, Biọdun. "Ritual, Anti-Ritual, and the Festival Complex in Soyinka's Dramatic Parables." In *Wole Soyinka: Politics, Poetics, and Postcolonialism*. Cambridge: Cambridge University Press, 2003.
Jeyifo, Biọdun. *Wole Soyinka: Politics, Poetics and Postcolonialism*. New York: Cambridge University Press, 2004.
Jones, Carolyn M., "Rethinking the Tragic Theory/ Rewriting Tragedy: Wole Soyinka's 'Death and the King's Horseman'." *World Literature Written in English* 35, no. 1 (1996): 78–94.
Jones, Eldred Durosimi. *The Writings of Wole Soyinka*. London: Heinemann Educational Books Ltd., 1973.
Joseph, C. L. "Wole Soyinka: Chronology and Selected Bibliography." *The Journal of Pan African Studies* 8, no. 5 (2015): 190–5.
Julien, Eileen. "African Literature." In *Africa*, edited by P. M. Martin and Patrick O'Meara, 295–312. Bloomington: Indiana University Press, 1995.
July, Robert W. "The Artist's Credo: The Political Philosophy of Wole Soyinka." *The Journal of Modern African Studies* 19, no. 3 (1981): 477–98.
Kachru, Braj B. "English as an Asian Language." *Links & Letters* 5 (1998): 89–108.
Karimi, Golnar. "Linguistic Imperialism: A Study of Language and Yoruba Rituals in Wole Soyinka's Death and the King's Horseman." PhD diss., Université de Montréal, 2015. https://core.ac.uk/download/pdf/55655298.pdf.
Kassem, Salsabeel. "Wole Soyinka, Bibliotheca Alexandrina." http://www.britannica.com/EBchecked/topic/557228/Wole-Soyinka.
Kassim, Ọmọlolu. "First Wife: Laide Speaks on Romance with Wole Soyinka." *The Spectator*, June 29, 2010.
Katrak, Ketu. "Theory and Social Responsibility: Soyinka's Essays." *Black American Literature Forum* 22. no. 3 (1988): 489–501.
Kelley, Kitty. *Oprah: Biography*. New York: Three Rivers Press, 2010.
King, Bruce. "Wole Soyinka and the Nobel Prize for Literature." *The Sewanee Review* 96, no. 2 (1988): 339–45.
Kirk-Greene, A. H. M. "His Eternity, His Eccentricity, or His Exemplarity: A Further Contribution of H. E. the African Head of State." *African Affairs* 90, no. 359 (1991): 163–87.
Klemp, Harold. *The Road to Spiritual Freedom: See a Greater Vision of Life*. Minneapolis: Eckankar, 2016.
Knipp, Thomas R. "Irony, Tragedy, and Myth: The Poetry of Wole Soyinka." *World Literature Written in English* 21, no. 1 (1982): 5–26.
Kodwo, Eshun. "Further Considerations of Afrofuturism." *The New Centennial Review* 3, no. 2 (2003): 287–302.
Kumar, K. Naveen. "Yoruba Tradition and Culture in Wole Soyinka's *The Lion and the Jewel*." *Journal of Arts, Science and Commerce* 2, no. 3 (2011): 88–97.
Layiwola, Dele. "Nigeria – Revisiting Language in Two Wole Soyinka Plays." *The IATC Journal/Revue de l'AICT* 15 (2017). http://www.critical-stages.org/15/nigeria-revisiting-language-in-two-wole-soyinka-plays/.
Lindberg, Stanley W., "Lasting Laurels, Enduring Words: A Salute to the Nobel Laureates of Literature." *The Georgia Review* 49, no. 1 (1995): 6–7.

Lindeborg, Ruth H. "Is This Guerilla Warfare? The Nature and Strategies of the Political Subject in Wole Soyinka's Aké." *Research in African Literatures* 21, no. 4 (1990): 55–69.
Lindfors, Bernth. "Africa and the Nobel Prize". *World Literature Today* 62, no. 2 (1988): 222–4.
Lindfors, Bernth. "Beating the White Man at his Own Game: Nigerian Reactions to the 1986 Nobel Prize in Literature." *Black American Literature Forum* 22, no. 3 (1988): 475–88.
Lindfors, Bernth. "Wole Soyinka, When Are You Coming Home?" *Yale French Studies*, no. 53 (1976): 197. https://doi.org/10.2307/2929658.
Lindfors, Bernth and M. Banham. "The Beginning of a Nigerian Literature in English." *Review of English* 3 (1962).
Lindfors, Bernth and Geoffrey V. Davis, *African Literature and Beyond: A Florilegium*. Amsterdam: Rodopi, 2013.
Lunga, Majahana John Chonsi. "A Critical Analysis of Wole Soyinka as a Dramatist, with Special Reference to his Engagement in Contemporary Issues." MA thesis, University of South Africa, 1994.
Longfellow, Henry Wadsworth, and H. J. Bruce. *A Psalm of Life*. Satara: Columbian Press, 1878.
Macebuh, Stanley. "Poetics and the Mythic Imagination." *Transition* 50 (1975): 79–84.
Maclean, Una. "Soyinka's International Drama." *Black Orpheus* 15 (1964): 46–51.
Maduakor, Obi. "The Political Content of Wole Soyinka's Plays." *Journal of Commonwealth Literature* 28, no. 1 (1993): 82–96.
Maduakor, Obi. "Soyinka as a Literary Critic." *Research in African Literatures, Special Issue on Criticism and Poetry* 17, no. 1 (1986): 1–38.
Maduakor, Obi. *Wole Soyinka: An Introduction to His Writings*. Lagos: Heinemann, 1986.
Maduakor, Obi. *Wole Soyinka: An Introduction to His Writings*. New York: Garland Press, 1986.
Maja-Pearce, Adewale. "Punching Holes Inside People: Words of Wole Soyinka." *Third World Quarterly* 9, no. 3 (1987): 986–92.
Makau, Kitata, "Narrative Techniques in Wole Soyinka's *The Interpreters*." Thesis Submitted to University of Nairobi, University of Nairobi Library, 2000.
Markham, James. "Soyinka, Nigerian Dramatist, Wins Nobel Literature Prize," October 17, 1986. https://www.nytimes.com/1986/10/17/books/soyinka-nigerian-dramatist-wins-nobel-literature-prize.html?searchResultPosition=4.
Maugham-Brown, David. "Interpreting and the Interpreters: Wole Soyinka and Practical Criticism." *English in Africa* 6, no. 2 (1979): 51–62.
May, Rollo. *Man's Search for Himself*. New York: W.W. Norton, 1953.
Maybury, Richard J. *Whatever Happened to Justice?* Placeville: Bluestocking Press, 1993.
Mazrui, Ali. "Wole Soyinka as a Television Critic: A Parable of Deception." *Transition* 54 (1991): 165–77.
Meyers, Jeffrey. "The Literary Politics of the Nobel Prize." *The Antioch Review* 65, no. 2 (2007): 214–23.
Mosobalaje, Adebayo. "Readers of Wole Soyinka's Political Drama and Theatre." *The African Symposium: An Online Journal of the Educational Research Network* 11, no. 1 (June 2011): 166–77.

Mouffe, Chantal. *Agnostics: Thinking the World Politically.* London: Verso, 2013.
Mpalive-Hangson, Msiska. "The Politics of Identity and the Identity of Politics: The Self as an Agent of Redemption in Wole Soyinka's *Camwood on the Leaves* and *The Strong Breed.*" *Journal of African Cultural Studies* 18, no. 2 (2006): 187–96.
Mphahlele, Es'kia. *Chirundu.* Johannesburg: Ravan Press,1979.
Mustapha, Kara. "The Inferior Sex: A Third World Feminist Approach to Wole Soyinka's *The Lion and the Jewel.*" *International Periodicals for the Languages, Literature and History of Turkish or Turkic* 10, no. 16 (2015): 847–62.
Nellickappilly, Sreekumar. "Aspects of Western Philosophy." National Programme on Technology Enhanced Learning (NPTEL). 2014.
Ngugi, James. "Preface." *The Black Hermit.* Essex: Heinemann, 1968.
Nkengasong, John N. "Samuel Beckett, Wole Soyinka, and the Theatre of Desolate Reality." *Journal of African Literature and Culture.* University of Yaounde, 2005.
Nyerere, Julius. *Ujamaa: Essays on Socialism.* London: Oxford University Press, 1968.
Obi, Joseph. "Art, Ideology, and the Militarized African Postcolony: A Sociological Reading of Wole Soyinka's 'Season of Anomy'." *Neohelicon* 25, no. 2 (1998): 403–15.
Obuke, Okpure O. "The Poetry of Wole Soyinka and J. P. Clark: A Comparative Analysis." *World Literature Today* 52, no. 2 (1978): 216–23.
Odom, Glenn. "'The End of Nigerian History:' Wole Soyinka and Yoruba Historiography." *Comparative Drama* 42, no. 2 (2008): 205–29.
Oduntan, Oluwatoyin. "*Elite Identity and Power: A Study of Social Change and Leadership among the Egba of Western Nigeria, 1860–950.*" Halifax: Dalhouseie University, 2002.
Ofeimun, Odia. *In Search of Ogun: Soyinka In Spite of Nietzsche.* Lagos: Hornbill, 2014.
Ofeimun, Odia. "Wole Soyinka: The Writer as Culture Hero." In *In Search of Ogun: Soyinka In Spite of Nietzsche*, edited by Odia Ofeimun, 114–6. Lagos: Hornbill, 2014.
Ogunba, Oyin. *The Movement of Transition: A Study of the Plays of Wole Soyinka.* Ibadan: Ibadan University Press, 1975.
Ogunba, Oyin. "Modern Drama in West Africa." *Perspective of African Literature.* Ibadan: Heinemann, 1977.
Ogundipe-Leslie, Molara. "A Comment on Ogun Abibiman." *Critical Perspectives on Wole Soyinka*, edited by James Gibbs, 198–9. Washington: Three Continents, 1980.
Ogundipe-Leslie, Molara. "Reflections on the 1986 Nobel Prize." *The Guardian.* October 27, 1986, 9.
Oguntayo, Ademola. *The Legion of Critics.* Lagos: African Concord, 1986.
Ojaide, Tanure. "Two Worlds: Influences on the Poetry of Wole Soyinka." *Black American Literature Forum* 22, no. 4 (1988): 767–76.
Ojoade, Femi. "De Origen Africano, Soy Cubano: African Elements in the Literature of Cuba." In *African Literature Today*, edited by Eldred Durosimi Jones, 48. New York: Africana, 1978.
Okpewho, Isidore. *Myth in Africa.* New York: Cambridge University Press, 1983.

Okpewho, Isidore. *Myth in Africa*. New York: Cambridge University Press, 1990.
Okpewho, Isidore. "The Mystic Essence." *The African Guardian*. October 30, 1986.
Olabode, Ibironke. "Fourth Stage: Wole Soyinka and the Social Character of Ibadan." *History Compass* 13, no. 11 (2015): 541–9.
Olaiya, Tope Templer. "Soyinka ... The 'Visiting' Husband, 'Absentee' Father, but Dotting [sic] Grandpa." July 13, 2014. https://topetempler.wordpress.com/2014/07/11/soyinka-the-visiting-husband-absentee-father-but-dotting-grandpa/.
Ọlaniyan, Tẹjumọla. "Dramatizing Postcoloniality: Wole Soyinka and Derek Walcott." *Theatre Journal* 44, no. 4 (1992): 485–99.
Ọlaniyan, Tẹjumọla. *Scars of Conquest/Masks of Resistance: The Invention of Cultural Identities in African, African-American, and Caribbean Drama*. New York: Oxford University Press, 1995.
Olatunji, Dare. "More Matters Arising." *The Guardian*. 1986.
Ọmọtọsọ, Kọle. *Achebe or Soyinka: A Study in Contrasts*. London: Hans Zell Publishers, 1996.
Ọmọtọsọ, Kọle. *Achebe or Soyinka: A Study in Contrasts*. Ibadan; Bookcraft, 2009.
Onanuga, Bayo, et al. "Soyinka Tells His Exile Story." In *Conversations with Wole Soyinka*, edited by Biọdun Jeyifo, 198–217. Jackson: University Press of Mississippi, 2001.
Osundare, Niyi. *The Writer as Righter*. Ibadan: Hope Publications Ltd., 2007.
Owomoyela, Oyekan. *A History of Twentieth Century African Literatures*. Lincoln: University of Nebraska Press, 1993.
Owomoyela, Oyekan, ed. "The Question of Language in African Literatures." In *A History of Twentieth Century African Literatures*. Nebraska: University of Nebraska Press, 1993.
Pallinder-Law, Agneta. "Aborted Modernization in West Africa? The Case of Abẹokuta." *Journal of African History* XV, no. 1 (1974): 65–82.
Parks, Tim. "What's Wrong with the Nobel Prize in Literature." *The New York Review of Books, NYR Daily*, October 2011. https://www.nybooks.com/daily/2011/10/06/why-nobel-prize-literature-silly/.
Peters, J. A. "English Language Fiction in West Africa." In *A History of Twentieth Century African Literatures*, edited by Oyekan Owomoyela, 9–48. Nebraska: University of Nebraska Press, 1993.
Phillips, Earl. *The Ẹgba at Abẹokuta: Acculturation and Political Change, 1830–1870*. Cambridge: Cambridge University Press, 2009.
Plunkett, Terry. "Longfellow's Verse: This World Is Only the Negative of the World to Come." In *Kennebec: A Portfolio of Maine Writing* 14 (1990): 2–3.
Poetry Foundation. "Wole Soyinka." *Poetry Foundation*, n.d. https://www.poetryfoundation.org/poets/wole-soyinka.
Povey, John F. "Contemporary West African Writing in English (1966)." *World Literature Today* 63, no. 2 (1989): 258–63.
Price, Amanda. "The Theatre of Promiscuity: A Comparative Study of the Dramatic Writings of Wole Soyinka and Howard Barker." *PhD thesis*, University of Leeds, April 1995.
Quayson, Ato. *Calibrations*. Minneapolis: University of Minnesota Press, 2003.

Rasheed, Biọdun Musa. "The Drama and Theatre of Wole Soyinka." *Encyclopedia of the Arts* 11, no. 3 (2006): 216–29.
Ready, Richard M. "Through the Intricacies of 'the Fourth Stage' to an Apprehension of Death and the King's Horseman." *Black American Literature Forum* 22, no. 4 (1988): 711–21.
Reed, Ishmael. "Soyinka among the Monoculturalists." *Black American Literature Forum* 22, no. 4 (1988): 705–9.
Roberts, Andrew. *Hitler and Churchill: Secrets of Leadership*. London: Weidenfeld & Nicolson, 2003.
Royal Society of Literature. "The Benson Medal." https://rsliterature.org/award/the-benson-medal/.
Sadiq, Deji. "Meet Prof. Wole Soyinka's Wife and 4 of His Children." *News*, July 11, 2014.
Said, E. W. *Orientalism*. New York: Vintage Books, 1979.
Scholes, Roberts. "In the Brothel of Modernism: Picasso and Joyce." *American Journal of Semiotics* 8, no. 1 & 2 (1991): 5–25.
Shakespeare, William. *Complete Works of Shakespeare*. London: Collins, 2007.
Smethurst, James. *The African American Roots of Modernism: From Reconstruction to the Harlem Renaissance*. North Carolina: University of North Carolina Press, 2011.
Sow, Alioune. "Political Intuition and African Autobiographies of Childhood." *Biography* 33, no. 3 (2010): 498–517.
Soyinka, Wole. *A Dance of the Forests*. London: Oxford University Press, 1963.
Soyinka, Wole. *A Play of Giants*. London: Methuen, 1984.
Soyinka, Wole. *A Shuttle in the Crypt*. London: Rex Collings/Methuen, 1971.
Soyinka, Wole. "Abiku." In *The Penguin Book of Modern African Poetry*, edited by Gerald Moore and Ulli Beier, 193. London: Penguin Books, 1963; 1984.
Soyinka, Wole. *Aké: The Years of Childhood*. New York: Vintage International Edition, 1981.
Soyinka, Wole. *Aké: The Years of Childhood*. Ibadan: Bookcraft, 2014.
Soyinka, Wole. *Art, Dialogue and Outrage: Essays on Literature and Culture*. New York: Pantheon Books, 1993.
Soyinka, Wole. *Art, Dialogue and Outrage: Essays in Literature and Culture*. Ibadan: New Horn Press, 1998.
Soyinka, Wole. "Between Defective Memory and the Public Lie: A Personal Odyssey in the Republic of Liars." *Interventions* 5 (2015): 135–6.
Soyinka, Wole. "Between Law and Responsibility." In *The Unappeasable Price of Appeasement, Interventions* 3 (2012): 45.
Soyinka, Wole. "Between Nation Space and Nationhood." Public Lecture Delivered at the Obafemi Awolowo Foundation, 2009.
Soyinka, Wole. *Death and the King's Horseman*. London: Secker and Warburg, 1975.
Soyinka, Wole. *Death and the King's Horseman*. London: Secker and Warburg, 1998.
Soyinka, Wole. "Ethics and Aesthetics of Chichidodo." *Guardian*, December 7, 1985.
Soyinka, Wole. "From Growing Pains to Terminal Disease?" In *The Unappeasable Price of Appeasement, Interventions* 3 (2012): 75–109.

Soyinka, Wole. *From Zia, with Love; and, A Scourge of Hyacinths (a Methuen Modern Play)*. London: Methuen Drama, 1992.
Soyinka, Wole. *Ibadan: The Penkelemes Years: A Memoir: 1946–65*. London: Methuen, 1994.
Soyinka, Wole. *Ibadan: The Penkelemes Years*. Ibadan: Bookcraft, 2014.
Soyinka, Wole. *Idanre and Other Poems*. London: Methuen, 1967.
Soyinka, Wole. *Introduction, Art, Dialogue, and Outrage*. Ibadan: New Horn Press Limited, 1988.
Soyinka, Wole. *Isara: A Voyage Around Essay*. Ibadan: Fountain Publications, 1989.
Soyinka, Wole. *Isara: A Voyage Around Essay*. Ibadan: Bookcraft, 2014.
Soyinka, Wole. *Kongi's Harvest*. London: Oxford University Press, 1967.
Soyinka, Wole. *Mandela's Earth and Other Poems*. New York: Random House, 1989.
Soyinka, Wole. *Myth, Literature and the African World*. Cambridge: Cambridge University Press, 1976.
Soyinka, Wole. "Neo-Tarzanism: The Poetics of Pseudo-Tradition." *Transition* 48 (1975): 38–44.
Soyinka, Wole. "Nobel Prize Banquet Speech, 10 December 1986." *Black American Literature Forum* 22, no. 3 (1988): 447–8.
Soyinka, Wole. *Of Africa*. New Haven: Yale University Press, 2014.
Soyinka, Wole. *Ogun Abibiman*. London: Rex Collings, 1976.
Soyinka, Wole. "Pen for Hire." *Présence Africaine*, Nouvelle série no. 163/164 (2001): 122.
Soyinka, Wole. *Poems from Prison*. London: Rex Collings, 1969.
Soyinka, Wole. "Profile: Wole Soyinka." *The Guardian*, November 2, 2002.
Soyinka, Wole. "Red Card, Green Card: Notes Towards the Management of Hysteria." http://saharareporters.com/2016/11/12/red-card-green-card-notes-towards-management-hysteria-wole-soyinka.
Soyinka, Wole. *Requiem for a Futurologist*. London: Rex Collings, 1985.
Soyinka, Wole. *Season of Anomy*. New York: Third Press, 1973.
Soyinka, Wole. *Six Plays (The Trials of Brother Jero; Jero's Metamorphosis; Camwood on the Leaves; Death and the King's Horseman; Madmen and Specialists; Opera Wonyosi)*. London: Methuen, 1984.
Soyinka, Wole. *Soyinka Collected Plays 1&2*. Ibadan: Oxford University, 1976.
Soyinka, Wole. "Telephone Conversation." In *The Penguin Book of Modern African Poetry*, edited by Gerald Moore and Ulli Beier, 187. London: Penguin Books, 1963.
Soyinka, Wole. *The Bacchae of Euripides*. London: Eyre Methuen, 1973.
Soyinka, Wole. *The Beatification of Area Boy: A Lagosian Kaleidoscope*. London: Methuen, 1995.
Soyinka, Wole. *The Beatification of Area Boy*. Ibadan: Spectrum Books, 1999.
Soyinka, Wole. *The Deceptive Silence of Stolen Voices*. Ibadan: Spectrum Books, 2003.
Soyinka, Wole. *The Interpreters*. New York: Africana Pub. Corp., 1965.
Soyinka, Wole. *The Lion and the Jewel*. London: Oxford University Press, 1963.
Soyinka, Wole. *The Man Died: Prison Notes of Wole Soyinka*. Harmondsworth: Penguin, 1975.

Soyinka, Wole. *The Man Died: Prison Notes of Wole Soyinka*. Ibadan: Bookcraft, 2014.
Soyinka, Wole. "The Precursors of Boko Haram." In *The Unappeasable Price of Appeasement, Interventions* 3 (2011): 1–42.
Soyinka, Wole. "The Precursors of Boko Haram," In *The Unappeasable Price of Appeasement, Interventions* 3 (2011): 40–1.
Soyinka, Wole. *The Road*. London: Oxford University Press, 1965.
Soyinka, Wole. *The Trials of Brother Jero*. London: Eyre, 1973.
Soyinka, Wole. "The Writer in a Modern African State." In *Art, Dialogue and Outrage* (1968), edited by Biọdun Jeyifo (Ibadan: New Horn Press, 1988).
Soyinka, Wole. "The Writer in an African State." *Transition* 31, no. 6 (1967): 11–3.
Soyinka, Wole. "The Writer and the Road: Wole Soyinka and Those Who Cause Death by Dangerous Driving." *The Journal of Modern African Studies* 33, no. 3 (1995): 469–98.
Soyinka, Wole. "Wole Soyinka: A Transition Interview." *Transition* 42 (1973): 62–4.
Soyinka, Wole. "Wole Soyinka on 'Identity': A Conversation with Ulli Beier." Reprinted in Jeyifo, *Conversations with Wole Soyinka*. Jackson: University of Mississippi Press, 2001.
Soyinka, Wole. *You Must Set Forth at Dawn*. New York: Random House, 2006.
Soyinka, Wole. *You Must Set Forth at Dawn*. Ibadan: Bookcraft, 2014.
Soyinka, Wole and Biọdun Jeyifo. *Conversations with Wole Soyinka*. Jackson: University of Mississippi Press, 2001.
Soyinka, Wole and James Gibbs. *Critical Perspectives on Wole Soyinka*. Boulder: Lynne Rienner Publishers, 1980.
Stanford, Simon. "The Nobel Prize in Literature 1986." NobelPrize.org. https://www.nobelprize.org/prizes/literature/1986/soyinka/25230-interview-transcript-1986/.
Stanford, Simon. *Transcript from an Interview with Wole Soyinka*. https://www.nobelprize.org/prizes/literature/1986/soyinka/25230-interview-transcript-1986/
Straton, Florence. "Wole Soyinka: A Writer's Social Vision." *Black American Literature Forum* 22, no. 3 (1988): 531–53.
Taleb, Nassim Nicholas. "Prologue." *The Black Swan: The Impact of the Highly Improbable*. London: Penguin Books, 2007.
The Nobel Prize. "Wole Soyinka Biographical." https://www.nobelprize.org/prizes/literature/1986/soyinka/biographical/.
Thomson, Jeff. "The Politics of the Shuttle: Soyinka's Poetic Space." *Research in African Literatures* 27, no. 2 (1996): 94–101.
Tidjani-Serpos, Noureini. "The Postcolonial Condition: The Archeology of African Knowledge: From the Feat of Ogun and Ṣango to the Postcolonial Creativity of Ọbatala." *Research in African Literatures* 27, no. 1 (1996): 3–18.
Tikkanen, Amy. "Wole Soyinka: Nigerian Author." *Encyclopaedia Britannica*, n.d. https://www.britannica.com/biography/Wole-Soyinka.
Ugwuanyi, Lawrence Ogbo. "I Am Therefore You Are: An Existentialist Perspective on Wole Soyinka's Writings." *UJAH: Unizik Journal of Arts and Humanities* 12, no. 2 (2011): 65–90.

UNESCO. "Funmilayọ Ransome-Kuti and the Women's Union of Abẹokuta." *UNESCO Series on Women in African History*, 2014.
Uzoatu, Uzor Maxim. "The Essential Soyinka." African Writing Online, n.d. http://www.african-writing.com/seven/uzoruzoatu.htm.
Vincent, Theo. "Africanity in Modern African Literature." In *The Arts and civilization of Black and African Peoples. Black Civilization and Literature* (vol. 3), edited by J. O. Okpaku, A. E. Opubor and B. O. Oloruntimehin, 35–58. New York: Third Press International. 1986.
Waitley, Denis. *Seeds of Greatness: The Ten Best-Kept Secrets of Total Success*. London: Cedar, 1983.
Wasson, Tyler and Gert H. Breiger. *Nobel Prize Winners: An H.W. Wilson Biographical Dictionary* (vol. 1). New York: H. W. Wilson, 1987.
Wa Thiong'o, Ngũgĩ. "The Conscience of Africa." In *Crucible of the Ages: Essays in Honour of Wole Soyinka at 80*, edited by Ivor Agyeman-Duah and Ogochukwu Promise, 3–7. Ibadan: Bookcraft, 2014.
Westcott, Nicholas. "Soyinka's Cultural Antiphonies." In *Crucible of the Ages: Essays in Honour of Wole Soyinka at 80*, edited by Ivor Agyeman-Duah and Ogochukwu Promise, 27–9. Ibadan: Bookcraft, 2014.
Whitehead, Anne. "Journeying Through Hell: Wole Soyinka, Trauma, and Postcolonial Nigeria." *Studies in the Novel* 40, no. 1/2 (2008): 13–30.
Wikipedia. "Abẹokuta." https://en.m.wikipedia.org/wiki/Abẹokuta.
Wikipedia. "Wole Soyinka." https://en.wikipedia.org/wiki/Wole_Soyinka.
Wilkinson, Jane. "Daring the Abyss: The Art of Wole Soyinka." *Africa: Rivista trimestrale di studi e documentazione dell'Istituto italiano per l'Africa e l'Oriente* 41, no. 4 (1986): 603–11.
"Wole Soyinka." Academy of Achievement, July 3, 2009. https://www.achievement.org/achiever/wole-soyinka/#interview.
Wright, Derek. "The Festive Year: Wole Soyinka's Annus Mirabilis." *The Journal of Modern African Studies* 28, no. 3 (1990): 511–9.
Wright, Derek. "Soyinka's Smoking Shotgun: The Later Satires." *World Literature Today* 66, no. 1 (1992): 27–34.
Wright, Derek. *Wole Soyinka Revisited*. New York: Twayne, 1993.

INDEX

Abacha, General Sani 39, 44, 74, 88, 92, 97, 124, 129, 213, 244, 245, 263, 271
Abẹokuta 13, 51–78, 80, 85, 88, 89, 107–9, 239, 244, 253, 262, 263
Abẹokuta Women's Union *see* AWU
Abiọla, Moshood Kashimawo 74–6, 192, 213, 254
Aboyade, Bimpe 152
Achebe, Chinua 16, 17, 26, 96, 101, 102, 127, 131, 142, 144, 145, 202, 203, 246, 252, 262, 267
Adegbenro, Alhaji Dauda 76
Adeniran, Tunde 80, 86, 87, 91, 269
Adiche, Chimamanda 145
Adichie, Chimamanda 136, 143
Adubi War 55
African Cultural Revolution 17
African epistemology 5, 17, 23, 138
African literature 84, 137–44, 146, 148, 149, 157, 159, 160, 163, 175, 188, 189, 197, 198, 202, 207, 210, 228, 231, 234, 247, 249, 263, 267
Ajantala 204
Akintọla, Chief S. L. 15
Akintọla, Samuel Ladoke 15, 81, 110, 124, 252
Allende, Isabel 128
Aluko, Timothy 145
Amadi, Elechi 145
Amaechi, Rotimi 270
Aminm Idi 124, 213, 242
Amuta, Chidi 111, 126
Anieke, Dr. Sylvester 110
anti-Negritudism 11
Anyadike, Chima 149

apartheid 124, 239, 240, 271
Appiah, Kwame Anthony 96, 97
Apter, Peter 106
Arimah, Leslie Nneka 230
Awẹ, Olumuyiwa 80, 120, 269
Awolowo, Obafemi 98, 105, 245, 274
AWU 68
Azikiwe, Dr. Nnamdi 99, 110, 119, 262, 271

Babalola, S. A. 138
Babangida, Ibrahim Badamasi 75, 97, 110, 213
Bakhtin, Mikhail 256
Banda, Hastings 124
Banham, Martin 46
Bannister, Roger 259
Baraka, Amiri 5
Belasco, Bernard 98
Benin 54
Benson, A. C. 81, 250
Biafran leaders 21
Biafran struggle 10
Biko, Steve 243
Biobaku, Professor Saburi 62, 76
Black and African Festival of Arts and Culture 243, 266
Bokassa, Jean-Bedel 242
Boko Haram 99
Brecht, Bertolt 243
Brennan, Timothy 128
Brodie, Clara 16
Brunschwig, Henri 52
Brutus, Dennis 242
Busby, Margaret 97
Buzan, Tony 117, 118

Camilla, Duchess of Cornwall 119
Castro, Fidel 92
Chain, Ernst Boris 259
Chief Sodeke 56
China 92
Chinweizu 24, 148, 189, 190, 191,
 202, 204, 260
Christianity 13, 17, 18, 21–3, 40, 57, 58,
 68, 70, 73, 76, 77, 82, 83, 86, 88,
 90, 108, 115, 116, 118, 119, 129,
 156, 166, 210, 271, 273, 274
Church Missionary Society 58
Churchill, Winston 81, 85, 89, 115,
 116, 242, 252, 259
Clark, Pepper 96, 160, 184, 217, 272
Cole, Teju 145
colonialism 9, 30, 80, 81, 83, 84, 88,
 89, 104, 105, 136–41, 143, 145,
 149, 155, 161–3, 169, 199, 209,
 210, 224, 232, 233, 254, 262,
 263, 271–3, 275
 British 161
colonization 9, 20, 23, 30, 130, 140, 258
Cooper, Brenda 126, 128
Coquard, Father Jean Marie 60
Covey, Stephen 86
Crowther, Rev. Ajayi 57, 58
Cuba 92, 154
Cudeback, Wade 104, 266
Curie, Madam 259

d'Azeglio, Massimo 106
Dahomey people 54
Dauda, Bola 76, 274
Davies, Lanre 62
decolonization 81, 82, 105, 116, 126,
 129, 140, 141, 263
Delanọ, Isaac 26, 76
Democratic Front for a People's
 Federation 186
Dickens, Charles 136
Dionysus 8, 189, 203, 252
Djelloul, Bourahla 24

Ẹgba 5–31, 33–47, 49, 51–55, 58, 61–4,
 71, 85, 104, 268
Ẹgba Alake 61
Ẹgba Gbagura 61

Ẹgba Oke Ọna 61
Ẹgba uprising see Adubi War
Ẹgbaland 71
Egypt 90
Einstein, Albert 130, 259, 275
Ẹlẹṣin Ọba 127, 227, 228
Elitism 80
Emecheta, Buchi 145, 149
England 13, 14, 106, 111, 124, 225,
 232, 240, 244
Equatorial Guinea 124, 213
Esu 204
EUBM 64, 66
EUG 64–6
Eurocentrism 5, 7, 8, 16, 36, 41, 42,
 70, 77, 188, 189, 192, 197, 204
Ezeliora, Osita 142

Fagunwa, D. O. 26, 136, 139, 144, 241
Fanon, Frantz 6, 96
Fatai Rolling Dollars 73
Federal Road Safety Commission 269
Festival of Black and African Arts 213
Figueiredo, Rosa 97, 103, 265
Fleming, Alexander 259
Florey, Howard Walter 259
Fourth Stage 179, 185, 190, 196, 197,
 222, 229–31, 233–6, 241
France, Peter 106, 120
FRSC see Federal Road Safety
 Commission
Fulani 54, 64

Gates Jr., Henry Louis 111, 123
Gay, John 243
Gibbs, James 12, 108, 271
Godwin, Peter 112
Goleman, Daniel 90, 91
Gowon, General Yakubu 97, 187, 200,
 241, 242, 262
Great Britain 10, 35, 69, 89, 271
Great Depression 82, 105
Greco-Roman mythology 188
Greenwich Mews Theater 241

Hallowell, Terry Plunkett 86
Hitler, Adolf 115, 259
Holocaust 259

Ibironke, Olabode 232, 234
Ijẹbu 51, 85, 104, 268
Ike, Chukwuemeka 142
Ilọri, Oluwakẹmi Atanda 20, 24
Imodu, Michael 88
Iṣara 13, 23, 82, 83, 88, 101, 103, 104, 107, 108, 112, 121, 123, 127, 266, 268
Islam 21, 274
Italy 106, 241, 244

Jemie, Onwuchekwa 24, 202
Jesus 18
Jeyifo, Biọdun 9, 31, 84, 101, 102, 111, 121-3, 146, 153, 201, 206, 221, 272, 273, 275
John, Elnathan 145
Jones, Eldred Durosimi 102, 197
Josiah, Pa 82
Julien, Eileen 137, 139, 148

Karimi, Golnar 28, 29, 30
Katrak, Ketu 122, 197, 198
Keene, Raymond 117
Kikuyu language 128
King George V 116, 119, 121
King Gezo 54
King Kosoko 72
Kirk-Greene, A. H. M. 98, 99
Knipp, Thomas 218
Kuti, Fela Anikulapo 55, 61, 62, 72, 73, 75-7, 118

Lagos 54, 56, 68, 71, 75, 86, 88, 99, 106, 162, 174, 239, 241, 243, 244, 245
Lambo, Professor Thomas Adeoye 76
Lindfors, Bernth 125, 127-9, 260
Lisabi 63, 64
Llosa, Mario Vargas 128
Lugard, Frederick 220

Macaulay, Herbert 99
Macron, Emmanuel 119, 120, 121
Madam Tinubu 56, 68, 71, 75, 76
Maduakor, Obi 150, 196, 204, 206, 211, 212
Madubuike, Ihechukwu 24, 202

Malawi 124
Marquez, Gabriel Garcia 128
Marx, Karl 206
Marxism 171, 206, 207
massacre of Iva Valley miners 88
May, Rollo 47, 120, 129, 262
Modern Literature 142
modernism 24-7, 161, 199, 201, 235, 261, 263, 264, 270
Mohammed, General Muritala 74
Muhammed, Murtala 242, 243, 262
Mukherjee, Bharati 128

National Democratic Organization 186
National Liberation Council of Nigeria 186
Negritude 30, 101, 131, 155, 181, 202-4, 210, 224, 225
neo-Negritudist 11
Neo-Tarzanists 205, 251
Nguema, Macias 124, 213, 242
Nigerian Civil war 167
Nigerian political landscape 27
Nigerian society 15, 21, 24, 25, 27, 30, 73, 76, 80, 162, 199, 243, 250, 254, 270
Nobel Prize 81, 95, 96, 98, 148, 169, 189, 190, 196, 205, 208, 231, 244-7, 249, 250, 254, 258, 259, 260, 261
Norman, Derine 230
Nwapa, Flora 145

Ọbasanjọ, Chief Oluṣẹgun 74-6, 98, 114, 243, 262, 271
Obey, Ebenezer 73, 75
Odegbami, Segun 76
Ọdẹmọ 83, 88, 103, 107, 108, 266
Ofeimun, Odia 98, 99, 101, 102, 115
Ogboni 40, 61, 62, 77
Ogun 4, 12, 21, 22, 41, 52, 53, 68, 70, 115, 129, 130, 138, 148, 151-4, 182-6, 197, 199, 204, 226, 231, 243, 248, 249, 274
Ogunba, Oyin 174
Ogunba, Oyinade 146
Ogunde, Hubert 88, 118, 266
Ojukwu, Col. Odumegwu 110, 262

Okara, Gabriel 145
Okigbo, Christopher 44, 160, 217, 272
Okorafor, Nnedi 145
Okoroafor, Nnedi 230
Okpewho, Isidore 153, 192, 226
Okri, Ben 145
Old Ọyọ 53, 56, 63, 76
Olegbe, Pius 80
Omotoso, Kọle 101, 102, 104, 127, 145–7, 268
Opara, Ralph 80
Orinshala 204
Orisa 122, 129, 154, 183
Orunmila 183, 204
Osofisan, Femi 30, 145, 206, 207
Osundare, Niyi 148
Ọyọ Empire 53, 56, 63

Pallinder-Law, Agneta 57, 62
Pan-Africanism 101, 224, 263
Pentecostalism 108, 274
Peters, Johnathan 139, 144
Pilkings, Simon 29, 30, 170, 273
Piper, Anne 240
postcolonialism 4, 12, 14, 19, 20, 23, 29, 30, 31, 42, 47, 72, 76, 79, 100, 114, 128–30, 141, 144, 146, 147, 155, 156, 163–5, 167, 169, 182, 185, 186, 192, 197–200, 209–11, 214, 225, 232–6, 250, 262, 267, 269, 273, 274
Prince Charles 119, 121
Princess Diana 119
Pro-National Conference Organization 186
Pyrates Confraternity 80, 109, 272, 273

racism 7, 13, 59, 70, 82, 88, 89, 103, 240, 251, 262
Ramsome- Kuti, Rev. A. O. 109
Rannsome-Kuti, Reverend Israel Oludotun 107
Ransome-Kuti, Funmilayọ 59, 61, 67, 70, 75, 77, 85, 107
Ransome-Kuti, Reverend J. J. 107
Roberts, Andrew 115, 116

Romanticism 26
Royal Society of Literature 250
Rushdie, Salman 128, 271

Sadiq, Deji 118
Ṣango 115, 129, 138, 183, 204, 274
Saro 44, 58, 271
Saro-Wiwa, Ken 44, 271
Scholes, Robert 26
Schopenhauer, Arthur 135
Senghor, Leopold Sedar 131, 142, 155, 181, 202, 203, 210
Shakespeare, William 3, 88, 111, 136, 159, 196, 244, 263, 264
Shange, Ntozake 5
Shoneyin, Lola 145
Sierra Leone 58, 63
South Africa 92, 124, 239, 243, 253
Soyinka, Adefolake 120, 121
Soyinka, Chief Laide 119, 120
Soyinka, Grace Eniola 239
Soyinka, Samuel Ayodele 239
Soyinka, Wole
  A Dance of the Forests 12, 24, 102, 111, 126, 128, 199, 201, 204, 208, 210, 211, 240, 264, 270, 274
  A Play of Giants 46, 188, 198, 211, 212, 213, 223, 230, 244, 264, 272, 274
  A Scourge of Hyacinths 244
  A Shuttle in the Crypt 112, 184, 186, 188, 200, 211, 242, 272, 274
  A Voyage Around Essay 23, 101, 104, 112, 117, 123, 127, 268
  Abiku 103, 151, 183, 184
  Agip Prize for literature 249
  Aké: The Years of Childhood 23, 65, 77, 78, 82, 84, 90, 104, 112, 156, 244, 251
  Alapata Apata 162, 171, 173, 245
  And After the Narcissist? Of Power and Change 241
  Anisfield Wolf Book Award 245
  Anisfield-Wolf Lifetime Achievement Award 250

arrest 38
Before the Blowout 243
Benson Medal 81, 250
Camwood on the Leaves 240, 242, 244
childhood 8, 13, 22, 23, 36, 46, 77, 82–6, 89, 107–9, 239, 261, 272
Civilian and Soldier 38
Climate of Fear? The Quest of Dignity in a Dehumanized World 245
confinement without trial 44
Death and the King's Horseman 12, 18, 24, 28, 29, 41, 81, 112, 123, 127, 130, 160, 169, 170, 171, 197, 207, 223, 224, 227, 242, 243, 244, 248, 256, 264, 272, 273, 274
Death in the Dawn 183, 185
Dedication 184
Die Still, Dr Godspeed 244
earliest literary prizes 80
early works 12, 126
Europe Theatre Prize 251
Felix Valera Medal of Honor 92
For Her Who Rejoiced 241
Forest of a Thousand Demons 139
George Benson Medal of the Royal Society of Literature 81
harassment 44
  Ibadan The Penkelemes Years 23, 90, 100, 101, 109, 112, 117, 119, 123
imprisoned 112
International Humanist Award 245
Intervention Series 99, 101
Jero's Metamorphosis 161, 165, 212, 242, 254, 264
Jock Campbell New Statesman Literary Award 45
Jock Campbell-New Statesman Literary Award 245
John Whiting Drama Prize 245
Kaduna Prison 242
King Baabu 39, 212, 213, 245, 272
Kongi's Harvest 24, 111, 128, 160, 161, 211, 212, 241, 242
literary genius 36
literary protests 47

literary radicalism 9
Madame Etienne's Establishment 46
Madmen and Specialists 24, 46, 112, 126, 128, 199, 211, 212, 223, 229, 242, 270, 272, 274
Massacre October "66" 241
Myth, Literature and the African World 222, 226, 243
Nobel Laureate 17, 47, 81, 82, 84, 95, 96, 98, 116, 130, 148, 169, 189, 190, 196, 205, 208, 231, 244, 245, 246, 247, 249, 250, 254, 258, 259, 260, 261, 263
Ogun Abibiman 12, 183, 184, 243
Opera Wonyosi 15, 112, 188, 207, 211, 212, 243, 264, 274
Poems of Black Africa 12
Political views 4
Requiem for a Futurologist 198, 244, 264
Rice Unlimited 243
Season of Anomy 112, 137, 150, 151, 154, 155, 156, 157, 211, 223, 242, 272
Second World War 9, 19, 69, 82, 105, 116, 131, 259, 261, 262
self-imposed exile 242, 252
Telephone Conversation 89, 103, 186
The Academy of Achievement Golden Plate Award 245, 250
The Bacchae of Euripides 223, 242, 264
The Beatification of Area Boy 165, 167, 244
The Biko Inquest 243
The Credo of Being and Nothingness 245
The Future of West African Writing 12
The Interpreters 12, 19, 24, 26, 27, 108, 111, 137, 150, 153, 154, 155, 156, 157, 200, 241
The Invention 5, 111, 240
The Lion and the Jewel 16, 25, 42, 46, 104, 123, 127, 128, 131, 199, 240, 254, 266, 268, 270, 272, 274

The Man Died 104, 112, 120, 126, 131, 188, 209, 224, 242, 267, 272, 274
The Road 24, 111, 124, 126, 128, 160, 162, 174, 223, 229, 241, 271, 272
The Strong Breed 12, 24, 241
The Swamp Dwellers 12, 24, 46, 111, 160, 240
The Tortoise 240
The Trials of Brother Jero 16, 111, 161, 165, 174, 199, 240, 241, 254, 264, 270
Towards a True Theatre 12
UNESCO Medal of Arts 81
University College 14
Whatever Happened to Justice? 131
You Must Set Forth at Dawn 112, 121, 151, 156, 245
Stoppard, Tom 245
Sweden 95, 106, 130, 241
Swedish Academy 95, 96, 169, 190, 244, 245, 246, 248
Synge, J. M. 196, 253

Talabi, Wale 230
Thiong'o, Ngũgĩ wa 84, 96, 128
Third World writers 218
Thomson, Jeff 187
Townsend, Rev. Henry 57, 59
tribalism 80
Trogneux, Brigitte 120, 121
Trump, Donald 92, 124, 271

Tunlewa, Soyinka 270
Tutuola, Amos 136, 142, 144, 145, 267

Uganda 124, 213
Uganda National Troupe 213
Ugwuanyi, Lawrence Ogbo 130
UN *see* United Nations
United Board of Management *see* EUBM
United Kingdom 52, 81, 89, 116, 250; *see also* Great Britain
United Nations 46, 114, 131, 162
United States of America 92

Walcott, Derek 5, 128
Westcott, Nicholas 97
Wole Soyinka (book) 15
Wolf, Edith Anisfield 251
World Bank 89
Wright Brothers 259

Yoruba 13, 18, 19, 21–3, 28, 29, 36, 39, 40–2, 51–4, 56, 58, 63, 66, 68, 71, 73, 76, 77, 79, 97, 98, 102–4, 107, 108, 111, 114, 115, 122–6, 129, 137–9, 144, 146, 147, 150–4, 157, 160, 161, 169–71, 174, 181–4, 193, 196, 197, 199, 203, 204, 206, 209, 219–23, 227, 239–41, 246–9, 252, 253, 255–8, 261, 263, 266–8, 270, 271, 274
Yorubaland 8, 23, 56, 123, 151, 174

FIGURE 14.1 *Wole Soyinka. Illustration by Olasunmade Akano.*